Edwin Hodder

The History of South Australia

From its foundation to the year of its jubilee. With a chronological summary of all the principal events of interest up to date. Vol. 1

Edwin Hodder

The History of South Australia
From its foundation to the year of its jubilee. With a chronological summary of all the principal events of interest up to date. Vol. 1

ISBN/EAN: 9783337314682

Printed in Europe, USA, Canada, Australia, Japan

Cover: Foto ©ninafisch / pixelio.de

More available books at **www.hansebooks.com**

THE HISTORY

OF

SOUTH AUSTRALIA

*FROM ITS FOUNDATION TO THE
YEAR OF ITS JUBILEE.*

WITH A

CHRONOLOGICAL SUMMARY

OF ALL THE PRINCIPAL EVENTS OF INTEREST
UP TO DATE.

BY

EDWIN HODDER,

AUTHOR OF
"MEMORIES OF NEW ZEALAND LIFE," "CITIES OF THE WORLD,"
"GEORGE FIFE ANGAS, FATHER AND FOUNDER OF SOUTH AUSTRALIA," ETC.

WITH TWO MAPS.

VOL. I.

LONDON:
SAMPSON LOW, MARSTON & COMPANY
LIMITED,
St. Dunstan's House,
FETTER LANE, FLEET STREET, E.C.
1893.

[*All rights reserved.*]

PREFACE.

It was the lifelong wish of Mr. George Fife Angas, one of the Fathers and Founders of South Australia, that a History of the Colony of his adoption, and which he was mainly instrumental in establishing, should be written. To this end he collected a vast number of documents from all available sources, and for many years employed a secretary to set them in order, hoping some day to write the History himself. But that day never came, and in 1879 Mr. Angas passed away. Among his papers several were found that showed how intensely keen his desire was that a full and comprehensive History, giving the story of the rise and progress of the colony, should be written. His son, the Hon. J. H. Angas, Member of the Legislative Council of South Australia, determined that the wish should be fulfilled, and kindly placed in my hands the whole of the valuable and voluminous papers. Of this material I have availed myself freely, and I have also drawn from Memoirs, Diaries, Travels, Parliamentary Debates, as well as from the Colonial Newspapers.

For the sake of easy reference, I have divided the work into chapters dealing with the successive Administrations of the various Governors, and have given fuller detail in the earlier than in the later chapters.

A special feature is the "Chronological Summary of Events," divided in like manner under the Administration of each Governor; and it is suggested that, after reading a chapter of the History, the corresponding portion of the Summary may be glanced through with advantage. It has been impossible to verify every date, the source from which a fact has been gleaned having perhaps contained only vague phrases, such as "recently" or "a short time since," in which case an approximate date has been given. Neither has it been possible to include *every* event of interest, and therefore those only have been chosen which appeared to me best worth recording, as marking progressive stages in the development of the colony. The Summary cannot fail to prove of interest to colonists, as it will keep alive the memory of events in which many of them were personally concerned, while the Obituary notices will recall the names and deeds of men and women who, like themselves, have been the "Makers" of the Colony.

I have to express my very hearty thanks to the Hon. J. H. Angas for his untiring assistance during the whole period covered in the preparation of this work. I also gladly acknowledge my indebtedness to the columns of the *South Australian Register*, to the valuable library of the Royal Colonial Institute, and to the kindness and courtesy of Mr. J. S. O'Halloran, the Secretary to the Institute.

EDWIN HODDER.

St. Aubyns, Shortlands, Kent.

CONTENTS OF VOL. I.

CHAPTER I.

EARLY EXPLORATIONS.

PAGE

Matthew Flinders and George Bass.—Bass's Straits.—The *Investigator*.—Discoveries of Flinders.—Lincolnshire Names.—A Missing Cutter.—Fate of Thistle and Taylor.—Spencer's Gulf.—Kangaroo Island.—Gulf of St. Vincent.—Encounter Bay.—*Le Géographe* and M. Baudin.—*Le Naturaliste* and M. Peron.—Circumnavigation of Australia.—Flinders sails for England in Colonial Cutter.—Imprisoned at Mauritius.—Conduct of M. Peron.—Death of Flinders.—Minor Explorers.—Captain Sturt and the Murray River.—Confirms Discoveries of Flinders.—Suffering and Courage.—Captain Barker.—Ascent of Mount Lofty.—Murder of Captain Barker.—The Future Site of Adelaide 1

CHAPTER II.

ATTEMPTS TO FOUND A COLONY.

How Colonial Questions became popular.—Edward Gibbon Wakefield.—New Principles in Colonization.—The Colonization Society.—Mr. Gouger and Colonel Torrens draw up a Scheme.—Lord Goderich annihilates it.—The Error of asking too much or too little.—Further Schemes.—Official Rebuffs.—The South Australian Association.—Chartered Colony *v.* Crown Colony.—Leading Features of the South Australian Act.—Stringent Provisions.—A Difficult Problem and how it was solved 19

CHAPTER III.

HOW THE COLONY WAS FOUNDED.

Mr. George Fife Angas.—Necessity for a Joint Stock Company.—Purchase of the stipulated £35,000 worth of Land.—Raising the Guarantee Sum of £20,000.—Formation of the South Australian Company.—Objects contemplated.—Fleet of the South Australian Company.—Choice of a Governor.—Colonel Charles James Napier.—Money and Troops.—Captain J. Hindmarsh.—His Remarkable Career.—First Colonial Officers and their Salaries.—H.M.S. *Buffalo*.—Colonel Light and his Instructions.—The Founders of South Australia 34

CHAPTER IV.

THE PIONEER SETTLERS.

Arrival of Pioneer Vessels.—"Governor" Walker.—Mr. Samuel Stephens.—Kingscote, Kangaroo Island.—Colonel Light and the Survey Staff.—Examination of St. Vincent's Gulf and Spencer's Gulf.—First Contact with Natives.—Holdfast Bay.—Lost in the Bush.—Removal of Settlers from Kangaroo Island.—Captain Light decides against Shores of Port Lincoln for Site of Capital.—Arrival of Governor Hindmarsh.—Proclamation of the Colony.—First Banquet in South Australia.—The "Makers" of the Colony 47

CHAPTER V.

ADMINISTRATION OF CAPTAIN HINDMARSH.

DECEMBER 28TH, 1836—JULY 14TH, 1838.

The Governor and the Resident Commissioner.—Site of the Capital.—Discussions thereon.—Appeal to the Board of Commissioners.—Selections of Land.—First Land Boom.—Removal of Settlers from Kangaroo Island.—Hard Work and Poor Pay.—Delay in the Surveys.—Too Rapid Immigration and its Consequences.—Harbour proclaimed a Free Port.—First Buildings in Adelaide.—Operations of the South Australian Company.—The First Bank.—The

Company's Land.—Rise of Religious Institutions.—
—Schools and Schoolmasters.—The Aborigines; Origin,
Manners, and Customs.—Protector of Aborigines.—Early
Pastoral Pursuits.—Overland Arrivals of Stock.—First
General Gaol Delivery.—Newspapers.—Recall of Captain
Hindmarsh.—Interim Administration of Mr. G. M.
Stephens.—Tribute to the Pioneer Colonists 61

CHAPTER VI.

ADMINISTRATION OF COLONEL GAWLER.

OCTOBER 17TH, 1838—MAY 10TH, 1841.

Offices of Governor and Resident Commissioner combined.—
Difficulties of Colonel Gawler's Position.—Financial Embarrassments.—Resignation of Colonel Light and the Survey Staff.—Death of Colonel Light.—Rapid Immigration and Unemployed Labour.—Erection of Public Buildings.—Special Surveys.—Explorations.—Mr. E. J. Eyre's Attempt to open up Overland Route to Western Australia.—A Story of Heroism.—Murder of John Baxter.—Board of South Australian Commissioners disbanded.—Formation of South Australian Society.—The "Company's" Road to the Port.—McLaren Wharf.—Bushrangers.—Massacres by Natives.—Treatment and Punishment of Criminal Aborigines.—Missionaries.—Question of Colonial Chaplains.—Arrival of Germans.—A Story of Religious Persecution.—Pastor Kavel.—Fruits and Vegetables.—Prosperity.—A Coming Storm.—Colonel Gawler's Bills dishonoured.—A Critical Time.—Colonel Gawler's Defence.—His Recall.—Universal Bankruptcy in Colony 107

CHAPTER VII.

ADMINISTRATION OF CAPTAIN GEORGE GREY.

MAY 10TH, 1841—OCTOBER 26TH, 1845.

The Financial Crisis.—Views of Mr. G. F. Angas thereon.
—South Australia a Crown Colony.—The Governor and the Imperial Government.—Errors of the Commissioners.—Retrenchment.—Unemployed Immigrants.—Agitation.—Reports of Select Committee of House of Commons.—A Loan guaranteed.—Colonial Creditors.—Outrages by

Natives.—Mr. E. J. Eyre.—Native Schools.—A Tide of Commercial Misfortune.—Universal Bankruptcy.—Its Causes.—Governor Grey's Bills dishonoured.—Serious Consequences.—New Waste Lands Act.—Act for Better Government of South Australia.—Signs of Improvement.—Ridley's Reaping Machine.—Mineral Wealth.—Mr. Mengé.—Kapunda Copper Mine.—Explorations.—Captain Sturt.—Mr. Drake.—Ecclesiastical Affairs.—Convictism.—Bush Fires.—Burra-Burra Copper Mine.—Port Adelaide a Free Port.—Popularity of Sir George Grey.—Eulogies 150

CHAPTER VIII.

ADMINISTRATION OF MAJOR ROBE.

OCTOBER 25TH, 1845—AUGUST 12TH, 1848.

A Tory of the Tories.—A Bad Beginning.—A Royalty on Minerals proposed.—Public Excitement thereon.—Mr. W. E. Gladstone on the Position of Colonial Governors.—Import Duty on Corn.—Canada and South Australia.—Imposition of Royalty on Minerals.—Specimen of South Australian Oratory.—Historical Scene in Legislative Council.—Unpopularity of the Governor.—State Aid to Religion.—Political Dissenters.—League for the Maintenance of Religious Freedom.—State Aid granted.—Return of Captain Sturt from Interior.—Geological Observations of the Governor.—Explorations of Mr. J. A. Horrocks.—Education Bill.—Steam Communication with England.—Arrival of Dr. Short, Bishop of Adelaide ... 208

CHAPTER IX.

ADMINISTRATION OF SIR HENRY EDWARD FOX YOUNG.

AUGUST, 1848—DECEMBER, 1854.

Antecedents.—Suspension of Royalties on Minerals.—Irish Orphans.—A Policy of Progress.—Municipal Corporation for Adelaide.—A New Constitution.—Federation proposed and rejected.—The "Political Association."—Universal Suffrage and the Ballot.—A Lost Constitution.—Elections to New Legislative Council.—Statistics.—State Aid to Religion permanently abolished.—Education.—City

and Port Railway Bill.—Pensions.—Californian Gold.—
Anti-Transportation League.—The Victorian Gold-fields.
—Exodus from South Australia.—State of Adelaide and
Suburbs.—A Drain on the Banks.—Proposed Assay of
Gold into Stamped Ingots.—The Bullion Act.—Government Assay Office opened.—Mr. Tolmer and the Overland Gold Escort.—Exciting Adventures.—Gold at
Echunga.—Increased Cost of Living.—Navigation of the
Murray.—Captain Cadell.—The Governor explores the
Murray.—The "Murray Hundreds."—Dreams that never
came true.—A Parliament for South Australia proposed.
—Opinions on a Nominee Upper House.—A Civil List Bill.
—Establishment of District Councils.—Roads and Railways.—Defence of the Colony.—Military Ardour ... 236

CHAPTER X.

ADMINISTRATION OF SIR RICHARD GRAVES MACDONNELL.

JUNE, 1855—MARCH, 1862.

Antecedents of Sir R. G. MacDonnell.—Unemployed Irish
Female Immigrants.—An Amusing Incident.—The Parliament Bill.—Election Riots.—Opening of the New
Legislative Council.—Depression in Trade.—Retrenchment and the Civil Service.—A Mania for Select Committees.—Adelaide Waterworks and Drainage.—New
Constitution Act.—Ballot and Universal Suffrage.—The
First South Australian Parliament.—A Noble Record.—
Questions of Privilege.—Originating Money Bills.—
Frequent Changes in Ministry.—Torrens' Real Property
Act.—Mr. Justice Boothby.—Australian Federation.—
Poll Tax on Chinese.—Colony attains its Majority.—
Assessment on Stock.—Free Immigration.—The Political
Association.—The Destitute Asylum.—Labour Tests.—
The Working Men's Association.—Defences of the Colony.
—Wreck of the *Admella*.—A Terrible Week.—Political
Parties.—Ministerial Programmes.—Archdeacon Hale
and the Aborigines.—Poonindie.—Mr. G. F. Angas and
Missions to Natives.—The Great Murray Railway Scheme.
—Explorations.—Sir R. G. MacDonnell on the Murray.
—Mr. B. H. Babbage.—A Fearful Death.—Mr. Stephen
Hack.—Major Warburton.—John McDouall Stuart.—
Journeys to the Interior.—Mining Discoveries.—Yorke's
Peninsula.—Wallaroo and Moonta.—A Mining Mania.—
South Australian Wines.—A Review of Six Years ... 289

CHAPTER XI.

ADMINISTRATION OF SIR DOMINICK DALY.

MARCH, 1862—FEBRUARY, 1868.

Coming and Departing Guests.—An Irish Gentleman.—Warlike Times.—Volunteering.—Explorations.—McKinlay.—Burke and Wills.—Return of J. M. Stuart after crossing and recrossing the Continent.—A Great Ovation.—Geological Survey by Mr. Hargreaves.—"No Man's Land."—Ministerial Difficulties.—The English Mail Service.—An Intercolonial Conference.—"No Confidence" Motions.—Retirement of M.P.'s.—Red Rust in Wheat.—Party Spirit.—The Northern Territory.—A Terrible Responsibility.—Waste Lands in North Australia.—A Survey Expedition.—Mr. B. T. Finniss Government Resident.—A Pioneer Expedition.—Misunderstandings.—Recall of Mr. Finnis.—Mr. G. W. Goyder sent out.—The Squatter Question.—Revaluations of Land.—Unprecedented Drought.—Loss of Stock.—Visit of H.R.H. the Duke of Edinburgh.—A Round of Gaieties.—Attempted Assassination of the Duke of Edinburgh at Sydney.—Death of Sir Dominick Daly.—Funeral.—Review of his Administration 354

THE HISTORY

OF

SOUTH AUSTRALIA.

CHAPTER I.

EARLY EXPLORATIONS.

Matthew Flinders and George Bass.—Bass's Straits.—The *Investigator*.— Discoveries of Flinders. — Lincolnshire Names.— A missing Cutter.—Fate of Thistle and Taylor.—Spencer's Gulf. —Kangaroo Island.—Gulf of St. Vincent.—Encounter Bay.— *Le Géographe* and M. Baudin.—*Le Naturaliste* and M. Peron. Circumnavigation of Australia.—Flinders sails for England in Colonial Cutter.—Imprisoned at Mauritius.—Conduct of M. Peron.—Death of Flinders.—Minor Explorers.— Captain Sturt and the Murray River.—Confirms discoveries of Flinders.— Suffering and Courage.—Captain Barker.—Ascent of Mount Lofty.—Murder of Captain Barker.—The Future Site of Adelaide.

THE first authenticated discovery of Australia by a European is believed to have been made by Manoel Godinho de Eredia, a Portuguese, in 1601. Five years later, Louis de Torres, a Spaniard, passed through the Straits that still bear his name. In 1609 De Quiros, also a Spaniard, saw the land and is said to have called it Australia. Then followed several Dutch exploratory expeditions, and in 1664 the island-continent was named New Holland by the Dutch Government.

Dampier, in 1686, is supposed to have been the first Englishman who visited Terra Australis, as it was also called. In 1770 Captain Cook carefully explored the east coast, gave names to several localities, and took possession of the country for Great Britain.

Before the commencement of the present century, Bligh, Edwards, Portlock, Bampton, Alt, Vancouver, Furneaux, and others had visited various parts of the coast, but there were still 250 leagues of the Southern and Western seaboard marked on the maps as the "Unknown Coast." The honour of filling up this blank in the chart of the Great South Land is due to Matthew Flinders.

In August, 1794, Captain John Hunter set sail in the *Reliance* for the then newly formed penal settlement at Port Jackson, to succeed the first Governor, Captain Phillip. There were on board the vessel two daring young men panting for adventurous exploration—George Bass, surgeon, and Matthew Flinders, midshipman. Soon after arrival at Sydney some scope was given to their ambition; they launched a little boat, eight feet long, named the *Tom Thumb*, and with no other crew than a small boy they sailed across Botany Bay and ascended twenty miles further up George's River than had been previously reached. At another time in the same boat they explored the Illawarra coast. After sundry trips, taken together or separately, during one of which Mr. Bass had observed a supposed inlet between Van Diemen's Land and the mainland, the Governor gave his consent to the proper fitting out of a boat expedition for further explorations; and Flinders and Bass set sail in the *Norfolk*, a deck-built boat of twenty-five tons, with a crew of eight men. As a result of this voyage, Van Diemen's Land was proved to be an island separated from the mainland by a strait ever since known as Bass's Strait.

In 1800 Flinders returned to England in the *Reliance*, and so successfully urged upon the Government the importance of prosecuting the survey of the Unknown Coast, that an expedition was at once fitted out, a war-vessel, the *Xenophon*, renamed the *Investigator* on account of the service in which she was to be employed, being set apart for the purpose, and Flinders was promoted to the rank of Commander. Every care was taken in the outfit, and besides the provision made by Government, the Honourable East India Company gave the sum of £600 for any additional necessities. The crew was composed of picked men; amongst the midshipmen was Mr. (afterwards Sir) John Franklin, the great Arctic navigator, and attached to the scientific staff was Robert Brown, the able botanist, and William Westall, a celebrated landscape painter.*

Owing to the war between France and England then in progress, a passport was obtained from the French Government ensuring the expedition from molestation by any of the armed ships of the enemy.

The *Investigator* arrived off Cape Leeuwin (or Lioness, so named after a Dutch vessel that had made the headland in 1622) on the 6th of December, 1801, and after proceeding to King George's Sound to refit, Captain Flinders set forth on his voyage of discovery. The map of South Australia still marks the course of his route. Fowler's Bay was named after his first lieutenant; Streaky Bay on account of the colour of the water; Smoky Bay from the smoke of bush fires; Denial Bay because of its proximity to St. Peter's Island; Investigator's Group, one of which was called Flinders' Island, after the second lieutenant (the captain's brother), and Coffin Bay named after Vice-Admiral Sir Isaac Coffin.

On the 20th of February, 1802, Flinders arrived at an inlet since known as Sleaford Bay. He was a Lincolnshire man, and this was one of a series of places he named after spots in his well-loved native county. At Sleaford Bay he found that the coast took a sudden turn, trending to the north, but that no land was visible to the north-east, from which quarter a strong tide was setting in. This gave rise to many wild conjectures.

* Westall's original sketches are now in the library of the Royal Colonial Institute, London.

"Large rivers, deep inlets, inland seas, and passages into the Gulf of Carpentaria," says Flinders, "were terms frequently used in our conversations of this evening, and the prospect of making an interesting discovery inspired new life into every man in the ship." Next morning Flinders went on shore, accompanied by Mr. Thistle, the mate, and satisfied himself of the insularity of the land. Soon after this a cutter was sent on shore in charge of Mr. Thistle with a midshipman named Taylor and others, to search for an anchorage and water. It was a fatal voyage. For a long time the little boat had been watched sailing hither and thither in her search, and towards dusk she was seen returning from the land. Then suddenly she was lost to sight, and Lieutenant Fowler went in a boat with a lantern to ascertain the cause. Two hours passed without any tidings. A gun was then fired, and Lieutenant Fowler returned soon afterwards, but alone. Near the situation where the cutter had been last seen he met with so strong a rippling of tide that he himself narrowly escaped being capsized, and there was reason to fear that this was what had actually happened to Mr. Thistle and his companions. Had there been daylight, some or all of the crew might have been saved, although only two out of the eight were good swimmers. But the tide was running strong, the night was pitchy dark, and hope was abandoned.

Next morning the missing cutter was found bottom upwards, and although most careful and diligent search was made in every direction, not a trace was ever discovered of any of the crew. The sight of a large number of sharks in the immediate neighbourhood furnished a horrible suggestion of their fate.

Flinders called the island on which he had landed Thistle Island, and caused an inscription to be engraved on a sheet of copper, and set up on a post at the head of the little inlet, which in commemoration of the sad event he named Memory Cove; the adjacent headland he called Cape Catastrophe, and the surrounding islands Grindal, Hopkins, Williams, Taylor, after men lost in the cutter. When all attempts to find any survivor of the missing boat's crew had proved ineffectual, Flinders entered a magnificent harbour, Port Lincoln, where he determined to refit and take in water. Almost every place in this neighbourhood he named after localities familiar to him in Lincolnshire. Thus the bay, an island, and a point of land bore the name Boston; Cape Donnington commemorated his native village; Louth Bay, Spalding Cove, Kirton Point, Stamford Hill, Reevesby, Sibsey, Grantham and Spilsby Islands, Sleaford Bay and Mere—all memorialize more or less the county of the fens.

On the 6th of March he left Port Lincoln and proceeded northwards. A cluster of islands was named after Sir Joseph Banks, whose good offices with the Admiralty had procured the equipment of the expedition; Barn Hill, Mount Young, Middle Mount, Point Lowly, Mount Brown, Mount Arden, and other places further marked the course of his explorations, while the whole range, of which these mountains formed a part, was honoured with the name of Flinders himself.

The great gulf he was exploring pursued a northerly direction, and Flinders entertained a strong hope that a channel would be found by which he could reach the Gulf of Carpentaria. Soon, however, the land began to lose its bold appearance, and eventually the gulf was found to terminate in desolate mud flats. On the return of the *Investigator* on the east side of the gulf two capes were named Points Riley and Pearce, after two gentlemen in the Admiralty, and on the 19th of February he entered a bay and named it after the Earl of Hardwicke. On the following day he was again at the head of the gulf named Spencer's Gulf, after Earl Spencer who was First Lord of the Admiralty at the time the expedition of the *Investigator* was determined upon. The eastern point of land he called Cape Spencer, and three islands near, the Althorpes.

Land was now seen from south to south-west, but whether it was an island or part of the continent was as uncertain as whether the wide opening seen at the same time was an inlet or a strait. Overtaken in a storm, Flinders stood across to the land, and, after rounding the headland (named Point Marsden, after the Second Secretary of the Admiralty), a bay was found beyond offering good shelter, and here they anchored, naming it Nepean Bay, after Sir E. Nepean, First Secretary of the Admiralty.

On the 22nd Flinders went ashore, and found a number of dark-brown kangaroos feeding beside a wood. "It would be difficult to guess how many kangaroos were seen," he wrote, "but I killed ten; the rest of the party made up the number to thirty-one taken on board in the course of the day, the least of them weighing 69 and the largest 125 pounds. . . . I scrambled with difficulty through the brushwood and over fallen trees to reach the higher land with the surveying instruments, but the thickness and height of the wood prevented anything else from being distinguished. There was little doubt, however, that this extensive piece of land was separated from the continent, for the extraordinary tameness of the kangaroos, and the presence of seals upon the shore, concurred with the absence of all traces of men to show that it was not inhabited. . . . The whole ship's company," he adds, "was employed this afternoon in skinning and cleaning the kangaroos, and a delightful regale they afforded after four months' privation from almost any fresh provisions. Half a hundredweight of heads, forequarters, and tails were stewed down into soup for dinner on this and the succeeding days, and as much steaks given, moreover, to both officers and men as they could consume by day and by night. In gratitude for so seasonable a supply I named the southern land Kangaroo Island." And here, as we shall presently see, the first settlers in South Australia landed in 1836.

While off Kangaroo Island the captain named the nearest headland Cape Jervis, and the highest land seen to the north-east Mount Lofty. Leaving Kangaroo Island, he stood across for Cape Spencer, naming the straits between, Investigator's Straits, and on the 29th of February found himself in another gulf with land right ahead as well as on both sides. A rise at the head of the gulf he named Hummock Mount, and in honour of the admiral who presided at the Board of Admiralty when he left England, he called his new discovery the Gulf of St. Vincent; the peninsula separating the two gulfs he designated Yorke's Peninsula, after the Right Honourable Charles Philip Yorke, and a dangerous shoal at the entrance of Gulf St. Vincent, Troubridge Shoal.

Flinders pronounced the country round the Gulf of St. Vincent to be generally superior to that on the borders of Spencer's Gulf, but the only notice he gives of its eastern side, destined to become a few years afterwards an important British settlement, was as follows: "The nearest part of the coast was distant three leagues, mostly low, and composed of sand and rock, with a few small trees scattered over it; but a few miles inland, where the back mountains rise, the country was well clothed with forest timber, and had a fertile appearance."

The *Investigator* touched once more at Kangaroo Island, "where not less than thirty emus were seen on shore at one time," and then proceeded through what Flinders called Backstairs Passage and anchored in Antechamber Bay. The headland at its eastern end, where now a fine lighthouse stands, he named Cape Willoughby. Leaving here, he passed three small islands, The Pages, and soon after a report from aloft announced a white rock ahead. "On approaching nearer," says Flinders, "it proved to be a ship standing towards us, and we cleared for action in case of being attacked. The stranger was a heavy-looking ship without any topgallant masts up, and, on colours being hoisted, she showed a French ensign, and afterwards an English jack forward, as we did a white flag. At half-past five, the land being then five miles distant to the north-east, I hove-to, and learned, as the stranger passed to leeward with a fair wind, that it was the French national ship *Le Géographe*, under the command of

Captain Nicholas Baudin. We veered round as *Le Géographe* was passing, so as to keep our broadside to her, lest the flag of truce should be a deception, and having come to the wind on the other tack, a boat was hoisted out, and I went on board the French ship, which had also hove-to." The passports of both captains were exchanged and read, and Flinders learned that his fellow-navigator had parted company from his consort-ship *Le Naturaliste* in a heavy gale in Bass's Straits, had lost his geographical engineer with the largest boat and its crew, and that he had examined part of Van Diemen's Land and part of the south coast of Australia. The navigators communicated their discoveries to each other, and Flinders presented Baudin with some charts. In honour of this friendly meeting Flinders named the locality Encounter Bay, and in passing along the southern coast adopted the nomenclature of Baudin, except in the case of two headlands discovered by Grant in December, 1800, and named respectively Capes Northumberland and Bridgewater.

Monsieur Peron, the naturalist to the French expedition, pursued a very different course with regard to the discoveries of Flinders, not only laying a claim to them on behalf of his nation, but renaming nearly all of them. Kangaroo Island he called L'Isle Décres, Spencer's Gulf Golfe Bonaparte, Gulf St. Vincent Golfe Joséphine, and so on.

This attempt to rob Captain Flinders of the honour so justly due to him was, as we shall see, afterwards exposed and condemned.

The first lieutenant of *Le Géographe* was far more honourable than Monsieur Peron; on meeting Flinders some time after at Port Jackson, he said to the English navigator, "Captain, if we had not been kept so long picking up shells and catching butterflies at Van Diemen's Land, you would not have discovered the South Coast before us."

On the 9th of May, 1802, the *Investigator* anchored at Port Jackson, where Flinders was heartily welcomed by the Governor, to whom he communicated the important discoveries he had made, and also sent an account of them to England by the South Sea whaler *Speedy*.

On the 22nd of July, 1802, he sailed from Port Jackson with the *Investigator* and the *Lady Nelson*, for the purpose of visiting Torres Straits and the north coast of Australia.

During this voyage—with the details of which we shall not concern ourselves here, although he explored some portions of the Northern Territory which in 1863 was added to the province of South Australia—he circumnavigated Australia and returned to Port Jackson on the 9th of June, 1803. The *Investigator* was now found to be unfit for further service, and as there was no other vessel in the harbour ready for exploring purposes, Flinders determined to proceed to England and lay his charts and journals before the Lords Commissioners of the Admiralty, and if possible obtain another ship.

A series of disasters now befell the heroic explorer. Soon after leaving Port Jackson in the *Porpoise*—accompanied by the *Bridgewater* and the *Cato*—he was wrecked on the Barrier Reef, the *Cato* sharing a similar fate. The *Bridgewater* escaped, and proceeded on her voyage to India. The crews of the two wrecked vessels contrived to get upon a sandbank, where they remained while Flinders returned to Sydney, a distance of seven hundred miles, in one of the ship's boats to procure assistance.

The Governor placed two small ships at his disposal, and with them he proceeded to the reef, and rescued all his companions. One of the two ships was a colonial cutter, the *Cumberland*, of twenty-nine tons, and on his return to Sydney Flinders conceived the idea of proceeding in this frail craft, only a little larger than a river-boat, to England. On making his plan known to the Governor, it was, strange to say, favourably entertained.

Flinders proposed to put into whatever port lay in his route for supplies of provisions and water, and seemed to entertain no doubt of a successful issue to his voyage; but in course of time his little vessel sprung a leak, and he steered to Mauritius for repairs. But here, being unprovided with any other passport than the one issued for the *Investigator*, he and his crew were taken prisoners. By an unlucky chance, *Le Géographe*, with the members of the French expedition who could have established his identity, had sailed from Mauritius on the day before his arrival. Having come from Australia, he was asked if he had seen or heard of "Flinders" the navigator, and the Governor of the island refused to believe his reply that he was the man, or that any Australian Governor would have sanctioned a voyage to England in such a small and dangerous craft.

Flinders, therefore, was detained a prisoner, and his papers were taken from him. For six weary years he suffered incarceration, and was only set at liberty when, in 1810, the island was capitulated to the English.

While Flinders was a prisoner at Mauritius, Monsieur Peron, the naturalist of Baudin's expedition, issued one volume of voyages and discoveries in Australia, in which he made the audacious attempt to deprive Flinders of the honour of his discoveries by giving French names to most of the places the English navigator had already visited and named.

This ungenerous attempt to appropriate the result of the labours of another was unsuccessful. The account of his discoveries which, owing to his incarceration, Flinders was unable to publish until 1814, completely set at rest for ever the justness of his claims, and there is a fine ring in the generous words of the heroic sailor when, in his published work, "Account of a Voyage to Terra Australis," he says, "How, then, came Monsieur Peron to advance what was so contrary to truth? Was he a man destitute of all principle? My answer is, that I believe his candour to have been equal to his acknowledged abilities, and that what he wrote was from an overruling authority, and smote him to the heart, for he did not live to print his second volume."

Flinders died on the 14th of July, 1814, the very

day on which his book was published. A monument to his memory was erected at Port Lincoln by Sir John Franklin when he was Governor of Tasmania.

From the time that Flinders and Baudin visited and explored parts of the coast-line of South Australia, several years elapsed before any further important discoveries were made. Captain Dillon, the discoverer of the remains of La Pérouse, visited Port Lincoln and Encounter Bay; Captain Sutherland, in command of a whaler, visited Kangaroo Island, which became in process of time partly inhabited by convicts who had escaped from the neighbouring penal settlements, and by runaway seamen, and one Captain Jones is said to have discovered the harbour now known as Port Adelaide.

In 1830, twenty-eight years after Flinders set forth on his memorable voyages, a vast addition to the knowledge of Australian geography in general and of South Australia in particular was made by the discoveries of Captain Charles Sturt.

In September, 1829, the Government of New South Wales, being anxious to trace the flow of the waters of the Murrumbidgee, or of such rivers as might be connected with it, instructed Captain Sturt to make the necessary preparations for a second descent into the interior for this purpose.

On the 14th of January, 1830, while pursuing the objects of the expedition down the Murrumbidgee, he came " suddenly and unexpectedly at the conflux of that river with a noble stream, flowing," as he says, " from east to west at the rate of two and a half knots an hour over a clear and sandy bed of a medium width of from three hundred to four hundred feet."

The river into which the whaleboat and her exploring party had been launched, Captain Sturt named the Murray after Sir George Murray, who at that time presided over the Colonial Department. Pursuing his onward course down the Murray, which Captain Sturt at first supposed was the Darling—a river he had previously discovered and named after General Darling

Governor of New South Wales—he arrived on the 23rd of January, greatly to his surprise and satisfaction, at the junction of the Darling with his new discovery, the Murray.

The Darling at this point was found to be about one hundred yards wide and twelve feet deep, and in 140° 56" of east longitude, that is to say, just without the boundary afterwards fixed for the province of South Australia. In 140° 29" he found another considerable junction of a river, which he named the Lindesay, after the colonel of his regiment. A little lower down he passed another, which he named the Rufus, after the red hair of his companion, Mr. (afterwards Sir George) MacLeay.

On the 9th of March, finding the horizon getting clearer to the south, Captain Sturt landed to survey the country. Referring to this circumstance, he wrote—

"I still retained a strong impression on my mind that some change was at hand, and on this occasion I was not disappointed; but the view was one for which I was not altogether prepared. We had at length arrived at the termination of the Murray. Immediately below me was a beautiful lake which appeared to be a fitting reservoir for the noble stream that had led us to it, and which was now ruffled by the breeze that swept over it. The ranges were more distinctly visible, stretching from south to north, and were certainly distant forty miles. They had a regular, unbroken outline, declining gradually to the south, but terminating abruptly at a lofty mountain northerly. I had no doubt in my mind of this being the Mount Lofty of Captain Flinders, or that the range was that immediately to the eastward of St. Vincent's Gulf. Between us and the ranges a beautiful promontory shot out into the lake, being a continuation of the right bank of the Murray. Over this promontory the waters stretched to the base of the ranges and formed an extensive bay. To the north-west the country was exceedingly low, but distant peaks were just visible over it. To the south-west a bold headland showed itself, beyond which, to the westward, there was a clear and open sea visible through a strait formed by this headland, and a point projecting from the opposite shore. To the east and south-east the country was low, excepting the left shore of the lake, which was backed by some minor elevations, crowned with cypresses. Even while gazing on this fine scene I could not but regret that the Murray had thus terminated, for I immediately foresaw that in all probability we should be disappointed in finding any practicable communication between the lake and the ocean, as it was evident that the former was not much influenced by tides."

The Murray at this depôt, and forty miles from its mouth, was found to be 350 yards wide, and from twenty to twenty-five feet deep. Finding the wind too boisterous to cross the lake, tents were pitched on a low tract of land that stretched apparently for many miles to the eastward. It was of the richest soil, being a black vegetable deposit. Encouraged by the appearance of the country, Captain Sturt, accompanied by MacLeay, walked out to examine it from some hills a little to the south-east of their camp, and found that the flat extended over about fifty miles, and was bounded by the elevations that continued easterly from the left bank of the Murray to the north, and by a line of rising ground to the south, the whole being lightly wooded and covered with grass.

"Thirty-three days had now passed over our heads," says Captain Sturt, "since we left the depôt on the Murrumbidgee, twenty-six of which had been passed upon the Murray. We had at length arrived at the grand reservoir of those waters whose course and fate had previously been involved in such obscurity. It remained for us to ascertain whether the extensive sheet of water upon whose bosom we had embarked had any practicable communication with the ocean, and whether the country in the neighbourhood of the coast corresponded with that immediately behind our camp, or kept up its sandy and sterile character to the very verge of the sea."

In crossing the lake a south-westerly course was pursued, leaving the great expanse of waters to the north-west, and the adjacent country unexplored on the downward voyage. A neck of land extending several miles into the lake was supposed to be an island from the indentation which takes place near the present township of Milang. This point, and the one on the opposite shore, have appropriately been named respectively Point Sturt and Point MacLeay.

When Sturt reached the shore of Encounter Bay, he found his stock of provisions so short that he had only just time to visit the mouth of the Murray and retrace his steps with all possible speed. The scarcity of provisions was not the only difficulty the party had to anticipate; some of the native tribes on the banks of the Murray and down to the sea-coast had shown themselves hostile to the expedition on its downward journey, and it was not to be expected that they would be friendly on its return.

The whole of the voyage back was one protracted course of suffering, but courage never flagged.

"The men were indeed so exhausted in strength," wrote Captain Sturt, "and their provisions so much reduced by the time they gained the coast, that I doubted much whether either could hold out to such place as we might hope for relief. Yet reduced as the whole of us were from previous exertion, beset as our homeward path was by difficulty and danger, and involved as our eventual safety was in obscurity and doubt, I could not but deplore the necessity that obliged me to recross the Lake Alexandrina (as I had named it, in honour of the heir-apparent to the British Crown), and to relinquish the examination of its western shores. . . . We were borne over its ruffled and agitated surface with such rapidity that I had scarcely time to view it as we passed, but, cursory as my glance was, I could not but think I was leaving behind me the fullest reward of our toil in a country that would ultimately render our discoveries valuable, and benefit the colony for whose interests we were engaged. Hurried, I would repeat, as my view of it was, my eye never fell on a country of more promising aspect or of more favourable position than that which occupies the space between the lake and the ranges of St. Vincent's Gulf, and continuing northerly from Mount Barker stretches away without any visible boundary."

Exactly six months after their departure, Captain Sturt and his gallant men were all safely back in Sydney, but in an utterly exhausted state. They had passed through terrible sufferings, but their indomitable courage had prevented them from sinking into despair, which would have resulted in certain death.

In his report to the Colonial Government of New South Wales, Captain Sturt strongly urged that a further examination of the coast should be made from the most eastern coast of Encounter Bay to the head of St. Vincent's Gulf, to ascertain with certainty if there were any other outlet for the waters of the Murray than the one he had discovered; the large body of water in the north-west part of the lake leading him to entertain the hope that there was a channel in that direction.

Governor Darling lost no time in carrying out this recommendation, and determined to avail himself of the services of Captain Collet Barker, who had been Commandant at Raffles Bay, and more recently had occupied a similar post at the settlement in Western Australia. He was directed to proceed to Cape Jervis and carry on his survey from that point. He was accompanied by Dr. Davis, an assistant-surgeon of his regiment (the 39th Foot), and Mr. Kent of the Commissariat.

On the 13th of April, 1831, the expedition arrived off Cape Jervis and proceeded up the eastern side of St. Vincent's Gulf.

On the 17th Captain Barker, accompanied by Mr. Kent, his servant Mills, and two soldiers, went on shore. They entered a narrow inlet at the base of the Mount Lofty ranges and were delighted with the beauty of the scenery, bearing the appearance of natural meadows lightly timbered and covered with a variety of grasses. Finding a rocky glen at the head of the inlet where there was abundance of water, the party bivouacked for the night, and on the following morning, leaving the two soldiers at the resting-place, Captain Barker, Mr. Kent, and the servant kept along the ridge of the range gradually ascending in the direction of Mount Lofty. In the course of the day they passed round the head of a deep ravine whose smooth and grassy sides presented a beautiful appearance. A few miles from this ravine the party encamped for the night, and on the following morning passed over Mount Lofty. After sleeping another night on the ranges, they rejoined the soldiers, who had obtained an abundant supply of fish in the mean time. While on Mount Lofty Captain Barker had observed an indentation in the coast to the north-west, and now proceeded to examine it. Little, of course, did he imagine that this inlet would, in a few years, become the harbour of the capital of a flourishing colony, and still less did he suppose that, within the same period, the uninhabited plains he had seen from the summit of Mount Lofty would be teeming with a busy population, and be skirted with the villa residences of the more wealthy and successful of the colonists. Between the inlet just referred to, and the one entered by the party on the 17th, Captain Barker discovered a small clear stream to which he gave the name of the "Sturt," after the gallant discoverer of the Murray.

Captain Barker and his former land-party next went ashore in a small bay behind Cape Jervis, and found themselves, on landing, in a rich and fertile valley, probably the Rapid Bay of a later date. Crossing over the ranges, they obtained a view of Encounter Bay, and proceeding still further to the north-east along the summit of the hill, they saw Lake Alexandrina and the channel of its communication with the sea. From this they descended towards the channel close to the sand hillock upon which Captain Sturt had pitched his tent before his return journey up the Murray, and then kept along the beach until they reached the sea mouth.

Captain Barker judged the breadth of the channel to be a quarter of a mile, and being anxious to take bearings, and to ascertain the nature of the strand beyond it to the eastward, he determined, notwithstanding the remonstrances of his people, to swim across. Unfortunately he was the only one of the party who could swim well enough for the purpose. He stripped and swam across with his compass fastened on his head, with difficulty gaining the opposite side, and then he was seen to ascend the hillock * and take several bearings. He then descended on the further side—and was never seen again. For a long time his comrades waited in anxious suspense; then some of them heard, or thought they heard, a sharp sudden cry. Evening advanced without any sign of Captain Barker's return, but when night set in the terrible explanation came. Upon the sandhill the doomed man had ascended, the natives had lighted a chain of small fires, around which their women were chanting a melancholy dirge. It struck upon the ears of the listeners with an ominous thrill, and assured them of the irreparable loss they had sustained.

As the only means of ascertaining definitely their leader's fate, they sought the assistance of the sealers on Kangaroo Island, when, for a certain reward, one of the men agreed to accompany Mr. Kent to the mainland with a native woman who would communicate with the tribe supposed to have committed the murder. It transpired that the natives, fearful, it was alleged, of the instrument Captain Barker carried in his hand, closed upon him and speared him to death, afterwards throwing the body into deep water, where the sea-tide would carry it away.

It was reported that the natives who committed this cruel act "were influenced by no other motive than curiosity to ascertain if they had power to kill a white man." "But," says Captain Sturt, who wrote an account of Captain Barker's expedition and its melancholy termination, "we must be careful in giving credit

* Now called Barker's Knoll.

to this, for it is much more probable that the cruelties exercised by the sealers towards the blacks along the south coast may have instigated the latter to take vengeance on the innocent as well as on the guilty." The sandhill on the right side of the mouth of the Murray has been appropriately designated Barker's Knoll, to commemorate the tragic event.

Sad as the termination was, good was effected by the expedition, and from the account furnished by Mr. Kent, Captain Sturt was able to report—

"It would appear that a spot has at length been found upon the south coast of New Holland to which the colonist might venture with every prospect of success, and in whose valleys the exile might hope to build for himself and for his family a peaceful and prosperous home. All who have ever landed upon the eastern shore of St. Vincent's Gulf agree as to the richness of its soil and the abundance of its pastures. Indeed, if we cast our eyes upon the chart and examine the natural features of the country behind Cape Jervis, we shall no longer wonder at its differing in soil and fertility from the low and sandy tracts that generally prevail along the shores of Australia."

The account of the discoveries of Sturt and Barker were received with enthusiasm in Great Britain, and led to practical steps being taken for the formation of a settlement on the southern shores of Australia.

CHAPTER II.

ATTEMPTS TO FOUND A COLONY.

How Colonial Questions became popular.—Edward Gibbon Wakefield.—New Principles in Colonization.—The Colonization Society.—Mr. Gouger and Colonel Torrens draw up a Scheme.—Lord Goderich annihilates it.—The Error of asking too much or too little.—Further Schemes.—Official Rebuffs.—The South Australian Association—Chartered Colony *v.* Crown Colony.—Leading Features of the South Australian Act.—Stringent Provisions.—A Difficult Problem and how it was solved.

THERE are no startling incidents to record in connection with the early attempts to found a colony in South Australia, although it is a story of protracted struggle against difficulties, of indomitable energy and perseverance, and of final success. The novelty of the scheme of colonization propounded, the untried character of the principles upon which it was proposed to establish the colony, the limited knowledge of the territory to be occupied, combined to give the Parliament and the public an idea that the well-meaning projectors were visionaries and enthusiasts seeking to establish a Utopian settlement. Nevertheless the development of the scheme was watched with interest, even by those who did not believe it would issue in success; while the opposition of a few, who had the prosperity of other colonies at heart, only tended to give impetus to the labours of the fathers and founders of South Australia.

It is not difficult to trace some of the causes leading

to the popularity of colonial questions in the early part of this century.

The conclusion of the European War in 1815 disposed the minds of the people to turn from foreign campaigns to the peaceful concerns of life, and colonization became a topic of general conversation.

Emphasis was given to it a few years later. The commerce of the country had suffered unwonted fluctuations, thousands of families were out of employment, population was rapidly increasing, trade was in an unsatisfactory state, and many who took a patriotic and benevolent interest in their fellows were asking, "What will the future present to the rising generation?"

Little was known generally in those days of the expansive nature of trade, which might be created by the lowering of duties upon imports and the removal of restrictions, and emigration appeared the most feasible remedy for the impending dangers. By removing the surplus population to some British colony the mother country would be relieved, and at the same time new markets would be originated for the manufactures of the parent state.

In course of time New South Wales and Van Diemen's Land began to attract attention; the climate was fine and salubrious, and particularly well adapted for pastoral pursuits; many of the early convicts who had obtained their freedom were making large fortunes by sheep-farming, and found a ready sale for their wool in the English markets. But with all these and other attractions, the fact that these places were penal settlements operated powerfully against any attempt to promote a free emigration to these colonies.

In August, 1829, the colonization of the Swan River Settlement, Western Australia, was commenced, and met with great favour from the public at the time, so that many respectable families joined the early expeditions there. But the colony was founded on a very imperfect basis, and proved a source of disappointment to almost all connected with it. Large grants of land were made to several persons, in one instance to the enormous extent of half a million of acres which the individual was allowed to select before the expedition sailed. Of course he chose his land in the immediate vicinity of the port, and consequently the other emigrants had to go beyond this vast tract before they could settle. The remainder of the land was sold at the low price of one shilling and sixpence per acre, enabling all to become purchasers. The consequence was that labourers taken out from England to cultivate the soil soon found that they could command their own prices, broke the engagements with their employers, and shortly became landed proprietors themselves. Thus there was land in abundance, but little capital, and comparatively no labour. Lacking these first essentials, the colony progressed so slowly that in 1848, nineteen years after its formation, the population, which in 1832 was 1540, had only increased to 4622.

A great impetus was given to colonization by Mr. Edward Gibbon Wakefield, who circulated a new theory as to the causes of failure and success in modern colonies, and laid down the principles which he conceived should be observed in their foundation and establishment. It was against the system of free grants and the low price of Crown lands that he grounded his chief objections in his works on colonization,* attributing the slow growth of the early English colonies mainly to these causes.

His argument was the futility of attempting to secure hired labour side by side with great cheapness of land; and that the exchange of land for labour was the only method of realizing a just proportion between land, labour, and capital. He contended strenuously for this principle—"the universal sale of land instead of land-grants, and the exclusive employment of the purchaser's money to promote emigration."

It was in the same year that the Swan River

---

* "A View of the Art of Colonization" (1829). "England and America: a Comparison of the Social and Political State of both Nations." 2 vols., 8vo. The second volume contained a treatise on colonization, published 1833.

Settlement was formed (1829) that Captain Sturt, the Government Surveyor in New South Wales, set forth from Sydney on the exploring expedition to trace the course of the Murrumbidgee River. When his discoveries were made known in Great Britain, they attracted the attention of a number of influential men who had long been favourable to emigration, and they determined to take active steps to found a new and free colony in South Australia on the plan put forth by Mr. Wakefield, to embrace the following principles: "That no free grants of land should be made, but that it should be sold at an upset price of not less than twelve shillings per acre nor more than twenty shillings. The money so obtained should form a fund for giving free passages to qualified labourers and mechanics with their wives and families; the colony to bear all its own charges, and to have the principal management of its own affairs." It was thought that the high price of land would prevent the purchase of more than was likely to be cultivated, that the supply of labourers would be in proportion to the land bought, and that the population would be concentrated.

The first practical attempt to found a colony on the southern shores of Australia was made by two or three parties of intending colonists, who were prepared to purchase a tract of land on certain conditions similar to those enumerated above. They placed themselves in communication with Mr. Robert Gouger, who was interested in colonization generally, and was an enthusiastic advocate of the principles laid down by Wakefield. Anxious to see them practically applied, he succeeded in forming two or three provisional committees, but failing to secure either a sufficient subscribed capital, or the adherence of well-known public men, the Government did not regard his proposals with favour, and the matter dropped for a time.

Little by little, however, attention to the subject grew. In 1830 the Colonization Society, formed for the purpose of collecting and diffusing information as to the best plans for establishing colonies, adopted the leading features of Wakefield's scheme as the basis of any operations of a fixed and definite character they might undertake, but no attempt to found a colony in South Australia was made by this society as such, although many of its members afterwards identified themselves with the South Australian Association.

In 1831, when the valuable discoveries of Captain Sturt became more fully known in England, a party of intending colonists at once made proposals to the Government, through the intervention of Major Bacon, for the establishment of a chartered colony in South Australia. But Mr. Hay, Under Secretary of State for the Colonies, promptly threw cold water on the scheme. It was understood, however, that his successor, Lord Howick,* regarded the project with favour.

About this time Mr. Wakefield and Major Bacon sought the co-operation of Colonel Torrens in Parliament. Under the impression that Lord Howick was favourable, Colonel Torrens entered warmly into the matter, and introduced to Lord Goderich, Secretary of State for the Colonies, a deputation including Major Bacon, Mr. Gouger, and Mr. Graham, when an outline of the proposed scheme was submitted to him, and it was inferred that his approval was also given. One part of the principle had already received the sanction of the Government, and had been put into operation in New South Wales, where, prior to 1831, the waste lands were granted free on certain conditions, but had since been put up for sale. "To Lord Howick," says Colonel Torrens, in the introduction to his work on "Colonization," "belongs the honour of having been the first to give practical operation to the principle of selling the colonial lands at the disposal of the Crown, and of employing the proceeds of the sale in conveying voluntary emigrants to the colonies."

In the belief that the Government approved the scheme of the intending colonists, the friends of the movement proceeded to carry it out, and an advertisement appeared in the *Spectator* to the effect that the

* Afterwards Earl Grey.

Government had given its sanction to the plan. But when this advertisement caught the eye of Lord Howick, he issued a memorandum, stating "it was a mistake to affirm that the Government had given its sanction to the plan proposed, and that the terms of approbation in which he expressed himself individually to Major Bacon ought not to have been so construed." He added that he considered it necessary for the Government to have some guarantee in the shape of a subscription list before the matter could be entertained.

To this end Mr. Gouger, with others, again set to work. A provisional committee was formed, and in June, 1832, Colonel Torrens, the chairman, drew up and submitted to Lord Goderich the draft of a charter. It was much too comprehensive a document, fixing the boundaries of the proposed settlement, the sources of capital, the classes of emigrants to be sent out, the powers to be granted to the company, the form of government, and many other details with regard to the emigration of foreigners, the sale of land, the raising of a militia, and the levying of a land tax.

Lord Goderich, "having bestowed the most careful attention upon the various provisions of the instrument," stated in reply that "the transmission of the proposed charter afforded the first occasion which had presented itself during the discussions on this subject for taking a clear and comprehensive view of the plan in all its bearings," and then proceeded to cut the whole scheme to pieces. He objected to the charter on the ground, among other things, that it would virtually transfer to a company the sovereignty of a vast unexplored territory; that it would encroach upon the limits of existing colonies; that the proposal to throw open the settlement to foreigners would give them an equality with British subjects; that the objects of the corporation were defined with far too much latitude as to the employment of their capital; that the investiture of the power of legislation was not sufficiently safeguarded; that they would exclude the King from imposing duties of custom; that a freedom of trade was proposed to which the Navigation and Trades Acts were in opposition; that it was proposed to erect within the British monarchy a government purely republican; and, finally, that they would be the receivers of large sums of public money for the due application of which they did not propose to give any specific security.

Upon Colonel Torrens the task devolved of seeking to remove some of these objections, and of placing matters in a less objectionable light; but although a lengthy correspondence ensued, and a willingness was expressed by the colonel, on behalf of the provisional committee, to considerably modify the draft charter as might be deemed proper and expedient, reserving only the principle of land sales, the application of the proceeds to emigration, and the eventual privilege of a legislative assembly, the main gist of Lord Goderich's reply was that "as the committee were so ready to abandon essential provisions of their scheme, he had serious misgivings as to the maturity of their knowledge and counsel on the very important subject which they had submitted to his consideration."

So ended the negotiations with his Majesty's Government in 1832. The error was in asking too much, and then too little, the result being that they got nothing at all. The provisional committee was broken up, and the intending emigrants took their departure to America and the United States instead of to South Australia.

On the 6th of July, 1833, negotiations with the Government were resumed, and a modified plan for establishing a colony on the southern coast of Australia was submitted by Mr. W. Woolrych Whitmore, M.P., to Mr. E. G. Stanley, successor to Lord Goderich in the Colonial Office. It contemplated the purchase of land by a joint stock company, and by private individuals, and with the proceeds arising from such sales to send out the pauper or unemployed population of the United Kingdom; the expense of establishing the colony to be borne by the company, and a land tax levied to defray the cost of government, the company having the right of pre-emption of one million acres of land at five shillings per acre.

It is not necessary to give the whole scheme in detail, which to a certain extent the Secretary of State received with favour, but suggested so many hard conditions and modifications that the negotiations were abruptly broken off.

Official rebuffs did not in any way damp the ardour of the persistent band of men who had the colonization scheme at heart, and they determined, with the assistance of Mr. Gouger, to make renewed efforts, and enlarge the sphere of their influence. Accordingly, in the early part of 1834, a powerful and influential body—at least, so far as names were concerned—was formed, under the designation of "The South Australian Association," of which Mr. W. W. Whitmore, M.P., was chairman, George Grote, M.P. (the historian of Greece), treasurer, and Mr. Robert Gouger secretary.

The provisional committee—all of whom were, of course, in sympathy with the movement, although, as is usual in such cases, the active work devolved upon a few—was composed of the following well-known men:—

A. Beauclerk, M.P.
Abraham Borradaile, M.P.
Charles Buller, M.P.
H. L. Bulwer, M.P.
J. W. Childers, M.P.
William Clay, M.P.
Raikes Currie.
William Gowan.
George Grote, M.P.
Benjamin Hawes, M.P.
J. H. Hawkins, M.P.
Rowland Hill.
Matthew D. Hill, M.P.
William Hutt, M.P.
John Melville.
Samuel Mills.
Sir S. W. Molesworth, Bart., M.P.
Jacob Montefiore.
George Warde Norman.
G. Poulett Scrope, M.P.
Dr. Southwood Smith.
Edward Strutt, M.P.
Colonel Torrens, M.P.
Daniel Wakefield, Jun.
Henry Warburton, M.P.
Henry G. Ward, M.P.
John Wilkes, M.P.
Joseph Wilson, M.P.
John Ashton Yates.

A draft charter of incorporation was very carefully drawn up and submitted to the Colonial Secretary, and then ensued the inevitable correspondence and discussion. One of the points in dispute was whether the proposed settlement should be a chartered colony or a Crown colony, the difference being, according to the definition of Mr. Grote, that "a colony founded by charter is an example of that delegation of authority which, in perpetual succession, has for ages been a leading principle of the British Government,* while a colony founded by the Crown is an example of that central authority, acting at whatever distance from the seat of Government, by means of temporary agents, which is a leading principle of the French Government."

The association soon found that there was little hope of the Government consenting to the foundation of a chartered colony in South Australia, and accordingly they passed a resolution to the effect that if his Majesty's Government would obtain from Parliament the authority necessary for planting a Crown colony there, provision being made in the Act for the permanent establishment of that mode of disposing of waste land, and of the purchase of such land, which had been recommended by the committee, coupled with provision for good government, the South Australian Association should continue its existence as a private and temporary society for the purpose of promoting the success of the measure.

Matters were now on a fair footing, and Mr. Gouger soon afterwards forwarded to the Colonial Secretary a rough draft of the proposed Bill. Just as the energetic and persevering friends of South Australia were, as it appeared, on the eve of success, there was a change of administration in the Colonial Office, Mr. Spring Rice † succeeding Mr. Stanley as Secretary of State for the Colonies, and a delay arose.

But it was not for long, and in the end it was not disadvantageous, for Mr. Spring Rice took up the matter energetically, and at once expressed his willingness to recommend, on certain unprohibitive conditions,

---

* Cases were cited from the year 1578 to 1791.
† Afterwards Lord Monteagle.

the passing of a Bill on the principles laid down by Mr. Gouger in his rough draft.

The long-looked-for day at length arrived, when "a Bill to erect South Australia into a British province, and to provide for the colonization and government thereof," was brought before the House of Commons by Mr. Whitmore, with the sanction and approval of the Colonial Secretary. Here it had many friends and supporters—Lord Howick, Mr. J. Shaw Lefevre, Lord Stanley, and Mr. Spring Rice, together with some of the parliamentary members of the provisional committee, doing yeomen's service; and it passed the third reading without any serious hindrance. In the House of Lords the Bill was introduced by the Marquis of Normanby, and was so warmly supported by the Duke of Wellington that the opposition, which at one time threatened to be dangerous, was overcome.* He expressed himself as deeply interested in this new experiment in colonization, and desired that it might have a fair trial. He also recommended that Colonel Light, his companion in arms, should be the first surveyor-general of the new colony.

On the 15th of August, 1834, the last day of the session, the Bill received the royal assent.

The leading features of the Act (4 & 5 Will. IV. cap. 95) were briefly as follows:—

The territory to extend from the 132nd to the 141st degree of east longitude, and from the south coast, including the adjacent islands, northwards to the tropic of Capricorn; the whole of the territory within the above limits to be open to settlement by British subjects; it was not to be subject to the laws of other colonies, but only to those expressly enacted for itself; in no case were convicted felons to be landed on its shores; all public lands were to be open for purchase by cash, the minimum price being twelve shillings per acre; the sale of such lands to be under the manage-

---

* For these good services Wakefield was anxious that the capital of the new colony should be named Wellington, but in this he was, as he says, "shabbily frustrated."

ment of a Board of Commissioners empowered to give a title in fee-simple to each purchaser; the whole of the money derived from the sale of waste lands to be employed in conveying labourers, natives of Great Britain and Ireland, to the colony, the labourers so conveyed to be an equal number of both sexes, preference being given to young married people without children, so that purchasers of land might obtain labour for its cultivation; the affairs of the colony to be regulated by the Commissioners until a certain population was reached, at which time a representative assembly should be entrusted with the duties of government, upon the condition that it undertook to discharge any existing colonial debt.

So far all was smooth sailing. But, carefully sandwiched between clauses which could not fail to give satisfaction, the Act further provided that no part of the expense of founding or governing the colony should fall on the mother country, and it authorized the Commissioners to borrow money *on security of the colony* to the extent of £200,000, but £20,000 of the money so borrowed was to be invested in exchequer bills in the names of trustees to be appointed by his Majesty.

The concluding clause of the Act nearly rendered the whole measure inoperative; it restrained the Commissioners from entering upon the exercise of their general powers until they had invested the required £20,000 in exchequer bills, and until £35,000 worth of land had been sold.

This was the *crux*. However desirable the country might be considered for emigration, no sane person could be expected to invest his money in land there until he had the assurance that a colony would be founded and a government established.

A glance at the Act (a rough outline only is given above) will show that the original propositions of the projectors of the colony had, in the course of the negotiations and the passage of the Bill through Parliament, undergone many important revisions, until almost the only things granted that were at first asked were the disposal of the waste lands at a uniform price, and the application of the proceeds to the purposes of emigration. Some of the features of a chartered colony were retained, but in the main they were those of a Crown colony, the Crown, however, agreeing to delegate almost absolute power and authority to a Board of Commissioners.

The provisions for the disposal of public lands presented two or three marked peculiarities. The title in the first instance was not to be direct from the Crown, but from the Commissioners, to whom the Act gave the power of sale; it was to be in fee-simple, and no royalty or reservation whatever was to be made by the Crown, so that all above and below the soil was to be unreservedly the property of the purchaser.

Although the Act did not in all respects meet the wishes or the anticipations of the projectors, it nevertheless embodied certain admirable and novel principles. It provided for the sale of *all* public lands at a uniform price, and the possibility of free grants being thereby precluded, it seemed that the chief cause of previous failure in planting colonies was obviated. The colony was never to be subjected to the curse of convictism. The settlement of population was to be regulated in groups, in order to secure the advantages of neighbouring communities. To this end lands generally were to be surveyed in small blocks of eighty acres. The sales were to be by public auction, so that the evils of large monopolies might,to a great extent, be avoided.

"In the old colonies," said Mr. John Stephens,[*] "vast tracts of land were granted to favourites; in South Australia no land whatever is granted on any other terms than the payment of a fixed price per acre. In the old colonies there has always been a deficiency of labourers, and, if capitalists imported them, land was so cheap that they immediately ceased to work for hire, and without adequate capital began to be farmers on their own account; the result of which was, that the

[*] "Rise and Progress of South Australia" (1839).

largest possible quantity of land was cultivated in the worst possible manner. But in South Australia a remedy, at once simple and effectual, has been provided, the whole net proceeds of the sales of land being appropriated to give a free passage to young and industrious emigrants of both sexes, by which means the capitalists will be ensured an adequate supply of labour. Thus the purchaser does not buy land so much as the facility of obtaining combined labour—that which alone makes land valuable. Here, then, is the first attempt, in the history of colonization, to plant a colony upon correct principles—to ensure to the labourer employment, and to the capitalist an ample supply of labour."

Colonel Torrens, expatiating on this grand feature in the new sphere of colonization, a few years later in the House of Commons, said, as the result of the experiment, "I am not merely prepared to show that emigration would cost less than maintaining paupers in their parishes at home, and would thus prove a measure of permanent economy and retrenchment; I am prepared to go much further than this. I am prepared to prove both theoretically and practically that emigration may be so conducted as to replace with interest the whole of the expenditure incurred in effecting it, and to aid the finances of the country by opening new and not inconsiderable sources of direct public revenue."

The difficulties of the projectors of the new colony did not cease, as some had been sanguine enough to imagine, with the passing of the Act.

A Board of Commissioners was duly appointed,* and at once the question arose how the money required to be invested before any valid steps could be taken, was to be raised. For six months they met at intervals to discuss the problem, but as they did not come any

---

* The first Board of Commissioners was composed as follows: J. W. Childers, M.P., W. Clay, M.P., G. Grote, M.P., G. W. Norman, Colonel Torrens, M.P., and W. W. Whitmore, M.P., chairman. Mr. Rowland Hill (afterwards Sir Rowland Hill, who introduced the Penny Postal System) was appointed secretary to the board.

nearer to a solution, they availed themselves of a change of ministry at the end of 1834 as a fitting opportunity for tendering their resignations, although, of course, they were appointed to give effect to the Act of the Legislature, and their functions as Colonization Commissioners had nothing whatever to do with party politics.

On the 5th of May, 1835, the first public act of Lord Glenelg, on taking office as Secretary of State for the Colonies, after the change of ministry, was to gazette as Colonization Commissioners the following: G. F. Angas, E. Barnard * (Agent-General for the Australian colonies), W. Hutt,* John Shaw Lefevre * (late Under Secretary of State), W. A. Mackinnon, M.P., S. Mills, Jacob Montefiore, G. Palmer, jun., J. Wright, Colonel Torrens, chairman, and Rowland Hill, secretary.

The difficulties which their predecessors had regarded as insurmountable, the new Board faced with courage and resolution. They had to raise the required guarantees before any act of theirs would be valid. "The difficulty of accomplishing these objects," said Colonel Torrens, "will be immediately perceived when it is considered that South Australia was at that period an unexplored wilderness, and that the colony, the revenue of which was to be the security for the proposed loan, was not then in existence. But this was not all. Before they could proceed to sell land in the wilderness, or raise a loan upon the security of revenues which remained to be created, it was necessary that considerable expense should be incurred in providing offices, engaging clerks and agents, and in explaining to the public the principles and the prospects of the new colony by printed papers and advertisements."

Application was made to the Colonial Department for the use of offices and the privilege of free postage, but even these small requests were not granted. A loan of £1000 was soon raised to meet the preliminary expenses, but the graver matter was not so easily disposed of.

* Those gentlemen against whose names an asterisk is placed were nominees of Lord Glenelg.

The first regulations for the sale of South Australian lands were published by the Commissioners in June, 1835. They had "considered it their duty to attempt realizing a price considerably higher than the minimum of 12s. per acre required in the Act of Parliament," and, "after mature consideration," the price was fixed at 20s. per acre in the first instance, or for a lot consisting of one town acre, and a country section of 80 acres, £80. Priority of choice with regard to both town acres and country sections was to be given to the holders of the first 437 land orders secured in England. In addition to the 81-acre allotments, any one paying the price of 4000 acres of land, or upwards, was to have the right of a special survey in any compact district not exceeding 16,000 acres, and select his 4000 acres from such district before any other application would be entertained. Brilliant opportunities! but no one seemed to care to avail himself of them.

For two months the Commissioners exerted all their energies to promote the sale of land, and every effort was made to give the experiment a fair trial. Circulars were issued with maps and pressing appeals; the best agents were appointed, and it was proposed to delegate some of the powers and honours of the Commissioners to gentlemen of rank, talent, and influence in the counties who might form the members of future associations. But all to no purpose. Not half of the required quantity had been disposed of when there came a pause; the length of their tether had been reached, and it seemed that, as there was nothing further they could do, the whole thing must collapse.

It was at this juncture that one of the Commissioners, Mr. George Fife Angas, a wealthy merchant, who had for some years been quietly working in the interests of the proposed new colony, came forward as leader of the forlorn hope—brought forward and carried into effect a scheme without which the colonization of South Australia, under the conditions of the Act of Parliament, would have been utterly impossible.

CHAPTER III.

HOW THE COLONY WAS FOUNDED.

Mr. George Fife Angas.—Necessity for a Joint Stock Company.—Purchase of the stipulated £35,000 worth of Land.—Raising the Guarantee Sum of £20,000.— Formation of the South Australian Company.—Objects contemplated.—Fleet of the South Australian Company.—Choice of a Governor.—Colonel Charles James Napier.—Money and Troops.—Captain J. Hindmarsh.—His remarkable Career.—First Colonial Officers and their Salaries.—H.M.S. *Buffalo.*—Colonel Light and his Instructions.—The Founders of South Australia.

"WITHOUT some collateral association to assist the Commissioners," said Mr. George Fife Angas to his colleagues on the Board, "I do not see how the Act is to be carried into effect." He then proceeded to unfold a scheme, which was, in brief, that a joint stock company should be formed with sufficient capital to purchase the requisite quantity of land; to take out its own agents, servants, and other emigrants, and supply them with provisions while they carried on operations of a reproductive and remunerative character; and to provide the capital for the working of the colonial Government.

At first the Commissioners strongly demurred to the suggestion of Mr. Angas, but when at length they saw that without such assistance they were powerless to act, and might as well tender their resignations, they confessed this happy thought was the only practical idea that had come before them, and they gave their unanimous consent to the effort being made.

Mr. Angas was ready to act on the moment, and, assisted by Mr. Henry Kingscote and Mr. Thomas Smith, at once subscribed sufficient capital to purchase the whole of the unsold land, to be handed over to the Company, when formed, at cost price, with interest at five per cent. This purchase was the basis of the operations of the Company, and, as a matter of fact, of all future operations of the Commissioners, and thus the initial difficulty in founding a colony under the Act was overcome. But a concession had to be made by the Commissioners to effect it. The offer for the purchase of the land was at the reduced rate of 12s. per acre, partly because it was evident there were no more purchasers to be obtained at £1 per acre, and partly because this reduced price would be an incentive to capitalists to invest in the proposed Company. This offer was accepted, and, to avoid clashing with the previous sales, the size of the country sections was altered to 134 acres and one town acre, instead of eighty acres and one town acre; hence the difference between a "preliminary land order" and one subsequently granted. In addition, the Commissioners resolved to sell at 12s. per acre to any who could give proof that they were prepared to take out adequate capital for the improvement of the colony; but this price was only available until the 1st of March, 1836, after which date the price was to be £1 per acre, the sections to consist of eighty acres as at first, and the sales to take place in the colony.

Having disposed, so far, of difficulty number one, the next question was how to raise the required guarantee sum of £20,000 to invest in the names of trustees. Having power to raise £200,000 if they could, the Commissioners threw open for tender by the public the sum of £80,000, as offering greater inducements to capitalists than the smaller sum. The proposals were well advertised in the London papers and by circular, but at the end of the time specified, only six tenders were sent in for a total amount of £13,000, at not less than ten per cent. interest, and with conditions that could not possibly be accepted.

The Commissioners then appealed to Mr. Wright, one of the members of their Board, to undertake the formation of a list, and after much trouble he was at length able to offer terms to the Commissioners—not such as they approved, but, as there was no alternative, they agreed to accept, and on the 19th of November, 1835, the £20,000 was invested in the names of three trustees in the three per cent. consols. The two great difficulties having now been overcome, the Commissioners at last saw a prospect of putting the necessary machinery in motion for founding the colony.

The origin of the South Australian Company is so intimately associated with the establishment of the colony, that we must now turn our attention to its operations.

It was no easy matter to start it. The capital was fixed at £500,000, with power to increase it to £1,000,000; but operations were to commence when the subscriptions reached £200,000. No smaller sum would suffice, for Mr. Angas was persuaded that no capitalists would embark their money in the distant colony unless the Company engaged to introduce ample capital and labour; and this, of course, enhanced the difficulty.

"We had," said Mr. Angas, upon whose shoulders the whole burden of the undertaking rested—"we had, as it were, to go to the capitalists of this kingdom and say, 'Gentlemen, lend us your money to carry out this scheme, notwithstanding there has not yet been an acre of land surveyed, nor a British harbour formed. Advance it to us on the faith of our settled conviction, notwithstanding its difficulties, that the project is quite practicable; that from the information we possess of the country we believe it must succeed; for the Act of Parliament presents advantages in the secure title it gives to the property, and the liberal principles of its government, that, under the blessing of Providence and the use of proper means, will eventually lead to a rich reward for your confidence.' This appeal," he continues, "we had to make, not only with public opinion adverse to us (a strong prejudice existed against some of the early projectors of the new system of colonization, of which we had in some degree to endure the consequences), the Government at that time lukewarm, and many of the members of each House of Parliament opposed to the whole project, but also a formidable opposition from powerful individuals resident in this country, who were deeply interested in the rival colonies of Western Australia, Van Diemen's Land, and New South Wales, besides the contempt thrown on the plan by the public press of these colonies themselves, although the writers should have seen that, if successful, it would of necessity become an important element of their own advancement. Above all, we had to meet the prejudices of many who, not having studied the principles and plans of our undertaking, concluded that it was purely Utopian."

In spite of all difficulties, on the 22nd of January, 1836, the South Australian Company was formed, with a subscribed capital of £200,000. The original directors of the Company were—George Fife Angas (chairman), Raikes Currie, M.P., Charles Hindley, M.P., James Hyde, Henry Kingscote, John Pirie (alderman), John Rundle, M.P., Thomas Smith, James Ruddall Todd, and Henry Waymouth.

The objects contemplated by the proprietary were: (1) The erection upon their town land of wharves, warehouses, and dwelling-houses, and letting the same to the colonists, or otherwise disposing of them. (2) The improvement and cultivation of their country land, and the leasing or sale of part of it if deemed expedient. (3) The laying out of farms, the erection of suitable buildings thereon, and letting the same to industrious tenants on lease, with the right of purchase before the expiration of such lease at a price to be fixed at the time of the tenant taking possession. (4) The growth of wool for the European markets. (5) The pursuit of whale, seal, and other fisheries in the gulfs and seas around the colony, and the curing and salting of fish suitable for exportation. (6) The salting and curing of beef and pork for the stores of ships and for the purpose of general export. (7) The establishment of a bank or banks in, or connected with, the colony, making loans on the security of land or produce, and the conducting of such banking operations as the directors might think expedient.

Although these were set forth as the primary objects of the Company, it was soon found that they were not sufficiently comprehensive. In order to give confidence to intending shareholders, and to ensure the successful establishment of the infant settlement, the directors had to consider what trades would be imperatively required, so as not to leave their manager without needful aid; to select, contract with, and provide the requisite tools for carpenters, brickmakers, lime-burners, blacksmiths, boat-builders, fishermen, and others, and generally to supply everything that would be needful, from the keels of whale-ships to pins and needles.

With the formation of the South Australian Company, as none of his Majesty's Commissioners were allowed to have any pecuniary interest in the colony they were appointed to establish, Mr. Angas felt it to be his duty at once to tender his resignation as a member of that Board. He was requested, however, to retain his position until the end of the year 1835, and was thus able to see all the preliminary measures required by the Act completed, and was permitted to nominate his successor, Mr. Josiah Roberts. Mr. Wright also, and on the same grounds, retired from the Board.

Such was the vigour with which the directors of the South Australian Company entered upon their work, that on the 22nd of February, exactly one month from the formation of the Company, not only had all the preliminaries been successfully arranged—secretary, clerks for London office, colonial manager, and overseers for each department appointed, and instructed in the measures they were to adopt on their arrival in the colony—but, what is almost incredible, the ship *John Pirie* had been chartered, and was under weigh fully laden with goods, live stock, and twenty-three adult passengers. Two days later the *Duke of York*, freighted with whaling stores and having on board forty-two passengers, including the colonial manager, Mr. S. Stephens, and other officers and servants of the Company, was also ready for sea, and both vessels immediately proceeded on their voyage.

Two other ships, the *Lady Mary Pelham* and the *Emma*, freighted with whaling and general stores, and together taking out fifty-one passengers, left England in March and April respectively.

All the Company's vessels were supplied with provisions equal to one year's consumption, and in the event of accident or loss sustained on the voyage or otherwise, the officers were furnished with the means of supplying themselves from Van Diemen's Land, and arrangements were also made for a regular supply of provisions from Hamburg. Besides the requisites for the voyage, sheep, cattle, pigs, and other live stock were sent out, so that the colonists on landing might have an immediate supply of fresh food, without which they would probably have suffered as did the early settlers in the North American colonies.

The whole of the early proceedings of the Company were characterized by great energy, mainly through the zeal and liberality of Mr. Angas, its founder and chairman, who allowed the necessary business to be carried on in his own offices, placed at its disposal at prime cost several vessels with their equipments and provisions for employment in the South Sea whale-fishery, handed over at cost price the land which he and his colleagues had purchased, and in every particular became the prime mover in the whole concern. "He made more sacrifices in time, health, and property," says Mr. John Stephens, in his "Rise and Progress of South Australia," "for the accomplishment of a public object, than many more wealthy merchants would have made in the prosecution of a hopeful private enterprise."

Meanwhile the Colonization Commissioners, having succeeded by the aid of the South Australian Company in fulfilling the requirements of the Act as regarded the sale of land, and raising the stipulated loan, proceeded to obtain the Orders in Council and letters patent for establishing the colony, and to this end Colonel Torrens, the chairman of the Board, successfully negotiated with Lord Glenelg, who entered with spirit into the whole matter, and rendered important service to the Commissioners.

The next steps were to make choice of a Governor and other officers, and to provide for their equipment and departure.

The choice of the Commissioners fell upon Colonel Charles James Napier (afterwards the hero of Scinde) for the office of Governor. In reply to the invitation of the Board, the colonel stated that he could not accept the Governorship of South Australia without troops, and the power to draw upon the British Government for money in case of need.

With regard to money matters, he observed "that while sufficient security exists for the supply of labour in the colony, there does not appear to be any security that the supply of capital will be sufficient to employ that labour, and if it be not employed the consequences must be disastrous. I therefore deem it necessary to have the means of meeting this, and other accidents which cannot be foreseen, but which inevitably arise in the execution of all experiments; and the plan of the colony is an experiment."

As to the troops, he wrote, "I will not attempt to govern a large body of people in a desert, where they must suffer considerable inconvenience (if not hardships), without I have a force to protect what is good against that which is bad; and such a force is the more necessary where, as in Australia, the supply of spirituous liquors will be abundant. The colony will be a small colony without discipline, suffering more or less from privation, and with plenty of liquor. Experience has taught me what scenes this would produce unless the leader had a controlling physical force. Such," he concluded, "are my demands and my motives for making them."

As both these demands were at variance with the self-supporting principle on which the colony was to be established, the negotiations with Colonel Napier fell through, and Captain (afterwards Admiral Sir John) Hindmarsh, R.N., was selected and appointed Governor. His career had been remarkable and adventurous. "He was with Lord Howe on the 1st of June, 1794; with Admiral Cornwallis in his glorious retreat; with Sir James Saumarez at Algeciras and in the Straits of Gibraltar; at the capture of Flushing, of the Isle of France and of Java; with Lord Cochrane at Basque Roads; and with Nelson both at the Nile and at Trafalgar.

"At the battle of the Nile he was a midshipman on board the *Bellerophon*, and so destructive was the fire of the enemy, that for some time he was the only officer left upon the quarter-deck. He received a wound in the head which deprived him of the sight of one eye, but he did not quit his post. The enemy's ship, *L'Orient*, caught fire, and the flames threatened to communicate to the *Bellerophon*, when Hindmarsh, being the only officer on deck, ordered the topsail to be set and the cable to be cut, and thus saved the ship from destruction. He had his proud reward; Nelson himself thanked the young hero before the assembled officers and crew, and repeated these thanks upon the deck of the *Victory* when presenting him with his lieutenant's commission."

The question of salaries to colonial officers was a difficult one for the Commissioners to settle, as they were anxious to obtain the services of the most efficient men at the lowest possible cost; but eventually it was arranged that the salary of the Governor should be £800 per annum, and an allowance of £500 for outfit.

The following gentlemen were appointed to hold offices in the colony :—

Office.	Name.	Salary.
Resident Commissioner and Registrar	Mr. James Hurtle Fisher	£400
Colonial Secretary	Mr. Robert Gouger	400
Judge	Sir John William Jeffcott	500
Advocate-General and Crown Solicitor	Mr. Charles Mann	300
Naval Officer and Harbour Master	Captain Thomas Lipson, R.N.	200
Governor's Secretary and Clerk of the Council	Mr. George Stevenson	200
Colonial Treasurer, also Collector of Revenue and Accountant-General	Mr. Osmond Gilles	300
Commissioner of Immigration, also Auditor-General	Mr. John Brown	250
Surveyor-General	Colonel William Light	400
Deputy-Surveyor	Mr. George Strickland Kingston	200
Assistant-Surveyors	Mr. Boyle Travers Finniss Mr. William Jacob Mr. Neale Mr. Claughton Mr. Pullen	100
Junior Assistant-Surveyors	Mr. R. G. Symonds Mr. John Cannan Mr. Alfred Hardy	50
Colonial Storekeeper	Mr. Thomas Gilbert	100
Colonial Surgeon	Dr. Cotter	100
Survey Surgeon	John Woodforde	

The appointment of colonial chaplain was made subsequently, when the Rev. Charles Beaumont Howard was selected, at a salary of £250.

The next step of the Commissioners was to apply to Lord Glenelg for a vessel of war to convey the Governor and survey party to South Australia, and afterwards to be used, for a time, for surveying purposes. But the application was not entertained; whereupon the chairman of the South Australian Company, annoyed, in common with his colleagues, not only at the parsimony of the Government, but also at the vexatious delay at a critical time, offered to place one of the Company's pioneer vessels at the disposal of the Governor and his officers—an offer which was, of course, declined, but it had the effect of stirring up the Colonial Office generally. Meanwhile Captain Hindmarsh had been beforehand, and had obtained the offer of the *Buffalo*, a heavy transport about to proceed to New Zealand for spars. But this old tub was totally unfit for surveying purposes, and as in the circumstances the Commissioners considered it desirable that the survey party should precede the Governor, the fast-sailing brig *Rapid*, of a hundred and sixty-two tons, was purchased, and despatched on the 4th of May, under the command of Colonel Light, the surveyor-general. Owing to the indisposition of Colonel Light and other causes, the *Cygnet*, another vessel chartered by the Commissioners for use in the colony during the progress of the surveys, preceded the *Rapid* by about six weeks (24th of March), having on board eighty-four passengers and a division of the survey party.

The officers sent out by the Commissioners were furnished with very explicit instructions how they were to act on reaching their destination. Colonel Light was to land two or three gardeners on Kangaroo Island, and direct them to bring a small piece of land into immediate cultivation, stocking it with vegetables for the use of the colonists generally. He was also to leave the wives and families of the officers and men with stores and a force sufficient to protect them from attack.

The colonel was then to make a careful examination of the coast in the central parts of the colony, excepting only those places where the previous explorations of Captain Flinders and others clearly showed that no harbour was to be found. His attention was to be particularly directed to Nepean Bay and Port Lincoln, but more especially to the line of coast extending from the eastern point of Encounter Bay to the northern point of Gulf St. Vincent. An inlet and harbour reported to have been discovered by one Captain Jones was to be examined, and Lake Alexandrina was also to be skirted, with a view to finding an outlet other than that discovered by Captain Sturt. Further, he was instructed to find out and survey the best sites for towns and settlements, and especially for the site of the capital; so that on the arrival of the Governor and the first body of emigrants, the whole machinery of the new colony might be at once set in motion.

As an example of the care taken by the Commissioners, and particularly by Colonel Torrens, the chairman, who drew up most of the instructions, a few details may be inserted here of the directions given to Colonel Light to assist him in determining the choice of a site for the capital: "In the opinion of the Commissioners the best site for the first town would be that which combined in the highest degree the following advantages: A commodious harbour, safe and accessible at all seasons of the year; a considerable tract of fertile land immediately adjoining; an abundant supply of fresh water; facilities for internal communication and for communication with the port; distance from the limit of the colony as a means of avoiding interference from without in the principle of colonization; distance from the neighbourhood of extensive sheepwalks. All the foregoing are to be considered of primary importance, and the following of secondary value: A supply of building material, as timber, stone, or brick, earth, and lime; facilities for draining, and coal."

In the exercise of the important duties intrusted to him, Colonel Light was to make himself acquainted, as far as possible, with the circumstances which had determined the sites of new towns in the United States of America, in Canada, and more especially in the Australian colonies, and he was to pay particular attention to those which, in the latter colonies, had led to an actual change, or to the desire for change in the sites after their first settlement.

Throughout all his proceedings he was to exercise the utmost caution to prevent collision with the natives, and with this view he was to avoid any unnecessary division of his party, and take care that each detachment was placed under the charge of an officer upon whose intelligence, humanity, caution, temper, and courage he could fully rely. Wild animals were to be considered the property of the natives, and, if required for food, to be purchased. Sporting was accordingly to be discouraged, and in any parts inhabited by natives prohibited. The colonel was reminded that not only the safety of his party, but the future security of the colonists generally, and the state of feeling which would afterwards exist between the two races, would depend largely on the attention paid to these instructions.

To the Resident Commissioner and other officers the instructions prepared by the Commissioners were equally full and explicit, and they display great judgment, foresight, and ability.

On the 30th of July, H.M.S. *Buffalo*, the third vessel sent out by the Commissioners, followed, with Captain Hindmarsh and one hundred and seventy-six other passengers on board. The place of rendezvous, whither eight vessels in all had preceded the *Buffalo*, was Nepean Bay, Kangaroo Island.

"Colonization," wrote Coleridge in 1834 (the year of his death, and a month after attending the meeting of the British Association of Science at Cambridge)—"colonization is an imperative duty on Great Britain. God seems to hold out His fingers to us over the sea. But it must be colonization of hope; not, as has happened, of despair."

And it was so. South Australia was not doomed to the penalty of land monopoly as in the case of the Swan River Settlement, or to the contamination and curse of being a penal colony like New South Wales and Van Diemen's Land. Prinsep, in his "Letters from Van Diemen's Land," draws a graphic picture of the moral contagion to which the family of a right-minded emigrant might be subjected there. "Freemen find so many ways of making money here, that they will not take service, and so the convicts, or, as they are delicately called, 'the prisoners,' supply all demands of this nation; and if the histories of every house were made public, you would shudder; even in our small *ménage*, our cook has committed murder, our footman burglary, and our housemaid bigamy!"*

It was also a distinct advantage that the regulations for the government of the new colony rested almost entirely in a Board of Commissioners, whose whole attention could be given to the subject, instead of being placed, as was the case in the older colonies, under the Colonial Secretary for the time being—"a functionary who has upon his hands the destinies of millions of people of every clime and every race, and whose office, being a political one, is changed with every change of ministry."

Honours are divided among the claimants to be founders of South Australia. Edward Gibbon Wakefield was the first to set forth the principles of the new form of colonization; Mr. Gouger, the secretary of the South Australian Association, took up the idea, and worked it into practical shape; Colonel Torrens brought experience and influence to bear to make the scheme popular, and ensure its acceptance by the Government; while Mr. George Fife Angas made the working of the Act of Parliament possible.

* Quoted in Stephens' "Rise and Progress of South Australia" (1839).

CHAPTER IV.

THE PIONEER SETTLERS.

Arrival of Pioneer Vessels.—"Governor" Walker.—Mr. Samuel Stephens.—Kingscote, Kangaroo Island.—Colonel Light and the Survey Staff.—Examination of St. Vincent's Gulf and Spencer's Gulf.—First Contact with Natives.—Holdfast Bay.—Lost in the Bush.—Removal of Settlers from Kangaroo Island.—Captain Light decides against Shores of Port Lincoln for Site of Capital.—Arrival of Governor Hindmarsh. — Proclamation of the Colony.—First Banquet in South Australia.—The "Makers" of the Colony.

THE first of the South Australian Company's vessels to arrive at Nepean Bay, Kangaroo Island, was the *Duke of York*, freighted with whaling stores and implements, and having on board Mr. Samuel Stephens, colonial manager of the Company, eight other passengers of independent means, and twenty-nine labourers.* She dropped anchor in the bay on the 27th of July, 1836. Three days later, another of the Company's fleet, the *Lady Mary Pelham*, with two settlers and twenty-nine labourers on board, made her appearance;

* Mr. Thomas Hudson Beare, second in command under the Company; Mrs. Beare and four children; Miss C. H. Beare, afterwards Mrs. Samuel Stephens; Mr. D. H. Schryvogle, clerk; Henry Mitchell, butcher; C. Powell, gardener; Neale, carpenter; Wm. West, labourer—the last four being emigrants. The first duty performed on setting foot ashore was to read the Church of England Service, in which all joined, the captain (Morgan) concluding with an extempore thanksgiving prayer for the prosperous voyage.

while the *John Pirie*, the first to leave England, laden with twenty-eight labourers, provisions, and general stores, did not arrive until the 16th of August.

All three vessels, however, reached the colony before the *Rapid*, the first ship sent out by the Board of Commissioners. The first colonist to set foot on the island was Mr. Samuel Stephens, whose first act was to select a site, and then to erect upon it a mud hut, surround it by a small battery, and plant upon the roof the British ensign. But Mr. Stephens and the first settlers soon found that they were not "monarchs of all they surveyed," for they were shortly afterwards interviewed by the lord of the isle, one " Governor" Walker, who had lived there for many years. His hut stood on a piece of good land some distance from the shore, in the neighbourhood of fresh water, and was surrounded with a cleared and well-cultivated piece of ground.* The only other residents on the island were a few sealers, whalers, and convicts who had escaped from the neighbouring penal settlements.

In the face of many difficulties—such as lack of water near at hand, tent-life in an inclement winter, salt beef and pork as the only meat obtainable, the proximity of convicts and whalers, apprehensive imaginations, and uncertainty as to the site of the chief town—a pleasant picture is given by a visitor to the island shortly after the first colonists landed. "Before us," he says, "were the hills, on the slope of which lies the town 'Kingscote.' These hills are covered entirely with wood, having, from the sea, the appearance of an impenetrable jungle, with here and there a group of dead trees rearing their gaunt and withered limbs above their fellows. A little patch had been cleared at the slope of one of these hills, and there stood a solitary white cottage, the property of Mr. Samuel Stephens. On the brow of the hill, looking down a steep precipice into the sea, were some half-dozen wooden huts of former immigrants.

* "Governor" Walker continued to reside on the island for nearly ten years after the first settlers landed, and died while on a visit to Adelaide, in 1856.

On the beach was the skeleton of a storehouse then under erection, around which were four or five huts built of bushes; in one of them they were performing Divine service, the summons to attend which was given by means of a bell hung up in a tree."

This is a pleasant picture, but, unfortunately, it was soon found that the settlement on Kangaroo Island was a mistake. Flinders, it will be remembered, had given a flourishing account of it as an eligible site for a settlement, and this had been confirmed in much stronger terms by one Captain Sutherland, who visited the island in 1819. He described the land and timber as excellent, and intimated his intention of settling there when the colony was founded. Flinders spoke chiefly of the number of kangaroos and other animals he found, and his account of the prodigious number of pelicans on a lagoon of the island inspired James Montgomery's imaginative poem, "The Pelican Island." Sutherland, on the other hand, described in glowing terms the interior, the fertility of the soil, and its beautiful tracts of level ground. As a matter of fact, it was little better than a desert island, deficient of every resource, except abundance of salt, and in every respect unsuitable for settlement, and incapable of repaying the South Australian Company for its outlay of money. But early lessons had to be learnt by experience, and the Company, influenced by the favourable reports they had received, could hardly be held responsible for the mistake of placing their first colonists on this wretched island. Moreover, they had other motives. At Kangaroo Island was the only port of the new province where there were any European settlers; the eastern shore of the Gulf of St. Vincent, which afterwards became the great centre of population, was practically unknown. In addition to this it was imperative that the first settlers should have a means of livelihood, and the island had long been known as an eligible station for the whale-fishery, a branch of industry which the Company intended to largely develop.

It was, however, soon to be demonstrated that with

the mainland before them, almost boundless in extent, and rich in every kind of natural wealth, it was a fatal error for the settlers to remain on Kangaroo Island.

On the 20th of August the brig *Rapid*, with Colonel Light and the survey staff on board — including Lieutenant Field, R.N., Mr. J. S. Pullen (afterwards vice-admiral), Messrs. W. Hill, Wm. Jacob, and G. Claughton, surveyors; Dr. Woodforde, and Mr. Alfred Baker, mate—arrived at Nepean Bay. The colonel was no ordinary man, and his life had been full of romantic adventure. He was of mixed race—half European, half Malay—and was born in 1784, at Malacca. His mother was the daughter of King Quedah, sovereign of the Malacca territory. Young Light was brought up in England, entered the navy and afterwards the military service as a cavalry officer, and served in the Peninsular War as lieutenant of the 4th Light Dragoons. He was an excellent linguist, and in the Intelligence Department of the army rendered important service to Lord Wellesley by his thorough knowledge of French and Spanish. Some of his remarkable adventures are recorded in Napier's "Peninsular War." He left the army soon after the battle of Waterloo, and married the daughter of the Duke of Richmond. He next accompanied Sir Robert Wilton to Spain to aid in the Spanish revolutionary war, and received the rank of colonel in the Spanish forces. Later on he accepted service in the navy of the Pasha of Egypt, where he became acquainted with Captain Hindmarsh, Governor-Elect of South Australia.

After examining the South Australian Company's settlement at Kingscote, and satisfying himself that it was an impossible place for colonization, Colonel Light proceeded to a bay which he named Rapid Bay, after his brig, and thence to St. Vincent's Gulf, landing occasionally to ascertain the nature of the coast. Several days were spent in fruitless search for the harbour, said to have been visited by Captain Jones. He could not identify it, however, but found one which he considered would be valuable at a future time.

After exploring the gulf he returned to Rapid Bay, where he was met by Mr. (afterwards Sir) John Morphett and Mr. Samuel Stephens, who brought the news that the *Cygnet* had arrived in Nepean Bay. The *Rapid* was at once sent thither to bring over the assistant-surveyors.

The *Cygnet* had brought over eighty-four passengers, namely, fifteen cabin and sixty-nine steerage. Mr. (afterwards Sir) G. S. Kingston, deputy-surveyor, was in command of the division of the survey party brought out in this vessel, and among others on board were Mr. B. T. Finniss, assistant-surveyor; Captain Lipson, R.N., harbour-master; Mr. Edward Wright, surgeon; and Messrs. Morphett and Powys, unattached. According to instructions, the passengers and stores were landed at Kingscote Harbour, but after hearing from Colonel Light that Kangaroo Island was totally unfit for colonization, they were reshipped, and the *Cygnet* proceeded up the gulf and anchored in Holdfast Bay. Here the passengers and stores were landed, and the tents pitched on the beach near the creek. One of the first cases unpacked contained twenty-four muskets, which were distributed, and a watch set to guard against a sudden attack by the natives, whose encampment was known to be at no great distance. The precautions were unnecessary, as the natives were very shy, and did not venture to approach the new-comers, until Mr. W. Williams went to their encampment, and induced one of them to return with him to the settlement, where the man remained for four days, and then suddenly disappeared to tell his tribe of the wonders he had seen, and to bring them back with him to behold some of the novelties of civilization. A friendly feeling thus sprung up between the sable children of the forest and the new-comers.

The camp of the first settlers at Holdfast Bay, viewed as the nucleus of a nation, was novel and interesting. The dwellings, like those on Kangaroo Island, were frail, tents predominating, but interspersed with huts constructed of reeds, bark, and branches of trees. Boxes and trunks served for tables and chairs. As there were neither vehicles nor animals, all wood had to be carried, and water conveyed on skids, or sledges; cooking operations were carried on in the open air, the triangle with hook and chain, the three-legged pot and camp-oven, the hook-pot and frying-pan being the utensils most in use.

There was work for everybody to do in providing the necessaries of life—baking, cooking, hunting, and fishing. Daily discoveries were made of fresh phases in the features and character of the country and its singular inhabitants, and, in the absence of any newspaper, every one took up his parable and told of exploits in killing kangaroos, emus, opossums, snakes, lizards, wild dogs, or other animals and reptiles.

Meanwhile Colonel Light was making important explorations and examinations of the plains on the eastern side of the gulf. On the 4th of October he wrote—

"I cannot express my delight at seeing no bounds to a flat of fine rich-looking country, with an abundance of fresh-water lagoons, which, if dry in summer, convinced me that we need not dig a deep well to gain a sufficient supply. The little river, too, was deep, and it struck me that much might hereafter be made of this little stream." On the 5th Messrs. Claughton and Jacob were sent on shore to trace the river up, if they could, until they found fresh water in it. On their return they reported that the river was fresh about four miles from the mouth, and that it was then a narrow stream bearing to the north-east, and appeared to have its source in the plains. "A circumstance," wrote Colonel Light, "that led me to suppose that more of these lagoons existed in that direction, and as every appearance indicated that these lagoons would be dry in summer, I felt convinced that the torrents from the mountains would be the fountain from whence they were now filled. My previous observations at sea, before I saw this country, were, that all the vapours from the prevalent south-westerly winds would rest on the mountains here, and that we should, if we could locate this side the gulf, be never in dread of those droughts so often experienced on the eastern coast of Australia. And I was now fully persuaded by the evidence here shown, as well as the repeated collection of clouds, and by rain falling on the hills even at this season of the year."

Such were the observations made, and the impressions formed by Colonel Light on visiting for the first time the arm of the sea, or salt-water creek, which was destined to become the principal harbour of South Australia. In his further examinations along the coast, can be traced, from his journals, visits to what are now known as Torrens River, the Reedbeds, Holdfast Bay, the creek at Glenelg with the little river Sturt flowing into it, and so on.

A highly favourable opinion of the locality was impressed on his mind, and, although he had not yet fixed upon any part of it as the site for the capital, his examination of other localities confirmed him in the opinion that the land-locked creek he had entered on the eastern side of the gulf was the best harbour in the most suitable locality of any he had seen.

Early in November the *Africaine*, commanded by Captain Duff, and having on board, amongst others, Mr. Gouger, the colonial secretary; Mr. Brown, emigration agent; and Mr. Thomas, printer of the *Gazette and Register*, arrived off Kangaroo Island. Deceived by the glowing language of Captain Sutherland in his description of the island, six of the passengers landed on its western side, with the intention of proceeding overland to the new settlement. They took with them two days' provisions, but soon found that the dense underwood made their progress slower than they had expected. With hatchets they chopped their way through scrub and bush, until, becoming exhausted, they made for the beach, hoping to reach the settlement by the sea-coast. But here their course was checked by the heavy surf beating against the high cliffs, and again they were compelled to force their way through the bush. For the first three days they found fresh water, but not a drop afterwards, and on one occasion they had to quench their thirst with the blood of sea-gulls. After being out for nine days, four of the party, in an exhausted state, reached Nepean Bay, but the other two (Dr. Slater and Mr. Osborne), being unable to keep up with their companions, perished in the bush.

On finding that Colonel Light had ordered all the surveying party and stores away from Nepean Bay, the *Africaine* proceeded forthwith to Rapid Bay, where the colonel happened to be on her arrival. He went on board, and was at once besieged with inquiries.

"Mr. Gouger was, of course, very anxious to know where we should settle—a question I was by no means prepared to answer; and the only thing I could do was to recommend his proceeding to Holdfast Bay for the present. This was not at all satisfactory, every one in such circumstances being anxious not to move again after landing all his embarked property. I could only recommend this place as one from which they were the least likely to re-embark, but stating strongly, at the same time, that I could not guarantee permanent settlement there. To make the best of a doubtful case, both Mr. Gouger and Mr. Brown agreed to take their chance, and Captain Duff having very kindly offered me a passage, I embarked on the 7th of November."

Next day the *Africaine* arrived at Holdfast Bay, where the *Rapid* was lying at anchor, and, in company with Captain Duff, Mr. Gouger, and Mr. Brown, Colonel Light set forth to examine, and, if possible, ascertain the mouth of the river Yatala, afterwards called the Torrens, which had been discovered by Messrs. Field, Kingston, and Morphett. But the river was found to exhaust itself in the lagoons afterwards known as the Reedbeds. As they were returning to their ships they observed the *Cygnet* standing in for the bay, and soon after it blew a gale of wind. Referring to this, the colonel wrote in his journal, "It is impossible to describe my feelings on this occasion, seeing three

English vessels on a lee shore, riding safely at the roadstead."

Many difficulties were in the way of Colonel Light at this time. Scurvy was breaking out among the newcomers from long abstinence from fresh food, and he had to enter into arrangements with Captain Duff to proceed to Hobart Town for a supply of fresh provisions; there were no proper appliances for penetrating into the interior with stores and baggage, and he had to write full and urgent letters to the Commissioners for vehicles and animals.

After more vain searching for Jones' harbour * (which was probably identical with Captain Barker's "sixteen mile creek" seen under a different aspect), Colonel Light again visited the localities on the eastern coast of Gulf St. Vincent, and became more and more confirmed in his opinion as to this being the most eligible site for the capital. Nevertheless, as the letter of his instructions bound him to look at other places before he finally fixed upon a locality, although, as he said, he felt assured he should only be losing time, he proceeded on the 25th of November down the gulf, and after touching at Rapid and Nepean Bays, sailed for Port Lincoln. In a report to the Commissioners, he wrote—

"I am decidedly of opinion that Port Lincoln is no harbour for merchant-ships; looking at it as a port for men-of-war, well manned, plenty of boats, etc., it is very well. It is capacious, and there is excellent holding ground, but the strong gusts of wind shifting all round the compass render the entrance not altogether so safe as the plan of it on paper would indicate."
Later on he added—

"I have been considering much of this gulf (Spencer's), and I think it best to give it up entirely for the present, for should there be a good harbour, and good soil higher up, yet the dangers that surround the entrance are too many for a new colony."

* From relying on the exaggerated report of Captain Jones, Colonel Light twice turned his back upon what was ultimately adopted as Port Adelaide.

These were wise and sagacious words, and, as we shall see, it would have been well had they been accepted without question. On the 17th of December, Colonel Light returned from his visit to Port Lincoln and the western side of Spencer's Gulf. He wrote—

"The time now lost in much extra labour, and the arrival of many people from England, makes me anxious to find some place to locate the land purchasers and others, and from every answer to my inquiries of the sealers, as well as the practical view of the coast I had to the westward, I felt convinced I should not find anything more eligible than the neighbourhood of Holdfast Bay." And so, on the 24th of December, the colonel returned to Holdfast Bay, and went on shore for the purpose of examining the river, and, if possible, of fixing the actual site of the capital.

The crowning moments of excitement in the life of the settlers were when tidings came of a sail in sight, or the arrival of an English vessel, and many were the visits paid to the highest sandhill in the hope of descrying a visitor. Especially was this the case when the arrival of the Governor was anticipated, and his non-arrival at the expected date greatly increased the excitement.

It is reported that, one Sunday morning, when Mr. Kingston was reading prayers with Mr. T. Gilbert for his clerk, a whisper went round that an English vessel was in sight. Those nearest the door began to quietly move out, followed by others, until at last the officiating minister was left alone with his assistant, when the former threw down the book, saying, "Come, Gilbert, it's no use our staying here," and the two went forth to join the throng.

On the same day that Colonel Light returned to Holdfast Bay, H.M.S. *Buffalo*, with the Governor, Captain Hindmarsh, and the Resident Commissioner, Mr. J. Hurtle Fisher, on board, entered the magnificent harbour of Port Lincoln, and found the *Cygnet* at anchor in Spalding Cove. Here Captain Lipson, R.N., the harbour-master, came on board, and presented a letter from Colonel Light, announcing that the most desirable site for the capital was to be found on the eastern side of Gulf St. Vincent.

The Governor landed at the head of Spalding Cove, and was greatly impressed with the scenery and general aspect of Port Lincoln. As, however, it was known that the officers of the Government who had preceded him were anxiously awaiting his arrival on the plains near Mount Lofty, he could not linger in that earthly paradise, and set sail without delay.

Early in the morning of the 28th the little band of pioneers at Holdfast Bay were gladdened by the sight of the *Buffalo* and the *Cygnet* standing across the gulf, and coming to anchor in the roadstead. At two o'clock the excitement culminated, when Captain Hindmarsh and his family, attended by Mr. J. H. Fisher, Mr. Stevenson, Mr. Osmond Gilles, and the Rev. C. B. Howard, with their families, proceeded to the shore in three boats, escorted by a party of marines from the *Buffalo*.

They were received and cordially welcomed by the settlers on the Glenelg plains, headed by Messrs. Gouger (colonial secretary), Brown (emigration agent), Gilbert (storekeeper), Kingston (deputy-surveyor), John Morphett, and Robert Thomas,—men who were destined to have their names indelibly associated with the annals of the colony.

The Company, or at least all the officials, assembled in Mr. Gouger's hut, when the Governor read aloud the Orders in Council erecting South Australia into a British province, and appointing the colonial officers. The commission of Captain Hindmarsh as Governor and Commander-in-Chief was then read, and the customary oaths were administered to the Governor, members of council, and other officers present.

But Mr. Gouger's tent was only constructed to hold about a dozen persons, and at least two hundred, nearly the entire population, were present. Therefore, as only a very few had heard what was passing in the tent, Mr. George Stevenson, the Governor's private secretary, clerk of the council, and embryo editor of the *South Australian Gazette*, assembled the people under the shade of an old gum tree, which still remains, though in a state of decay, and read aloud the proclamation establishing South Australia the only free British province of New Holland. The official account of the proceedings, as given in the *South Australian Gazette and Colonial Register* of June 3, 1837, was as follows: "The commission was afterwards read to the settlers, of whom about two hundred were present. The British flag was displayed under a royal salute. The marines fired a *feu de joie*, and the *Buffalo* saluted the Governor with fifteen guns. A cold collation, provided for the occasion, was laid out in the open air, of which the party partook."

In less stately language, by the same writer, the scene is thus described: "A dozen or so of drunken marines of H.M.S. *Buffalo* discharged several muskets in honour of the occasion; a table manufactured impromptu out of boards supported on barrels, salt beef, salt pork, and an indifferent ham, a few bottles of porter and ale, and about the same quantity of port and sherry from the crypts of the *Buffalo*, completed the official banquet which graced the advent of British rule to the shores of South Australia. In the evening kind and hospitable hands—alas! now no more—prepared the grateful herb. . . ."*

---

* The following is from the diary of Mrs. Robert Thomas:—

"*December 28th*, 1836.—This was a proud and I hope will prove a happy day for South Australia. Early in the morning it was announced that the *Buffalo* had arrived from Port Lincoln, accompanied by the *Cygnet*, which had gone thither to escort the Governor to Holdfast Bay. This made us all alive; and soon after Mr. Thomas received notice to attend at the tent of Mr. Gouger, the colonial secretary, where his Excellency the Governor was expected to be at three o'clock to read his commission and proclaim the colony. Mr. Thomas then went to the Company's store, and soon returned with a request that he would procure a ham, as Mr. Gilbert was not provided with one, which was done, and a fine Hampshire ham was dressed for the occasion. It was also requested that we should prepare ourselves to meet the procession, as all who could were expected to attend. We went accordingly, and found

So ended an ever-memorable day in the history of the colony. It was the day of small things, although no one would have so regarded it on reading the enthusiastic literature of the time. The *South Australian Record*, a monthly journal published in London, broke

the largest company assembled we had yet seen in the colony—perhaps two hundred persons. The Governor's private secretary read the proclamation under a large gum tree, and a party of marines from the *Buffalo* fired a *feu de joie*, and loud hurrahs succeeded. A cold collation followed in the open air, of which we partook. The Governor was very affable, shaking hands with the colonists, and congratulating them on having such a fine country. After the repast he mounted on a chair, and gave the first toast, 'The King,' which was received with three times three, and followed by the National Anthem, led by Mr. Gilles; but the old royal appellation of George is so natural to Englishmen after four successive reigns of kings of that name, that it was forgotten at the moment we have now a William on the throne, and the first line was sung as formerly—

'God save great George, our king,'

which excited a smile, and yet I believe that William IV. has not more loyal subjects throughout his wide dominions than those who were there assembled to welcome the arrival of the first Governor of South Australia. The health of his Excellency was then proposed and drunk with loud and universal cheering, followed by 'Rule Britannia.' Then 'Mrs. Hindmarsh and the ladies,' proposed by Mr. Gilbert, which also received great applause, as did several other toasts. The Governor then gave the following: 'May the present unanimity continue as long as South Australia exists,' which made the plain ring with acclamations; and at about five o'clock his Excellency and lady departed to the ship, and some officers and others followed in another boat. They all seemed highly delighted with our village, as I may call it, consisting now of about forty tents and huts, though scattered about without any regularity, as every family fixed their present abode wherever they pleased, knowing it would not be of long duration. We took coffee in Mr. Kingston's hut, and returned home about seven. The evening, as well as the day and the preceding one, was very hot, and the night continued so, insomuch that it was impossible to sleep, the thermometer having been sometimes upwards of 100° in the tent, and it seemed that some of the colonists did not even go to bed, for we heard singing and shouting from different parties at intervals till long after daylight. And here I may remark that, from the exceeding stillness of the night, except when the wind disturbs the trees near us, we can distinctly hear almost every sound that occurs, though at a considerable distance."

forth into singing the praises of the event in these amusing terms—

"The landing of the little band in their new country recalls the awful emigration of Noah, and the promise that painted his horizon, and that of Moses. It reminds us of the Tyrians at Carthage; of Æneas and the dominion of the West, which tradition tells us was founded by him; of the stout-hearted Britons who built up the great, though still young, nations of America, and, nearer to the present scene, the colonies of Australia, whose errors of constitutions have served as an impressive lesson, while their unexampled prosperity points to the commercial fortune of the newer settlement."

Apart from all bathos, it was a day long to be remembered. A band of brave-hearted men and women had staked their fortunes, left home and friends and country, and journeyed to the antipodes to settle in a land almost uninhabited, unsurveyed, with no town laid out, nor even the site of the intended capital selected.* And amongst the number assembled that day on the Glenelg plains were men who were to be the "Makers" of the new colony—men who were to bear the burden and heat of the day, and by their toil, judgment, and persistence lay the foundations of healthy, political, social, and religious life in one of the finest lands on which the sun ever shone.

It is no wonder that to the present day thousands of people go forth on the 28th of December to the old gum tree at Glenelg to celebrate Foundation Day, or, as it is generally termed, "Proclamation Day."

* During the year 1836 fifteen vessels arrived from England, bringing nearly a thousand men, women, and children, a large number of whom settled in the first instance at Kangaroo Island.

CHAPTER V.

ADMINISTRATION OF CAPTAIN HINDMARSH.

December 28, 1836—July 14, 1838.

The Governor and the Resident Commissioner.—Site of the Capital.—Discussions thereon.—Appeal to the Board of Commissioners.—Selections of Land.—First Land Boom.—Removal of Settlers from Kangaroo Island.—Hard Work and Poor Pay.—Delay in the Surveys.—Too Rapid Immigration and its Consequences.—Harbour proclaimed a Free Port.—First Buildings in Adelaide.—Operations of the South Australian Company.—The First Bank.—The Company's Land.—Rise of Religious Institutions.—Schools and Schoolmasters.—The Aborigines; Origin, Manners, and Customs.—Protector of Aborigines.—Early Pastoral Pursuits.—Overland Arrivals of Stock.—First General Gaol Delivery.—Newspapers.—Recall of Captain Hindmarsh.—Interim Administration of Mr. G. M. Stephens.—Tribute to the Pioneer Colonists.

Excellent as the speeches were on the day of proclamation, and harmonious as everything seemed to be, it was unfortunately the fact that the relations between the Governor and the Resident Commissioner were strained, the difficulties between them being as to the exercise of the powers entrusted to each. The breach, commenced on shipboard, soon widened on shore, and resulted in the formation of a Governor's party and a Commissioner's party, greatly to the hindrance of the general welfare.

Matters were further complicated by grievous dissensions with Colonel Light, the surveyor-general, regarding the proposed site of the principal settlement. The selection was left solely to him, and this duty he was not only authorized but required to discharge, the Commissioners purposely avoiding all minute instructions, and desiring that he would consider himself at liberty to deviate even from the more general instructions given, if, in the discharge of his duty, new facts should arise which, in his opinion, justified so strong a measure. Should, however, the Governor arrive sufficiently early in the colony, Colonel Light was instructed to confer with him on the subject, and pay due regard to his opinions and suggestions, but he was warned against yielding to any influence which could have the effect of diverting him in any way from the sole responsibility of the decision.

On the 30th of December the Governor went with Colonel Light to inspect the proposed site for the capital, and, in common with many others at that time, expressed dissatisfaction, his ground of objection being that it was too far from the harbour. The colonel, therefore, sought a site not so far out; but as there were evident marks of the river overflowing its banks on the place fixed upon by the Governor, Colonel Light resolved to go back to the first site. "My instructions from the Commissioners were peremptory as to the responsibility of this choice devolving upon myself," he wrote; "for although I was allowed to pay respect to the Governor's opinion, yet my own judgment on this point was to be paramount and conclusive." *

---

* The following letter from Captain Hindmarsh to Mr. G. F. Angas is not without interest:—

"H.M.S. *Buffalo*, at anchor off Glenelg Plains,
"January 5, 1837.

"MY DEAR SIR,

"We reached Port Lincoln on the 24th ult., where, according to my expectation, I found Captain Lipson waiting for me with a letter from Colonel Light, informing me that he had found a good harbour and plenty of excellent land on the eastern side of Gulf St. Vincent. I immediately proceeded to join him, in doing which I was two nights and two days in beating out of Spencer's Gulf, which I entered without any fear. I should, how-

Having definitely made up his mind, he spent several days in looking over the ground, and mentally laying it out according to the course of the river and the nature of the surroundings.

The site selected is in latitude 34° 57" south, and comprises a southern and northern elevation, with a small valley and river between them. The northern rise is the spur of a low range of hills, of limestone formation, and the southern elevation is a piece of table-land which, at the time the first settlers arrived, was tolerably well wooded.

The country all along that part of the coast presented a most attractive aspect, resembling English park scenery. The land required little clearing, and was fit for immediate occupation for tillage or sheep-runs, well watered, and covered with luxuriant grass. The ground sloped backwards for several miles from the coast, terminating in the Mount Lofty range, behind which lay Lake Alexandrina and the country of the Murray. So many combined advantages decided Colonel Light in fixing upon this spot as the site of the principal settlement, but it was hardly to be expected that it should include every requisite, and still less that it should answer all the expectations of the colonists. One fancied drawback was that it was six miles from the port, and some urged that the first settlement

ever, be very sorry to try the same navigation again until that very dangerous gulf is surveyed. Flinders' survey is good as far as it goes; but his own track is the only thing to be depended upon. Gulf St. Vincent, on the contrary, appears to be perfectly clear, with regular soundings and good anchorage all over it, not one danger having yet been discovered. Each sandy beach, however, seems to have a small reef running off it, according to Colonel Light's report. I am now at anchor off the Mount Lofty of Flinders, about three miles from the shore, in seven fathom. Most of the people who preceded me are located temporarily on the plains abreast of the ship, which I have named after Lord Glenelg, and which for quality and beauty are well worthy to bear his lordship's name.

"Adelaide is to be on the bank of a beautiful stream, with thousands of acres of the richest land I ever saw. Altogether a more beautiful spot can hardly be imagined. . . ."

should be close to it. But at the port there was no fresh water, and Colonel Light had no hesitation in deciding that it was better to be obliged to carry all necessary commodities from the port to the town, than to convey all the water required for culinary and other purposes from the town to the port; and his wisdom and sagacity were soon justified.

There were others who still clamoured for the first town to be located in the neighbourhood of Encounter Bay, one of the chief advocates of this situation being the judge, Sir John Jeffcott. But Colonel Light would not yield to this suggestion for a moment; he was satisfied that even if a good harbour could be found, the tremendous rollers at the entrance of the bay would render it comparatively useless. And a tragic confirmation of his wisdom was soon to be given; one or two wrecks occurred in the dangerous neighbourhood, and Sir John Jeffcott and Captain Blinkinsopp, in attempting to prove that they were justified in their opposition, lost their lives by the upsetting of their boat in the turbulent waters.

Having selected the site, Colonel Light was instructed in laying it out to make the streets of ample width, arranging them with a due regard to convenience, salubrity, and beauty, and to make the necessary reserves for squares, public walks, and open spaces. Ten acres were to be reserved as a Government domain, and two hundred acres to be appropriated for a public park and gardens. He was also directed to reserve as a public road all land on the coast within a hundred feet of high-water mark, and a road sixty-six feet wide on each side of every navigable river.

No sooner had he commenced his task than he was subjected to a series of interferences from the Governor, his private secretary, and others in different spheres of authority; and, being of a sensitive nature, he was hurt that reflections were made in high quarters on his judgment and ability. Nor were matters much mended when a public meeting of the landowners and others concerned was called by the colonial secretary, at the command of the Governor, to discuss the proposed site of the capital, a wish having been expressed by many to stay any definite action being taken until all the coast had been surveyed.

At the meeting a resolution was submitted, "That it is the opinion of this meeting that the site at present selected for the chief town of the colony, being at a considerable distance from navigable waters, is not such as they were led to expect would be chosen." Considerable discussion followed, but happily an amendment was proposed: "That this meeting considers that in the site selected by the surveyor-general for the first town, he has secured in a most satisfactory manner those advantages which the Commissioners and the first purchasers in England contemplated as essential, namely, a central point in the province, in the neighbourhood of a safe and improvable harbour, abundance of fresh water on the spot, and of good land and pasturage in its vicinity, with a probable easy communication with the Murray, Lake Alexandrina, and the most fertile parts of New South Wales, without fear of any injury to the principles of the colony from too near an approach to the confines of the convict settlement." The voting was, for the amendment, 218; for the original motion, 137: giving a majority of 81 in favour of the amendment.

Notwithstanding this, the Governor was not satisfied. He had come to the colony with the impression that the capital should be somewhere in the locality of Encounter Bay, and he was injudicious enough to appeal to the Commissioners for the removal of the capital to that neighbourhood, and at the same time to give strong expressions of complaint against Colonel Light, who had only exercised the powers made binding upon him.

The answer received by Captain Hindmarsh was, that "when he applied for the office of Governor he was distinctly informed that the right of selecting the capital would be vested solely in the surveyor-general," and that when he pressed the Board to cede this right to him, he was "seeking for an extension of power inconsistent with the principle of the colony; and that a Governor of South Australia must be content to receive and to hold his appointment subject to the condition of non-interference with the officer appointed to execute the surveys, and to dispose of the public land." This was a judicious snub, but it had no abiding effect.

The survey and staking off of the town acres was commenced by Colonel Light and his assistants on the 11th of January, and was completed on the 10th of March.

On the 23rd of March, the method of drawing by lot having been fixed upon, and the plan of the town mapped out and exhibited for public inspection, those preliminary purchasers who had deposited money for land in England to enable the colony to be founded, made their selections. A few days afterwards the remaining acres were sold by auction. Then came the first land boom, when those acres which had cost from £2 2s. to £14 14s. each at auction, and those first selected at 12s., were selling at from £80 to £100 each, and for those considered to be well situated as much as £250 was demanded, resulting, as most land booms do, in disappointment to the majority, and in the witnessing of the resale, some four or five years afterwards, at prices not reaching more than one-fifth of those rates.

On the 28th of March permission was given to the public "to cut down and grub up trees in the public streets, except those within sixteen feet of the frontage of private property."

The naming of the streets and squares did not take place until the 23rd of May, and it was the occasion of a renewal of those bickerings and misunderstandings that had gone on from the first. Divided authority was the bane of every movement, and of course the Governor and the Resident Commissioner both claimed the right of naming localities and places as well as Colonel Light, the surveyor-general. Eventually the matter was settled by a combination of "authorities" and landed proprietors, and the names of those connected with the early history of the colony were handed down to posterity in the streets, squares, and terraces of Adelaide.

Fortunately there was no dispute, and could be none, as to the name of the capital, King William IV. having requested, before the first ships left England, that it should be called after his royal consort, Queen Adelaide.

Soon after the site was definitely settled, the emigrants who had been holding on at Kangaroo Island and elsewhere removed to the "city," in the hope that they would soon be able to take up their country sections. But in this they were disappointed, and many complications ensued. Amongst them was the question of food. Before the arrival of the Governor, when one of the most pressing wants of the colonists was a supply of fresh provisions, Colonel Light despatched the *Cygnet* to Van Diemen's Land for eight hundred sheep; but, in consequence of boisterous weather on the return journey, very few remained alive when the vessel reached Kangaroo Island. Then the matter was taken up by the Governor and council, and a sum of £5000 was voted for the purchase of flour, horses, bullocks, waggons, barges, etc., and a committee appointed to select and purchase the same. While in Sydney for this purpose, Messrs. Barnard and Fisher, two of the committee, made inquiries as to the practicability of conveying stock overland, when one Mr. Robert Clint offered, for the sum of £10,000, to convey to a given point 2000 young ewes in lamb, 300 mixed cattle, 30 horses, mares, and geldings, and 24 true-bred sheepdogs. The offer was not accepted, but, as we shall see, the transit of cattle overland soon became an accomplished fact. Meanwhile the vessels chartered by the Commissioners continued to bring in supplies of live stock from the Cape of Good Hope and elsewhere.

After completing the town surveys, Colonel Light directed his attention to the country lands, but his work was carried on under great difficulties. A spirit of disaffection was abroad; owing to the lack of means for transporting goods, rations often ran low; and the survey vehicles were diverted from their proper use to convey the luggage of new-comers from Holdfast Bay to Adelaide. The lack of fresh water at the harbour was a great drawback to progress. As an instance of the cost of conveying it to the bay, it may be mentioned that the *Buffalo* had twenty tons of water conveyed from Adelaide to Glenelg, the charge for which was £100, and nearly half this amount for bringing back the empty water-casks.

Alluding to his men, who were called "two-shilling-a-day slaves," Colonel Light wrote, "Their complaints had much truth. They had signed in England for twelve shillings a week and rations, the same in quality as allowed in his Majesty's navy, and they were sometimes many days with hardly anything but biscuit, sometimes not that. Had there been no difficulty with the men, we could not have detached a party from the town, as not a single working bullock could be had. The tents were all in use by the immigrants as well as by the surveying parties. The rations which came up from Holdfast Bay in small quantities were delivered almost immediately, not only to those entitled to them by agreement, but also to the immigrants, who had no other means of sustenance than from the Commissioners' stores, and the remaining part of the twelve months' stores purchased in England for the use of the survey alone were now shared out to all. Humanity required this, but the consequence was a cessation of work, and an apparent neglect of duty on the part of the surveyor-general, for which, of course, there were many quite ready to abuse him."

When the stores were better supplied, surveying recommenced under more favourable circumstances, and a party was formed under Mr. Finniss to commence on the western side of Adelaide, with the Torrens on the right, the range of hills to the left, and the sea in front, while Colonel Light began on the right bank of the river. Still the work was hindered by occasional strikes among the men and by bad weather. "During this period," wrote Colonel Light, "I began to feel a very evident change in my health, which, with anxieties of mind, wore me down very much, and I was obliged to neglect many days' working in consequence."

To the unavoidable delay in the progress of the country surveys may be mainly ascribed the overwhelming difficulties and disasters in the first years of the history of the colony; and, next to this, the error of the Commissioners in permitting emigration to take place to the extent it did before the country land was ready for selection. By the 25th of May, 1837, not quite a year after the arrival of the first vessel at Kangaroo Island, sixteen vessels from England had landed upwards of a thousand emigrants, and twenty-five vessels had left Sydney and Van Diemen's Land with supplies of provisions and merchandise, besides conveying many settlers. In November of the same year the population was estimated at 2500. All these people flocked to the city because, although they held land orders, they could not get possession, and therefore could not enter upon their proper business pursuits, or upon any productive labour. As a consequence there came a state of stagnation. The very implements required for agriculture and the utensils for dairy work soon crowded the auction-rooms, and were sold at absurdly low prices, that the vendors might support themselves on the proceeds. "The majority of the settlers were without income, and had to live upon their capital and by the sale of their town acres. Rents being very high, employment was given to artisans at extravagant wages to erect buildings in the city; but as houses soon increased and rents diminished, those who had embarked their capital in buildings had cause to regret making such investments." Provisions were imported at ruinous prices; hard cash intended to be used in "making a fortune" was squandered in idleness; and labourers were employed upon works premature, if not unnecessary, for the mere sake of giving them employment.

The Government was largely dependent upon what

it could make, and the principal source of its revenue, for emigration purposes only, was the sale of land, but the sales had not yet commenced; the duties upon spirits and wine licences yielded so small a sum that the Governor had not sufficient money to pay even the salaries of its officers. There were no other revenues. The Land Fund was sacred; the English Government could not be asked for money; the Colonial Treasury existed only in name.

On the 25th of May, 1837, the Governor, after much contention with the Resident Commissioner on the subject, proclaimed the harbour a legal port, but for some time afterwards it was not much used. At this early date there was neither wharf, pier, nor jetty at either Holdfast Bay or the harbour, and considerable damage and loss was sustained in consequence. At the bay heavily laden boats were sometimes in danger of being swamped, and if the water was smooth they could not approach near enough to the shore for the goods to be landed dry without great care. As soon as vehicles were obtained, the bullocks or horses were driven into the water as near as possible to the boats, but even then a submerging of the package or case in course of removal was no uncommon thing. A tradition of those days records that, among other casualties, Mrs. Hindmarsh, soon after her arrival, had the mortification of seeing her piano floating ashore at Glenelg.

One of the first public works undertaken at the port at the head of the creek was the cutting of a small canal to enable lighters to discharge their cargoes on *terra firma*. The silt and mud excavated formed a bank above the reach of ordinary tides, and upon this bank the goods landed were piled until removed by carts or drays to their destination.* The cost of this

* There were for the first few months so few vehicles, oxen, and horses, that it was a long time before the colonists could get their belongings together, and sledges, skids, wheelbarrows, and other impromptu devices were in requisition to convey luggage from the landing-place to Adelaide.

little canal, which would receive some six or eight barges, was about £800.

The arrival of large numbers of immigrants rendered a depôt for their immediate accommodation necessary, and a site was selected on a part of the western parklands, and wooden buildings, known as "Immigration Square," were erected. In one part of the square there was an infirmary and dispensary, and adjacent thereto the office of the immigration agent—a functionary who had by no means an easy time during the first few years of the colony's existence.

Up to the end of 1839 nearly all the large vessels arriving from England came to anchor in Holdfast Bay, and here, therefore, the immigrants were landed. Many were the strange and exciting scenes enacted there. In the absence of jetty or wharfs, passengers, luggage, and merchandise had to be landed in the surf on the beach, unless the bullock-drivers could persuade their teams to go sufficiently near to the boats to obviate this necessity. As a matter of course, the greater number of persons landed had either to be carried ashore, or to wade through the water. Soon the beach would be thronged with the wondering and inquiring new-comers; a number of bullock teams stood about waiting to convey the women, children, and luggage to the town; and here and there a group of natives would welcome the visitors with strange grimaces and modest appeals for "biccity," "'bacca," or "black money." Then the procession would move off, bound for Immigration Square.

The city presented a strange appearance in the early days. The temporary dwellings of the settlers who had removed from Glenelg were strewn about the valley, or lined the banks of the river, presenting the appearance of a large gipsy encampment. Some of the "buildings" were composed of mud and grass, others of brushwood, and some of wooden frames covered with canvas. One of the first residences close to the town was "the Vice-regal Mansion," as it was jokingly called—a building remarkable for its want of pretension to either elegance or comfort. It was built by the sailors of the *Buffalo*,* and consisted of three rooms, the walls being of mud and the roof of thatch. Unfortunately, "Jack" forgot to put in a chimney, which caused many a joke at his expense. Of stone and brick houses there were, of course, very few in the first instance, and these few were erected at great expense. But soon a building mania set in ; temporary erections gave way to proper houses, and almost within a year of its foundation Adelaide began to assume the characteristics of an established town. Unfortunately, it became the great centre of attraction, and, in addition to the mania for substantial buildings there, many were building castles in the air, instead of turning their attention to flocks and herds, the growth of grain and garden produce, and the development of the natural resources of the colony.

It was some time before the ordinary machinery of society got into proper working order, but the first year of the existence of the colony witnessed many interesting events and enterprises, important as being the foundations upon which great things were to be built in the future. It will be well in this place to see what attempts were made to evolve order out of chaos ; and we will first glance at some of the early operations of the South Australian Company. The Company, as we have shown, was the means of planting the colony. We have now to inquire how far it succeeded in fulfilling its further design to make the prosperity of the

---

* The marines of the *Buffalo* were left as a sort of body-guard to the Governor. But they were not a very sober or reliable set. Mr. Osmond Gilles used to tell a story of one of them who was left to act as guard over the Treasury—at that time only a tent in which was a safe, his own private property, lent to the Government. Returning home late one night, he passed the tent and found the guard helplessly intoxicated, his general impression being that he was on board the *Buffalo*. The treasurer dealt with him gently. "The truth is," he said, "as there was only one shilling and sixpence in the safe, a guard might have been spared." At that time the Government was completely aground as to cash, and remained so until the treasurer, from his private purse, brought a supply.

colonists possible. It will be remembered that the Company undertook to build and buy ships, to establish whaling fisheries and stations, to enter into agricultural and stock farming, to embark in pastoral pursuits, to lease land to farming tenants, and assist them to cultivate their holdings by advancing funds. It was pledged to build wharfs and storehouses, shops and houses; to buy and sell produce and manufactured goods; to work mines and quarries, flour and saw mills, and generally to open up all the possible avenues to prosperity.

On the 22nd of November, 1836, in a letter to Governor Hindmarsh, Mr. Angas mentions the departure of Mr. McLaren, chief commercial manager; Mr. Mildred, master ship-builder; Dr. Drescher, overseer of the Germans; Mr. Shepherdson, superintendent schoolmaster; Mr. Germein, master of the trawl-fishing vessel; Mr. Wright, master of the white fisheries; two vine-dressers; one flax-grower from Germany; with their respective families, and others in the Company's service.

Besides the officers already mentioned, Messrs. W. Giles, C. S. Hare, W. Prescott, W. B. Randell, and E. Stephens were among the first engaged in various departments of the Company's colonial service. To Mr. McLaren the directors committed the entire management of the banks, shipping, fisheries, ship-building, and commercial affairs of the Company, while Mr. S. Stephens had the entire charge of the agricultural department.

The letters of instructions furnished by Mr. Angas, the chairman of the Company, to Messrs. McLaren and Stephens, are models of what such documents should be—clear, graphic, explicit, and as complete and comprehensive as if the establishment of the infant settlement had been entrusted solely to the South Australian Company. Nothing conducive to the progress and well-being of the colony was overlooked.

It was patent from the first that a banking establishment would be an imperative necessity, and the prospectus of the South Australian Company stated, as one of its objects, "the establishment of a bank or banks in or connected with the new colony of South Australia, making loans on land or produce in the colony, and the conducting of such banking operations as the directors may think expedient." But it was equally clear that it should not form a branch of a commercial company, and therefore, with great wisdom and forethought, it was omitted from the original plan submitted by Mr. Angas to intending shareholders. Negotiations were then opened up with the Bank of Australasia, but they fell through; and as applications were being received by persons wishing to proceed to the colony to transmit their money, the original £50 shares in the Company were divided into two of £25 each, and additional shares were issued at a premium to afford sufficient capital for the commencement of a bank or banks in the colony.

Accordingly, a supply of specie and small notes was sent out in one of the first vessels despatched by the Company; and the entire plant of the bank, together with a framed banking-house, iron chests, and so forth, were forwarded by the ship *Coromandel*, in charge of Mr. Edward Stephens as cashier and accountant. This vessel arrived in South Australia on the 12th of January, 1837, a few days after the colony had been proclaimed a British province, and in March the bank commenced operations. The notes, which were engraved in London, varied in value from ten shillings to ten pounds, and represented in the aggregate £10,000.

In a letter of instructions, drawn up by Mr. Angas, Mr. Stephens was advised that the bank was to be one of issue, discount, deposit, and loan, and that it would also undertake the collection of debts and receipt of moneys by commission; give in exchange for the notes of the bank, bills on England, and open up a system of exchange between the colony and the mother country. Besides the ordinary business of a bank, it was also practically a savings bank, the smallest deposits, when they reached £1, bearing interest at 5 per cent. Loans were also to be advanced on the security of property at moderate rates of interest, although, when the mania for speculation in town lands took place shortly after the colony was established, the Company gave no encouragement to the proceeding, either in disposing of their own property or in making advances to private individuals.

To the early settlers, however, these loans were a great boon, and enabled them to commence farming operations and pastoral pursuits which they could not have done without such assistance; while a place of security for their savings was also a desideratum in those days of tents and mud cottages. As soon as capitalists arrived, these subsidiary operations of the bank ceased.

For the first three or four years the rate of discount charged on bills having three months to run was 10 per cent., and 12 per cent. for those of longer periods. Interest at 4 per cent. was allowed on the daily balance of current accounts, and 7 per cent. on cash deposited.

The bank at once became a medium of exchange between Great Britain and the colony, and in course of time secured agencies at Sydney, Hobart Town, Launceston, Canton, Calcutta, Bombay, Madras, Ceylon, Mauritius, Cape of Good Hope, St. Helena, and Hamburg.

It was foreseen from the first that the Government would need the aid of the bank, and the directors intimated to their agent that, as the Governor had only taken out £1000 in specie, both he and the Resident Commissioner might require assistance, in which case it was to be given within reasonable limits. Events soon justified that anticipation. On one occasion, during the administration of Governor Hindmarsh, the bank advanced the sum of £5000 when there were no funds whatever in hand. An important arrangement was made with the Commissioners that the notes of the bank should be received in payment for land, and for any taxes to be levied for the support of the Government.

All these facilities for transacting monetary affairs

should have been, and, as a matter of fact, were, of great benefit to the early colonists; but, unfortunately, owing to the open hostility between the Governor's party and the Resident Commissioner's party, neither the Company nor its bank were regarded with favour by the authorities in the colony. Nevertheless the bank outlived this petty opposition, and became a permanent and useful institution. From the first it more than justified its existence. During the first year of its operations moneys were lodged at the London office of the Company for repayment in South Australia amounting to upwards of £15,000, while the drafts drawn on England in the colony amounted to nearly £7000. In 1840 the business of the bank had increased to nearly a quarter of a million, and was yielding a profit to the Company of 15 per cent.; but as it was an obstacle in the way of the Company in its efforts to obtain a charter of incorporation, it was in the following year transferred from the Company and established upon an independent footing as "The South Australian Banking Company." Mr. McLaren, the general manager of the South Australian Company, on his return to England in 1841, stated to the shareholders, "I do not hesitate to say that the progress of the colony, and the success of individual colonists, has been more owing to the Bank of South Australia than to any other cause whatever—perhaps I might say, than to all other causes put together."

The total quantity of land possessed by the Company in the first instance was 102 town acres, 13,770 country acres, and 330 acres for the first settlement at Kangaroo Island. At the sale of town land in March, 1837, sixty-six acres more were purchased in the "city," making a total of 168 town acres, including six at the port.

Pastoral pursuits were among the first labours entered into by the Company in the colony. Pure merino rams and ewes, selected with great care and at much expense in Saxony, were early sent out, as well as some pure

Leicesters and South Down sheep and Cashmere goats. Later on choice stock of various kinds were sent out by the Board in London to improve the breeds in the colony. The number of prizes awarded from time to time to the exhibitors of the Company's live stock was evidence of the value of the importations.*

In horticulture the Company introduced the vine, Zante currant, olive and other fruits, but beyond establishing the fact that the soil and climate were suitable for their growth and culture, and the formation of a small nursery, no attempt was made to enter into competition with the settlers in the production of fruit and vegetables.

The fishery operations of the Company were on an extensive scale, and embraced the sperm, black, and off-shore whale-fisheries, besides white fishing for home consumption, salting, and exportation. Five of the Company's vessels were employed in this industry; off-shore stations were established at Encounter Bay and Thistle Island, the former soon after the landing of the first settlers, and the latter at an early period of the Company's existence.

The loss of the *South Australian* and the stranding of the *John Pirie* in Encounter Bay, and also the loss of three other vessels engaged in this service, led to the relinquishing of what had once been a profitable pursuit. Some of the produce of the Company's fisheries constituted the first export from the colony to the mother country, and as early as the 26th of December, 1836 (two days before the colony was proclaimed), the Company's manager shipped at Kingscote for exportation to Van Diemen's Land three barrels of salted fish, containing 1359 mullets and 605 lbs. of skipjacks. The trade did not, however, prove profitable, and was soon abandoned.

One of the largest and most beneficial of the early undertakings of the Company was the laying out and opening up of the New Port, as it was called; the

* In May, 1851, the Company relinquished its pastoral pursuits altogether, and disposed of the whole of its flocks and herds.

erection of wharfs and warehouses, and the construction of a good road across the swamp to connect the port with the city. The road was formed at a cost of about £13,000, and soon after its completion the Company took in exchange an equivalent in land of the Government at the upset price, so that the road might become available for public purposes. This spirited undertaking greatly enhanced the value of the Company's property, and was also of incalculable benefit to the young colony.

The Company in its early days was largely engaged in the erection of buildings; but these operations, like many others, were relinquished in course of time, the idea of the founder being that the Company might be compared to a scaffolding, needful to the erection of a large building, but to be taken down when the building is completed.

In the early days the Company held a prominent place in the estimation of the first settlers, who were indebted to its various establishments for much of their supplies; hence the "Company's Stores," the "Company's Cattle Station," the "Company's Ship Station," the "Company's Dairy," the "Company's Steam Flour Mills," the "Company's Buildings," the "Company's Wharf," and the "Company's Bank," were familiar as household words. Many of the Company's servants became most useful colonists, and attained to wealth and influence.

Enough has been shown here to prove that all the operations of the Company were favourable to the advancement of the colony; in fact, but for its large capital—vastly beyond any other available for similar objects—employed judiciously in giving remunerative occupation to the people, and in developing the resources of the country, there would have been a dead-lock at the outset. Unfortunately little unity of action characterized the proceedings of the Commissioners and the Company, and if these two bodies could have worked together more harmoniously, beneficial results would even more speedily have followed, and some serious evils would have been averted. The Company was too energetic and expeditious in its movements for the Commissioners, and they, in turn, were too much so for the Colonial Office, and consequently none acted in concert.

Having glanced thus far at the operations of the South Australian Company, we must turn again to the early settlers, and the administration of the first Governor.

The history of the rise and progress of religious institutions in South Australia is of exceptional interest. One of the main points for which the early friends and founders of the colony contended was that there should be no dominant Church; that no provision should be made by the State for the promotion of religion, but that the voluntary principle should be put fairly to the test. Nevertheless, there crept into the South Australian Act of 1834 a clause giving power to persons appointed by the Privy Council to appoint chaplains and clergymen of the Established Churches of England and Scotland, and under this Act the first colonial chaplain, the Rev. C. B. Howard, was appointed by Lord Glenelg, on the recommendation of the Bishop of Chester. A strong protest was made by the "founders" against the appointment, not on personal grounds, but as being an evasion of the non-establishment principle; and in the amended Act, passed shortly afterwards, the clauses relating to such appointments were omitted.

Mr. Howard arrived in the *Buffalo* with the Governor and other Government officers, and being anxious to commence work at once, religious services were held under a huge sail, borrowed from a captain in port, until a temporary building could be erected. To get the sail from the port, some miles away, was a "labour" of love, and it is on record that the worthy clergyman, assisted by Mr. Osmond Gilles, the colonial treasurer, accomplished the task by drawing it on a truck with ropes over their shoulders along the dusty track in blazing hot weather.

Better accommodation was, however, in store for the worshippers. An association had been formed in England, in connection with the Society for the Propagation of the Gospel, to assist the colonists in providing for themselves the means of public worship and religious instruction, and, subscriptions amounting to over £800 having been collected, a wooden church, capable of accommodating 350 persons, and provided with communion plate and books, was sent out in frame, together with a parsonage house. It was soon found that the wooden church did not answer the purpose, and it was determined to erect a stone structure. Mr. Pascoe St. Leger Grenfell, having offered a town acre for the erection of a church and parsonage house, acre No. 9, at the corner of Morphett Street and North Terrace, was selected, and on the 26th of January, 1838, the foundation-stone of "the Church of the Holy Trinity" was laid by the Governor.

Shortly after Mr. Howard's arrival, it was rumoured that the Bishop of Sydney regarded the new province as a part of his diocese, and had appointed the colonial chaplain as his surrogate for granting marriage licences, and examining the certificates of clergymen. This gave rise to the first religious dissension in the colony; but it was found that the bishop and the colonial chaplain, without any wish to violate the provisions of the South Australian Act, had been under a misapprehension, as the Act distinctly stipulated that South Australia should not be subject to any law passed for any other part of Australia, and consequently the letters patent of the Bishop of Sydney could have no force in Adelaide. A frank explanation settled the little storm, but a watchful eye was kept for a time upon the movements of the Church party. It was soon found, however, that Mr. Howard was a warm-hearted catholic man, whose one object in life was to do good, and he succeeded in winning the confidence and affections of the colonists of all classes and creeds.

South Australia having been designed as a "Paradise for Nonconformists," the various religious denominations were soon well represented. The Wesleyans were among the first in the field, and early in 1837 a few individuals set to work to provide funds for a chapel and schools. Through the liberality of Mr. E. Stephens and others, a neat brick building was soon erected in Hindley Street, at the back of the South Australian Bank, and here Mr. D. McLaren, manager of the South Australian Company, conducted service in the morning, and other laymen in the afternoon and evening. But in course of time they felt the need of a regular minister, and early in 1838 one was sent to them in a singular fashion.

The Rev. William Longbottom, Wesleyan minister, sailing in the *Fanny* with his wife and child from Tasmania to fill a vacancy in Western Australia, fell in with a gale which increased in fury, until at midnight the vessel struck on an unknown coast, and they were landed through the surf by means of a rope. They suffered for want of a fire, till on the second day of their escape some friendly natives ventured near them. After a fortnight spent in a forlorn condition, and not knowing whither to turn, a crew of shipwrecked mariners found them. By means of a chart they had saved they had travelled a hundred miles, and were going fifty more in search of a whaling station. The two companies made common cause, and for forty-five days they wandered through the bush, and, reaching the station, they were taken by sea to Adelaide, where the pastorless society of sixty members welcomed the minister, and would not let him go. He lost all his worldly possessions by the disaster, but a subscription was set on foot to recoup him for some of his losses. He soon commenced his ministrations among the people, and carried them on with such success, that he may be regarded as the founder of Wesleyan Methodism in South Australia.

The first minister of the Congregationalists—a body destined to play a very important part in the political as well as in the religious history of the colony—was the Rev. Thomas Quentin Stow, for several years pastor of an Independent chapel at Halstead, Essex. He was selected for the colony by the Colonial Missionary Society, whose attention had from the outset been directed to the new settlement, with its peculiar constitution in regard to religion, as an important sphere of labour for Independents. Until, however, the infant settlement was in a position to maintain Mr. Stow, the London Missionary Society agreed to grant him £100 per annum, and Mr. George Fife Angas made himself responsible for his outfit and other expenses.

In a letter to friends in the old country, Mr. Stow thus describes his early labours in the colony:—

"March, 1838. . . . I am pleased to say the clergyman is evangelical and active. The Methodists, too, I rejoice to add, have a society and are doing good. I have been kindly received by all persons, and hope, by God's grace, to be enabled to do something here. Mr. Giles is at Kangaroo Island, where he preaches, and where his services are much needed.

"Mr. McLaren is sometimes there and sometimes here; he is a Baptist, manager for the Company, and is said to be an excellent preacher. I am gathering a congregation, though, of course, not very fast. Our Church has been formed about two months, consisting of thirteen members and two candidates. We have also begun a Sunday school, which promises well. The Governor and most of the officials have been to hear me. It is well you allowed us a tent, for no house was to be had. I determined, therefore, to build on the same acre where my house stands (a most eligible spot for worship) a temporary place of gum-wood posts, pine rafters, and reed thatch, and the walls, at present, of old sail-cloth canvas. The size is forty feet by twenty, besides a schoolroom at one end fourteen feet by twelve, and can be opened into the main building in half an hour, if called for, thus giving us a building of more than fifty feet in length. To pay for this I sell the tent. It is a good edifice of its kind, and is reported to be the best thatched place in the colony. It was done by two Halstead men of my Church there.

I worked regularly with them, felling the pines, cutting the reeds miles from the town, thatching, etc. . . ."

The first Baptist Church in the colony was under the care of Mr. D. McLaren, the members belonging to various sections of the Baptist body. They met at first for worship in the School Society's building in the park-lands, but after a time they removed to a chapel in Hindley Street, vacated by the Wesleyans.

In course of time other religious communities came upon the scene, until scarcely a section of any denomination remained unrepresented.

In those early days of which we now write, comparatively little was done with regard to education, although Mr. George Fife Angas, as representing the South Australian Company, had from the first made it a leading consideration. It will not be uninteresting to "set in order" the story of the introduction of schools into the new colony.

Among the earliest settlers was a man whose main object in life was, strange to say, not to make money, but to assist in forming the new community on a moral and religious basis. This was Captain Bromley, who for nearly a quarter of a century had been the unsalaried agent of the British and Foreign Bible and School Societies, and had in 1813 established the first British School in British North America. He was living on his little freehold property in Boston, Lincolnshire, when he heard of the South Australian enterprise, and foreseeing a field for his own peculiar benevolent, and to a great extent self-sacrificing, labour, he was among the first to depart for the new settlement. In December, 1836, he commenced his work on Kangaroo Island, and the following is the first educational report from South Australia:—

"I collected," he says, in a letter home, "all the children I possibly could, but the whole number only amounted to twenty-four, and nearly half of these were infants; they were, therefore, taught on the infant-school system, and all except one, a mere babe, could either spell or read before I came away. While thus employed I could hardly obtain money enough to purchase bread and cheese, the weekly pay of the children not amounting to more than ten shillings, so that, instead of building a hut, I was obliged to buy common necessaries to live upon. I had, therefore, no alternative but to teach the children under the shade of a large and beautiful tree, which would have accommodated forty or fifty more." Captain Bromley afterwards contrived to erect a hut with his own hands, so that, "when a change of weather drove them from the tree, he was able to shelter his little flock from the rain." He left the island for the mainland in May, 1837, when he was appointed Protector of Aborigines, and in May of the following year was accidentally drowned in the river Torrens.

Such is the history of the first school and schoolmaster in South Australia.

Long before Captain Bromley went to the colony, however, Mr. G. F. Angas had elaborated an educational system for the new settlement, and had established in England "The South Australian School Society," to create and sustain an interest in education in that colony. Mr. J. B. Shepherdson was selected to make himself acquainted with the best school systems in operation in the mother country, and at the end of 1836 he set sail for South Australia with strong recommendations to the Governor, and backed by sufficient voluntary contributions to make a good start.

In April, 1838, the school-house, a wooden building in the park-lands nearly opposite Trinity Church, was opened for the reception of children over five years of age. The school continued under the management of Mr. Shepherdson until July, 1840, when he resigned the appointment.

The cause of education was greatly indebted to the ministers of the various places of worship, who, in addition to organizing Sunday schools, night classes, and so forth, undertook in some instances to teach the higher branches of learning. It should be remembered that all these powerful influences for good were being exercised at a time when, in the early history of several other colonies, the thoughts of the settlers were almost exclusively engrossed in matters far other than those of a religious and educational character.

Nor was the welfare of the aborigines overlooked. In the Act of 1834 South Australia was declared to consist of "waste and unoccupied lands," thus failing to recognize the existence of the aborigines. Further than this, the Act declared all the lands of the province to be public lands open to purchase by "British subjects," and thus excluding the natives from any possession in or advantage arising from the land.

Nevertheless, from the outset of all negotiations for colonizing South Australia, the Commissioners made special provision for their welfare, while in the plans of the South Australian Company the chairman invariably set the claims of the natives, and the duty of the servants of the Company in regard to them, in the forefront.

One of the earliest appointments made by the home Government was that of a "Protector of aborigines," whose duty was to study their interests generally, to see that no violence was done to them by the colonists, that their grievances were, as far as possible, redressed, and that food, shelter, medical treatment, and education were afforded when necessary. Certain lands were reserved for their use, but, as we shall see, the wild children of the forest never took kindly to "eighty-acre sections."

We need not discuss here the many theories that have been put forth as to their origin, or whether they were descended from a higher or a lower race, but there seems little doubt that all the aboriginal tribes of Australia originally belonged to one and the same branch of the human family; the root of the language spoken throughout the entire coast-line of the continent, the personal appearance of the people, their rites and ceremonies, manners and customs, all point to a common origin; and all are alike in having neither legend nor tradition, scrip nor inscription as to how, when, or whence they came. Like most other savages, the Australian looks upon his wife as a slave. To her belongs the duty of collecting and preparing the daily food, of making the camp or hut for the night, of gathering and bringing in firewood, and of procuring water. She must also attend to the children, and in travelling carry all the movable property, and frequently the weapons of her lord and master. In wet weather she attends to all the outside work, while he is snugly seated at the fire. If there is a scarcity of food, it is she who has to endure the pangs of hunger in addition to ill-treatment and abuse.

The natives, although robust in appearance, do not possess muscular strength in a proportionate degree. In expertness they will successfully rival most white men, and even in the case of a brief trial of strength; but they are no match for the white man in long-continued hard labour. Six or eight days' consecutive work generally taxes their endurance to the utmost limit.

When first known they appeared to have been free from any hereditary diseases, and were comparatively free from those of an epidemic character. In the treatment of their ailments they resorted to sorcery or witchcraft.

In those days they had ample resources, according to the localities they were in, for finding food, which consisted of fish, indigenous vegetables, roots, birds, snakes, lizards, luscious grubs, manna, honey, emu and other eggs, kangaroos, opossums, wallabies, pelicans, swans, geese, ducks, and other fowl. Their dress in their natural condition was very simple, consisting of the skins of the opossum, kangaroo, or wallaby; or, on the sea-coast, if these could not be procured, seaweed and rushes were manufactured into garments. Their dwellings consisted, in fine weather, of a few bushes laid one upon the other in the form of a semicircle, as a protection to the head from the wind, and in the winter of rough huts supported by branches, or the protection of projecting or overhanging rocks, caverns, or the hollows of large trees. They were, however, almost always on the move, and their buildings were in consequence of a very temporary character, intended only for a few weeks' occupation at most.

In their domestic arrangements polygamy was practised to its fullest extent, and wives were considered the absolute property of their husbands. Little real affection existed between them, and in innumerable instances women, children, and old people were known to be treated with gross inhumanity, especially when helpless and infirm. Few women were to be found free from frightful scars upon the head, or marks of spearwounds about the body. Infanticide was very common, and was practised solely to get rid of the trouble of rearing children, and to enable the woman to follow her husband in his wanderings, which she frequently could not do if encumbered with a child.

The natives had several superstitious ceremonies and customs peculiar to themselves—varying in different localities—relating to circumcision, marriage, death, and burial; but their religious ideas were of the most meagre kind. That they had a notion of immortality may be gathered from the fact that they regarded Europeans as dead blacks resuscitated, and who had changed colour in the process! They had a wholesome dread of evil spirits, believed in sorcery and witchcraft, but had no knowledge whatever of God, nor had they any special objects of adoration or worship.

Dancing was one of their principal amusements, and throughout the entire continent there were points of resemblance in the manner of conducting the dances, such as the practice of painting the body with white and red ochre, carrying boughs in their hands, or tying them round their limbs, adorning the head with feathers or down, beating time upon sticks or folded skins, and in the dance representing the actions of animals, the circumstances of the chase, of war or of love.

Their songs were of a very rude and unmeaning character, consisting of endless repetitions of one or two meagre ideas. One of the most fruitful sources of strife and warfare was the meeting of different tribes, for however friendly they may have been in the first instance, they rarely parted without a quarrel or bloodshed.

Such, briefly, were the lords of the soil on whose territory the all-conquering Europeans had come to live; and one of the earliest questions the friends of the new colony had to consider was how to civilize and Christianize the natives, and secure to them the due observance of justice and the preservation of their rights.

In the first report of the Commissioners, published in 1836, the subject was made one of chief importance, and their benevolent intentions with regard to the natives took this form—to establish asylums for them, consisting of weather-proof sheds, in which they might at all times obtain gratuitous shelter and lodging; to train them in the use of European eating and clothing, and in habits of useful industry as assistants to the settlers.

An account of their first contact with "the higher civilization," in the person of the representative of Majesty, is given in letters written by Captain Hindmarsh to Mr. G. F. Angas, from which we quote—

"February 15, 1837.

". . . Many natives have visited us, bringing with them their women and children, and altogether exhibiting confidence that is quite pleasing. Instead of being the ugly, stupid race the New Hollanders are generally supposed to be, these are intelligent, active, and handsome people, being far better looking than the majority of Africans; not perhaps so good looking as the East Indian, but an intermediate between the two. The women exhibit a considerable degree of modesty. A party of about twenty, who came down a few weeks ago, and who brought the first women and children I had seen, were placed under the shade of a tree in little family groups. When I first came up to them I soon became well acquainted with their names, which were musical and pretty, such as Alata, Ateon, Atare, and Melanie."

Later on in the same year he wrote—

"September 3, 1837.

"We have a very grave case now under our consideration. A sailor left Encounter Bay a few weeks ago under the guidance of a native and his two women. At about six miles from Encounter Bay the native murdered the sailor for the sole purpose, it would appear, of possessing himself of the poor man's bundle. The murderer is now a prisoner on board the *South Australian*. We have not yet decided how to proceed with him, but evidence is being collected. It would, however, be worse than useless to bring him before a jury unless there is almost a certainty of his conviction. To release him under any circumstances (his tribe knowing him to be guilty) would be naturally ascribed by the natives to fear. We hardly know what evil this may lead to, as they make a practice of taking the life of one of any tribe who may have taken one of theirs, and this without regard to right or wrong. I am sorry to tell you that from the examination of the women, who have acquired a little English by living with the whalers, murder appears not to be considered a crime, and does not entail any disgrace, but only the retribution of the avenger of blood, whose right to exercise his office is known, and once exercised no more is thought about it. As to this prisoner, had the whites knocked him on the head on discovering his guilt, I believe his relatives would have considered it quite in the way of business, and then thought no more about it. Not so, I fear, should a regular process condemn him. And yet 'the bull must be taken by the horns.' The colonists must be protected, and we must do all that we can to show these poor people that justice is equal between us.

"I have not yet been able to discover that these aborigines have any notion of a Supreme Being, though it is clear they believe in an evil spirit, who they consider the author of ill, and who they fear, but do not worship. Indeed, we know but little about their notions on this head. One fact, however, that occurred the other day was interesting. A boy who had acquired a little English was accused of having committed a theft. He denied it very stoutly, and appealed for a confirmation of his denial to his father and mother, both of whom are dead."

If the Governor was in doubt how he should deal with an individual native, it is not to be wondered at that Mr. William Wyatt, Protector of Aborigines, should find it difficult to deal with all the tribes of the province, and his first report is unwittingly amusing. After announcing that twelve huts in the aborigines "location" were nearly ready for habitation, and that rations of biscuit were distributed twice a day to whomsoever might apply, the report proceeded—

"Many natives, especially children, are becoming acquainted with a great number of English words"—it was proverbial that they swore like troopers—"and are very eager to learn the names of everything which attracts their attention. But their general indifference to whatever is valued by civilized men, whether it be clothing, the luxuries of food and comfortable habitations, or the more worthy gratifications of the intellect, makes it no easy matter to stimulate them to that degree of industry necessary for acquiring such advantages; and the salubrious climate of their native land predisposes very considerably to this indolent condition of mind and body."

During the administration of Captain Hindmarsh, there were no serious conflicts between the natives and the colonists, nor were any really practical steps taken to educate the natives within that period.

By the end of 1837 the population of the colony had reached about 2500, and Adelaide boasted about fifty substantial buildings and a hundred and fifty inferior houses or huts; the rates of wages for mechanics and others had materially risen, and there were signs of general prosperity.*

The activity in town presented a striking contrast to the little progress made in the country around, due in great measure to delay in the surveys. Unfortunately, Colonel Light, instead of having the assistance of the Governor, appears to have experienced much harassing interference and interruption from him. An appeal was made, therefore, to the Resident Commissioner to expedite the surveys. Colonel Light having made known his requirements, it was decided to report to the Commissioners, and to send Mr. Kingston to procure additional assistance and implements. He sailed in October, taking with him the first exports from the colony to the mother country, consisting of oil from the fisheries of the South Australian Company.

* Mr. Morphett, in a letter home, written in December of this year, says, "It is not a twelvemonth since the governor proclaimed the province on the plains of Glenelg, and very little more than that time since the first body of emigrants landed on the beach at Holdfast Bay—the forlorn hope, as it might be termed, of a large, wealthy, and intelligent community of Englishmen, who had fixed upon this country as the scene of an experiment in colonization. I recollect the disconcerted and dismal look with which most of the party regarded from the deck of the ship the dried and scorched appearance of the plains, which to their English ideas betokened little short of barrenness. . . . All this has given way to approval of the place, confidence in the capabilities of the soil, and fitness of the climate, with the most perfect satisfaction at the steps we have taken, and a full confidence in the ultimate benefits that will be reaped by those who are pecuniarily interested in our adventure. . . . The activity which prevails in business is healthy and likely to last. Business in Adelaide has already been systematized after the fashion of large towns in England. At first the retail trade was in the hands of half a dozen individuals, who both sold 'the staff of life' and prepared the 'trappings of woe;' now we have butchers, bakers, tailors, shoemakers, dressmakers, and a variety of tradesmen, each class following its own particular calling. There never was a colony which, within the same time, had assumed one-tenth of the outward signs of an independent community that this now does. Visitors from the sister settlements in Australia are surprised at the forward state of our town, at the evidence of capital which they see, at the energy and spirit which prevail, at the amount and character of stock, and at the comforts which most have collected around them."

Meanwhile, the settlers who could not obtain possession of their lands were allowed the free use of the Glenelg plains, where they pitched their tents, tended their flocks and herds, and made away with the dingo, or wild dog, for which the Government offered a reward of five shillings per head for the male, and seven and sixpence for the female; these prowling depredators being most audacious in their attacks on sheep, poultry, and other live stock.

When the first settlers landed on the Glenelg plains, grave doubts were entertained as to the agricultural capabilities of the soil. Only two experiments had as yet been made, one by Mr. Mengé at Kangaroo Island, and the other by Captain Light's survey party at Rapid Bay; and as the suburban and country sections were not surveyed in 1837, the cultivation of the soil was almost at a standstill. Under these circumstances an attempt was made to raise a small crop of wheat on one of the South Australian Company's acres on North Terrace, and although the crop was not a heavy one, the yield was quite sufficient to remove the general impression that the plains around the city were unsuited to the growth of grain.*

During the year (1837) the settlers visited the neighbourhoods of Hurtle, Morphett, and McLaren vales in the south, Mount Barker in the east, and Lyndoch valley in the north-east and elsewhere, and satisfied themselves that there were large tracts of land admirably adapted for agricultural pursuits, although the most sanguine never imagined that in the course of a few years South Australian wheat would carry off the prize in the Great Exhibition of the products of the world.

When the country lands were surveyed and allotted, the settlers found, in commencing operations, that they had almost everything to learn, for experience gained in the mother country was of comparatively little use

---

* Colonel Light never had any doubt on the subject, and was wont to say to grumblers, "This country will not only produce cereals, but all the products of Spain and Portugal."

in the infant colony. The climate, seasons, and soil were quite different; there were no hedges or fences; oxen and horses were very scarce; provisions and labour were exorbitantly high. The land first occupied, on the Glenelg, Gilles, and Gawler plains, was but lightly timbered, and as the greater part of it did not bear sufficient for fencing, posts and rails had to be brought from a distance—namely, from the "tiers," as the timbered hills were called.

In this work the "splitters" from Van Diemen's Land rendered good service until the labour market became stocked by new-comers from Great Britain.*

After fencing his land and building his house or hut, the next process was "clearing." If the wood could be sent into Adelaide at a paying price, this was done; if not, the farmer would select sufficient for his own wants and burn the rest. Then came the grubbing of the stumps or roots, although those were often left in the ground until the first crop had been raised. Many with limited capital depended upon this crop for carrying on future operations, and if it proved a failure, or gave but a small return, they were thrown back for years. A "first crop" has determined the whole future of many a colonist.

These small growers, who constituted the majority of the agriculturists of the colony, were rarely freeholders in the first instance; they leased a section for three or more years with a right of purchase, the rental being so much per cent. per annum on the purchase-money, or so much per acre according to agreement. Every nerve was strained to become possessors of the land; the strictest economy was practised; but if the first crop failed, there followed, in many instances, the forfeiture of the land through inability to carry out the terms of the agreement. It was for some years a common practice for merchants and storekeepers in

---

* More recently wire fences were very largely used, horned cattle having become adepts at working out wooden slip-panel rails with their horns—the patience, perseverance, and ingenuity displayed in getting access to a field of standing corn being truly surprising.

Adelaide to supply these impecunious settlers with provisions till harvest-time, when wheat would be taken in exchange.

The fact that so many of these small growers succeeded and became men of position in the colony, after commencing with little capital and less experience, speaks well, not only for the productiveness of the soil, but for their own indomitable energy and perseverance.

A large proportion of those who were termed farmers became, as a matter of fact, only growers of wheat; instead of improving and extending their homesteads, they aimed mainly at adding section after section of land for wheat-growing purposes, without devoting even a small plot to the production of fruit and vegetables, which when planted require very little attention.

The question of raising stock was one of absorbing interest, and the first beginnings of pastoral pursuits deserve some notice here.

In 1836 the arrivals of stock from England consisted of half a dozen rams of the Merino and Leicester breeds, sent out by the South Australian Company, two cows brought out by the *Africaine*, and a few goats. With the exception of one cow, these importations were landed at Kangaroo Island, the one cow being taken to the mainland, where it was sold for fifty guineas, and calved a few days afterwards. Her progeny, a bull calf, was actually put to work within a twelvemonth afterwards, and earned for its owner, Mr. F. Garden, thirteen pounds per week in drawing water and building materials.

In the same year seventy sheep were brought over from Hobart Town, where they had been purchased at twelve shillings per head; a fine mare for the use of Mr. S. Stephens, first manager of the Company; and a grey gelding, which was lost in what was then called " the bush," the skeleton being found some three years after in Coromandel Valley.

The locality first occupied by the imported stock was the plains near Glenelg and around the embryo city of

Adelaide. Here the emu and the kangaroo gave place to flocks of sheep, while the dingo, or wild dog, found himself "in clover," greatly to the annoyance of the shepherd and to the loss of the importer or owner. For a few years certain localities around Adelaide were known as No. 1 Sheep Station, No. 2 Sheep Station, and so on; but these were destined soon to become the sites of flourishing suburban townships. In 1837 fresh arrivals of stock were landed from Hobart Town, the Cape, and elsewhere, and it was soon found that South Australia was eminently suitable for pastoral pursuits. The promoters and founders of the colony gave the subject of common pasturage early attention, and the Commissioners afforded facilities to those desirous of engaging in such pursuits, by providing for the occupation of land on lease at the rate of ten shillings per square mile, two square miles being allowed for each country section.

On the 3rd of April, 1838, Mr. Joseph Hawdon arrived at Adelaide with a party of nine men, and announced the fact that he had succeeded in bringing overland from New South Wales 325 bullocks, cows, heifers, and horses, all in good condition after a journey of nearly one thousand miles, which had occupied about ten weeks. The cattle were driven from their station on the Hume to the Port Phillip mail establishment on the Goulburn, at which place the drays from Port Phillip, carrying supplies for the party, joined the expedition. The tracks of Major Mitchell, the explorer, were next followed for some distance, and then, descending the left bank of the Murrumbidgee and crossing the Murray at the ford near its junction with the Darling, Mr. Hawdon discovered a lake at the head of the Rufus, which he named Victoria (after her Majesty), and another which he called Lake Bonney, after his friend, Mr. C. Bonney. Four bullocks were killed on the road by lightning, and many natives were seen, but all were quite friendly.

Mr. Hawdon was the first to open up the overland communication for stock; three months later, however

Mr. E. J. Eyre, with three hundred head of cattle, arrived in Adelaide, having made the journey from New South Wales by an almost entirely different route. He discovered a lake, and named it Lake Hindmarsh; on leaving it he found no more fresh water, and was for three weeks engaged in attempting to reach the Murray. At length, after many adventures, he fell in with Mr. Hawdon's tracks, which he followed.

A third overland party, under the command of Captain Sturt, arrived in Adelaide in August, with four hundred head of stock. Sturt had fallen in with the tracks of both Hawdon and Eyre, and considered that Mr. Hawdon's route was the best that could be taken. In this second visit to South Australia, Captain Sturt was confirmed in his first impressions, and gave a glowing report of the great pastoral capabilities of the country at the base of Mount Barker, "far exceeding in richness," he says, "any portion of New South Wales that I ever saw."

In addition to these overland arrivals of stock, large numbers of sheep and cattle were sent by ship from Van Diemen's Land and New South Wales. To further promote such importations, a "Joint Stock Sheep and Cattle Company" was formed, with a capital of £20,000, and large purchases were made. In October, 1838, it was estimated that there were in the colony 22,500 sheep and lambs, 2175 head of cattle, and 233 horses.

We must now go back a little in the narrative to follow the fortunes of "the dwellers in the city." Although in the very early days of the colony those in authority might not always have been very loyal to one another, there was never a period when South Australia was not absolutely loyal to the throne.

In 1837 the birthday of King William IV. was celebrated by a ball and a supper and other demonstrations, but within a few days of these rejoicings the King had ceased to be, and the Princess Victoria had acceded to the throne. On the 19th of October a "Gazette Extraordinary" was issued, informing the colonists of the fact, and on the day appointed the members of Council, magistrates, officers of Government, and a number of the principal inhabitants of the province assembled in front of "Government House," when the Governor read the following:—

"Whereas it hath pleased Almighty God to call to His mercy our late Sovereign Lord King William the Fourth of blessed and glorious memory, by whose decease the Imperial Crown of the United Kingdom of Great Britain and Ireland and all other his late Majesty's dominions is solely and rightfully come to the High and Mighty Princess Alexandrina Victoria, saving the right of any issue of his late Majesty King William the Fourth which may be born of his late Majesty's Consort, we, John Hindmarsh, Knight of the Royal Hanoverian Guelphic Order, Captain in her Majesty's Royal Navy, Governor and Commander-in-chief of the Province of South Australia, assisted by the Honourable Members of Council of the said Province, the Magistrates, Officers of Government, and numbers of the principal inhabitants of Adelaide, therefore do now hereby, with our full voice and consent of tongue and heart, publish and proclaim that the High and Mighty Princess Alexandrina Victoria has now, by the death of our late Sovereign of happy and glorious memory, become our only lawful and rightful liege Sovereign Victoria, by the grace of God, Queen of the United Kingdom of Great Britain and Ireland, Defender of the Faith, saving as aforesaid, Supreme Lady of her Majesty's province of South Australia and its Dependencies, to whom, saving as aforesaid, we do acknowledge all faith and constant obedience, with all hearty and humble affection, beseeching God, by whom kings and queens do reign, to bless the Royal Princess Victoria with long and happy years to reign over us. God save the Queen!"

Among the early Bills passed by the Council were the following—"For establishing a Court of General or Quarter and Petty Sessions; For fixing the qualification of jurors; For the summary determination of disputes between masters and servants; For granting licences for the sale of wine, beer, and spirituous liquors; For the promotion of good order in public-houses; For the establishment of a Court to be called "The Supreme Court of the Province of South Australia."

The plan adopted for announcing any Bill about to be passed was to issue a notice that "the said Bill could be inspected at the office of the Colonial Secretary," and affixing such notice to a tree opposite "Government Hut."

But this early legislation was not regarded with favour in England, and only the last-named Act was permitted to occupy a place in the statute-book of the colony. Meanwhile the young community was to be governed by the laws of the mother country so far as those laws would apply.

Although the early colonists in South Australia were probably the most reputable that had ever gone forth as pioneers to a new land, in the matter of crime the infant settlement was not entirely free, and on the 13th of May seven prisoners were brought before the "Court of General Gaol Delivery" for trial. In addressing the grand jury the judge, Sir J. W. Jeffcott, said—

"You are aware that in the neighbouring colonies it has been considered inexpedient to concede the full right of trial by jury. The reasons which have been considered as justifying such a restriction elsewhere do not, however, happily prevail here; and I feel no slight degree of satisfaction in being able to congratulate the free inhabitants of South Australia, not on being admitted to, but in being able to claim as their birthright the full and unrestricted privileges of the British constitution amongst which not the least valuable is that which has justly been styled the palladium of English liberty, trial by jury, an institution which, however it may have been occasionally abused (and no human institution is free from imperfection), has been proved by the experience of ages in our native land to have well deserved that appellation. This valuable institution, in the fullest sense of the term—that is, trial by the grand and petit jury—will from this day—the first on which a court is held in this province—be in operation, and I again congratulate you on it."

In continuing his charge to the grand jury, Judge Jeffcott said, "I am sorry to find that the vice of drunkenness, notwithstanding the exertions of the Governor and the authorities to check it, prevails here to an alarming extent. It must, however, be checked amongst our own population, and if the fine of £2, which the colonial Act directs to be imposed upon every man who is proved to be drunk, be not sufficient, other and still more coercive means must be resorted to."

It was easy to talk of more coercive measures, but it would have been very difficult to put them in force. Three months earlier than the date of this charge, the Governor had written to Mr. G. F. Angas—

"February 15, 1837.

"What I shall do without a small military force I do not know. It is true I can institute a police force, but who am I to make policemen? Those of sufficiently respectable character are able to earn much higher wages than I dare offer, and I am restricted in the salary to a police magistrate to £100 a year. Where shall I get a gentleman fit to do such duty who will give up his time for so small a sum? I have suggested to Lord Glenelg that he should allow me to make it £200. . . ."

About this time, settlers as well as Government officials had to employ banished men, ex-convicts, who were in many cases skilful splitters, sawyers, fencers, and hut-builders. High wages were paid to them, but it was considered undesirable to inquire too closely whether they were "expirees" or "runaways." As the Port was free and drink abundant, there was much disorderly conduct at times. On one occasion a serious disturbance occurred, and after the reading of the Riot Act the marines were ordered to load and fire with ball cartridges, when some of the rioters were wounded, and a few taken into custody. Not long after this the

Government store was broken into, and food, ammunition, and other goods stolen; the hut of the sheriff, Mr. S. Smart, of Tasmania, was attacked, and a pistol was fired at the sheriff. Volunteers were at once sworn in as special constables, the delinquents were captured, and a man named Magee, who fired the ball, was hanged.

It is almost a matter of surprise that, with the bad example set at this time by those in authority, there was not more lawlessness among the people. The colonial secretary had assaulted the colonial treasurer for violent language, and the former was suspended. The emigration agent had been charged with disobedience to the Governor's commands, and was suspended. One official was charged with inciting the people to sedition, and another with setting the judge at defiance, and so on.

As an illustration of the state of the times, an incident of a visit to Kangaroo Island, made by the Governor in June, 1838, may be recorded. While he was there a mail arrived, and the captain of H.M.S. *Pelorus*, in which the Governor had voyaged, was anxious to know if there were any despatches for him. Captain Hindmarsh, in the presence of an officer, who for the nonce he dubbed postmaster-general, opened the mail. At a meeting at Adelaide, his action was very strongly condemned

Apropos of this, it may be stated that postal irregularities were a source of very great trouble to the colonists at this time, and the following curious advertisement in the *Sydney Monitor* was intended to give a friendly hint as to where the missing letters went :—
" Post office in South Australia. The Governor ought to be reminded that owners and masters of vessels trading to new colonies are deeply interested in destroying all letters between the new colony and the colonies they trade with, and that until a judicious law regulating the mails between Adelaide and these colonies be passed and regularly enforced, letters and newspapers will continue to be purloined, as they have hitherto been, and now are."

The dissensions in high places were soon to be aggravated by the freedom of the press. The first number of the first South Australian newspaper was published in London, on the 18th of June, 1836, before the first vessel sent out had sighted the shores of the new colony. The newspaper dealt more largely with probabilities than certainties, but it was the wish of Messrs. Robert Thomas and Co., the proprietors, and Mr. George Stevenson, the editor, "to print the first number of the *South Australian Gazette and Colonial Register* in the capital of the civilized world, and the second number in a city of the wilderness," the site of which was then unknown.

Printers, presses, type, and paper, identical with that used in the first number, were shipped to South Australia, and on the 3rd of June, 1837, the second number was issued under many difficulties, the printers and workmen engaged in England having "bettered themselves" in other employments. Moreover, the printing-office was only a tent. But by degrees all difficulties were overcome, and the *Gazette and Register* occupied its well-earned position.

The first colonial issue, however, was not well received by all, nor indeed could it have been, for the dissensions and disputes consequent upon the divided authority of the Governor and the Resident Commissioner had, as we have said, led to the formation of two parties, and as the *Gazette and Register* stood by the Governor's party, it became necessary to establish another newspaper, and the *Southern Australian*, edited by Mr. Charles Mann, at that time advocate-general and Crown solicitor, came into existence, as a party organ on the other side. Official matters were sufficiently complicated before the press asserted its liberty—they became more so when the two newspapers took up their parables, and commenced wordy warfares not infrequently in strong language, garnished with personalities.

While such was the state of affairs in South Australia, matters at home were taking a serious turn for some of the colonists. Reports unfavourable to the administrative conduct of the Governor had reached the Commissioners from so many quarters, that they were constrained to lay the matter before Lord Glenelg. The principal complaints were that he had retarded the progress of the surveys by interfering with the surveyor-general; that he had assumed some of the powers delegated to the Resident Commissioner; that he had incurred expenses without authority, and that he had suspended and discharged a number of public officers without sufficient cause. The letter addressed by the Commissioners to Lord Glenelg concluded by stating that "however much they might respect the rank of Captain Hindmarsh as a distinguished officer of the British navy, they were compelled by a paramount sense of duty respectfully to recommend, on the several grounds which they had endeavoured to explain to his lordship, that he might be immediately recalled from the government of South Australia."

Pending a reply, several of the most influential friends of the colony met in London to discuss the position, and a deputation waited on the Secretary of State in reference to the appointment of a new Governor.

The choice of the Commissioners fell upon Lieutenant-Colonel Gawler, a distinguished officer under the Duke of Wellington in the Peninsular campaign.

No sooner had the Commissioners completed their arrangements with regard to the new Governor, than they received a series of grave complaints against the Resident Commissioner, and somewhat hastily they dismissed him from his office,* and having experienced the evils of divided authority in the colony, the Board submitted that henceforth the office of Resident Commissioner should be merged in that of the Governor. In this Lord Glenelg concurred, and later on Colonel Gawler was gazetted Governor and Resident Commissioner.

In June, 1838, the news reached the colony of the

* It may here be stated that during the administration of Captain Grey inquiries were instituted relative to these charges, resulting in a complete exoneration of the Resident Commissioner, communicated to him by Earl Grey, Secretary of State for the Colonies.

recall of Captain Hindmarsh, and a large number of the colonists at once presented him with an address expressing personal attachment, and regretting his loss as " a colonist who had in so many instances set a bright example of patient self-denial and energetic exercise of manly accomplishments." In the course of his reply to this address, Captain Hindmarsh read as follows :—

"I receive your expressions of attachment in the same sincerity of feeling with which I believe they are offered, and I assure you that the regret I feel deeply at this moment is influenced less by the political change to which you refer, or by the reflection that such change has been effected by unworthy means, than by the necessity I am under of leaving you for a time to vindicate my public conduct and justify in England my administration of the government of the province. The share which a Governor of South Australia possesses in conducting the new experiment in colonization is so small that under no circumstance can he be justly responsible for its result. That responsibility rests with the Colonization Commissioners, to whom the charge of working out so peculiar a constitution is entrusted. The principle, though novel, is simple, as I believe it to be sound. Its successful practical application, however, depends, not on the Colonial Government, but on the integrity and ability of the individuals entrusted by the Colonial Commissioners with its development, and it must be to a deficiency of those qualities alone that anything approaching failure ought to be attributed. . . ."

Captain Hindmarsh left the colony on the 14th of July, in H.M.S. *Alligator*, for Sydney, intending to proceed from thence to England. It was evident that he anticipated a return after he had made his defence in England. Those most opposed to his administration never doubted that to the best of his judgment he had endeavoured to promote the welfare of the community, and with this conviction he was confident that he could make a fair representation of his proceedings at head-quarters. And there is little doubt that if he had been so situated as to have been able to act on his own responsibility and exercise an independent judgment, he would have proved a much more successful administrator of the affairs of the infant colony.

He was appointed Governor of Heligoland in 1840. In 1849 he received the war medal and seven clasps, and other honorary distinctions, for his long and distinguished services in the navy. In 1851 the honour of knighthood was conferred upon him, and in 1856 he returned to England, where he died, on the 29th of July, 1860, at the advanced age of seventy-eight.

Interim Administration of Mr. G. M. Stephens.

Pending the arrival of the new Governor, the temporary administration of affairs was undertaken by Mr. George Milner Stephens, advocate-general, and son-in-law of Captain Hindmarsh. His position was not enviable. In his first address to the Council he drew this melancholy picture of affairs: " I have to announce with regret that there are no funds in the treasury, and that the quarter's salaries due to the whole of the public servants on the 30th of June last are unpaid. We have, therefore, to fear that the tempting remuneration held out for the exercise of ability in private undertakings in this province, added to the distress which they are beginning to experience from the want of money, will induce many indispensable public officers to leave the service of the Government. Secondly, by the departure of the marines on H.M.S. *Alligator*, this province, with a population exceeding four thousand persons, is abandoned to the protection of eighteen policemen, lately embodied by Governor Hindmarsh, while there are now twenty-one prisoners confined in the weather-boarded building used as a gaol, and perhaps double that number of desperate runaway convicts in the neighbourhood of the town. At the same time, as I have observed, there are no funds for the support of the force now constituting our only protection, and the Resident

Commissioner is restricted by his instructions from providing money for such a purpose. . . . We have happily no immediate cause to apprehend hostility from the aborigines, or our situation would indeed be deplorable; but they have ere now sacrificed two fellow-creatures, and you have too recently witnessed the outrages that terminated in a public execution, to regard with indifference our present unprotected state. . . ."

The brief administration of Mr. G. M. Stephens as acting Governor was a very successful one, inasmuch as he was the means of arresting the progress of party spirit and of quelling much of the strife that had unfortunately sprung up. From his private funds he liberally relieved the treasury from its embarrassment and effectually re-organized the police force.

It would be unfair to conclude this chapter without some direct reference to the character, as a whole, of the colonists who bore the burden and heat of the day at this important time and in the more exciting times soon to follow, and we cannot do better than quote the language of Sir Henry Ayers, K.C.M.G.*—

"The early settlers evinced great boldness in coming to this country when they did, for it was no light undertaking for men and women, with their children, to leave the comforts and conveniences of civilization and venture to settle in a country whose geographical position was not very generally understood, and of whose productive powers absolutely nothing was known; and it was the possession of like courage, when they were surrounded with difficulties, which enabled them successfully to withstand them. I have always urged and am still of opinion that the greatest factor in overcoming our difficulties was the sterling qualities of our pioneers.†

* From a lecture on " Pioneer Difficulties in South Australia," by Sir Henry Ayers, K.C.M.G., delivered in Adelaide in June, 1891.

† According to the classification of colonists made by the Old Colonists' Association, " pioneers " included those who arrived prior to the 28th of December, 1846, that being the tenth anniversary of the day South Australia was proclaimed a British colony, and " old colonists " were those who arrived between December 28th, 1846, and December 28th, 1856.

"Taking all classes together they were a superior sample of the people of the mother country. . . . Our pioneer colonists had their privations, their disappointments, and their losses, which they bravely met. Most of them were extremely capable and intelligent, possessed of sturdy endurance and self-reliance, determined to succeed if success were possible. In short, they were made of the right sort of stuff, and well worthy of the grand old country whose sons they were. It was these qualities which enabled them to meet and surmount the reverses with which they were environed. They were, in numerous instances, young and recently married, many marriages having been hastened to enable the young people to cast their lot and try their fortunes in this country. It is then, when men and women leave their homes and have to found new ones, that even the painfulness of the severance from their native land to do so is less felt than it would be after forming a home soon to be broken up again. It is a period, too, when men and women feel that they are all the world to each other, so that as long as they are together the locality of their residence is of less consequence. It is a time when new enterprises may be undertaken with better hope of success, for they are then possessed of double strength, with twice the amount of hope and exhilaration that they have at any other era of their existence, and there is no better period when a man may commence a great and important or an arduous undertaking than when he has the enthusiastic help and tender sympathy of a loving wife.

"With the prosperity that followed our adversity I should have liked to have been able to say that the early settlers, who worked so diligently and struggled so hard to sustain the settlement of the colony, met with the good fortune such conduct merited. Alas! it was not so. More fortunes were lost, or missed of making, than had been retained or secured. The coming of general prosperity was, so far as most of the pioneers were concerned, only the renewal of fresh efforts more or less empty-handed."

CHAPTER VI.

ADMINISTRATION OF COLONEL GAWLER.

OCTOBER 17th, 1838—MAY 10th, 1841.

Offices of Governor and Resident Commissioner combined.—Difficulties of Colonel Gawler's Position.—Financial Embarrassments.—Resignation of Colonel Light and the Survey Staff.—Death of Colonel Light.—Rapid Immigration and Unemployed Labour.—Erection of Public Buildings.—Special Surveys.—Explorations.—Mr. E. J. Eyre's Attempt to open up Overland Route to Western Australia.—A Story of Heroism.—Murder of John Baxter.—Board of South Australian Commissioners disbanded.—Formation of South Australian Society.—The "Company's" Road to the Port.—McLaren Wharf.—Bushrangers.—Massacres by Natives.—Treatment and Punishment of Criminal Aborigines. — Missionaries. — Question of Colonial Chaplains.—Arrival of Germans.—A Story of Religious Persecution—Pastor Kavel.—Fruits and Vegetables.—Prosperity.—A Coming Storm.—Colonel Gawler's Bills dishonoured.—A Critical Time.—Colonel Gawler's Defence.—His Recall.—Universal Bankruptcy in Colony.

COLONEL GEORGE GAWLER, the second Governor of South Australia, was a man of great ability, of calm determination, and withal of intense enthusiasm and vigour. When he arrived in the colony he was in his forty-second year, the prime of manhood. His previous career had been adventurous and notable. Leaving the Military College, Great Marlow, at the age of fifteen, he joined the 52nd Light Infantry, and served to the end of the Peninsular campaign. He was present at the battles and sieges of Badajoz, Vittoria, Nives, Nivelles,

Orthes, Toulouse, and Waterloo. As ensign he led the forlorn hope at the storming of Badajoz, where he was struck in the right knee by grapeshot, and fell from the parapet into the ditch below. Here he would have perished but for his timely rescue by a private of his own regiment, who laid down his life to serve his officer. At Waterloo Colonel Gawler performed signal service while commanding the right flank company of the 52nd Regiment during the great charge on the Imperial Guards, for which he received the war medal with seven clasps. After this he was in the Civil Service; then he occupied the post of Governor in one of the North American provinces for a period of three years, and subsequently he employed his time in literary pursuits.

When he was selected to supersede Captain Hindmarsh in the important office of Governor of South Australia, and to combine in himself the dual position of Governor and Resident Commissioner, it of course became necessary that new instructions should be issued, and these were clear and explicit. Enlarged financial powers were given him, but he was reminded that, in principle, South Australia was a self-supporting colony; therefore, when the balance in hand upon the revenue fund was not sufficient to pay accounts fully due, he could draw upon the Emigration Fund; and if that fund was not sufficient, he could draw a bill or bills of exchange upon the Commissioners; but that no accounts so drawn were to exceed in the aggregate a total of £2500 per quarter, or £10,000 in the year. At the date of his appointment the expenses of the authorized establishment of the colony amounted to £8322 12s. The power to draw to the extent of £10,000, therefore, the Commissioners reminded him, was in excess of the total fixed expenses of the colony, and he was requested to "distinctly understand that the right to exceed that expenditure was not thereby in any degree extended."

When intelligence of the appointment of Colonel Gawler reached South Australia, a gleam of hope, almost amounting to exultation, took the place of irritation and despondency. The settlers understood that they might be ruled somewhat despotically, but they welcomed any change from the irritation of being ruled almost entirely by men sixteen thousand miles away (by ship's course), for the most part ignorant of the wants of the colonists and of the physical capabilities of the country, and unaided by those improvements in the communication of orders which modern science has made known. Altogether, the position of the colonists was one of great difficulty and uneasiness, and when, on the 12th of October, 1838, the ship *Pestongee Bomangee*, with the new Governor on board, dropped anchor in Holdfast Bay, there went up a great sigh of relief, as if their burdens had already begun to roll away.

On the 17th the Governor was publicly received in Adelaide, about a thousand people meeting him on the Bay Road, and escorting him to Government House, or " Hut." * Here a Council was held, and the Governor took the oaths, which he afterwards administered to Mr. G. M. Stephens, on his receiving the appointment of colonial secretary; to Mr. H. Jickling, judge; and to Mr. R. Bernard, acting advocate-general and Crown solicitor.

The reception was enthusiastic, everybody hoping that a reign of peace and good-will would set in, now that they had an able and influential man invested with the powers of Governor and Resident Commissioner.

The routine addresses followed, but they were not of the routine kind. There was an intense desire among the settlers to develop the wonderful resources of the province, in which each individual seemed to take a special pride. They had long suffered from delays, hindrances, and vexations, inevitable in the circumstances, and they were eager to encourage every action on the part of the authorities which should throw

* When Colonel Gawler went to Government House, it was only a temporary erection of one story, with a thatched roof, the timbers principally of native pine, procured from what was then called the " Pine Forest," since known as Nailsworth.

open the country more widely to capitalists and settlers.

The position of Captain Hindmarsh was, as we have seen, an unenviable one, but that of Colonel Gawler was much more so. The task before him was one of supreme difficulty. The contentions, if they had not ceased altogether, were at least dormant, but there was a vast network of financial difficulty before him. As, later on, we shall have to consider the whole matter in detail, it will be well in this place to give the Governor's estimate of the situation in his own words, written within a fortnight of his arrival in the colony:—

"I must, in the strongest manner, solicit the Commissioners' most indulgent consideration. I am about to incur the heaviest responsibilities, from which I could not shrink without endangering the finest prospects of this most beautiful colony, and my duty to the Colonization Commissioners. I find the public offices established here much beyond the authorized number and force furnished to me in England, and yet I am persuaded that, with the consent of the Council, I must not only keep, but probably increase, the existing establishments. The surveys are altogether unequal to the demand for land; 21,000 acres of preliminary purchases remain unsurveyed, and, of course, the great mass of subsequent purchases unprovided for, and great disappointment has been experienced. It is my intention, with the consent of the Council, to put on every surveyor that I can procure, until the survey comes up, or nearly up, to the demand. The profits of capitalists are great; provisions, wages, and house rent are very high; all prosper but the servants of Government. To retain them in their places, it will be absolutely necessary to increase their salaries, at least of the junior classes, to something like a proportionate scale to those of private officers. My instructions permit me to draw on England to the amount of £10,000 per annum. Within this year (1838), upwards of £12,000 has been already drawn; the third quarter's salaries are still due; the treasury is absolutely empty, and public debts to a considerable amount have been incurred; urgent demands are made for payment, and the credit of Government is therefore injuriously low. The colony itself is most flourishing. I have great confidence that a proportionately large revenue may be raised from it, and that in many things public expenditure may be reduced. Care and exertion on my part shall not be spared to accomplish these objects, but, until they are attained, I must surpass my instructions, and look to England for considerable unauthorized pecuniary assistance."

These words were written, as we have said, within a fortnight of his arrival in the colony. The experience of a few more weeks convinced him much more strongly that he was involved in most aggravated and complicated difficulties. He found that the public offices were carried on with scarcely a pretension to system; "every man did as he would, and got on as he could." There were scarcely any records of past proceedings, of public accounts, or of issues of stores; innumerable complications had arisen in consequence of the non-fulfilment of one of the leading principles on which the regulations made for the disposal of land were based, namely, that "the surveys should be in advance of the demand," complications which the letter of the law as it stood could not by any possibility set right; the survey department was reduced to three individuals; immigrants were crowding into the town, and leaving the country districts; the principal business was in land-jobbing; capital was flowing out to Sydney and Van Diemen's Land for the necessaries of life, as rapidly as it was brought in by fresh arrivals from England; there was a dire necessity for new public buildings of every kind; the gaol, constructed for eight prisoners, always had an average of thirty persons; in the Government "Hut" there was not tolerable household or office accommodation; the two landing-places, Holdfast Bay and the Old Port, were of the most indifferent description; the cost of transport to and from these ports to Adelaide was simply ruinous, and in the midst of all this, the tide of immigration was flowing in with a rapidity which would have taxed the resources of any young colony, however perfect its organization might have been.

Colonel Gawler took an intense interest in the "experiment in colonization" under trial, and, in spite of difficulties, he threw all the strength of his great energy into the attempt to make the scheme successful. Soon after his arrival his Council was formed for the time being, and work began in earnest.

Amongst the first instructions sent out to Colonel Gawler by the Commissioners, was one giving him authority to reconstruct the survey staff, Colonel Light and his assistants having resigned their appointments.

It will be remembered that when the dissensions between Governor Hindmarsh and the surveyor-general were at their height, Mr. G. S. Kingston was despatched to England to confer with the Commissioners on the subject of the surveys. The Commissioners insisted upon the surveys being carried out in a particular way, distasteful to the surveyor-general, and in the event of his not complying, Mr. Kingston was to supersede him. On receiving this ultimatum, Colonel Light at once tendered his resignation, and his example was followed by the whole of the officers of the survey staff. For the awkward and unpleasant position in which he found himself placed Mr. Kingston was in no wise responsible, the action taken by the Board having been upon their own initiative. A public meeting was held in Adelaide, at which the overwhelming vote was in favour of the plan pursued by Colonel Light; but this was not sufficient to induce him to withdraw his resignation. He entered into business with Mr. B. T. Finniss, under the title of Light, Finniss, and Co., but Colonel Light's health had been for some time failing, and under the irritation of what he felt to be unrequited public services in the colony, his malady—consumption—soon became fatal, and he died shortly after Governor Gawler's arrival.*

* In his last illness his great anxiety was to be acknowledged as

On the subject of the reconstruction of the survey staff, the Board of Commissioners wrote to Colonel Gawler as follows:—

"The Commissioners are desirous of placing, and do hereby place, in your hands the fullest and most ample powers to reorganize the surveying staff in whatever manner and to whatever extent may appear to you most expedient, in order to render it efficient, and to remedy, as far as may be practicable, the interruption and delay in the progress of the surveys which these resignations have occasioned."

This unrestricted licence became the source of one of Colonel Gawler's greatest troubles, and led in no small measure to the difficulties which culminated in one of the most disastrous episodes in the history of the colony.

The possession of land, not for use or cultivation, but for speculation, became a mania, many acting as if the whole population of Great Britain were about to be suddenly transferred to South Australia. As each fresh exploring party found out the existence of good country, the desire to purchase became almost irresistible. But as, immediately after survey, the deposit for purchase had to be paid, the capital of the country, instead of being employed in cultivating the land already held and in effecting improvements, was either sent home to England for expenditure in emigration purposes, or to

the founder of Adelaide, and he requested that a copper plate, with an inscription to that effect, might be placed inside his coffin. He was buried in a vault in Light Square, where an obelisk to his memory was erected, bearing this inscription—

ERECTED BY
THE PIONEERS OF SOUTH AUSTRALIA,
IN MEMORY OF
COLONEL WILLIAM LIGHT,
FIRST SURVEYOR-GENERAL,
AND BY WHOM
THE SITE OF ADELAIDE WAS FIXED ON THE 29TH OF DECEMBER, 1836.
DIED 5TH OF OCTOBER, 1839,
AGED 54 YEARS.

A more worthy and imposing monument was erected in 1892.

the neighbouring colonies for the purchase of the necessaries of life, and even for timber, of which there was abundance in the colony. This was a double evil in many respects. The Colonization Commissioners, finding their coffers fill so rapidly, despatched emigrant ships accordingly,* and the arrival of these in quick succession led the Governor to incur expenses which the revenue of the province was quite inadequate to meet. For the accommodation of these immigrants some thirty or forty wooden houses had been erected to the westward of the city, and even these were wholly insufficient to afford the necessary shelter. In consequence of the speculation in land, and a total disregard to its cultivation, there was little employment for the new arrivals, and they, therefore, for the most part were kept in the neighbourhood of Adelaide; not only their shelter, but their provisions having to be provided by the Government.

What to do with this unemployed labour was the problem the gallant colonel at once set himself to solve. Impressed with an anxious desire to improve the colony, and feeling convinced that this could only be done by a liberal expenditure of money, he determined to embark in a series of enterprises. And truly he entered upon the execution of his plan with wonderful spirit and energy, and scattered money in a right royal manner. He built an extensive and well-finished Government House, commodious offices for the various Government departments, a custom house, gaol, and hospital; he remodelled and extended the survey department; enrolled a large police force, both foot and mounted; formed roads, sent out exploring parties, and introduced bold and decisive measures everywhere and in everything. This kept a large amount of money afloat, gave employment to numbers of immigrants, and produced what appeared at the time to be a state of general prosperity. But, unfortunately, the erection of

* In 1838 the total land sold was 47,932 acres, realizing £47,932; and the number of emigrants who left England for South Australia was 3154 souls.

Government works on this extensive scale induced the colonists to launch out into erecting shops and warehouses, and far-seeing men whispered that very soon wages would go up as well as the price of provisions, and that, for all the apparent prosperity, a day of reckoning was not far distant.

The bills drawn by Colonel Gawler on the Commissioners, and presented to them during the first half of the year 1839, amounted to £8560, and during the last half to £10,600.

Besides the erection of public buildings, the Governor tackled the subject of official salaries, which were absurdly small,* and raised them from the 1st of January,

* A committee was appointed to inquire and report on this subject, and one of the documents sent in by them, and afterwards transmitted by the Governor to the Commissioners, was the following statement of the weekly expenses of a single gentleman and his servant at that time:—

	£	s.	d.
15 lbs. fresh meat @ 1s.	0	15	0
14 lbs. bread @ 4½d.	0	5	3
7 pints of milk @ 4d.	0	2	4
Vegetables for one week	0	7	0
Wine and beer	1	1	0
Minor groceries	0	7	0
¼ lb. tea	0	2	0
1 lb. loaf sugar @ 1s. 3d., 2 lbs. moist @ 1s.	0	3	3
¾ lb. fresh butter @ 3s. 6d.	0	2	7½
1 lb. salt butter @ 2s. 6d.	0	2	6
3 lbs. soap @ 7d.	0	1	9
2 lbs. candles @ 1s. 6d., 1 lb. at 4s.	0	7	0
1½ load of wood @ 8s.	0	12	0
1½ load of water @ 4s.	0	6	0
Washing 3½ dozen @ 5s.	0	17	6
Per week	5	12	2½
Per annum	289	2	10
House rent	60	0	0
Man-servant's wages	45	0	0
Master's clothes, with economy	50	0	0
	£444	2	10

—If such were the necessary expenses of a single gentleman and

1839. He added also largely to the police force. In all these arrangements the Commissioners appear to have heartily concurred. In their despatches during 1839 the following and several similar passages occur:—

"I am directed to assure you" (wrote the secretary of the Board) "that the Commissioners will do everything in their power to sustain your proper authority; that so far as their information enables them to judge they fully approve of the steps you have hitherto taken, and that you may safely rely on their efficient co-operation in all measures calculated to promote the welfare of the colony."

Again—

"You will observe that while certain rules are laid down for your guidance, you are authorized to deviate from them under peculiar circumstances, and on certain conditions, one of the most important of which is that the grounds for such deviation shall be placed fully and without delay before the Board."

These sanctions and expressions of approval naturally led Colonel Gawler to conclude that his course of action gave satisfaction, and accordingly, therefore, he went on in the same way.

While matters in official quarters were thus in progress the colonists were seized with the same spirit of enterprise, and broke forth into various new undertakings. For example—

In January, 1839, the first "special survey" of four thousand acres was applied for by Mr. F. H. Dutton on behalf of himself, Mr. D. Macfarlane, and Captain Finniss, colonists of New South Wales. This was followed by several other applications of a similar kind, and the race for them became almost as great, in some instances, as it afterwards was for taking up mineral leases. In one case the manager of the South

---

his servant, what must have been those of a married man with a family? With the exception of the Governor and the judge, whose salaries at this time were £800 and £500 respectively, the highest were £400 per annum, and only two or three were in receipt of so much, the greater number varying from £250 to £100.

Australian Company proceeded to Port Lincoln to look out for a good locality, and before he returned the one fixed upon had been applied for and taken, the second best being then selected by the unfortunate manager. Soon a "rush" was made to Port Lincoln and a new settlement formed; trading vessels proceeded there with provisions, passengers, and building materials, and for a time it seemed as if the capital would be supplanted; the *Port Lincoln Herald* was established, and all went well until the bubble burst, and then people began to return to the capital.

In the times of the land-purchase mania the transactions were not always on a large scale; purchasers of preliminary or eighty-acre sections split them up into very small building allotments, ranging from £3 to £5 and upwards in value. Besides the usual sales by land agents there was an evening auction in Hindley Street, where fenders and fire-irons, spades and axes, or allotments of building land could be purchased. As in those days the mart was, with the exception of the little theatre and the public-house, the only resort for colonists when the day's work was done, the clever and witty auctioneer always kept a large audience in high good humour, besides doing a considerable trade.

Great enterprise was shown in many other directions, notably in the matter of minor explorations by parties in search of suitable localities for special surveys, as well as for sheep and cattle stations. In one instance Messrs. Strangways and Blunden discovered a fine river in the north, and named it the Gawler, and this gave an impetus to the occupation of the land in this direction. Other discoveries were made about the same time by Messrs. Cock and Jamieson, who visited Yorke's Peninsula, and penetrated into hitherto unknown parts of the country, and subsequently by Mr. R. Cook in a trip up Spencer's Gulf, where he discovered three harbours.

In 1839 a considerable knowledge of the south-east part of the colony was obtained from Mr. Charles Bonney, who opened up a new route overland from

New South Wales, and by Major (afterwards Sir) Thomas Mitchell, the explorer of a large portion of New South Wales and Australia Felix (Victoria), who reached the boundary of the South Australian colony on the Glenelg River, after proving the junction of the Darling, the Lachlan, and the Murrumbidgee with the Murray on its northern side. Governor Gawler made a flying visit to the north-west bend of the river Murray, accompanied by a young man named Bryan, a visitor at Government House. Mr. Bryan's horse gave up, and it was necessary that he should remain with it while the Governor and his attendant proceeded to find water for man and beast. The weather was fearfully hot. Before the searchers could reach the river they were so exhausted that one of the horses was killed and his blood drunk. On reaching the camp from whence they had started, men and horses were sent on their return tracks with all that was necessary to save man and horse. But Mr. Bryan was not to be found. Search was made in all directions for many miles, but although, years afterwards, the horse was found alive, "with his hoofs turned up like skates," no trace of the unfortunate visitor to Government House was ever discovered.* The Governor also visited that part of the Murray within the boundary of South Australia, and made some valuable geological observations.

But all these exploits sank into insignificance in comparison with the heroic attempt of Mr. E. J. Eyre to open up overland communication with Western Australia. The idea had been suggested by Captain (afterwards Sir) George Grey when on a visit to the new colony *en route* to England, and Colonel Gawler warmly encouraged the fitting out of the expedition. The story has been many times and splendidly told, but by no one better than the late Henry Kingsley.† We can only give a meagre outline of it here.

* Mount Bryant, in the locality where he was lost, is named after him.
† See *Macmillan's Magazine*, vol. xii. p. 502.

On the 18th of June, 1840, Mr. Eyre, accompanied by Mr. Scott, a personal friend and travelling companion, John Baxter, an overseer, Corporal Coles, of the Sappers and Miners, and two native boys, together with drays, horses, and sheep, started, amid the cheers of the whole populace, to explore the interior of South Australia. But in this he was unsuccessful. He forced his way for four hundred miles to the north of Adelaide, and got into what was then known as the basin of Lake Torrens, a fearful country of alternate mud, brackish water, and sand. Proceeding into the basin of the lake, he found it coated with an unbroken sheet of salt crust, into which the foot sank at every step. Beaten back from the north at all points, and bitterly disappointed, he came to the conclusion that he could proceed no further in that direction.

"I had one of three alternatives to choose," he wrote at this critical juncture, " either to give up the expedition altogether, to cross to the Murray to the east and follow up that river to the Darling, or, by crossing over to Streaky Bay to the westward, to endeavour to find some opening leading towards the interior in that direction. After weighing well the advantages and disadvantages of each (and there were many objections to them all), I determined upon adopting the last."

After many difficulties and dangers, he formed a depôt of his party at Streaky Bay, and spent weary months in trying to find a way to the westward or northward. His attempts to round the head of the Great Bight— a part of the coast described as "a hideous anomaly, a blot on the face of nature, the sort of place one gets into in bad dreams "—were desperate. Water was only to be obtained by digging, and then it was generally brackish; the heat was terrific; the cliffs were parched and barren; everything along that desolate coast, where for seven hundred miles no harbour fit to shelter a small boat, and for eleven hundred miles no rill of water so big as a child's finger, are to be found, was forbidding and horrible. After a journey of twenty-four days in an attempt to round the head of the

Bight, he returned to the camp unsuccessful, but only to start again with a dray-load of water, and after making a distance of 138 miles, to return again with his task unaccomplished, although within twelve miles of the Bight. A final effort was made, and he reached the head of the Bight. The actual distance was only 153 miles, but to reach the goal he had to ride 643 miles and to labour incessantly for forty days, while a dray laden with water was driven backwards and forwards for 238 miles. But the Bight was only one incident of the expedition. He was convinced he could not penetrate to the northward in that direction with drays, and he came to the heroic determination to reduce his followers and go westward to King George's Sound, the original goal of the expedition, with pack-horses only.

Then came a day when he informed his companion, Mr. Scott, that they must part, as he intended only to take three native boys—among whom was one named Wylie, of King George's Sound—as they would be of most service in the country to be passed over. To Baxter, the overseer, and for some years his faithful servant, Mr. Eyre pointed out the extreme peril of the undertaking, in which he was resolved to succeed or perish, and left it to him to decide whether he would go forward or return. The faithful fellow never hesitated for a moment, but resolved to go forward at all hazards. For some weeks the horses were fed up and rested for the task before them; meanwhile, those of the party who were to return to Adelaide had long since left in the cutter placed at the service of Eyre by the Government. But on the 24th of January, 1841, the day when Eyre was making his final preparations to leave, he was startled by the report of a gun. It was fired by Mr. Scott, who had returned from Adelaide bearing letters and verbal messages innumerable, urging Eyre to abandon his dangerous task. But he was not to be moved, and on the following day, after bidding a final farewell to Scott, he started with Baxter, Wylie, two other natives, nine horses, a Timor pony, and some sheep, on one of the most daring expeditions ever conceived.

Leaving Fowler's Bay, they kept along the coast, and, beyond the Bight, came upon high cliffs unbroken for many miles by a single ravine, and here the terrible part of the journey began. On one occasion they were four days without water, and the horses and sheep with scarcely a particle of food; on another they were reduced to such straits that Eyre found it necessary to cast away everything that was not essential to life; sometimes they were rejoicing over a quart or so of water collected by a sponge from the dew on the grass. Some of the horses died, some were abandoned; the sheep failed; two of the natives became disaffected and absconded, but, being unable to find food in the desert, returned apparently repentant.

One day—it was the 29th of April—having made an early start, and the weather being intensely hot, Baxter pleaded for an early halt. After some hesitation Eyre consented, and agreed to take the first watch. He saw Baxter and the boys lie down in their respective break-winds, and then went a short distance from the camp to look after his horses. It was a wild, cold night; the wind was blowing hard from the southwest, and scud was driving across the moon. Just as Eyre was leading his horses round, towards the end of his watch, he saw a flash, and heard the report of a gun. Calling out and receiving no answer, he ran towards the spot, and was met by Wylie, crying, "Oh, massa, massa, come here!" To his horror he found Baxter on the ground by the camp-fire, weltering in his blood, and in the last agonies of death. A glance around showed that the place had been ransacked by the two disaffected native boys, who, having aroused Baxter while securing the rifles and other things, had shot him in the breast as they decamped.

Alone in a waterless desert, five hundred miles away from all human aid, Eyre covered the body of his faithful friend, gathered together the few things left by the treacherous natives, and with the boy Wylie proceeded on his lonely journey overwhelmed with unutterable grief.

On the 3rd of May, water was found at a distance of a hundred and thirty miles from the last supply; on the 11th a hill was descried, the first properly so called that had been seen for many hundred miles, and then there was a marked change for the better in the character of the country; water became more abundant, and an occasional kangaroo was killed.

On the 2nd of June, while in Thistle Cove, Eyre, weak and exhausted, but bearing up against despair, beheld a gladsome sight. It was a boat being pulled towards a French whaler, the *Mississippi*. Almost wild with joy, the lonely man stood on the verge of a wave-worn rock, and made signals to the vessel. A boat was at once put off to take him and the boy on board, where they were treated with great kindness, supplied with a stock of clothes, and for twelve days enjoyed rest and boundless hospitality. Refreshed and invigorated, and furnished with an ample supply of provisions, the travellers started again on their journey. On the 4th of July some horse tracks showed them they were approaching the haunts of civilized men, and on the 7th they were received in the town of Albany with enthusiastic delight. "Wylie was in the bosom of his enraptured tribe, and 'Eyre was shaking hands with Lady Spencer," after his thousand miles' journey. A week later he left King George's Sound, and on the 26th of July, after an absence of little more than a year, was once more in Adelaide, the ideal hero of all classes.

The geographical knowledge gained by this remarkable expedition extended little beyond a description of the coast-line between Streaky Bay and King George's Sound, but the gain to South Australia in other respects was nevertheless incalculable. The minds of the settlers were moulded to delight in brave deeds and glorious enterprise; they were all more or less making history, all interested in one way or another in the development of the vast territory they had come across the seas to possess, all fired with ambition to do their best in their respective spheres, and the courage, piety, and self-sacrifice of Edward John Eyre set them an example and taught them a lesson that was worth the learning.

Leaving this field of stirring adventure, we must now return to follow the more prosaic course of events in Adelaide.

In January, 1840, in order to satisfy the Commissioners that the excessive expenditure during 1839 had been absolutely necessary, the Governor appointed a board of audit, consisting of three colonists not belonging to the Government, to act with the auditor-general. This course, he thought, would relieve him of some of the responsibility he felt in sanctioning so many overdrafts, and would justify him in entering into further engagements of an urgent character.

It was this question of urgency that was at the root of all the main difficulties of the Governor. He could not consult with any one. Those who held the reins were sixteen thousand miles away. "The regulations issued by the Commissioners in London, as published in their third annual report of April 23, 1839, look very complete and ingenious on paper, but they involved an amount of complexity and delay which rendered their observance in a new country an impossibility without an absolute stoppage of all government, and these are the extenuating circumstances with which all the financial proceedings of Governor Gawler must be regarded." *

As a means of partial relief the colonists in April memorialized the Secretary of State for an extension of the Legislative Council, urging only two points as essential to the good government of the province, namely, that there should be a certain number of non-official members chosen freely by the people, and that if any law were unanimously opposed by the non-official members it should not take effect without the sanction of her Majesty. Nothing, however, came

* "The Constitutional History of South Australia," by B. T Finniss.

immediately of this, and in the mean time South Australian affairs at home were undergoing considerable change.

In June tidings reached the colony that the Board of Commissioners had been disbanded, and that a new Commission of only three members had been appointed as a Colonial Land and Emigration Board.

Of course the members of the old Board were not very well pleased with their summary dismissal, especially when, about six months afterwards, they were asked to attach their signatures to a report of their proceedings not even drawn up by themselves. Mr. Jacob Montefiore declined absolutely to sign the document.

For five years the Commissioners had given the most faithful and zealous gratuitous attention to their arduous work, and now when, as it appeared, the colony was approaching a state of unparalleled prosperity, the action of Lord John Russell in disbanding them immediately an application had been made by some of their number to receive remuneration for their services, was very keenly felt.

Colonel Torrens, who had been chairman of the Board of Commissioners from the first (at a nominal salary of £600 per annum), occupied a similar position on the new Board. Not long after his appointment to the new Commission, he entered into correspondence with Lord John Russell on the propriety of resigning his seat in consequence of having interest in some land in South Australia to the value of £1000. Lord John took the same view of this case that Lord Glenelg had taken in the case of Mr. Angas, already cited, and all that Colonel Torrens could obtain was permission to hold office temporarily.

On the dismissal of the Board of Commissioners, an association was formed in London called "The South Australian Society," the members of which comprised several of the late Commissioners, directors of the South Australian Company, and other friends of the colony, its main object being to guard against any encroachment on the leading principles contained in the Act of Parliament upon which the province was founded. On many occasions this society, as we shall see, rendered the colony essential service in the mother-country.

While these matters were going on at home, affairs in the colony were in a very complicated state. The Governor was becoming more and more embarrassed with financial and other difficulties; speculators were pushing their schemes with redoubled vigour, as if fearing an approaching crisis; wages of mechanics and labourers had risen to almost fabulous rates, and the price of provisions was extravagantly high.

The position of the Governor was as peculiar as it was difficult. He had to work out new principles in a colony that had sprung into existence at a bound, and had advanced with a rapidity unequalled in the history of British colonization. Nevertheless, he stood firm to the policy he had initiated at the first, and watched the progress of events with alternate feelings of anxiety and good hope.

The important work undertaken by the South Australian Company in constructing an admirable road to the port over the old swamp, and in erecting a suitable and much-needed wharf and warehouses, was so far advanced that on the 14th of October, 1840, they were thrown open to the public, the event being celebrated by a fitting demonstration, at which the Governor presided. In honour of the manager of the South Australian Company, by whom these improvements were projected and successfully carried out, the wharf was named the "McLaren Wharf"—a name it retains to the present day. At the ceremony some five thousand people assembled, and the day's proceedings included a regatta, a novelty in the new settlement.

The apparently flourishing condition of the colony at this time not only attracted a number of the free population of the neighbouring convict settlements of New South Wales and Van Diemen's Land, but several of the convicts also whose rendezvous was in that part then known as the "Tiers" on the Mount Barker road, where dense forest and almost inaccessible gullies offered them a safe retreat. The unwelcome visitors made a large increase in the crime of the infant settlement, and kept the colonists, in some parts of the bush, in a constant state of alarm. And not there only. Mr. John Hutt, at that time Governor of Western Australia, wrote to a gentleman in South Australia as follows :—

"Perth, Western Australia, July 17th, 1840.

"I say nothing of the overland expedition which you vivacious folk are threatening us with; we propose offering, I believe, to meet you with provisions at some appointed place. Your stock will be very acceptable to us, but not so your bushrangers, who, I see, have begun their ravages near Adelaide. I wish to keep as wide a gulf as possible between us and them. We have nothing as yet much to tempt them, but this overland route would show them the way, and we have no police or money to raise a corps. The sea is quite sufficient, with common prudence in those who ship stock, for all communication between us; and although, when Mr. Eyre related to me the horrible country he passed over to and beyond Streaky Bay, I regretted to find that my favourite colony's fertile boundaries were so circumscribed, yet I could not help secretly rejoicing that you had quite enough to keep you employed for the present without looking further west, and that if you did that you would find no encouragement from Nature. I do not doubt that if this passage is to be effected South Australian energy and determination and eagerness will do it; but long may the south land flourish and spread its branches and saplings far and wide any way, save to the westward."

Of the state of crime in the colony at this period, Mr. Alexander Tolmer, then sub-inspector of mounted police, says, "No precautions had been adopted to prevent the importation of escaped convicts or ticket-of-leave men from the neighbouring penal settlements, and the consequence was that the colony was overrun with such persons, and the police found constant employment in hunting and apprehending them. That such was the state of things by the unchecked importation of this class of bandits may be gathered from the fact that, out of thirty prisoners tried at the gaol delivery on the 3rd of March, 1840, there was only one convicted who had come to the colony direct from England, and among the twenty-five prisoners who were awaiting their trial for different offences at the next sessions, there were but five English emigrants, the remaining twenty being either escaped convicts, ticket-of-leave men, or emancipists from New South Wales or Van Diemen's Land. There were no orders issued to the port police with regard to the crews and passengers of vessels arriving from the penal settlements, and not the slightest attention was paid to the subject, either at Glenelg or at the port, and a shipload of escaped convicts could at any time be landed without remark or remonstrance. Again, there was no check upon overland parties arriving with stock, and it was notorious that some of the worst desperadoes of New South Wales found their way hither by that route, and after squandering their money in drunkenness and debauchery in town, would retire to the 'Tiers' and join others who had preceded them, living in log-huts built in deep and almost inaccessible gullies and ravines, densely timbered and overgrown with scrub and vegetation. Under cover of dark nights they would thence sally forth, and commit daring black-faced robberies and burglaries in the city, and again find shelter in their fastnesses, and 'plant' the plunder, or otherwise be harboured by sympathizers and accomplices in town, creatures of the same type as themselves, some of whom were publicans."

Many thrilling stories of adventure and misadventure have been told of this period of lawlessness, and many more prosaic tales of loss, especially by owners of cattle.*

* A notorious bushranger, Patrick Murphy, *alias* Blue Cap, was believed to be in Adelaide, and the Government of New South

The South Australian Company were great losers in this respect, and it was an additional mortification to them to be aware that beasts innumerable belonging to them were being shot, skinned, the brands destroyed, and the meat salted and shipped to foreign markets.

Any number of picturesque and amusing stories might be told of proceedings in the law courts and courts of justice in the early days of the colony. Here is one as a specimen. On the 11th of November, 1840, Joseph Stagg, charged with the wilful murder of a man named John Gofton, an escaped prisoner, was brought up for trial at the Supreme Court—that is to say, at

Wales offered £100 for his capture. Mr. Alexander Tolmer was soon on his track, and received information that a suspicious-looking character had been seen on the way to the Tiers. How the capture was made may best be told in Mr. Tolmer's own words. The story gives a glimpse into the state of the times, and at the iron-nerved men who had to deal with the desperadoes of that day. "On turning the corner where the Stag Inn is now," says Mr. Tolmer. "I descried the individual some distance ahead on the track across the park-lands leading to Gleeson's Hill. On hearing me approach, he suddenly stopped and half turned, but, owing to my horse being hard in the mouth and excitable, I passed him a few paces. The glance I obtained of his face, however, satisfied me that he was the identical man whose description had been received from Sydney a few days before. The moment he stopped he placed himself in a peculiar attitude, with both hands under the lapels of his coat, and it struck me forcibly that he had a pistol in each hand. However, without hesitation, I gently urged my horse nearer the fellow and said, 'Why, I know you; you are Patrick Murphy!' to which he replied, 'Well, what do you want?' By this time I had managed to approach near enough to his person, and, quickly leaning forward, seized his collar, saying, 'You are my prisoner,' which action caused my right spur to touch my horse's side, when he made a sidelong plunge, and as the fellow threw himself back at the same time, I was dragged off the saddle to the ground, and in falling brought the prisoner down with me. We then both sprung up together, I still retaining a firm grip of the collar; he then struck me on the side of the head with his fist. Being then satisfied he had no pistols, I at once loosened hold of him and dealt him a heavy blow in the face, which knocked him down. He nimbly got up again, however, when we had a regular set-to, which lasted some minutes. He was no match for me, however, which he soon admitted, and surrendered, saying, 'Well, now you've got your £100!'"

the residence of his Honour Judge Cooper, in Whitmore Square. "The room used as the court contained two French windows, which opened into the garden, the judge's elevated seat being between the two. On the judge's left hand, along the side wall, were the jury; on his right, fronting the jury, was the prisoner in the dock, with Mr. Ashton, the governor of the gaol, standing on the left side; and opposite the witness-box immediately under the bench, at a large table covered with law books, briefs, etc., sat the sheriff, Mr. Newenham, the officers of the court, the advocate-general, Mr. Charles Mann, the counsel for the prisoner, Sir James Fisher, Messrs. Poulden, Nicholls, and others; and on the floor, on the right of the bench, were chairs occupied by ladies.

"Just as Mr. Tolmer of the police, the first witness in the case, was giving evidence, a sudden sharp report was heard, like that of a pistol or rifle, followed by repeated cries, 'He's shot at!' In an instant Mr. Tolmer drew his sword; the foreman of the jury, followed by the other eleven, dashed through one open window into the garden; judge, lawyers, and ladies rushed pell-mell through the other; the governor of the gaol locked the prisoner's left arm within his, and with the other held a pistol at his head, while Mr. Tolmer stayed beside him with drawn sword."

The general idea was that, as Mr. Tolmer was the principal witness, some confederate of the prisoner had fired at him to prevent his giving further evidence, but when the excitement and terror had subsided it was found that a defective beam in the floor, which was over the cellar, had snapped owing to the overcrowded state of the room! In a short time the break was made safe by means of supports, and the trial proceeded, ending in the death sentence on the unhappy man Joseph Stagg.

A startling and terrible episode occurred in July of this year. Tidings reached Adelaide that a vessel had been wrecked on the Coorong beach, near where the *Fanny* went ashore, and that ten white men, five women, and seven children had been brutally massacred by natives of the Melmenrura, or Big Murray, tribe. Mr. Pullen (afterwards Admiral Pullen) was immediately despatched in a whaleboat from Encounter Bay to ascertain the truth or otherwise of the ghastly rumour. He found the wrecked vessel was the *Maria*, which had left Port Adelaide a few weeks previously with a crew of nine persons and fifteen passengers. He found also several bodies of murdered persons, and having interred them he returned to report the case to the Government.

The gallant Major T. S. O'Halloran, Commissioner of Police—a man whose career was as full of adventure as that of a hero of romance—and a party of mounted police, accompanied by several colonists, at once set forth to make further investigations. Considerable difficulty was experienced in finding out the perpetrators of the horrible deed, but at length two were given up by the tribes as the actual murderers. It was deemed expedient to resort at once to some exemplary punishment in the immediate locality of the murders, and the two natives were, after a deliberate investigation on the spot, executed—a step that was severely censured in many quarters. Eventually twenty-three bodies in all were found of the twenty-four who had embarked in the *Maria*.

Through the instrumentality of "Peter," a friendly native, Dr. Penny, who visited the scene of the murders some months after the first executions, succeeded in obtaining from the aborigines eleven pounds in gold and silver, and a coin valued at four shillings. In his report to the Government he says, "I questioned the party, who consisted of two of the Melmenrura tribe and thirteen of the Tenkinyra and Toora tribes, through my natives, as to the murders, which they confessed to have perpetrated, but showed apparent regret for their crime. I gathered from them that they had brought the whole party up a long way, showed them water, fished, and carried their children for them for a considerable time. That when they came to this point, they could not take them any further, as their country ends there, and the 'Picannini Murray' begins. They then demanded some clothes and blankets for their trouble, but the white people refused to give them, yet said if they would take them to Adelaide they should have plenty. This they could not do, so they began to help themselves, and this being resisted, ended in the murder of the whole. The white men fought for some time, but the natives broke their arms with waddies and then speared them. They were also jealous of the next tribe, into whose territory they would then have passed, and who, being in the habit of visiting Adelaide, could have taken them up and have obtained the reward promised to them."

This native account seemed plausible, but it did not mitigate the regret felt for the unfortunate individuals, who, having escaped the dangers of shipwreck, lost their lives under such melancholy circumstances. It was the greatest calamity that had taken place in the colony, and it was long before the gloom was dissipated.

The punishment of the natives was considered by many to be almost as terrible as the crime, and this gave rise to much comment and censure in the colony and in the newspaper press everywhere.

The "Native Question" here, as in other colonies, bristled with difficulties, and moreover was always cropping up. This was not the first occasion when drastic measures had to be taken to protect the lives and property of the settlers. In the fourth report of the Commissioners (1839) the first fatal collision of the colonists with the natives was recorded. "The province," so ran the report, "has been the theatre of one of those appalling tragedies which, occasionally occurring in every region where man is found, bring home the conviction of his imperfect nature," a statement which could not lay claim to any marked originality. But the report continued—

"Three settlers have been murdered by the natives, and two natives have been tried, convicted, and executed for the crime. The perpetration of such crimes and their expiation by capital punishment are events which must, under any circumstances, be deeply deplored, and which in the present instance cannot be contemplated without exciting the most painful feelings. To subject savage tribes to the penalties of laws with which they are unacquainted, for offences which they may possibly regard as acts of justifiable retaliation for invaded rights, is a proceeding indefensible except under circumstances of urgent and extreme necessity. Such circumstances had unhappily occurred in the case under consideration. The authorities of South Australia had no choice but to pursue a course of judicial proceedings according to English law. The murder of the two settlers had excited amongst their brethren a violent sentiment of fear, as well as of anger, towards the aborigines. The prospect of further assassinations, in consequence of no punishment being inflicted upon the perpetrators of those which had taken place, would have been intolerable. If the murderers had not been tried, convicted, and legally punished, the settlers, unprotected by the governing authorities, would have been obliged to take the law into their own hands, and in their fear and rage might have commenced an exterminating warfare against the natives. The necessities of the case left but a choice of evils, and the authorities chose the least."

There was a great outcry in many quarters at the severity of the punishment inflicted in both the cases we have cited, and the Commissioners attempted to vindicate the carrying out of the British law in these words—

"In establishing a new colony it is one of the first and most sacred duties of the Government to protect the native races, but to protect the natives against the colonists without at the same time protecting the colonists against the natives would be impracticable. The aborigines cannot have the protection of British law without being amenable to British law. To place the European and native races under different codes would be to place them in hostility to each other. If it be necessary to inflict the punishment of death for the murder of a native, it is equally necessary to inflict that punishment for the murder of a settler by a native."

Unhappily the poor savage, conscious of his inferiority and his inability to bring those who offended against him to punishment, often had to submit to unkind and even brutal treatment, for which there was no redress, and, writhing under the wrongs he endured, he would entertain feelings of resentment, ending sometimes in his taking summary revenge on supposed, as well as on real, enemies.

"Can it be deemed surprising," asked Mr. Eyre, who knew the native character as well as any one, "that a rude, uncivilized being, driven from his home, deprived of all his ordinary means of subsistence, and pressed perhaps by a hostile tribe from behind, should occasionally be guilty of aggressions or injuries towards his oppressors? The wonder rather is, not that these things do sometimes occur, but that they occur so rarely. In addition to the many other inconsistencies in our conduct towards the aborigines, not the least extraordinary is that of placing them, on the plea of protection, under the influence of our laws, and of making them British subjects. Strange anomaly, which by the former makes them amenable to penalties they are ignorant of, for crimes which they do not consider as such, or which they may even have been driven to commit by our own injustice, and by the latter but mocks them with an empty sound, since the very laws under which we profess to place them, by their nature and constitution, are inoperative in affording redress to the injured. . . ."

In addition to the official Protector of Aborigines in the colony, the natives had the sympathy of an association in the mother country, established for the express purpose of affording such protection to them *as it could*. But seeing they were so far away, and had to rely upon reports not always well authenticated, they sometimes condemned actions taken on the spot, and thus, instead of being of any assistance to the aborigines, they unintentionally created a prejudice against those whom they were endeavouring to serve.

But the natives had friends nearer at hand, who were zealously labouring for their welfare. The first direct missionary efforts on their behalf were made by Messrs. C. G. Teichelmann and C. W. Schürmann, who were sent out by the Lutheran Missionary Society at Dresden, under the auspices and mainly at the expense of Mr. G. F. Angas, in 1838. They were followed in 1840 by two other missionaries from the same society, Messrs. H. A. C. Meyer and F. Klose.

In 1839 Messrs. Teichelmann and Schürmann, in conjunction with Mr. Moorhouse, Protector of Aborigines in succession to Mr. Wyatt, commenced school operations, and soon acquired a sufficient knowledge of the language to publish vocabularies. But although some of the children learned to read and to write, and adults came to listen to the gospel preached in their own tongue, it was always discouraging work, as they were constantly migrating from place to place.

In course of time it was found that teaching in the native tongue was a mistake, and a complete change in the plan of procedure was effected. The objections to imparting instruction in the native tongue were set forth by Mr. Eyre to this effect:—1. The length of time and labour required for the instructor to master the language. 2. The very few natives he could instruct, almost every tribe speaking a different dialect. 3. The sudden stop that would be put to all instruction if the preceptor became ill or died, as no one could supply his place. 4. If the children could not speak in the language ordinarily spoken by the colonists, they would be debarred from the advantage of casual instruction or information, and also from entering upon duties or relations with Europeans amongst whom they might be living. 5. By adhering to the native language they would become more deeply confirmed in their original feelings and prejudices, and more thoroughly kept under the influence and direction of their own people.

Schools were established in several places on this new

method, but no great success attended the efforts of the teachers; nevertheless, it is interesting to note that even at this early period in the history of the colony, when every nerve was being strained to increase commercial prosperity, the colonists were disposed to give time and attention to philanthropic subjects. The Governor watched the progress of the German missionaries with much interest, and wrote of them to Mr. Angas in July, 1840, thus:—

"I have very great reason to believe them to be sincere, intelligent, persevering Christian men, and if their efforts had not at all succeeded, they, I think, would have been blameless. The change of the aborigines, in any moderate time, even to mere civilization, would be an especial effect of the power of God. The deep-rooted prejudices of a very ancient people, agreeing universally throughout the whole island in the leading points of a very ancient system, are not to be overcome in a few years. The Protector and missionaries have done much to shake it, but the progress will be slow, and not very discernible to indifferent spectators."

The Governor was a religious man, and gladly supported all philanthropic workers, while, as a good Churchman, he naturally took a strong interest in all Church questions. It will be remembered that in the original South Australian Act of 1834 there had crept in a clause giving authority to create colonial chaplains, and the Rev. C. B. Howard had been sent out with the first Governor in this official capacity. But the friends of the voluntary system had from the first made it a *sine quâ non* that the new colony should be absolutely and entirely free from any connection whatever between Church and State, and they agitated with such effect that on the 31st of July, 1838, an amended South Australian Act passed the British Parliament, partly to set at rest certain doubts as to the powers vested in the Commissioners, but mainly to repeal that part of the previous Act which related to the appointment by the Crown of chaplains and clergymen. This was, of course, not regarded with favour by the Church party, and it became one of the burning questions of the day. The Governor's views on the religious outlook are well given in a letter he wrote to Mr. G. F. Angas:—

"July 10th, 1840.

"Many circumstances have arisen to force very strongly upon my attention the religious necessities of the colony. . . . Our deficiencies in places of worship and ministers of the gospel are very great; they do not keep pace with immigration. I lately made a careful calculation, and from it believe that the utmost limit of religious accommodation will not include the means of attendance for more than eighteen hundred persons: from these must be deducted at least one-sixth for the average of absentees, leaving an attendance of fifteen hundred out of a population of nearly fifteen thousand. Several of the buildings included in this calculation are private houses, others are very temporary erections, and some others are very much in debt. . . .

"The current voluntary system, I deliberately and conscientiously believe, will not in any reasonable degree supply the necessities of the population; it has not nearly done so as yet under most favourable circumstances. I see no probability that it can do so in the future. Without a colonial chaplain or chaplains there would be to me the insuperable objection that the fundamental doctrines of the gospel would not be acknowledged by the Government. . . . I do not wish for any corrupt, secularly political connection between the Church and State, but I cannot conceive that any sincere Christian man can be satisfied at being at the head of a Government which, as a Government, acknowledges no God and no doctrine.

"I have arrived at a plan which, if it be supported by the Government and Commissioners, will, I think, be a solid basis for the best of blessings to the province. It is in abstract this:—1. That the provision of the original Act requiring the appointment of chaplains of the Churches of England and Scotland should continue to be carried out, but with great moderation, as an acknowledgment on the part of the Government of the fundamental doctrines of the Christian faith—doctrines common to all really Christian denominations. 2. That for the maintenance of religion and the furtherance of education in the colony at large, land for religious and educational purposes should be sold to all applicants at a very low rate (say 5s. per acre), the property and proceeds of such land to be legally secured and applied according to the intentions of the donors."

Nothing could have been more moderate, but it was opposed to the principle for which so many of the fathers and founders of the colony had zealously contended, and the appeal had no effect. A worse thing, however, was to happen to the Dissenters in the not far distant future, as we shall presently see.

During the years 1839–40, very few English settlers turned their attention to agricultural pursuits. The high rate of wages, the dearness of provisions, and the disinclination to grapple with what really amounted to "bush-life," acted as deterrents, and the people still clung tenaciously to the city, the suburbs, and the port, a course which operated most unfavourably against the development of the agricultural resources of the country. But during these years the colony was greatly indebted to a large number of German immigrants, who arrived in the *Prince George* in 1838, and at once proceeding to the cultivation of the land, produced an abundant supply of vegetables for Adelaide, where there would otherwise have been scarcity.

The story of the circumstances under which these Germans obtained a footing in South Australia is interesting.*

In 1817 the union between the Reformed and Lutheran Churches in Prussia had nearly everywhere been effected; but the Church ritual being different in various places, it was thought desirable to introduce a regulation for uniform worship over the whole of the

* For a fuller account see "George Fife Angas, Father and Founder of South Australia," by Edwin Hodder. London, 1891.

evangelical part of the monarchy. Accordingly, in 1822, King Frederick William III. issued a new liturgy, introduced it by Cabinet order, caused it to be used in the royal chapel and the garrison churches, and recommended its adoption by all Protestant communities in the State. But as it clashed in some doctrinal particulars with the views of a certain portion of the Lutherans, they felt it to be their duty to withstand the innovation at all costs. So long, however, as the Government confined itself to a simple recommendation, the objections raised against it were not of great importance; but when, in 1825, it was in contemplation to make the use of the new liturgy compulsory, a strong agitation began. The Church party, with Schleiermacher at its head, fought bravely against Auguste, Marheinecke, and others, for the freedom and independence of the Church, and against the "Agenda" as being the work of the Government, without the consent of the respective Church communities.

The quarrel lasted until 1829, when a modified edition of the liturgy was prepared, and the 25th of June, 1830, was fixed as the date for its universal introduction.

The principle at stake was held by many to remain unaltered, and they combined to resist the innovation. This brought upon them the royal displeasure, and persecution, fines, and imprisonment followed their disobedience. In Silesia the tyranny was felt more than elsewhere, and many Lutherans determined, like the Pilgrim Fathers, to seek some part of the globe where they might worship God according to the dictates of conscience. To this end the Rev. Augustus Kavel, minister of the Evangelical Lutheran Church at Klemzig, having heard of the labours of Mr. G. F. Angas on behalf of the colony of South Australia, waited upon him to seek his advice. Mr. Angas was a backbone Nonconformist, and stood in the front rank of fighters for religious freedom; his sympathies were at once enlisted, and after two years of incessant labour, and at an enormous expense, he finally succeeded, despite the reluctance of the Prussian Government to grant passports to the emigrants, in sending out to South Australia some hundreds of these German Lutherans. The first batch of two hundred, with Pastor Kavel on board, left Plymouth Sound—the very harbour from which the Pilgrim Fathers set sail to lay the foundation of the great Western Republic—in the *Prince George*, and arrived in the colony in November, 1838. They settled upon some land belonging to Mr. Angas on the river Torrens, only a short distance from Adelaide, to which they gave the name of Klemzig, after their native town in Prussia. Vessel after vessel followed rapidly, carrying many hundreds to the new Land of Promise, and in course of time there sprung up the flourishing townships of Angaston, Blumberg, Greenock, Grünthal, Hahndorf, Lobethal, Lyndoch, Nairne, Nuriootpa, Rosenthal, and Tanunda, where, at the present time, many thousands of Germans, as well as English, are resident.

The thrifty, practical, hard-working Germans soon made their little wildernesses blossom as the rose, and there is no doubt that their success inspired others to turn attention to similar as well as other branches of husbandry and industry.

Activity became the order of the day in every branch of labour. Wheat, from the ease with which it could be grown, with the demand there was for it in the Victorian market, and the large profits it yielded, led many to embark in its cultivation; some more extensively than their capital warranted, and when bad and dry seasons set in, they were overtaken with misfortune, and found their way into the insolvent court. Many, therefore, began to look out for other sources of income, and it was found that the climate and soil were equally well adapted for the growth and production of wine, olive oil, hops, tobacco, and a variety of other articles required for exportation and home consumption. As early as 1840 Mr. Struthers cultivated a small quantity of Sea Island cotton, as an experiment, and it grew remarkably well.

It was believed that nearly all kinds of tropical plants, trees, fruits, and flowers, as well as those of temperate climes, could be successfully grown, and when the experiment was tried, it was found that the apple and the orange, the pear and the pine-apple, the gooseberry and the fig, the raspberry and the olive, and many other fruits would come to perfection within a short distance of each other.*

Nearly all kinds of vegetables have been successfully cultivated, and have attained to almost incredible sizes and weights, although the raids of insects have always been a source of unusual trouble.

The year 1841 opened with all the outward and visible signs of prosperity. The land sales had reached the enormous figure of 299,072 acres (of which, however, only 2503 were under cultivation); the population had reached sixteen thousand (but of these an overwhelming percentage were entirely dependent upon the Government for food or labour, the wherewithal to get food); immigration was continuing to pour in (although there were many labourers and few capitalists); Adelaide had thrown off almost every vestige of her first simplicity. Handsome public build-

---

* Fruits come to perfection and are in season in different districts somewhat as follows:—
Strawberries: September to December.
Raspberries: October to December.
Gooseberries, currants, cherries, and almonds: November and December.
Figs: December to March.
Mulberries: December and January.
Blackberries: January.
Grapes: January to May.
Nectarines and apricots: December to February.
Plums and peaches: December to April.
Late plums: May and June.
Guavas and granadillas: January and February.
Sweet and water melons: January to April.
Pie-melons: May to August.
Lemons, limes, citrons, and bananas: February and March.
Pomegranates: March.
Apples, pears, and quinces: February to August.
Oranges: nearly all the year.

ings, churches, meeting-houses, prisons, macadamized roads, bridges of magnificent span connecting the various suburbs of the picturesquely situated metropolis, custom houses, harbours, quays, gave the appearance of an almost unlimited revenue. It was as fine a capital and as complete a Government establishment as would have been the usual proportion of thirty times the number of population at home. And everything was done on a complete and lordly scale—no jerry-building, no stucco, no veneer. The prison, "the last of all places in a new colony that some might suppose needed elaborate architecture, had its high walls and strong doors; its angle towers surmounted with cutstone embattlements, the stone alone costing £2 2s. per cube foot to work, while for other services artificers were paid from £3 18s. to £4 4s. per week."

It was a grand time; everywhere there was planning and working, enlarging and improving, demolishing the brick and raising the marble; it was the old story, eating and drinking, marrying and giving in marriage, and then—the deluge!

Rumblings of the coming storm had been heard here and there, but little heed had been taken. The whole matter was in a nutshell—immigration was pouring in with every tide; the supply was unfortunately in excess of the demand; the immigrants could not be left to starve; to employ them on work even unnecessary at the time then present would be for the ultimate good of the colony, and as to the responsibility—well, it must rest on the shoulders of the Commissioners, and if they were not strong enough to bear it, on those of the Imperial Government. This was the dream, from which there was to be a rude awakening.

Early in February, when Governor Gawler was on a visit to Cape Jervis and Kangaroo Island, tidings reached the colony that some of the bills drawn by him on the Commissioners had been returned dishonoured.

The blow, feared and not altogether unexpected, had fallen, and the utter ruin of the colony seemed inevitable.

Colonel Gawler hastened back, and at once summoned the Council. They, desperately assuming, or pretending to assume, that the bills were dishonoured merely because the Commissioners had not, at the moment, the needful funds in hand to meet them, and that the whole question was simply a matter of time until the necessary funds should be forthcoming, recommended, "That the practice of drawing upon the Colonization Commissioners should be continued with the precautionary addition of a reference, in case of need, to the Lords of her Majesty's Treasury."

A little later, and there was another scare. In April a rumour reached Adelaide indirectly, by way of Tasmania, that Governor Gawler had been recalled and his successor appointed. The rumour was not generally credited, although it produced uneasiness in all quarters.

Shortly after this a despatch was received from the Commissioners, informing Colonel Gawler that the Board had no longer any funds to meet the bills that had been sent home, and that he must discontinue to draw upon them. He at once called the Council together, and stated that he must adopt one of two courses, "either at once to reduce the survey, harbour, immigrant, colonial store, and police departments, and confine the Government expenditure to the mere Government and judicial offices, customs, and absolute pauper immigrants which the revenue may at present support," or "act as every governor of a British colony is authorized by the instructions of the Colonial Office to do in case of *pressing emergency*, draw, in the capacity of Governor, directly on the Lords of the Treasury for the sums necessary in reason to preserve the colony, during the interval described, from disorder, ruin, and destitution." After giving the subject the most careful consideration, he determined to adopt, for the time being, the latter course.

The times were critical in the extreme; every individual in the colony had a personal interest in the questions at issue, and public meetings to discuss the financial position became the order of the day. Those held by the Chamber of Commerce were of the most practical importance, as it was resolved that "should his Excellency the Governor see fit to draw upon her Majesty's Treasury, they will accept such bills in payment of their ordinary business transactions."

It cannot be denied that the responsibility the Governor had taken upon himself throughout was, in a certain sense, unauthorized by the Commissioners, and was maintained contrary to their wish. But he had unbounded faith in the capabilities of the colony, and never entertained the shadow of a doubt as to a successful issue of his schemes. So long therefore as the Commissioners had funds, they yielded to his pressing demands for additional monetary help, under the conviction, it would seem, that his confident and sanguine expectations would shortly be realized and that they would be relieved from the constant drain on their finances.

In deference to the opinion expressed at certain public meetings and to instructions received from the Commissioners, the Governor commenced retrenchment as regarded special land surveys and the police department, but he had not proceeded far when, on the 10th of May, the *Lord Glenelg* arrived, bringing not only the recall of Colonel Gawler, but also his successor in the person of Captain Grey!

This was regarded by the friends of the Governor as an arbitrary and discourteous proceeding, more especially as the Commissioners, who had placed his conduct in the strongest light before the Government, had not in any of their despatches directly censured him, although perfectly aware of the ever-increasing expenditure. It is true that under date of the 13th of July, 1840, in reply to an application from Colonel Gawler for an increase in salary from £1000 to £2000 per annum, the Secretary of State (Lord John Russell) had written as follows:—

"It was not until I was placed in possession of the Commissioners' report that I was made aware of the actual embarrassments of the colony. Under the circumstances stated by the Commissioners, it is obviously impossible to make any increase in the incomes of the public officers of the colony; and I regret therefore that I cannot recommend to the Lords Commissioners of the Treasury to sanction the grant of the salary which you propose." After asking for a report upon the statements made by the Commissioners, Lord John concluded, "I cannot but express my surprise and concern at the large expense into which the colony has been plunged, and I most earnestly hope that you will use every endeavour to arrest the difficulties in which it is placed."

To this despatch, which was not received till December, 1840, Colonel Gawler made a lengthy and energetic reply, in which he not only endeavoured to justify his own position, but threw upon the shoulders of the Commissioners whatever blame was due. "The Commissioners," he wrote, "were desirous to form a fine colony, and abstractly they were willing to authorize the measures necessary to accomplish this end; but I must respectfully say, in my own defence, that they did not calculate the cost of them, nor had they any adequate conception of the difficulties arising from the state and requirements of a new and large community suddenly collected and planted in an unexplored wilderness."

Again:—" In all the documents and communications issued by the Commissioners from the date of my appointment to office until the report which your lordship has enclosed to me, there never was the slightest censure passed on any portion of the expenditure which I had directed. On the contrary, I was justified by the Commissioners in the greatest items of expenditure which I had incurred on my own responsibility—items which embrace almost all the extraordinary expenditure of the colony. Therefore I am in no wise guilty of the heavy charge which the Commissioners have made against me of 'setting their instructions at naught,' but that I simply stand on my own responsibility for correctness of judgment as to whether or not the cases referred to were really cases of emergency. In no other matter have I ever intended in any of my former official statements to confess responsibility. In speaking of unauthorized expenditure, I have always supposed it would be distinctly understood to mean expenditure unauthorized by detailed instructions. I came to this colony to conduct a great and first experiment. An experiment of necessity involves the possibility not only of success but of failure without blame to those who conduct it faithfully. The experiment in South Australia embraced two great considerations: (1) the success of the self-supporting system, and (2) the safety of the colony. I never doubted but that the safety of the colony was the point to be first maintained, and until the receipt of a semi-official letter from Colonel Torrens, dated 17th of June, 1840, and of the report of your lordship of the 7th of July, 1840, the instructions and correspondence of the Commissioners with regard to emergencies gave me the fullest reason to believe that their view and mine coincided. . . .

"I considered it emergency when the survey department could not keep pace with the demand; when the police force was not sufficient to suppress bushrangers and other lawless characters, to control the natives, and to check contraband trade; emergency, when public officers of value were leaving their situations on account of the insufficiency of their salaries, or were trading and really plundering the Government on what they called authorized principle; emergency, when the survey and land offices being burnt down, there was not a public office belonging to the Government in Adelaide, and none of reasonable permanent suitableness to be hired; emergency, when, with an immense pressure of business and harassment of all kinds upon me, I, my wife, family, secretary, office, and servants, were limited during the day to a mud cottage, fifty feet by twenty-seven in extreme dimensions; and emergency, when, with a really beautiful natural port, commerce was suffering almost indescribable hindrances from the difficulty of landing in a broad, triangular swamp. . . . These, in addition to immigrant sickness and destitution, are the great and leading objects which have been to my fullest conviction emergencies, and which have absorbed the greater part of the extraordinary expenditure."

Such were some of the lines of Colonel Gawler's defence, and whatever estimate may be put upon them, no one will deny that he acted from a high sense of the responsibilities attaching to his office.

"Governor Gawler," says Mr. B. T. Finniss, "did what Imperial legislation afterwards recognized as a valid employment of the land fund; that is, he promoted public works, and provided for the maintenance of the labour, which every Government is bound to do to guard against destitution. But in doing so, he violated his instructions and paid the penalty in removal from office with all its attendant consequences. Whether he was right or wrong, it may be asserted that the colonists of that period and of the present owe him a debt of gratitude for saving the colony from anarchy, and for the improvements in its condition which must have resulted from an expenditure not wastefully incurred, but spread amongst the community in the shape of wages for useful purposes. Governor Gawler was impelled by circumstances to act as he did. Moreover, his action led to a more practical system of land legislation, and struck a deathblow to the principle of applying all the proceeds of all the lands sold and alienated from the Crown to the introduction of labour." *

The exact amount of the excess of Colonel Gawler's expenditure over the revenue and the amount of bills drawn by him upon the Commissioners was stated to be £291,861 3s. 5½d. The total debt due in England on the 1st of May, 1841, and chargeable on the revenue of the colony, was £305,328 2s. 7d.!

When the news was received in the colony that the bills were dishonoured, there was a panic among the

* "Constitutional History of South Australia."

merchants who had purchased the Government paper to a large amount as remittances to their correspondents in England, and tradesmen and others who had been working for or supplying articles to the Government found themselves involved. The distress became general and was shared by all classes.

"Universal bankruptcy and great distress then prevailed throughout all Australia, such as had never occurred before or have been since experienced. The severe fall in land, stock, and all other property would appear at the present time as almost incredible. A song was composed and nightly sung, which was especially applicable to the then circumstances of New South Wales in describing the troubles of the period, which it did in the personal lamentations of a luckless individual named 'Billy Barlow,' amongst whose terrible misfortunes was 'the sale of his sheep at sixpence per head with the run given in'—a state of things not so very far from the truth. Emigration from other countries had ceased. The privations of the settlers were severe, and everything seemed to be at its lowest. The loss of capital incurred in founding the colony cannot be estimated, but it must have been very considerable, inasmuch as nearly all those engaged in the importation and distribution of merchandise, with many others, were ruined. A number of persons were in prison for debt, for whom there were no means of relief. It was found that the British bankruptcy and insolvency laws did not apply to South Australia, and so these unfortunate debtors continued in gaol until the Act for giving relief to insolvent debtors was passed on the 22nd of June, 1841, and an Insolvent Court was established, when there soon after followed what might be termed a 'general gaol delivery' for debtors." *

Much sympathy was felt for Colonel Gawler, and addresses, testimonials, and other marks of respect and good feeling poured in upon him from many quarters. When, on the 18th of June, he took his departure from the colony, he left behind him a memory which was

* Sir Henry Ayers, K.C.M.G.

treasured by many even of those who had suffered most from the policy he had pursued. Of the wisdom of that policy he never entertained a moment's doubt. Five years after he had left South Australia, he wrote to his old friend, Mr. G. F. Angas, in these terms :—

"June 4th, 1846.

"I laid, in the face of immense difficulties, the foundation of the finest colony, in proportion to its duration, that has appeared in modern times. I did so with full purpose and foresight of beneficial results, and without running the reckless risks that are attributed to me, and in England have obtained, as to my policy, nothing but reproaches. It is moreover, I believe, one of the cheapest, if not the very cheapest of the distant colonies that England has had. . . . I carried out with full foresight of results the 'self-supporting system' as far as it was possible to do it . . . at a cost less than even its original devisers calculated, for they thought of £375,000 for the political expenses of foundation (see Wakefield, vol. ii. p. 119), while the net cost of South Australia up to this moment is short of £300,000. Not, however, that I should desire that £300,000 to be laid upon the colony. I think it was the ruining error of the original plan that such a thing should ever have been contemplated. A parent State ought to pay for her colonies as a parent does for his children, or as States do themselves for their lines of battle ships; it is a beggarly spirit of penury alone which can lead them to fume and grumble as they have done about South Australia.

"You justly ask, 'Could not the effects have been produced for a less sum?' I would say not, in reasonable consideration and under the circumstances of the case and time. A novel system; an unknown climate; an unexplored country; public officers utterly inexperienced (some, from ill health or other causes, really useless— I mean men in the highest stations); population flowing in and land selling with fearful rapidity and a rapidity that the Commissioners were pledged to meet. I was their representative, a Commissioner under the same sign manual like themselves, and bound before God and man to maintain in good faith their engagements. I really laboured most continually and anxiously for economy, and Mr. Hall and I nearly destroyed ourselves with unceasing labour."

It was anticipated by many that after he had defended his actions "at home," Colonel Gawler would be reinstated in his office in South Australia. But this was not to be, and he remained an injured and unjustly treated man.

Of the immediate circumstances connected with his recall, and of the action of the Imperial Government in averting the utter ruin of the colony, threatened by their returning the bills drawn upon the Commissioners and the Lords of the Treasury dishonoured, we shall write more fully in the next chapter.

CHAPTER VII.

ADMINISTRATION OF CAPTAIN GEORGE GREY.

MAY 10TH, 1841—OCTOBER 26TH, 1845.

The Financial Crisis.—Views of Mr. G. F. Angas thereon.—South Australia a Crown Colony.—The Governor and the Imperial Government.—Errors of the Commissioners.—Retrenchment.—Unemployed Immigrants.—Agitation.—Reports of Select Committee of House of Commons.—A Loan guaranteed.—Colonial Creditors.—Outrages by Natives.—Mr. E. J. Eyre.—Native Schools.—A Tide of Commercial Misfortune.—Universal Bankruptcy.—Its Causes.—Governor Grey's Bills dishonoured.—Serious Consequences.—New Waste Lands Act.—Act for Better Government of South Australia.—Signs of Improvement.—Ridley's Reaping Machine.—Mineral Wealth.—Mr. Mengé.—Kapunda Copper Mine.—Explorations.—Captain Sturt.—Mr. Drake.—Ecclesiastical Affairs.—Convictism.—Bush Fires.—Burra-Burra Copper Mine.—Port Adelaide a Free Port.—Popularity of Sir George Grey.—Eulogies.

WHEN it became known to the friends of South Australia in England that the bills drawn by Colonel Gawler had been dishonoured, the greatest consternation prevailed. Ruin, irretrievable ruin as it seemed, stared the insolvent colony in the face. The Commissioners and the directors of the South Australian Company were alike terror-stricken. The blow had fallen with sudden and startling force.

One of the first to take action on behalf of the colony was Mr. G. F. Angas, the chairman of the South Australian Company, who wrote to Lord John

Russell, Secretary for the Colonies, a stirring letter, from which the following is an extract:—

"October 24, 1840.

". . . It is impossible for me to feel otherwise than greatly alarmed at the present dangerous position of the new colony, and the destruction that awaits it when the dishonoured drafts of the Governor, now under protest for non-acceptance, shall reach Adelaide in utter disgrace, with twenty per cent. damages for non-payment. From whatever causes, that colony is at this moment in a state of advancement and completeness in the fourth year of its existence, without a parallel in the history of the Empire, and if it should not continue to progress, the cause of its obstruction cannot be chargeable upon its inhabitants, or upon the professed friends of the colony in this country, who have nobly done their duty in the furtherance of this important experiment in colonization. Neither in the measures of the Government nor in the application of the finances have they had any power whatever, and they cannot understand how it is that with an unappropriated emigration fund of about £80,000, and the power given to Her Majesty's Commissioners by the South Australian Act to raise a loan of £200,000, of which £120,000 remain untouched, that the Governor's drafts should have been refused acceptance. Thus, in an instant, the public credit of the colony has been destroyed, and, if not restored by a timely interposition of the Government, must end in anarchy, confusion, and ruin.

"Most happily, the interval between the first presentation of the drafts and their maturity will afford time for your lordship's intervention, and the awful consequences of a general bankruptcy may be averted. Here is a colony, raised up within four years without trouble or expense to the mother country, with a population of 16,000 persons, whose seaports have, during the past few years, admitted about two hundred merchant ships, and where more than a million of British capital has been embarked, even at a distance of 14,000 miles. The celebrated colony of Pennsylvania, at one-third the distance, could not in seven years number half the population, or a fourth of its commerce."

This, and similar appeals, moved the Government to action. It was decided to guarantee a loan, and to recommend its adoption by Parliament, and orders were given to the Commissioners to make arrangements to meet the dishonoured drafts. A parliamentary inquiry upon the whole of the affairs of South Australia was to follow.

Meanwhile, punishment was to be meted out to the Governor whose lavish expenditure, it was said, had brought about all the mischief, and it was done in a manner as unpleasant as it was unjust.

Colonel Gawler's recall, dated Downing Street, December 26, 1840, and signed by the Secretary of State for the Colonies, was in these terms:—

"In consequence of the reports which have been made to her Majesty's Government by the Colonization Commissioners for South Australia, respecting the amount of the bills which you have drawn on the Commissioners in excess of the authority which you had received from them for that purpose, it has become my unwelcome duty to advise her Majesty to relieve you from the office of Governor and her Majesty's Resident Commissioner in that province. The Queen, having been pleased to approve of that advice, has appointed as your successor Captain Grey, who will proceed to South Australia in the vessel that carries this despatch."

The first official intimation received by Colonel Gawler of any direct censure of his policy by the Commissioners, or of dissatisfaction on the part of the Colonial Office, was this curt recall, and the appearance of Captain Grey at Government House as his successor!

Upon the appointment of Captain Grey, the management of the colony by the South Australian Commissioners in London practically ceased, the home Government taking it entirely into their own hands.

Apart from the objectionable manner in which it was done, it is questionable whether any better man could possibly have been selected than Captain Grey. He was the son of Colonel Grey, killed at the taking of Badajoz, and was born in Lisbon, Portugal, on the 14th of April, 1812. Educated at Sandhurst, he entered the army in 1829, but retired from his profession. From 1837 to 1840, he was employed in exploring the coast of Western Australia and tracing the sources of the Glenelg River. During his travels he received a severe spear-wound, which for many years was a cause of suffering to him. His "Journals of Discovery" give the romance of Australian exploration, and in an unobtrusive way reveal his character for courage, perseverance, and endurance under privation.*

Before assuming the reins of office, under "the most difficult and unpopular of all conditions, namely, the necessity of rigid retrenchment and the task of creating a revenue by the imposition of increased duties of customs," he determined to have a clear understanding as to the course he was to pursue generally, and the support he would receive from the Imperial Government, and he at once addressed a lengthy minute to the Secretary of State for the Colonies, his inquiries plainly showing that he was opposed to the policy of his predecessor, and was resolved to grapple with the financial difficulties sternly and resolutely. He wished to be informed whether official correspondence was to be addressed to the Commissioners, or to the Colonial Secretary; what was to be the mode of dealing with the different departments engaged in the receipt and issue of public moneys; what provision was to be made for paying the interest of the public debt; whether the system of special surveys was to be continued, and, if so, upon what principle; whether the public buildings in course of erection should be completed or not; whether, as the Government House was far too vast for his residence "without extreme imprudence," he

* "Explorations in Western and North-Western Australia," published 1841.

would be at liberty to appropriate it to some public object, and hire a smaller house as a residence; and then followed a string of queries as to salaries of Government officers (his own included), the creation of corporate bodies, and the employment of troops to do public duty, and to relieve the colony of this heavy item of expenditure.

To many of the inquiries Lord John Russell was unable to give direct replies; on others, however, he was definite and explicit. Thus: " It will be proper that you should address yourself to the Secretary of State on all questions relating to the legislative and executive duties of your Government; and, further, that under the existing circumstances of the colony, and until you receive further instructions, you shall communicate directly with me generally on all questions of finance. I will then make such communications as may be necessary on the subject of your despatches to the Colonization Commissioners." No objection was raised to the sale or letting of public buildings not actually required for the real exigencies of the public service, due care being taken not to alienate any buildings which might in the near future be required for such service, but all public outlay on buildings in course of erection was to be suspended, except in so far as might be necessary to prevent dilapidations. The hire of a smaller house for the Governor could only be allowed if accommodation could not be obtained in such of the public buildings as were to be retained and could not be disposed of. In reply to another query, Lord John said, "I entirely approve of the measure which you propose of creating corporate bodies, whether municipal or otherwise, and of investing them with the power of imposing rates and assessments, of levying wharfage and other duties with the view of relieving the public revenues, and of devolving, as far as possible, on the inhabitants of the towns and of the rural districts, the management and the charge of their concerns;" and, finally, the Lords of the Treasury concurred with Lord John Russell, that "no prospect of increase to the rate of salary at present assigned for the government of South Australia could be held out to Captain Grey."

The Commissioners being still a constituted body, possessing certain powers conferred by Act of Parliament, were allowed to have their say in reply to these inquiries, but foreseeing that their days were numbered, and that the colony would soon be placed under the entire care and control of the Crown, they did not press for their rights and privileges in the matter of official correspondence, while all questions relating to finance they were only too glad to leave to "my lords." With regard to Government House, if Lord John thought the Governor should not retain it for his residence, they suggested "that it might perhaps be expedient to dispose of the house to the Corporation of Adelaide for a Court House or Town Hall, should it be suitable for that purpose," adding, "it is not impossible that the Corporation might offer such a price as would cover the expense of the erection of the house."

This was only one of innumerable instances in which the utter incompetency of Commissioners in England to arrange and settle affairs in the distant colonies was shown. Little did those good gentlemen, seated in their armchairs in a snug board-room, imagine when they made their suggestion that the Corporation of Adelaide would soon be found in a state of insolvency, and that the messenger would seize the few chairs and tables belonging to that august body in part payment of his salary!

On the 10th of May, 1841, when as yet Colonel Gawler had received no official intimation of his recall, Captain Grey arrived in the *Lord Glenelg*, having been gazetted as Governor and Resident Commissioner on the previous 18th of December.[*]

Captain Grey, on his arrival in the colony, was kindly entertained by Colonel Gawler, and on the 15th of May took the oaths of office in front of Government House.

---

[*] "Thus at the early age of twenty-eight," says his biographer, "George Grey left England as the ruler of her youngest colony, himself the youngest Governor ever appointed to a similar position."

He began his career in the colony without any ostentation, as one who knew well that he had difficulties and annoyances of no ordinary kind to grapple with, and who had determined to exercise the strictest possible economy compatible with the efficiency of the public service and the state of the colony. From the first his trumpet gave no uncertain sound. He was opposed to any kind of extravagance in an infant settlement, and of course, therefore, he deprecated the policy of his predecessor. He maintained that in the early stage of a colony, as there were no producers either of the necessaries of life or of articles of export, a large outlay upon extensive public buildings and town improvements was of no further benefit to the colony than that those buildings and improvements were obtained, and that the whole of the money expended in labour was carried out of the colony to purchase food and clothing.

Moreover, as the colony was thus altogether dependent upon imports, and as the Government was monopolizing the labour market, the country settlers stood no chance of carrying on agricultural operations, their capital being eaten up by the high price of wages and of the necessaries of life. Disappointed agriculturists were, therefore, compelled to abandon their legitimate occupations and betake themselves to speculation in land and buildings, and instead of assisting the general prosperity, only hastened the inevitable ruin.

These facts had been fully and lamentably illustrated in the experience of South Australia, and the task of evolving order out of the universal chaos was the herculean task of Captain Grey. His first step was directed to obtaining exact information as to all claims upon the colonial Government and the Colonization Commissioners, in the hope that "he would shortly receive instructions from the Secretary of State, which would enable him to make the necessary arrangements for their liquidation." Meanwhile, the question how to procure funds for carrying on the Government was a burning one.

The estimated expenditure for the first quarter of his administration was £32,000, to which had to be added nearly £3000 due for Colonel Gawler's last quarter in office. Towards meeting this sum there was only £700 in the hands of the treasurer, and with the revenue decreasing and the land sales falling off considerably, there seemed little prospect of raising anything like a revenue to meet even the ordinary expenditure, to say nothing of a further sum of about £35,000, the amount of the outstanding claims. Nor, owing to the state of the times, was there, as Captain Grey had hoped, any chance of selling the elaborate new premises built for the Government by Colonel Gawler.

In his extremity Captain Grey applied to the bank for a loan, but as he was only offered £10,000, and that at twelve per cent. interest on his personal security, he resolved not to attempt the liquidation of any debts contracted by his predecessor until the result of the parliamentary inquiry into the affairs of the colony should be announced.

Meanwhile retrenchment must be made at once, but it was difficult to know where to begin, and the task was in any case an unpleasant one. The Great Eastern Road through Glen Osmond* was then in course of formation, and he proposed to stop the works; but against this step there was an instant remonstrance in the form of a memorial and the inevitable public meeting.

The discontinuance of the signals on West Terrace was another grievance; so was the increased rate on postage, and a tax of a penny on newspapers; but the most formidable discontent was on the part of the labouring classes. The Governor had addressed a letter to the bench of magistrates, asking them to take into consideration the position of such immigrants as were unable to obtain work other than that which the Government was obliged to provide for them, and to give their opinion as to the remuneration to be given to those immigrants with whom a stipulation had been

---

* Named after Mr. Osmond Gilles.

made, that in the event of their being unable to obtain work elsewhere, the Government would employ them at reduced wages.

The magistrates met and passed a series of resolutions in which the practice of inducing the labouring population to hover in and about the town was deprecated on the one hand, while on the other the magistrates considered that the Government was bound to afford them such means of subsistence as would put them above want. They recommended, as an adequate Government allowance, seven shillings a week for a single man, ten and sixpence for a man and his wife, and for every unemployed child in the family, up to three inclusive, two and sixpence each per week; that all immigrants employed by the Government should be obliged to work daily, including Saturday, from 6 a.m. to 6 p.m., deducting one hour for breakfast and another for dinner. During the winter months—May, June, July, and August—the hours to be from seven to five o'clock. It was further recommended that, in the event of any immigrant refusing from a settler employment at the rate of £20 per annum and rations, or any man and his wife refusing £30 and rations, they should be struck off from Government employment and not be taken on again.

These recommendations the Governor adopted, and the usual outcry arose, followed by public meetings, memorials, and deputations. To these succeeded the formation of organizations for self-protection, and a resolute determination not to accept the terms of the Government. But while the agitation was being kept up, the resources of the people were steadily going down, and distress, at the worst season of the year, became very general. In proportion as the Governor remained firm the dissatisfaction of the people increased, until on more than one occasion an outbreak was anticipated, which, in the absence of any military force, might have been serious. At one time several hundred men, in an organized body, marched to Government House and threatened the Governor with personal violence, but his firmness and coolness had the effect of quelling the disturbance.

Captain Grey had an advantage over his predecessor in this respect, that he was instructed to act, in all matters connected with the revenue and expenditure of the colony, in concert with the members of the Legislative Council, who were to share with him the responsibility of their action.

About the middle of July intelligence was received in the colony that a Select Committee of the House of Commons had been appointed, upon the motion of Lord John Russell, to consider the Acts relating to South Australia and the actual state of the colony. The committee was composed as follows:—Lord Howick, Lord Stanley, Sir George Grey, Mr. W. E. Gladstone, Mr. G. W. Wood, Lord Mahon, Mr. J. Parker, Lord Eliot, Mr. Ward, Captain A'Court, Mr. Vernon Smith, Mr. Raikes Currie, Mr. Sotheron, Lord Fitzalan, Mr. George Hope, and Sir William Molesworth.

The first report of the committee was brought up in March, and it was recommended that "provision ought to be made to meet the actual engagements incurred under the authority of the Resident Commissioner and the Commissioners appointed under the Act 4 Will. IV. c. 95, and to repay the sums due to the Emigration Fund; and that such provision should not be delayed until after this committee shall have completed the inquiry in which it is engaged into the South Australian Acts and the general state and prospects of the colony."

A few days later the further news reached the colony that the British Parliament had, upon the motion of Lord John Russell, voted the sum of £155,000 for South Australia, and that it was henceforth to be considered and treated as a Crown colony.

In moving this vote Lord John said—

"In proposing that Parliament should relieve the colony from its present financial embarrassments it was not perhaps necessary that he should state his opinions as to the manner in which the colony should be in future governed, but he had no hesitation in stating that he thought the principles of government which were applied to the other colonies should be applied to the colony of South Australia. That, making what provisions they thought proper with respect to the sale of land and the application of money derived therefrom, the provisions which placed the government of the colony in the hands of Commissioners, and directed that the whole of the expenses of the colony should be defrayed by their orders, and not by the Treasury, should be repealed so as to bring the colony into the same state as other colonies with regard to its government; that if the Crown was to do anything for the colony, the responsible ministers of the Crown should have a more direct control; that the Governor appointed by the Crown should correspond, not with the Commissioners, but with the Secretary of State and the Government; and with respect to the financial question, that when the Governor should write home, his application should be referred to the Treasury, and that their opinion, as well as that of the Secretary of State, should be taken before the directions of the Government were sent out. For himself he could see no good—indeed, he could see nothing but mischief—in that anomalous kind of government in which the Crown had a nominal direction, yet, in fact, left everything to the Commissioners, whilst the Commissioners felt bound by the Act of Parliament, so that neither could be considered as responsible. If the committee thought it proper that the colony of South Australia should govern itself, and that the persons there should have a representative constitution, although he confessed that that was not his opinion, he should feel no insuperable objection to it. He should feel that it would in time, though perhaps not until after a considerable time had elapsed, struggle through its difficulties and obtain considerable prosperity."

The second report of the Select Committee of the House of Commons reached South Australia in November. In it the committee called attention to certain fundamental defects in the South Australian Act, namely—

1. That the provisions of the Act were to be carried into effect by a Board of Commissioners, the members of which were to be appointed and removed by the Crown, but over whose movements the responsible members of the Crown could exercise no adequate control. 2. The inconvenient division of authority. "While one department," it was said, "was made responsible for the payment of the colonial debt, another had the management of the fund out of which it was to be paid, and whilst one was responsible for conducting the public service the money by means of which it was to be conducted was placed under the control of another. If the revenues of the colony were mismanaged by the local Government the Commissioners could not satisfy the public creditor; if the funds raised on the security of those revenues were mismanaged by the Commissioners the Government could not conduct the public service," and so on. 3. The uncertainty of the mode prescribed by the Act for obtaining the supplies on which the colony in its earlier years was entirely to depend. 4. The inadequate provision for securing the mother country against any loss which might eventually arise.

With regard to the administration of affairs by Colonel Gawler, the committee were of opinion that "the condition of the colony on his arrival made it absolutely necessary that he should assume a large responsibility in deviating from his instructions," and they "entertain no doubt that Colonel Gawler was actuated in the course which he pursued by the most earnest desire to advance the interests and promote the prosperity of the country, nor can they undertake to state to what extent he may have been justified by imperative necessity in involving the colony in an expenditure so far exceeding his authority." "But," continued the report, "it is due to Colonel Gawler to observe that the general character of his administration has been spoken of in terms of strong approval, even by those who have censured his expenditure as excessive, and that, among the witnesses examined, even those who have pronounced this censure most decidedly have been unable to point out any specific items by which it could have been considerably reduced without great public inconvenience."

The committee considered that the arrangements of the late Board of Commissioners had proved in many material points defective; that their instructions as to expenditure, "though minutely and elaborately drawn up, appear to have been framed without any clear foresight of the necessities of such a community placed in such circumstances, and on an estimate of the charges to be incurred and the objects to be provided for totally inadequate and bearing no proportion to the reality."

It was, however, distinctly stated in the report that the committee would be "doing injustice to the individuals upon whom the responsibility for the management of these affairs had fallen did they not add their opinion that the chief and original error was committed in the Act itself."

The gracefulness of this encomium was considerably discounted by a subsequent remark: "That the Commissioners have been unsuccessful in the execution of their charge is less a matter of surprise than that they should have entertained no apprehension of the result which has taken place, and that up to the termination of their official connection with the colony in 1840 they should have apparently conceived that the experiment was advancing to a successful issue."

Many of the measures recommended by the committee were subsequently embodied in a Bill passed on the 15th of July, 1842, entitled, "An Act for the Better Government of the Province of South Australia."

Under the impression that the recommendations of the Select Committee would be speedily carried into effect, Captain Grey felt confident himself, and endeavoured to inspire confidence in the colonists, that all claims would in the near future be settled. In addition to those due in England, he had found that there were considerable sums due in the colony, and he felt it to be his duty to commence paying off these, so that Government creditors in the colony might not be worse off there than elsewhere—a step cordially approved, not only by the Council, but also by the Chamber of Commerce. Accordingly, and without express authority, he drew bills upon her Majesty's Treasury, and in a despatch to Lord John Russell justified his actions in these words :—

"November 14th, 1841.

". . . A great deal of distress necessarily resulted from the non-payment of these bills, and this was more severely felt from the limited nature of the mercantile community in this province. The situation of these Government creditors was also peculiar. They had seen the supplies furnished by them appropriated to the uses of the Government; a pledge had been given to them which neither the late Governor nor myself had yet fulfilled, and they were not even in so good a position as the holders of the bills; if they had been so their claims would have been settled at the same time as those of the other creditors in England. When, therefore, I ascertained that all the bills drawn by Colonel Gawler were in course of payment in England, and found that had Colonel Gawler drawn bills for these precisely similar claims remaining unpaid in the colony, that then the creditors here would have been placed in the same position as those elsewhere; when also I saw the distress which the non-payment of those accounts was creating, I felt that I should be no longer justified in refraining from putting all the Government creditors upon an equal footing. I, accordingly, have commenced drawing drafts upon the Lords of the Treasury for the payment of these outstanding claims, and I trust that the line of policy I have pursued may meet with the approbation of her Majesty's Government."

But "my lords" did not approve, as we shall see later on.

Apart from financial matters, there were many

notable events to claim the serious attention of Governor Grey during the first year of his administration.

On the 21st of April news reached Adelaide that a ferocious attack had been made by about 300 to 400 natives on an overland party, led by Mr. Inman, about forty miles from Lake. Bonney. It was stated that the leader of the party and two shepherds had been speared and the sheep scattered. Major O'Halloran, the commissioner of police, was at once despatched to the scene of the affray with a body of mounted police, and accompanied by a surgeon to render assistance if necessary. Happily, there had been no loss of life, and the party had escaped to the nearest station.

On his return to Adelaide, Major O'Halloran left a corporal and four mounted troopers near the Great Bend for the protection of a party shortly expected overland, who had started from Mr. Dutton's station for the purpose of rescuing, if possible, the sheep belonging to Mr. Inman's party. They soon fell in with the natives, who approached to within fifty yards of them, when one of the leaders gave the signal of attack, by striking a spear into the ground and waving his hand. In an instant the war-cry was raised and the affray began. "The first man who threw a spear I shot through the head," says one of the party, "and gave the order to fire, hoping that when they saw two or three of the natives fall they would have retreated; but they did not appear in the slightest degree intimidated, but still advanced in the form of a crescent in a body of at least two hundred, while many more were partially seen in the thick part of the scrub. At this time, Mr. George Hawker called out to me that they were encircling us, and seeing that they were advancing both wings while the centre was engaged, a large lagoon being in our rear, I ordered the party to follow me and outflank them on the right. While effecting this, Mr. G. Hawker's horse fell over a tree, and he was dismounted; we wheeled round to protect him, and about this time Mr. John Jacob's horse received a second spear-wound and was soon unable to carry him further. He dismounted, and we were all engaged in covering his retreat, at the same time moving towards a dry creek, on the further side of which was rising ground. We succeeded in reaching this, and formed in line while Mr. Jacob mounted behind Mr. Edward Bagot. The affray had now lasted more than half an hour, and I directed the party to retreat in order. There were very few shots fired without effect, and the last man shot was one of their chiefs. Had not the gentlemen of the party displayed much steadiness and coolness Mr. Jacob must have fallen, as it was by frequently coming to the 'present,' but reserving our fire, that we kept the headmost men back, as on these occasions they adroitly double themselves up into the smallest possible compass, holding a shield before their heads. In covering Mr. Jacob's retreat a spear struck me in the fore part of the head, but as it passed through a thick tarpaulin hat, the wound was but slight; but the mare on which I rode was speared through the shoulder. When I was struck the natives gave a yell of triumph, as they did on every occasion when the advantage appeared to be on their side. Having retreated about a mile, we were obliged to halt to sew up the wound in my mare's shoulder, or she must soon have dropped from loss of blood; then, choosing the clearest ground, we joined our cart on the following day. I felt convinced that the sheep remaining were not far distant, and that the natives had assembled for the purpose of defending them; and it is my opinion that it would take a very large party to subdue them without loss of life, as their great activity and courage, combined with their numbers and the difficult character of that part of the country for horse attacks, render them a much more formidable enemy than the colonists have any idea of."

This report, typical of many, caused some stir in Adelaide. Another party being expected overland, Major O'Halloran, with a body of troopers, was again sent out to the locality. A large number of gentlemen volunteered their services and were sworn in as special constables, the funds of the local Government being altogether inadequate to pay for the protection of overland parties. They started, sixty-eight in all, on the 31st of May, and soon after their arrival at the Murray fell in with the expected overlanders. And a sorry lot they were. Only two days before, they had been attacked by the natives; four of their number had been killed and two wounded out of a party of sixteen, twenty head of cattle had been dispersed, others killed, and all their property and supplies filched. Meanwhile, the natives had cleared off; carcases of about a thousand slain sheep were lying about in heaps, but no living sheep could be found.

At one place a striking incident occurred. Some of the party came upon the body of a man with his faithful dog standing beside him, which, as the party approached, set up a pitiful wail. The poor animal itself was found to have been speared in two places, and it was concluded that it had bravely attacked the natives in the affray. The body of the unfortunate man, over whom the wounded dog had faithfully kept guard for two days, was found to be in a dreadfully mangled and lacerated condition, and the whole scene where the conflict had taken place was described by Major O'Halloran as a horrifying one.

All efforts to capture the natives were, owing to the facilities for escape offered by the nature of the country, found to be unavailing, but the expedition had nevertheless been fruitful; fifty-three out of seventy head of cattle were recovered, and seven hundred and ten saved from loss, while twelve men were rescued from inevitable death.

On several other occasions during the year outrages were committed by the natives, each fresh instance giving rise to increased uneasiness. In one of the attacks between thirty and forty of the natives were killed, and this led to a careful consideration by a full bench of magistrates of the whole subject. They recommended that an armed force should be placed at the ferry near to which the attacks were made, for the protection of overland parties. This was agreed to, and shortly afterwards a permanent police station was established at Morrundee, on the Murray, and Mr. E. J. Eyre, the experienced traveller, was appointed resident magistrate. To him was entrusted the difficult task of conciliating the natives, and of establishing, if possible, friendly relations between them and the intruding Europeans. He was furnished by the Government with provisions and blankets for distribution, and these were given once a month to the most deserving. For three years he resided at Morrundee, and during this time not a single case of serious aggression, either on the persons or property of the Europeans, occurred. He visited alone the most distant and hostile tribes, where, but a short time previously, large and well-armed bodies of Europeans could not pass uninterruptedly or in safety; and in many instances the natives showed him considerable kindness and attention, accompanying him as guides and interpreters, introducing him from one tribe to another, and explaining the amicable relations he wished to establish. Influence amounting to authority was obtained by treating them with uniform kindness, and this was demonstrated on one occasion in Adelaide, when a large body of the Murray natives collected to fight those from Encounter Bay. The Government directed Mr. Eyre to use his influence to prevent the affray, and he at once proceeded to their *wurleys*,* and requested them to leave without delay, and return to their own district, ninety miles away. In the course of a few hours, not a native was left in Adelaide, and the encounter was averted.

It was much to be regretted that in 1844, owing to a misapprehension by the Government of the wish of Mr. Eyre, he was released from an office he had so ably fulfilled, and that the successful experiment at Morrundee was abandoned, and the post made little better than a mere police-station.

* Native name for bush-huts.

Meanwhile, the native schools established by the Government in the park-lands at Adelaide and at Walkerville were making some progress; the children were apt to learn, took kindly to their trousers and shirts, or grey woollen frocks, and, so long as they could be kept away from the huts or wurleys of their elders, were teachable and contented. But the natural desire for a wandering and savage life could not be eradicated, and as the children advanced in years, they broke away from the restraints of school life, and plunged once again into the depths of the forest.

A typical case was that of "Nancy," who, after receiving instruction in the three R's, resided for several years at Government House in the capacity of a servant. She was always well dressed, spoke English fluently, and regularly attended a place of worship. But, after enjoying the comforts of civilized life, and the confidence and society of all in the establishment, she suddenly, without any apparent or sufficient reason, left her situation, returned to her tribe and, to a great extent, to her primitive mode of life.

It was mainly for the purpose of overcoming this tendency to revert to barbarism that Archdeacon Hale (afterwards Bishop of Perth, Western Australia) resolved to attempt the establishment of a native institution in some locality situated as far as possible from the centres of European population, and also at a distance from the usual haunts of the aborigines; but there was no practical outcome of this scheme until some years later.

Up to 1844 the general results of the previous experiments in teaching native children may be summed up as follows:—(1) That they possessed capacity for learning not inferior to the best class of European children to be found anywhere in a mixed community; (2) that they were eager to be instructed, and were easily kept at their school work except when parental influence was brought to bear upon predisposing inclinations; (3) that, apart from this influence, there was the probability that their vagrant habits might be overcome, and that they would cheerfully and voluntarily engage in industrial pursuits; (4) that an interesting field for religious instruction had been opened, which would amply repay the labours of zealous missionaries.

One event, trifling in itself, but interesting to South Australians, as it became a standard topic of conversation for many years, occurred in the early part of Captain Grey's administration, and may be mentioned here in passing.

On Sunday morning, the 24th of February, a large number of persons assembled at the port in a state of considerable excitement, a rumour having gone abroad that an expedition was being fitted out for the seizure of a French vessel in St. Vincent's Gulf. The vessel in question was the *Ville de Bordeaux*, which a few days previously had arrived in Holdfast Bay, the captain reporting that he had come from King George's Sound to take in sheep, but declined to produce satisfactory papers to Mr. Anthony, the boarding officer at Glenelg, or to Mr. Torrens, the collector of customs. It was, therefore, determined not to allow the sheep to be taken, and Mr. Anthony was sent on board for this purpose. The captain, after abusing and threatening him, set sail, boarding officer and all, across the gulf. The collector at once determined to start in pursuit, and the steamer *Courier*, the only one in the harbour, was requisitioned. As there was no coal at hand, shingles, palings, anything that would serve for fuel, was thrown on board to enable the little vessel to get up steam with all possible speed, and amid great excitement and not a little consternation, the *Courier*, with the collector on board, left the wharf on what appeared to be a very hazardous mission.

A war with France had for some time been thought probable, and if the French vessel in the gulf were really captured, a collision between France and England was deemed by the excited colonists inevitable.

But the sailing of the "Shingle Expedition," as it was afterwards called, was only a three days' wonder.

The crew of the Frenchman refused to obey the captain's orders, took the ship into their own hands, squared the yards, and stood back up the gulf, bringing the vessel safely to anchor in Holdfast Bay without the intervention of the *Courier*. But the matter did not end here. As the officers of customs had been obstructed in the execution of their duty, and the cost of the expedition was £800, a criminal information was laid against the captain of the Frenchman. The trial extended over two or three days, and resulted in a verdict justifying the collector of customs in holding the ship as a condemned vessel, the owners being permitted to come into court and try the legality of the forfeiture and condemnation. This was done in the following year, and after various applications, trials, hearings, and a reference to the Court of Appeals, the vessel was finally ordered to be forfeited.

For many years this fine ship lay quietly moored in the stream in charge of a custom-house officer, but was subsequently appropriated to the purposes of a lightship at the outer entrance of the harbour.

The year 1841 will ever remain memorable in the history of South Australia. It witnessed the greatest reverses it was almost possible for the colony to experience. At its commencement nearly every branch of industry, trade, and commerce appeared to be in a flourishing condition. Companies, societies, and institutions sprang rapidly into existence; exports of colonial produce and samples of minerals had been sent to Britain; great progress had been made in agriculture and horticulture; the country districts round about the capital had received many settlers; a fairly good harvest had been gathered in. Notwithstanding all these and many other signs of progress and prosperity, at a stroke the condition of the colony became one of absolute insolvency. As the tide of misfortune set in, bankruptcy became a matter of frequent occurrence, and brought to light, in a few cases, some very reckless and fraudulent transactions, with which the non-payment of the Governor's bills had nothing to do except to reveal them. The almost unlimited and indiscriminate credit given by merchants, who in their turn were mostly agents for English houses, presented a fine opening for adepts at fraud, and even gave novices an unusual chance of success. These cases quite perplexed the officers of the Insolvent Court, as well as the unfortunate creditors, inasmuch as several of the defaulters, seeing that the end of their palmy days was at hand, had carefully laid aside certain assets for contingencies, including the necessary funds for a bolt to Sydney or elsewhere by a favourite clipper, the *Dorset*. So successful were these bolters that few of them were captured, and, in fact, few efforts were put forth for that purpose.

Although the Governor had given his confident assurance that the debts of the colony would ultimately be paid, and had afforded temporary relief through the bills drawn upon her Majesty's Treasury, many leading merchants were completely paralyzed by the sudden check which trade and commerce had sustained. Large numbers of the working classes, dissatisfied with the low rate of wages obtainable, either left the colony or fell back upon the Government alternative in preference to seeking employment in the country districts. Several tradesmen and mechanics, who had sufficient means left to pay their passage-money, proceeded to the then recently established colony of New Zealand. As early as May, sixteen prisoners for debt petitioned the Governor to have a Bill prepared for their relief, some of them having suffered from protracted incarceration, and there being at that time no Act for regulating the imprisonment of insolvent debtors. A Bill was accordingly prepared, and during the first six months after it came into operation thirty-six insolvent debtors availed themselves of the benefit of the Act.

The widespread prevalence of distress and destitution led some benevolent colonists to establish a society to assist in relieving the wants of those suddenly overtaken by misfortune, and "The South Australian Philanthropic Association" was instrumental in effecting much good, especially in cases where Government aid was greatly needed, but had not been sought.

Towards the end of the year, nearly two thousand men, women, and children in destitute circumstances were being supported at the expense of the Government.

But with all the distress there was peace, and the public press of the colony even grew jocular over misfortunes, for when Foundation Day (28th of December) came round one of the journals said—

"Considering our present state, and the improvidence which our useless consumption of gunpowder would involve, perhaps the noisier modes of celebration were wisely omitted, while those so peculiarly appropriate at the present moment—the closing of the banks and public offices—were as widely retained."

The year 1842 was, from beginning to end, a year of trial and discontent. Of the four newspapers in existence at the beginning of the year, only one was in any way favourable to the Governor and his administration. Despondency was the prevailing tone. One writer, in drawing a comparison between the 1st of January, 1841, and the corresponding date in 1842, said—

"Then bankruptcy and insolvency were almost unknown—they were rare exceptions to the rule of prosperity; now they are themselves the rule and their opposite the exception; then the plough and the spade were busy in all directions; the merchant was a man of business, not of leisure; the counter of the storekeeper was thronged, and able-bodied labourers were for the most part employed. Now, 'the ruin, destitution, and dispersion,' apparently foreseen by Governor Gawler, are here and in full activity."

In another despairing journal the question "Shall we re-emigrate?" was fully discussed; but the conclusion arrived at was that it was better for the colonists to bear the ills they had than fly to others that they knew not of. Certainly vexations arose in every conceivable quarter. Such progress had been made in the survey department, under the able superintendence of Captain Frome, that all the special surveys claimed—namely, thirty-six of four thousand acres each—had been completed, and the quantity of land open for selection amounted to upwards of three hundred thousand acres; but just when this long-waited-for land was ready for sale there were few who had either money to buy or confidence to invest in it. Unquestionably the times were bad in other respects, and the spirit of discontent and dissatisfaction was so great that, in the absence of business and more profitable employment, public meetings and other demonstrations for the ventilation of grievances became the order of the day, the Chamber of Commerce taking the lead in these gatherings and inviting the colonists to meet and deliberate upon the financial position of the colony.

There was a curious misapprehension in some quarters as to the real cause of the embarrassment. The case was simply this: the rapid expenditure in the early days suddenly ceased at the very moment when the colony was most in need of such support. Since its foundation, five years previously, the local Government had expended between £400,000 and £500,000; the South Australian Company had invested an equal amount; the colonists had imported and expended upwards of a million; and the whole of this rapid and enormous expenditure stopped at the end of 1840. Capitalists ceased to come to the colony, and, worst of all, the colony lost its credit with the mother country. Hence the disastrous position. Depression in every article of merchandise and every kind of colonial property followed, and sixteen thousand persons were plunged in more or less of distress, which could be alleviated only by assistance from without, that is to say, the importation of capital into the colony.

In the press, and at public meetings, it was stated that the operations of agriculture were clogged almost to cessation; that the merchants only existed by sufferance of the banks and large companies; that the profitless pursuits of tradesmen were daily terminating in insolvency; that labourers were seeking other shores, or were sunk into the condition of pauperism; and that hundreds of families, not belonging to either of the before-mentioned classes, found that they had exchanged wholesome abundance in England for a bare and precarious subsistence in the colony.

And yet there was scarcely any step taken by the Governor and his Council for the improvement of affairs that did not meet with the opposition of the colonists! To increase the revenue, bills were passed imposing additional dues on the shipping visiting the port, and to protect the customs duties by preventing private distillation. There could be no doubt that it was desirable to discountenance as far as possible the import of those things which the colony could itself produce, but it was questionable whether it was wise to levy such high charges as would practically prohibit the importation of merchandise.* A meeting to protest was held in the Queen's Theatre, when it was stated that whereas formerly the charges on a vessel of five hundred tons were £10, under the new dues they were raised to £50. The imposition of high duties on spirits was also considered "to be opposed to the public interests."

Soon after this a reduction was made in the port charges, but not enough to satisfy those connected with the shipping interest; and later in the year the City Council took the unconstitutional course of drawing up a petition to her Majesty, for presentation through the Governor, praying for a disallowance of the Acts imposing the obnoxious rates and taxes. At the same time, a memorial was presented to the Governor, praying him to suspend the operation of those Acts until her Majesty's pleasure became known.

To the latter request Captain Grey replied—

"I have been in no slight degree surprised to find that the Corporation, who have shown themselves so jealous for the preservation of the British constitution,

---

* It was, however, very much a matter of "Hobson's choice," and the duties were temporarily imposed as the only available means of obtaining ready money.

should have solicited me to suspend certain laws, and thereby set all the principles of that constitution at defiance. A moment's consideration should have sufficed to show the Corporation that a Governor has no power to suspend the operation of the laws. . . ."

Throughout the year the Governor had been incurring great responsibilities by drawing on the Treasury for such sums as he considered necessary, without knowing what the consequences might be. These responsibilities were largely increased in August. He received instructions from the Colonial Office that, in the present critical state of affairs, all the unemployed labourers in the colony were to be sent forthwith to Sydney. This was regarded, not only by the Governor, but by nine-tenths of the people, as impolitic to the last degree; and, on the receipt of a numerously signed memorial praying him to prevent this great loss to the colony, he at once took upon himself the responsibility of disregarding the instruction, and also of continuing to draw on the British Treasury. With the example and fate of his predecessor before his eyes, this was even a bolder stroke than his unauthorized payment of the claims upon the local Government, and a general feeling of uneasiness took possession of men's minds. Colonel Gawler throughout all his dashing career carried the people with him and enjoyed their confidence and sympathy, but Captain Grey had not this advantage; his policy was unpopular in all quarters. Every step he took, therefore, was watched with suspicion; and even those who urged him on in the most perilous course of all that he had taken were foremost among those who, when the bolt fell, attacked him for the consequences of his action.

The storm that had been gathering through all the earlier months of the year broke in October, when tidings reached the colony that drafts drawn by Captain Grey on the British Treasury had been dishonoured. Unfortunately, no official despatches reached the Governor at the same time, and he was left in a most difficult and unenviable position—" naked to his enemies," as it were, every claimant holding him personally responsible. For the time his credit was totally destroyed; the banks refused to negotiate any more of his drafts, and he had to fall back upon the commissariat chest for £1800 to meet urgent current expenses of government.

It was not until Christmas Eve that the long-looked-for despatches arrived, and then there was a plentiful and important supply. They announced the passing of "An Act for the Better Government of South Australia," and "An Act for regulating the Sale of Waste Lands in the Australian Colonies and in New Zealand," and they also explained the reason why Captain Grey's bills, amounting to about £14,000, had been dishonoured.

The whole of the bills drawn for the current service of the colony would, it was intimated, be accepted, but those drawn in part payment of outstanding claims the Lords of the Treasury declined to accept, and directed the Governor to issue debentures to the holders in exchange for their bills, such debentures to bear interest at five per cent. from the date at which the bills became due.

In the despatch to Captain Grey making these intimations, Lord Stanley said—

"The justification which you have urged for the course taken by you is in substance this—that you understand that all the bills drawn by your predecessor were to be accepted and paid, and that the claims, in satisfaction of which you were about to draw those bills, were similar to those on account of which Governor Gawler drew his bills. It is true that, in order to sustain the credit of the colonial Government, the home Government ultimately consented to provide for the payment of Governor Gawler's bills, but you appear to have overlooked the fact that Governor Gawler's conduct in drawing those bills was strongly disapproved of, and that it formed one of the principal grounds of his recall. You were warned not to draw any bills without having previously received authority to do so, and not to take any measures on your own authority for the settlement of the debt."

This was strong and somewhat unjust, as Lord Stanley failed to take into consideration the fact that the bills drawn by Captain Grey were not for debts contracted by him but by his predecessor, and were, in fact, mainly for the fulfilment of contracts entered into before Colonel Gawler received positive instructions not to incur further liabilities or draw any more bills. There was, therefore, as Lord Stanley very well knew, no more reason for the rejection of these claims than those recognized and provided for, and in a private despatch, dated June 21, 1843, Captain Grey had the satisfaction, such as it was, of receiving from Lord Stanley an acknowledgment of this. "It would, indeed, be an ill return," he wrote, "for the essential and most effective services which you have rendered in reducing the expenditure and re-establishing the finances of South Australia if you should be left to discharge from your own private fortune a debt originally contracted, not by yourself, but by your predecessor, for the public service of that colony."

The consequences of the rejection of the bills were very serious. In the first place, the colonists concerned had been kept waiting for eighteen months before they had any settlement at all; their claims were then arranged by the Governor's bills on the Lords of the Treasury, to get which cashed they were obliged to pay the bank five per cent. discount. The bills were sent to England and refused acceptance; then the lawyers got hold of them and, in addition to the expense of noting protest, there was the charge of twenty per cent. for re-exchange, which, according to the commercial laws of the colony, every endorser of a bill on England was liable for if that bill was not paid. The lawyers in the colony were then instructed by the banks to request an early reimbursement from the unfortunate endorsers, who were powerless to do more than to hand over the debentures bearing five per cent. interest, whilst the current rate of bank interest in the colony was at that time from ten to twelve per cent. "A child," says Mr.

Dutton in his work on South Australia,* "might guess the consequences to nine out of ten of the holders of these bills—the expenses on the returned bills, being nearly half the amount of the bills themselves, are finally settled by an advertisement of the sheriff in the public papers announcing the property of A., B., or C. for peremptory sale!"

Of course there was a great outcry against Captain Grey, and he was made the scapegoat to bear all the responsibility and all the difficulty of the position. How he came through the embarrassment we shall see later on. Meanwhile attention was diverted by the publication of the two important Acts passed by the Imperial Legislature and the despatches accompanying them.

The "Act for regulating the Sale of Waste Lands in the Australian Colonies and New Zealand" was passed on the 22nd of June, and made, as suggested by the Select Committee of the House of Commons, an important alteration in the mode of applying the proceeds arising from the sale of lands. By the original Act it was provided that all lands should be disposed of at the uniform price of £1 per acre, and the entire proceeds be applied to emigration. The new Act provided that all waste lands, except blocks of 20,000 acres, should be put up to public auction at the minimum price of £1 per acre, and that only one-half of the proceeds should be applied to the purposes of emigration, the other half being applicable to local improvements, the aborigines, and so forth.

Under the new Act the power of sale and conveyance was vested in the Governor, who was authorized to divide the colony into any number of territorial districts not exceeding four, in the event of its being deemed expedient to adopt different sums respectively as the minimum for the upset price of land in different parts.

The most important despatch was that conveying a copy of the Act passed on the 15th of July, entitled "An

* "South Australia and its Mines," by Francis Dutton. 1846.

Act for the Better Government of South Australia." Its first section repealed altogether the two former Acts, and with them the authority under which the Board of South Australian Commissioners and the Resident Commissioner exercised their functions; the fifth section empowered her Majesty to establish a form of legislature similar to that previously in force in all the other Australian colonies, and instructions were sent to the Governor, under the royal sign manual, constituting such a Council as being, at least for the present, best suited to the wants and conditions of the colony, the hope being held out that at an early period it might be expedient to grant to the inhabitants of the colony a certain degree of control over its resources and expenditure by means of popular representation in the local Legislature.

A few days previous to the passing of this Act—which transferred the colony from the Commissioners into the hands of the Crown—Lord Stanley laid a statement of the financial affairs of the colony before the House of Commons, embracing not only the main items of the debt, in a classified form, but the manner in which he intended to dispose of the several sums. The total amount of liabilities was stated to be £405,433. Of the first item, namely, the Parliamentary grant of £155,000 advanced the previous year, he asked the House to forego the payment. Colonel Gawler's remaining unpaid bills, amounting to £27,290, and Captain Grey's bills on account of emigrants' maintenance, amounting to £17,646, he recommended should be paid. The £85,000 borrowed by the Commissioners, bearing interest at from six to ten per cent., to remain outstanding at three and a half per cent. interest, the bondholders being guaranteed payment by the British Treasury out of the Consolidated Fund. The £35,000 outstanding debts of Colonel Gawler, and the £84,697 borrowed from the Land and Emigration Fund, were not at present to be made good, but, as we have seen, Captain Grey was instructed to issue debentures in the colony at interest not exceeding five per cent. Lord Stanley further signified his intention of moving for the sum of £15,000 to be placed upon the estimates for carrying on the government, and with that amount he thought the colony would be in a healthy and prosperous condition.

Despite all drawbacks, by the end of the year (1842) Captain Grey had succeeded in getting the machinery of his Government in good working order, and many important measures had been taken in the interest of the colony. A Board of Audit was appointed, and all public accounts were submitted to their careful scrutiny; an Emigration Board had been established for hearing and judging cases requiring relief; the road across the swamp to the port was purchased from the South Australian Company for 12,000 acres of land, in lieu of the £13,000 paid by the Company for its construction; new roads had been made and streets repaired, 37,814 acres of land had been surveyed for selection, and large tracts of fresh land had been discovered in the north; the raids of the natives upon overland traders had been checked by the appointment of Mr. Eyre as resident magistrate at Morrundee, and friendly intercourse to some extent established; a system of tender had been adopted for the supply of everything required for the public service; provision had been made for the regular fortnightly transmission of an overland mail between Sydney, Melbourne and Adelaide, the service to be performed by mounted police, who would gather up intermediate intelligence along the line of route, and extend some protection to settlers on the overland track; and other arrangements and improvements had been effected. As a set off, there were the dishonoured bills drawn by Captain Grey; but had he not drawn those bills, the numerous Government creditors who hung about Adelaide would never have dispersed into the country. As it was, the country districts became the chief scenes of activity and progress; 19,641 acres of land were brought under cultivation during the year, owned by 873 proprietors.

When harvest came, rich and bountiful, there was some difficulty in gathering it in, so large a number of the male population having left the colony; but the military were permitted to give their assistance, and the tradesmen of Adelaide and many gentlemen not otherwise occupied lent a helping hand, and so it was garnered.

While, however, the country districts were enjoying a small degree of prosperity, the city was suffering most severely, not only from the withdrawal of its population, but also from want of capital. At the end of the year, 642 out of 1915 houses were vacant, and 216 more were neglected, or had fallen into decay. During the year no less than 136 writs for the recovery of debts had passed through the hands of the sheriff, and 37 fiats of insolvency had been issued. Money in most cases had ceased to pass as a circulating medium for the purchase of the necessaries of life, and a system of barter and "truck" was almost universal. The various trading and commercial interests had become curiously interwoven with one another to enable the "order" system to be carried out extensively and with facility. Tradesmen had "orders" upon merchants, and servants upon tradesmen, and as the holders had to take the article supplied, however inferior, there was a perpetual murmuring and dissatisfaction.

Depressing as these things were, there could be little doubt that at the close of 1842 the financial crisis was practically over, and that the colony had passed through its greatest trial. But there was no room for boasting; the clouds still hung heavy in the horizon, and it was evident that neither the troubles of the Governor nor those of the people were at an end.

It was discouraging to read in the newspapers statements like the following:—"Property is now selling by auction in Adelaide and the neighbourhood, in many cases for less than the title-deeds cost two years ago. Houses are gladly let to respectable persons rent free, and notwithstanding this, nearly half the tenements are empty and falling to pieces. . . ." And again : "The *Countess of Durham* will take back a large number of persons to England, and as many as twenty passages have been paid for in that vessel. Every ship that leaves for the other colonies takes from fifteen to twenty passengers, whilst the arrivals are *nil*." There were glints of sunshine through the gloom, and the same newspapers were able to report at the same time : " The rural districts of the province present a pleasing contrast to the town. There everything is activity, and farms are spreading almost like the work of enchantment over the land, raised up by the industry of our settlers."

On the 4th of January the Governor called his Council together, and submitted to them the accounts of the last year : receipts from all sources, £81,813 19s. 5d.; expenditure, £84,531 16s. 10d., of which £18,069 10s. 5d. had been spent in the immigration department, the greater part for the maintenance of destitute persons, and £26,013 had been paid in liquidation of outstanding claims; these two items making more than half the total expenditure, while the entire proceeds of the land had been included in the total revenue.

Expenditure being still in excess of receipts, the Governor determined to still further cut down expenses in every practicable quarter. It is a curious illustration of the state of the times to find reductions in the salaries of public servants to. the amount of £4000, and that even the master of the signal station at West Terrace was to be dismissed unless the public provided the necessary funds by subscription, in which case " the Government would allow the use of house, staff, and signals." During the time of the suspension of the signal master, Messrs. Thomas and Co., the proprietors of the *Register*, signalled the arrival of vessels from the flag-staff erected on their premises in Hindley Street.

Even more significant were the notices that tenders would be received for leasing to the public the Government wharf at the port, and that the leases of premises held by the Government for bonded stores, for the building used by the Supreme Court in Whitmore Street, and for the house used for the resident magistrates' court in Currie Street, would each be abandoned! But the crowning humiliation was perhaps the announcement that, "in consequence of the reduction in the post-office department, the services of the letter-carrier to North Adelaide would be dispensed with!" A "cheeseparing" policy is always hateful to the majority, and it was so in South Australia.

On the 20th of February, 1843, the "Act for the Better Government of the Australian Colonies" came into force, but in the midst of somewhat troublous times. The *Examiner* opened a heavy fire upon the Governor, alleging in strong language that all the disasters of the colony were attributable to him and his policy. The inflammatory articles worked upon those who had suffered in the crisis and others, and as one result a "monster indignation meeting" was called, and, on the 16th of March, in the Queen's Theatre, a crowded assembly of malcontents moved "total want of confidence in the administration of his Excellency Captain Grey," and a petition to her Majesty was drawn up, humbly praying "that your Majesty will be graciously pleased to take the case into your most gracious consideration, and either recall his Excellency the Governor, or issue directions for such an amended mode of administering the Government of the province as shall to your Majesty seem meet."

Captain Grey was well aware of the odium that was being cast upon him in so many quarters, and he had the good sense to take it calmly. He knew that the majority of the colonists were interested in the maintenance of a lavish Government expenditure. During the twelve months preceding his arrival, about £150,000 had been distributed, in the form of salaries, allowances, and lucrative contracts, amongst a population of 14,061 people, who only contributed £30,000 towards their own support; in other words, the British Treasury had paid to every man, woman, and child in the province upwards of £10 per head per annum, or, if only the males of twenty-one years and upwards were considered, more than £12 each per annum was paid by Great Britain for the support of themselves and their families.

No wonder that, when this liberal annual contribution was withdrawn, the people should break forth into lamentation at their indignation meeting!

Even the natives took the cue and were wont to say, "No good, Gubner Grey, berry good Gubner Gawler— plenty tuck out."

It was not until the 20th of June that the new Council was called together. It consisted of eight members, four official (including the Governor) and four non-official.* In his inaugural address the Governor announced that, in order to give the public the greatest facility for becoming acquainted with the minutest details of the financial arrangements of the Government, and of increasing their knowledge of its legislative measures, he sanctioned the admission of strangers to the Council chamber to hear the debates.

This formal meeting was mainly for the purpose of administering the oaths to the members who had been gazetted, and of hearing a lengthy address from the Governor. But on the 10th of October the Legislative Council met for the transaction of business in the new building in North Terrace erected for their use, the gallery and also the body of the house being crowded by strangers, it being the first time that the public had ever been admitted to the privilege of hearing the deliberations of the Council, and the first time that non-official members had taken part in its proceedings.

During the session which came to a close on the 14th of November, sixteen Bills embracing some important and useful measures were passed, including "An Ordinance for avoiding Unnecessary Repetitions in the

* The following were the first members of the new Legislative Council:—A. M. Mundy (colonial secretary), W. Smillie (advocate-general), C. Sturt (colonial treasurer), T. S. O'Halloran, T. Williams, J. Morphett, and G. F. Dashwood. Mr. Williams resigned shortly afterwards, and Mr. Jacob Hagan was nominated to fill the vacancy.

Ordinances of the Governor and the Legislative Council;" "An Ordinance to facilitate the Adoption of the Laws of England in the Administration of Justice;" "An Ordinance to avoid Trifling and Frivolous Suits at Law;" "An Ordinance to regulate the Profession of the Law;" "An Ordinance for the Limitation of Actions and Suits relating to Real Property, and for simplifying the Remedies for trying the Rights thereto," and so on.

By the end of the year 1843 it was becoming evident that, despite all the struggle it had gone through, the colony was in reality in a healthier and more flourishing condition than it had been since its foundation. For one thing, it had become a grain-exporting instead of a grain-importing country, owing to the fact that thirteen hundred proprietors were now settled upon their properties in the country districts. Other sources of wealth and prosperity were opening up on every hand. The year was remarkable, to an extraordinary degree, for colonial inventions and improvements in machinery, and for the introduction of new manufactures. During the time of enforced leisure, while the general depression lasted, many of the colonists had been turning their attention to the invention of machinery to facilitate work when the prosperous days should return. The offer of a premium for the best reaping-machine resulted in the production of about fifteen models and designs, and, ultimately, to the general adoption of Mr. John Ridley's celebrated machine, which gave an unprecedented impetus to agriculture. Mr. Ridley was a miller at Hindmarsh, and erected there one of the first steam flour-mills that had been put up in the colony. He was not a competitor for the premium, but mechanism was a hobby with him, and although his knowledge was self-acquired, he was successful in introducing an implement which revolutionized the agricultural interests of the colony.*

---

* "The greatest invention ever produced for the agriculturists of South Australia is Ridley's reaping machine, which reaps and thrashes the wheat by one simple process. A machine of this kind could be used only where the climate is dry, and where the grain

His invention sinks all others into insignificance, but at about the same period Mr. Pettit invented an extraordinary plough; Messrs. Swingler and Dent were on the track for finding out a new motive power; Mr. Pitaway discovered a new method for propelling boats; Messrs. Harding and Bankhead produced excellent models of an aërial machine (the subject being then much under discussion in England); many colonists followed the example of their neighbours in New South Wales by boiling down sheep and cattle for the sake of the tallow; Messrs. Owen and Warner commenced the manufacture of blacking; Dr. Davey succeeded in manufacturing starch equal, if not superior, to any imported. It was an era of progress and enterprise, and all these attempts to develop the talent and resources of the colony had a beneficial effect.

But there was another source of wealth which had been gradually developing, and was destined to be one of the most potent factors in the continuous prosperity of the colony.

One of the early arrivals at Kangaroo Island in 1836 was "Professor" Mengé, an experienced German geologist and mineralogist, who, finding no scope in the settlement for his particular studies, commenced the cultivation of a plot of land, and became so engrossed in it as to be oblivious to everything else. His little garden was his study, and, notwithstanding the ravages of the wallaby and other wild animals, he tended it with an enthusiasm incomprehensible to his fellows.

But in 1837 Mr. Mengé, with most of the other settlers, was obliged to remove to the mainland, and he at once turned his attention to those studies to which he had devoted the greater part of his life. He made

is allowed to ripen and harden in the ear. In some of the Australian colonies the machine cannot be used in consequence of the moisture in the air. In South Australia, however, as soon as the crop is fully ripe, the machine is put into the field and the wheat is reaped and thrashed with amazing rapidity, and at a very small expenditure. It may safely be said that the cost of farming has been reduced to the minimum in South Australia."—Harcus's "South Australia," p. 61.

an investigation of the ranges from Cape Jervis upwards to the Barossa, and was delighted with the indications he discovered of the existence of gold, silver, copper, lead, iron, and nearly every variety of precious stones. In a short time he had collected 100 specimens of rocks and minerals, which he arranged and classified. But the fact of his not opening up a single mine led most people to doubt his assertions that the colony possessed great mineral wealth. This fact can, however, be easily accounted for; he was a mineralogist and not a miner, a collector rather than a trader, and it would have afforded him more pleasure to discover a variety of specimens than to have come upon one or two rich mines.

He was an eccentric individual, and took his own line in life without reference to others. He made no important practical discoveries, but he earned for himself the title of "Father of Mineralogy" in the colony, as there is no doubt that he was the first to arouse inquiry into its mineral resources.*

The first undoubted indication of the existence of silver-lead ore was made in 1838, on a section belonging to Mr. Osmond Gilles, at the foot of the hills near Adelaide, but no attempt was made at that time to open up the mine; while the trade in land, scarcity of labour, the want of means of transit, diverted attention from copper, afterwards to become one of the chief sources of wealth to the colony.

But in 1841 public attention was, for the first time in a practical manner, directed to mining operations by

---

* On the first day Mr. Mengé set foot in the colony he said that copper and gold abounded—"the hills are full of them."

To him belongs the honour of having proved to a demonstration that precious stones abound in the colony, and in the course of his residence there he discovered the following:—

Amethyst.	Chrysolite.	Emerald.	Opal.
Aquamarine.	Chrysoprase.	Garnet.	Smaragdine.
Beryl.	Cornelian.	Jasper.	Tourmaline.
Chalcedony.	Diamond.	Mocha-stone.	Topaz.

Specimens of these were sent to the Great Exhibition of 1851, and attracted considerable attention.

the formation of the South Australian Mining Association to work the Wheal Gawler Silver and Lead Mine, which had just then been discovered by some practical miners near Glen Osmond. A few tons of the ore were sent to England in the *Cygnet* as a sample, and an assay made in the colony resulted in giving 12,526 ounces of silver to the ton of ore and 75 per cent. of lead.*
Mr. J. B. Neales was an active worker in the mining association.

Much about the same time, a lode of copper was discovered on the banks of the Onkaparinga, near Noarlunga, in a section belonging to the South Australian Company, and shortly afterwards the Wheal Watkins Lead Mine.

But the great discovery of this period—the valuable Kapunda Copper Mine—was made in the latter part of 1842, first by Mr. C. S. Bagot, youngest son of Captain C. H. Bagot, whilst gathering some wild flowers, and shortly afterwards by Mr. F. S. Dutton, who, in his work on the mines of South Australia, thus describes his part of the discovery. A flock of sheep had been dispersed in a thunderstorm, and Mr. Dutton while searching for them rode to the top of a hillock to view the surrounding country. "After being out nearly the whole day in drenching rain," says Mr. Dutton, "I ascended this little hill prior to returning home, for one last view of the surrounding country. The very spot I pulled the horse up at was beside a large protruding mass of clay-slate, strongly tinged and impregnated with the green carbonate of copper. My first impression was that the rock was covered with a beautiful green moss, but on getting off the horse I quickly found, by breaking off a piece from it, that the tinge was as bright in the fracture as on the surface. My acquaintance with mineralogy was not sufficient to enable me to pronounce on the precise character of the rock, but I had little doubt that it

* It is recorded that the first piece of silver discovered in this mine was applied to the singular use of stopping the tooth of a member of the Bar in the colony.

was tinged with copper from the close resemblance of the colour to verdigris."

The steps taken by Mr. Dutton to secure the land containing the newly discovered mineral led to a curious coincidence. He says, "To Captain Bagot, with whom I had long been on intimate terms, I confided my discovery, when he also produced a specimen which was found by his son, and on a subsequent visit to the place we found that the two spots were in close proximity, although at first, from the one being on a hill and the other in a plain, we thought they were two different places. To make a long story short, we soon ascertained that the specimens were undoubtedly copper ores; the discovery was of course kept secret; we got eighty acres surveyed; all the forms as laid down by the old land-sales regulations were complied with; the section was advertised for a whole month in the Government *Gazette*, and we became the purchasers of it at the fixed Government price for waste lands of £1 per acre."

Having secured the services of a few Cornish miners, a considerable quantity of rich ore was raised,* and it soon became evident that the mine was of unusual value.

In purchasing the eighty acres Mr. Dutton thought he had taken in all the copper deposit, but some other out-croppings were observed, not only by his own miners, but by other people. When the next section of one hundred acres was put up to auction in April, 1845, it was bought by Captain Bagot for the large sum of £2210, so keen was the competition.

While excitement was still running high on the

* Previous to the erection of smelting works and the construction of a railway to Kapunda, the ore was carted to the Port on drays holding two tons each, and drawn in dry weather by six bullocks and in wet by eight. They reached Gawler Town (eighteen miles) on the first night, the Dry Creek (eighteen miles more) on the next night, and arrived at the Port early on the following morning. The convoys consisted of eight or ten teams, and made the journey with ease once every ten days, besides carrying up to the mines on their return all supplies required there.

subject of the Kapunda mines, the Montacute Mine, in the Mount Lofty Range, ten miles from Adelaide and sixteen from the Port, was discovered by one Andrew Henderson, overseer of Mr. Fortnum, when searching for a bullock which had strayed. Mr. Fortnum was a chemist and mineralogist, and he at once pronounced the specimen shown him by his overseer to be copper ore of a rich quality. Instead of keeping his own counsel, the secret was divulged, first to one, then to another, until it reached the survey office, and the chance of securing the land without the competition of a public sale was lost. It was brought to the hammer on the 16th of February, 1844, when the new regulations had come into operation. Mr. Baker was deputed by a small syndicate to bid as high as £4000 for the eighty-acre section, but at that time little was known about the value of the Kapunda ores, and the bidding was not very high, and when the price reached £1550 it was knocked down to Mr. Baker for that sum. Within a few hours, the syndicate resold thirty hundred parts for £5000, and the property became merged into the Montacute Mining Company.

Several other mines were discovered and partially worked about this time, such as the Yattagolinga, the Onkaparinga, and others; but all these were practically abandoned when, in 1845, the great discovery of the Burra-Burra Mine was made, which threw all the other mines into insignificance, and gave an enormous impetus to the mining interests of the colony.

Notwithstanding the abuse poured upon Sir George Grey, he pursued the even tenor of his course, and many felt no little surprise that he never alluded to the stinging articles which were constantly issuing from the local press. The explanation is to be found in a letter addressed to an old friend in England, Mr. George Fife Angas.

"With regard to the articles in the ——, to which you allude," he says, "I have never read them, and am sometimes quite surprised, when I receive papers from

England, to find what abuse has been heaped upon me here. If I had not pursued this course I could hardly have avoided being annoyed."

How chagrined those editors would have felt if they had only known this, and what a flood of light it throws upon the quiet, self-contained man, upon whom so much responsibility rested.*

The year 1844 opened with great activity in business and industrial concerns generally. The depression was now so far over as to enable all classes of the community to breathe more freely; Governor Grey was no longer regarded by the majority as the enemy of the colony, and the opposite conviction was strengthened by one of his first acts at the beginning of the year, namely, a reduction of the heavy port charges—a concession which gave general satisfaction.

With the comparative leisure consequent upon a partial cessation of hostilities, he was able to give attention to many matters which had hitherto been impossible. His well-known advocacy of the rights of the aborigines found expression in his opening address to the Legislative Council, when he announced his intention to bring in a Bill for the reception of the evidence of aborigines without oath. In urging the necessity of endeavouring to remedy their disabilities he said—

"One of the most distinguishing features of modern colonization is the anxiety manifested by the immigrants to render their occupation of the ancient territory of the aborigines productive of the blessings of Christianity and civilization to the people whose country they enter,

---

* "He ever maintained," says his biographer, "that it was the duty of a servant of the Crown to go on in the performance of the public service without devoting time and energy to the refutation of attacks made upon him. He held that such attacks would always be made when public duties were faithfully performed, and that they would meet with adequate and proper judgment when time had afforded the evidence upon which public opinion could be fully expressed. And he considered that the energies of those to whom had been committed great responsibilities, were too valuable to be wasted in useless apologies or lengthened arguments, and should be applied exclusively to useful and beneficial purposes."

and the settlers in this colony have ever lent the Government a zealous aid in the promotion of any plans having for their object the civilization and welfare of the native population. It is obviously one of the most important duties of the Legislature of a country circumstanced as this is, to promote this feeling by every means in their power, and to endeavour to induce each member of the community to perform, within the sphere of his individual influence, those duties towards the aborigines for the fulfilment of which he rendered himself morally responsible when he entered the territory. No prouder or brighter distinction could adorn the history of South Australia than the fact of its first European occupants bequeathing to their children a territory unsullied by deeds of violence and crime, and I rely upon your bestowing the most careful consideration upon the measures I am about to introduce into the Council with the object of giving increased means of ameliorating the condition of the aborigines, both to the Government and to the settlers, upon whose Christian and benevolent sentiments towards them the welfare of the scattered and wandering native population must mainly depend."

In addition to the bill for the reception of evidence without oath, another was brought in for the care of the orphans of aborigines. In recommending it, Governor Grey said he considered that the care of such orphans afforded the best chance of civilizing the race, by educating the children and attaching them to our customs. It was a plan that had been tried at Swan River with satisfactory results.

It was a sign of the improvement of the times that attention was once more seriously directed towards exploration. In April the Governor was able to accomplish a long-cherished wish of visiting the south-eastern districts and that part of the overland route to Port Phillip lying within the boundary of the colony. Accompanied by Mr. Charles Bonney, commissioner of Crown lands, Mr. Burr, deputy surveyor-general, Mr. George French Angas, and Mr. Gisborne, the Governor set forth on his travels. The results of the journey were very satisfactory, as it was ascertained that by keeping near the sea-coast, instead of pursuing the line of route previously traversed, there was an almost uninterrupted tract of good country between the rivers Murray and Glenelg, widening as it approached the boundaries of New South Wales, until it formed one of the most extensive and continuous tracts of good country at that time known to exist within the limits of South Australia. Moreover, the south-eastern portion of the province was as fertile as any other part of it, capable of easy communication in all directions by drays, and with good bays on the coast for the shipment of produce.

Another expedition, under the command of Captain Sturt, was fitted out this year with the object of obtaining some knowledge of the interior of the continent. Captain Sturt was one of the idols of the people, the discoverer of their province, the father of South Australian exploration, a fellow-settler, and withal a man whose courage, energy, and scientific attainments won the admiration of all. He started on the 10th of August, when business was suspended in the city to do honour to the leader and his adventurous band. Among the objects of the expedition was the discovery of a supposed chain of mountains lying parallel with the Darling and running north-west, with rivers rising from them. Great preparations had been made for the expedition, and when the cavalcade set forth down King William Street towards the Torrens, escorted by over a hundred horsemen, who accompanied the party as far as Dry Creek, it seemed that all the city and the regions round about had assembled to do honour to the occasion. At German Pass, where now the township of Angaston stands, the travellers were hospitably entertained by Mr. J. H. Angas.

Despatches were received from time to time, detailing how Captain Sturt had found that "the flats of the Darling exceeded in luxuriant verdure those of the

Murray;" how, on the way to the hills, the wind blew with the constancy and intensity of a hot blast from a furnace, insomuch that they had great difficulty in breathing so rarefied an atmosphere; how scurvy broke out, and illness set in; and how, in one part of the journey, the thermometer, fixed in the shade of a large tree four feet from the ground, stationary at 135° Fahr., at 2.30 p.m. rose in the direct rays of the sun to 157°. The travellers proceeded as far northward as water was known to exist, and then had to carry forward a supply. On the 13th of February Captain Sturt reported: "I was then nearly abreast of Moreton Bay in point of latitude, more than two hundred miles to the westward of the Darling, and in longitude 141° 22' as near as I could judge; and yet, as I looked around, and from the top of a small sand-hill I had ascended, I could see no change in the terrible desert into which I had penetrated. The horizon was unbroken by a single mound from north round to north again, and it was as level as the ocean. . . ."

"I returned from this excursion," he continues later, "with the full conviction on my mind that I had twice been within fifty, perhaps thirty, miles of an inland sea. It was, in truth, impossible that such a country, from which the very birds of the air shrank away, should continue much further; but whether such really was the case remains yet to be ascertained."

He determined to make another attempt to reach the north or north-western interior as soon as the rains would enable him to do so; but on account of the shortness of provisions he deemed it expedient to send back a third of his men in charge of Mr. Poole, his chief assistant, who had suffered much from scurvy. The party left the depôt on the 13th of June, 1845; and on the following day Mr. Poole suddenly expired, from internal hemorrhage, and his place was supplied by Mr. Piesse, the storekeeper.

After their departure, Captain Sturt again and again made excursions, in the hope of finding a practicable route to the north, but was each time driven back from some uncontrollable cause. On the last occasion he rode eight hundred and forty-three miles in five weeks, and for twelve weeks was exposed to the perils of excessive heat, insufficient food, and loathsome water, which resulted in a severe attack of scurvy and a painful affection of the eyes. At the end of January, 1846, he arrived in Adelaide. The results of the expedition may be summed up as follows:— Knowledge was gained of an immense stony desert in the interior, which it was found impossible to penetrate or even to skirt sufficiently to ascertain its extent in any direction attempted at that time; a large creek was discovered (named by Captain Sturt "Cooper's Creek," in honour of Sir Charles Cooper, the Chief Justice), and which was afterwards found to be a continuation of the Victoria of Mitchell. It was satisfactory also for South Australians to know that most of the good country seen while out on this expedition was within the boundary of their own country.

In the same month of the same year that Captain Sturt started to explore the interior (namely, August, 1844), another expedition, the result of private enterprise, under the leadership of Mr. Darke, set forth from Port Lincoln and proceeded in the direction of Fowler's Bay, from whence a report had come, brought by runaway sailors, that good country was to be found. The explorers penetrated for about three hundred miles into the interior and found excellent country, but on the return journey their leader, Mr. Darke, was killed by the natives.

Not only was returning prosperity shown in the matter of exploration, but in various other departments there were signs of progress, probably in none more than in ecclesiastical affairs. Large accessions were made to the ministerial staff of the various religious bodies. The Church of Scotland had erected a new place of worship in Grenfell Street, and the Congregationalists an auxiliary one in Franklin Street. The members of the Church of Rome had welcomed their bishop, and commenced the erection of a place of worship on West Terrace. The Methodist New Connexion had re-opened the chapel in Hindley Street, and opened another in the village of Walkerville; the Primitive Methodists had received two new ministers; and other denominations either commenced operations or extended those already begun.

A picture of early days and scenes in a country Nonconformist chapel is graphically drawn up by an early settler thus:—

"It was in the very wet winter of 1849 that we first attended the little church at McLaren Vale. No place of worship in all Christendom could have been more bare or unadorned than that. A barn-like building, the thatch the only ceiling, broad square windows letting in the sunshine to waken sleepers, and a very shaky deal structure called a pulpit.

"There were two square pews with doors, which were thought much of by the two families who sat in them; two benches with arms and backs occupied by families next in honour, while ordinary folk sat on slabs of wood propped up on bricks. At one time a sofa-bedstead, and at another a chest of drawers with a saddle on the top, were kept in the church.

"But if the place was primitive, the people were also. The drone of the singing, the waving of the peppermint-gum branches to keep away the flies, the minister's little boy on the pulpit-step catching flies by the dozen by that slow movement of the hand peculiar to the young colonial, the old-fashioned toilets, and the dogs! Very cheerful chat used to go on outside the door before and after service, and sometimes dinner was taken there, so as to be ready for school in the afternoon. The children were marvels of unknowing freshness. A teacher showing a picture to a little boy in the Sunday school, of a man cutting down a tree, the child examined it with the keenest interest, and then said, 'I reckon he'll have it down by next Sunday.'" *

* Quoted in "Jubilee Record of Congregationalism," by Rev. F. W. Cox.

The affairs of the Church of England had not, prior to this year (1845), been in so flourishing a condition as might have been expected. The Rev. C. B. Howard had laboured alone till 1840, when the Rev. James Farrell arrived to share in the work, which had largely increased. In addition to the Church of the Holy Trinity, there was by that time St. John's, in the eastern part of the city, and shortly afterwards places of worship were erected at the Port and on the Sturt, and these two clergymen performed the services at the two city churches regularly, and at the other two occasionally.

In 1840 the South Australian Church Building Society was formed for the purpose of aiding in the erection of churches and Sunday schools. Mr. Howard worked very arduously and earnestly in this cause, and his death in July, 1843, at the early age of thirty-six, was attributed in large measure to anxiety with regard to the responsibility he had undertaken as a trustee in this matter. On the 23rd of July he was buried. The Government offices were closed; the Governor and most of the officials, the soldiery, police, ministers of all denominations, citizens, and Sunday-school children, formed part of the imposing funeral *cortége*, and it is scarcely an exaggeration to say that his loss was mourned by every man, woman, and child in the place. After the death of Mr. Howard, the Rev. J. Farrell was the only clergyman in the colony, and remained so for two or three years. By his energy in raising funds, Trinity Church, which had become heavily encumbered by debt, was saved from being disposed of as a granary or store, or from falling into the hands of the Roman Catholics—both dangers being imminent.

The year 1845 was one of marked tranquillity, although not without alarms of various kinds. On two occasions the colonists were greatly agitated on the question of convictism. Early in the year, it was announced that the home Government intended to send out a shipment of the Parkhurst prison boys. This was regarded as a gross infraction of the principles upon which the colony was founded, and at once a large meeting was called, which pledged itself to resist by all lawful means the introduction of such characters into the province. A memorial to Lord Stanley was drawn up, and in the end the memorialists carried the day.

Later in the year (September), there was another scare, and this time the threatened danger was the proposed introduction of conditionally pardoned men from Van Diemen's Land.

The following notice had been published in the Tasmanian newspapers:—" Notice is hereby given to all holders of conditional pardons who may be desirous of having such pardons extended to the limits of the Australian colonies and New Zealand, that upon making their application for the said extension of indulgence to this office, they will be laid before the Lieutenant-General in order that those approved of by his Excellency may be immediately granted."

The ordeal of trial by public meeting was again resorted to, and a vigorous protest was made with good effect; the conditionally pardoned men never came to the colony.

Another source of anxiety was the extraordinary prevalence of bush-fires. They generally occurred on the Mount Lofty ranges, and in the height of summer presented a scene of great grandeur. They had a singular effect on the atmosphere, sometimes reproducing an Etna or a Vesuvius, at others extending for a considerable distance along the sides or tops of the hills, causing a lurid glare, and sending up dense volumes of smoke. In proportion as population increased, great damage was done to property, and active steps were taken to prevent these fires; but their origin was always involved in doubt, many ascribing them to ignition by friction of the long dry grass, to the firing of the country by the natives in order the more readily to obtain wild animals, to the carelessness of travellers who did not properly stamp out their camp-fires, or to smokers scattering the live ashes of their pipes on the dry grass or other inflammable substances.

The greatest event of the year had to do, not with fears and alarms, but with a discovery which was to prove a source of incalculable wealth and prosperity to the colony.

Towards the middle of June, it was reported that in the far north a shepherd had accidentally stumbled on a lump of copper ore, of almost incredible richness and purity, cropping out of the surface, and that he had brought specimens into Adelaide. It was further stated that the deposit of copper was traceable for fifteen miles, and was visible for a breadth of from fifteen to twenty feet. There was so much secrecy kept as to the locality that many pretended to regard the affair as a hoax; those in the secret assured themselves, however, of the correctness of the shepherd's report, and an application was forthwith made to the Governor for a special survey of twenty thousand acres in one block, in accordance with the Crown lands regulations. Captain Grey was willing enough to further the object, but a monetary difficulty arose. How was the requisite £20,000 to be raised? The colony was only beginning to recover from its financial embarrassments, and hard cash was a very scarce commodity, the banks collectively having at that time only about £25,000 in coin and bullion, and neither bank-notes, promissory notes, nor anything short of gold, silver, or copper coin was accepted at the Treasury in payment for land. There was no time to be lost, for if the news of the discovery reached England, or even one or more of the other colonies, the prize might pass out of the hands of South Australians altogether.

As the first applicants were unable to raise the necessary funds, one or two other parties combined and made the attempt, but were also unsuccessful. The first applicants, as might be supposed, entered their protest against the second party, and as neither could succeed, war waged between them. Those two organised parties were known familiarly as the "Nobs" and the "Snobs," the former being leading capitalists, and the latter, for the most part, tradesmen.

Mr. William Giles, the manager of the South Australian Company, might be considered as a third party, he having offered to advance £10,000, leaving the Nobs, or capitalists, to make up the remainder. But even this was not forthcoming, and the tradesmen tried to coalesce with Mr. Giles. As, however, their offer was not accepted, they determined to prevent the other side from entering the field by withdrawing from the bank the amount of their united funds in specie!

At this stage the Governor, seeing there was so wide a division in the camp, postponed for a few days the time for receiving tenders for the coveted block of land, and this gave the rival parties an opportunity to mature their plans — no easy matter, while excitement remained at white heat and suspense almost unbearable. Previous to the Governor's determination becoming known, Mr. Giles and his party had offered £12,000 in sovereigns and the cheque of the bank for the remaining £8000. Another party followed with a somewhat similar offer, having raised the sum of £10,000 by the sale of property and the payment of exorbitant premiums for money, the bank having refused to discount their bills, or make them any advance for the projected speculation.

Ultimately Mr. Giles withdrew from the contest, leaving the two rival parties in possession of the field, and as neither could separately obtain the prize, they agreed to become joint purchasers and participators in the coveted treasure. Their application for the twenty thousand acres at Burra Creek was lodged with the Governor on the 18th of August, only two days prior to the limit of time allowed by the Government for completing the purchase, and the £20,000 in specie was duly paid into the Treasury.

Although the two parties agreed to unite for the purchase of the land, they did not intend to work the mine in concert, and arrangements were therefore made for a division of the property into northern and southern blocks, the possession to be decided by lot. The northern and richest half fell to the "Snobs," or tradesmen's party, who were henceforth known as the South Australian Mining Association, and their mine as the Burra, while the southern half was called the Princess Royal Mine.*

The Burra Mine is situated about a hundred miles from Adelaide, the road being for the most part over level or gently undulating ground. The hills in the mineral district range generally north and south, and vary from 2000 to 2500 feet above the sea-level.

In the course of two or three years the £5 shares became worth £220, a fact in the history of mining at that time probably unparalleled. For the first six years the produce of the mines amounted to nearly 80,000 tons of copper ore, and the profit obtained on the working for that period was no less than £438,552, or nearly half a million. These results were arrived at under several disadvantages, but chiefly from the absence of machinery, the amount of unskilled labour, and the distance the ore had to be conveyed over unmade roads.

When at the end of June, 1845, and shortly after the discovery of the Burra Mine, Captain Grey called the Legislative Council together for the despatch of public business, his opening address was of a highly gratifying character. He was able to announce that the finances of the colony were in a very satisfactory state; the Government was able to make prompt payment of all obligations it had contracted, and rapid progress was being made in the general wealth and prosperity. One of the most important measures brought forward in the Legislative Council in this year by the Governor, was a Bill for the repeal of the pilotage, tonnage, wharfage, and all other port

* "The effect of the combination to purchase the Burra-Burra mines was," says the biographer of Sir George Grey, "that the ownership was thus distributed amongst a very large number of deserving people, who, with their families, enjoyed considerable benefits from these rich mines for many years. This effort to spread as widely as possible the advantages arising from the ownership of lands or mines, or, indeed, any of the forces of Nature, was typical of Captain Grey's lifelong desire."

and harbour dues and charges, thus opening Port Adelaide and all other ports within the province to ships of all nations, free of expense in entering, remaining, and departing. To make up for any monetary deficiency certain judicious customs duties were imposed. It was a measure that not only created great surprise, but gave unqualified satisfaction, and a public meeting was held to accord the thanks of all classes of the community to the Governor, and to pledge themselves to give him their support. As a matter of fact he stood in the proud position of being the first in the Australian colonies to follow the enlightened policy originally adopted by Sir Stamford Raffles at Singapore. Besides the increase of trade and traffic that would ensue, it would also ensure a sufficient supply of shipping to convey the export produce of the colony to the British or other markets. During the previous export season there had been some 6000 tons of colonial produce for shipment, and there was only the prospect of sufficient shipping to convey 3000 tons, while the want of hundreds of tons of shipping was actually experienced.

It was a curious fact that whereas during the period of the financial crisis the colonists could not say anything severe enough with regard to the administration of the Governor, in 1844-45, when it was found that he had successfully tided them over their difficulties, they were equally at a loss to find adequate words of praise.

At the close of the session, the members of the Council thanked him for his kind bearing to them individually and collectively, and expressed their conviction that "the urbanity of his manners to them, and the courteous attention he had given to their opinions and suggestions, had conduced to that perfect freedom of discussion which was necessary to the efficiency of the Council as a legislative body, and so essential to its obtaining the confidence of the whole community."

Alas! that the recognition of merit came so late in this case as in so many others. Only two months later, and the rumour ran through the colony that Captain Grey had been appointed to the Governorship of New Zealand, on the ground of his peculiar qualifications for dealing with the natives, who were in a disturbed state, and that Major Robe was to succeed him.

A forensic mania had set in. The English newspapers brought an account of the addresses in the Imperial Parliament on the appointment; how Lord John Russell, in an excellent speech, had said that, in giving Captain Grey the government of South Australia, he had given him as difficult a problem in colonial administration as could be committed to any man. "And I must say," added Lord John, "that, after four or five years' experience of his administration there, he has solved that problem with a degree of energy and success which I could hardly have expected from any one. He has extricated the colony and gained the good will both of settlers and aborigines."

Not less flattering was the testimony borne by Sir Robert Peel to the character and efficient services of Captain Grey.

When, therefore, on the 20th of October, he announced to the Legislative Council that so soon as the *Elphinstone* would be ready to proceed to sea he would, in pursuance of her Majesty's commands, hand over the administration of the Government to the officer who had been sent out to relieve him, the voice of the whole people was heard in lamentation for their loss and praise for the leader they had so little appreciated, and all the intervening days of his sojourn in Adelaide were spent in receiving and replying to addresses.

On Sunday, the 26th of October, the *Elphinstone* weighed anchor and proceeded on her voyage with Captain Grey on board, bound for the scene of his new, but at that time not very promising field of labour, and bearing with him the respect, good will, and good wishes of almost every settler in South Australia.

He had lived down incessant, flagrant, and altogether

unmerited abuse and opposition, conscious that he was in the right and that his motives were pure; he had proceeded from first to last in a straight line of policy, with judgment, decision, and firmness, and his reward was in the fact that he had saved the colony from a chaotic state, and placed it on a sound and solid basis, and had proved himself one of the foremost political and financial reformers of his day.

From the day when Captain Grey received the first inkling of his appointment to the Governorship of South Australia, to the day when he quitted it to take office in New Zealand, he was greatly indebted to the wisdom, experience, and sagacity of Mr. George Fife Angas, who probably knew more of the actual condition of the colony than any other man then living. A series of valuable letters, many of which are preserved in the public library at Auckland, New Zealand,* were written by him, and were extremely helpful to the Governor throughout his administration.

"The friendship of these two men," says the biographer of Sir George Grey, "commenced when the young explorer was in England, in 1840. Anxious to learn the views of a man so interested and experienced in questions of colonization, on the Government project of founding a colony on the north coast of Australia, Grey sought and obtained an interview with Mr. Angas. The latter strenuously opposed the plan, foreseeing many difficulties and disasters. Years afterwards, he raised his voice in the Legislative Council of South Australia against the proposed settlement being made, except as a purely tropical colony, with aid from Calcutta and London.

"Mr. G. F. Angas was one of the most sincere and untiring friends a young colony ever had. A director of the Company under whose auspices South Australia was founded, he lost no opportunity of doing it a service, sparing neither time, money, nor personal effort in its

---

* This voluminous correspondence, and certified copies of the letters in the Auckland library, are in the present possession of the writer, but instead of quoting it, an extract from the " Life of Sir George Grey " is given in preference.

cause. At the same time, he strongly disapproved of the extravagance which characterized the new community. No words can be more decided than those he used on this subject in writing to Captain Grey, in 1843 :—

"'You know my views as to the absolute necessity of settlers in a new colony adopting the most rigid economy in all their establishments and expenditure. A neglect of this has been the curse of South Australia, and the ruin of its best interests, and nothing has made it greater enemies at home and abroad.'

"These letters are remarkably interesting. They contain an account of the formation of the South Australian Society, and its first prospectus. They form a record of what was done by this one man during the term of Captain Grey's Governorship and residence at Adelaide. He was indeed helped and cheered by the co-operation and sympathy of the Governor, who furnished him with statistics and other information concerning the colony; but, in the details of his work, he was practically single-handed.

"He wrote pamphlets, publishing and circulating them at his own expense; he obtained interviews with Cabinet Ministers and other leaders of public opinion; he delivered lectures in every town through which he passed in travelling about Great Britain; he appointed agents, who were, he wrote, 'men of influence and devoted to South Australia,' to perform the same duties; he kept up an active correspondence for over three years with the owners of six or seven hundred American ships engaged in the South Sea whale-fisheries, with the object of inducing them to put into South Australia for their supplies.

"He was in constant communication with European States, with commercial houses in China, Mauritius, and Bombay, and with the various missionary societies; approaching the latter with a plan for establishing colleges in Adelaide, at which young men might receive a suitable training for future work amongst the heathen of the Pacific islands.

"In every direction from which prosperity might flow to the colony, Mr. Angas thus laboriously made a channel for its passage, turning up the sods of ignorance and apathy. He met with discouragements which would have caused one who had the real interests of the young community and of humanity less at heart, to give up the weary struggle in despair. But, foiled at one point, Mr. Angas only turned with fresh energy to another.

"Thus he wrote: 'When I found our Government resolved upon doing nothing for us, I commenced an active correspondence with the Continent, and I do confidently expect that we shall get out one hundred Germans this spring to Adelaide. Often enough, my spirit sinks under my incessant labour, on the one hand from the shameful, cruel, and ungrateful treatment I have met with from many persons in the colony, who have thereby amply repaid me for having been their best and most generous friend, and on the other hand from the utter apathy which universally exists in this country towards the colony. Still, I will never abandon the work as long as God enables me to continue it. I began it with the best of intentions, and I shall not leave it in this extremity.'

"In February, 1844, he wrote that if his resources had not been crippled by the dishonesty of agents in South Australia, he would have been able to send out from one to two thousand Germans as settlers. 'But,' he added, 'beaten down as I am with all my troubles, I will not rest until you have emigration renewed from this country.'

"Mr. Angas was successful in his introduction of German colonists, and, at his own expense, settled large tracts of agricultural country. Many of these communities still retain their Teutonic character. This experiment worked so well that years afterwards Sir George Grey, when Governor of Cape Colony, carried it out on a larger scale, under somewhat different conditions, and with still more marked success. . . .

"It is a mournful criticism upon the justice of human judgment to find that after the lapse of a quarter of a century, when Mr. Angas was upwards of eighty years of age, his claims to the gratitude of South Australia and the South Australians were treated with contempt, his long years of faithful service depreciated, and his lavish expenditure of money and zeal turned into derision.

"In 1869 Sir George Grey himself, smarting under unmerited coldness and neglect, received from his old fellow-worker in South Australia a pathetic letter claiming his sympathy, and asking Sir George Grey to bear testimony to the unselfishness of his efforts for the well-being of the colony, for which, in years long gone by, they had worked so zealously together. The answer given must have done much to soothe the wounded feelings of Mr. Angas, and to vindicate his undoubted services to the colony.

"The instability of human affairs was thus strikingly exemplified. Mr. Angas had served the people with a loyal and unswerving faith, and the people had forsaken him. Sir George Grey had served the Government of Great Britain with unexampled vigour and success, and, as a reward, was dismissed contemptuously. Yet history will record the deeds and achievements of both when the names of their detractors are forgotten."[*]

Of the subsequent brilliant career of Sir George Grey we cannot concern ourselves in detail here. After settling the New Zealand difficulty, and bringing the war to a successful termination, he was made a baronet and a D.C.L. of the Oxford University. He was appointed Governor of Cape Colony, and some years later, by special request of the Colonial Office, again became Governor of New Zealand, when the long Maori War at Taranaki was raging. Eventually he took up his residence in New Zealand as a private citizen, accepted an office and a seat in the colonial Legislature, an instance probably without a parallel of a statesman entering the political arena in the very colony where he had himself been twice the Governor.

[*] "Life and Times of Sir George Grey, K.C.B.," by W. L. Rees and L. Rees. London: 1892.

CHAPTER VIII.

ADMINISTRATION OF MAJOR ROBE.

OCTOBER 25TH, 1845—AUGUST 12TH, 1848.

A Tory of the Tories.—A Bad Beginning.—A Royalty on Minerals proposed.—Public Excitement thereon.—Mr. W. E. Gladstone on the Position of Colonial Governors.—Import Duty on Corn—Canada and South Australia.—Imposition of Royalty on Minerals.—Specimen of South Australian Oratory.—Historical Scene in Legislative Council.—Unpopularity of the Governor.—State Aid to Religion.—Political Dissenters.—League for the Maintenance of Religious Freedom.—State Aid granted.—Return of Captain Sturt from Interior.—Geological Observations of the Governor.—Explorations of Mr. J. A. Horrocks.—Education Bill.—Steam Communication with England.—Arrival of Dr. Short, Bishop of Adelaide.

ON the 14th of October, 1845, all conjectures as to the successor of Captain Grey were set at rest by the arrival in the colony of Major Frederick Holt Robe, of the 87th Royal Irish Fusiliers, who had been appointed by her Majesty to the Governorship of South Australia. He had at one time held the office of military secretary at Mauritius, under Major-General Sir William Nicolay, and at the date of his appointment to South Australia he was holding a similar office at Gibraltar. In order to obtain the services of Captain Grey in New Zealand as quickly as possible—for affairs were in a disturbed and critical state there—Major Robe was instructed to proceed direct from Gibraltar, *via* Alexandria and the Isthmus of Suez, to Bombay, where the *Elphinstone* was in readiness to convey him to South Australia, the vessel then to proceed forthwith to New Zealand with Captain Grey.

Major Robe was in almost every respect a startling contrast to his predecessor. He was a blunt, honest soldier, well versed in his profession, but his manners were not prepossessing, nor had he those gifts and graces which tend to make men popular. He knew nothing of the art of public speaking, and this in itself created a prejudice against him in many quarters; he was unfortunately a bachelor, and this, from a social point of view, was a great drawback, as a lady should always accompany a Governor, and take her place as leader of society; he was a Tory of the Tories, and proclaimed from the housetop his "aversion to popular tendencies;" he was an undisguised advocate of High Church principles, and took no pains whatever to conceal his abhorrence of Nonconformity.

There are many things in heaven and on earth and in the Colonial Office which are not dreamed of in the philosophy of ordinary mortals, and how Major Robe could have been selected to fill the office of Governor in "the Paradise of Dissent" will probably ever remain a mystery. It is only just to add in this place that he was an honourable, upright man, greatly respected in the limited sphere of his personal friendships, and true as steel to his Sovereign and to the political party whose views he was determined, if it lay in his power, should predominate throughout the colony.

For prudential reasons Major Robe was gazetted *Lieutenant*-Governor, the object being to protect Captain Grey from any proceedings that might be taken against him by the holders of certain dishonoured bills drawn upon the British Government, and for which the parties refused to take debentures. So long, therefore, as Captain Grey retained official connection with the colony as "Governor," he was entitled to the protection which pertained to that office.

Shortly after Major Robe assumed the government of the province a notice appeared in the *Gazette* informing all who had claims upon the Government that debentures would be made and issued with the interest due thereon to the 31st of March, 1846, that they could be obtained on application, and that no further interest would be allowed after that date. This intimation was satisfactory enough for those whose claims were admitted, but its obligatory character did not prevent those whose accounts were disputed from subsequently obtaining the whole or a portion of the amount due to them.

One of his first acts was to rescind certain resolutions, issued shortly before by his predecessor, for regulating the disposal of waste lands, on the ground that in most cases the regulations had operated disadvantageously to the colonial interests. He claimed the right to submit any lands that had passed the hammer, but had acquired a higher value than the upset price first put upon them, a second time to public auction, instead of allowing them to be selected by private contract. This measure, as a matter of course, met with considerable disapprobation, the *Observer* dubbing the new Governor as " principal Land-Jobber and Auctioneer-in-chief (by appointment) to her Majesty."

This was a bad beginning, but it was no fault of the Governor—it was simply his misfortune. He was a military man of the old school, and had been accustomed to rule and to be obeyed; he was totally unable to realize the genius of a rising colony or to sympathize with the liberal views and sturdy independence of the men over whom he was officially placed, and thus it was that from first to last he was continually "in hot water," and aroused the controversial spirit among the colonists to its highest degree.

In November news was received that Lord Stanley had made an attempt to introduce a new Waste Lands Bill into the Imperial Parliament, containing clauses imposing a royalty or reservation on the minerals raised, in violation of an Act previously passed and which had been in operation some years. The Bill was stated to have been defeated by Lords Lansdowne and Monteagle, who thus laid the colony under a deep obligation. But the matter did not rest here. Lord Stanley prepared an altered measure, submitted it to members during the recess, and in the mean time obtained the opinion of the law officers of the Crown, who considered that the existing Act would bear the construction that a royalty on, or reservation of, minerals might be admitted; whereupon he sent a despatch to the Lieutenant-Governor advising the imposition, forwarding at the same time the text of the legal opinion.

The colonists were up in arms, and at once a public meeting was called to express regret that such a Bill as the one Lord Stanley had brought forward should ever have been devised; that it was an uncalled-for interference with the proper duties of the Legislative Council as it related to the internal government of the province; that it was a breach of public faith under which most of the colonists had emigrated to South Australia, and that, if any such alteration as that proposed of the perfect tenure under which the waste lands had hitherto been purchased were carried into effect, it would discourage all further introduction and investment of capital, and in other respects be fatal to the interests and prosperity of the colony. It was resolved that appeal should be made to her Majesty for protection, and that, until the Queen's action should be made known, the Governor should be strongly entreated to suspend or defer the operation of the measure.*

A little glimpse into the mental attitudes of Governor and people may be obtained from the speeches made when the petition to her Majesty, signed by seven hundred colonists, was presented, with a memorial to the Governor, by a deputation consisting of a number of members of the Legislature, justices of the peace, and leading colonists. Major O'Halloran was the spokesman on behalf of the deputation, and in concluding his speech he said—" We yield to none in

---

* It may be noted in passing that at this meeting Mr. John Baker, destined to take a leading part hereafter in the Legislature, made his maiden speech in public.

attachment to our Sovereign and her Crown, but we are not prepared to bow the knee to the present or any other minister who may be disposed to trample on our rights or tamper with our interests."

Then uprose the Governor, cold and stern, and said—

"Your memorial stigmatizes as oppressive certain proposed measures of the Queen's Government having reference to her Majesty's waste lands in this part of her dominions, and you entreat me, in the event of those measures having actually passed the Houses of Parliament, to interpose such authority as may be confided to me in order to frustrate for a period the intentions of the Queen and of the Parliament. It is barely consistent with common sense to imagine that such large discretion would in any case be confided to a local governor of so distant a possession of the Crown, and you make this request at a time when it is a matter of public notoriety that the measures of which you complain have not met the sanction of the Imperial Parliament. Under these circumstances you will not be surprised at my declining to give any other reply to your memorial than an assurance that I will at all times feel pleasure in being made the medium of transmitting, for presentation to the Queen, the dutiful and loyal petitions and addresses which her Majesty's subjects in this province may desire to have laid at the foot of the throne."

A traveller once said of Niagara, "No picture can give you any true idea of it; you may paint the Falls, but you cannot paint the *roar* of the waters!" In like manner, type may give the words of Major Robe, but it is impossible to reproduce the austere tone and the irritating style in which his simplest utterances were given. As a matter of fact, in the instance under notice the colonists were premature; the measure did not receive the sanction of the Imperial Parliament, and the Bill of Lord Stanley was thrown out. So ended the first skirmish on the royalty question. The great battle was to be fought at a future period.

In December, Mr. W. Giles, on behalf of the South

Australian Company, brought an action against the Lieutenant-Governor for refusing to allow him (Mr. Giles) to exercise certain preliminary land orders in the selection of some mineral sections near the Montacute Mine. The judge refused to allow the action to proceed, alleging that the Company had not used due diligence after Captain Grey's proclamation to the holders of land orders in which the time was fixed for making the selection.

At that time Mr. Gladstone was Secretary of State for the Colonies, and as soon as he became aware that an action had been brought against the Governor, he forwarded a despatch to him expressing strong disapprobation of the course pursued. Adverting to the refusal of the Court to grant the injunction, he said—

"It is fortunate that such was the decision of the Court. An opposite judgment might have raised many embarrassing difficulties. But," he added, "I cannot sanction the course which you followed in this case. By appearing, or permitting any officer of the Crown to appear, in defence of such a suit, you virtually acknowledged that the head of the local Government was amenable to the jurisdiction of the courts of the colony which he governs. It does not follow that because the question of jurisdiction was not discussed on this occasion, it was therefore not decided or compromised. On the contrary, the absence of any such discussion, resulting as it did from the absence on your part of any such objection, was a clear though tacit acknowledgment that the asserted jurisdiction really existed. I object to that acknowledgment, not on any ground of mere dignity, or usage, or precedent, but because thus to break down the barriers which separate the judicial and administrative authorities must result in great practical evils. The immunities of the Sovereign in this country, and the corresponding immunities of a Governor in the colony he rules, exist for the good of the people at large. If it were admitted that you, as Governor of South Australia, were amenable to the courts of the colony, you would of course be liable to fine, to distress, and imprisonment at their bidding."

The despatch concluded—

"I must therefore desire that the precedent which has been established in this case be avoided in all future cases, and that no act be done (except with the express previous sanction of her Majesty's Government) from which it could be inferred that you are amenable to the jurisdiction of any court in South Australia so long as you retain her Majesty's commission for the administration of the government of that colony."

It is somewhat singular that Major Robe, who had assumed the title of Lieutenant-Governor expressly for the protection of his predecessor, should have overlooked the position which the Governor of the colony is generally supposed to occupy, and of which his own case furnished such a striking illustration.

Towards the end of the year intelligence arrived that the Imperial Parliament had taken some action upon certain memorials sent home from the Australian colonies generally, praying for the removal of import duty on their corn. In the debate Lord Howick pointed out the injustice of admitting corn from Canada free of duty, characterizing the concession as a bribe to secure the good will of that colony towards Britain, but admitting that the boon was a conditional one requiring the Canadians to levy a duty on American corn, so that the United States should not send their produce to Britain through Canada. He urged that there need be no apprehension of foreign grain reaching Britain through the Australian colonies, as Chili, the nearest country from which these colonies could obtain a supply, was too far off to admit of any such traffic being carried on profitably.

In the course of a very able speech Lord Howick said—

"I maintain that by refusing this concession to Australia you are teaching Canada that it has nothing to be grateful for. You teach it that what you have done has not been from a sense of justice, or for the common advantage of the Empire, but that it was a bribe for acquiescing in the continuance of your Government. It is like the money given by the Roman Empire in its decline to the barbarians who were threatening at the gates—it is sure to purchase only further demands. On the other hand, if you now act to Australia, from which you have nothing to fear, as you have acted towards Canada, you are showing to your colonies generally that you are acting on the principle of a large and liberal policy and a desire to promote their welfare as integral portions of the British Empire."

It was certainly a hard case that Canada, near to the United States, dissatisfied and rebellious, should have the duty on her corn reduced, while Australia, patient and loyal, with no dangerous neighbour, had no relief or indulgence. Lord Howick had shot his arrows at the right mark. If the colonies were integral parts of the Empire, and not mere excrescences, what need was there for any commercial restrictions? And the Australians felt and complained that whilst they had soil and climate for the ample growth of corn, they were checked by Britain denying them a market, and they reasonably urged that if such a market were allowed it would enable the settlers to consume British manufactured goods—their chief article of import—to a greatly enlarged extent.*

It must always be borne in mind that South Australia was well represented in England by able men deeply interested in everything that concerned her welfare, and in many cases financially pledged to her prosperity, so that questions discussed in the colony were more

* "The singularity of the necessity for such an Act is only equalled by the novelty of the measure itself, which is probably without precedent, in delegating to an officer, irresponsible to the people, the power of taxation, without limit as to the amount or time, on the export of any article enumerated in the Act. And one can hardly realize in the present day that a country that was reduced to such an extremity should, after a lapse of a few years, become for the number of its people the greatest exporters of wheat and flour in the world."—Sir Henry Ayers.

or less re-echoed in the mother country, and *vice versá*. The South Australian Association, too, was still in existence, and its members were active both in and out of Parliament on her behalf, and through the persevering labours of these combined forces the obnoxious tax on corn, as well as many other well-founded grievances, was in process of time removed.

The year 1846 opened prosperously with a balance in hand of £50,000 applicable to the purposes of immigration, local improvements, and the satisfaction of outstanding claims. One matter that gave rise to mingled hope and apprehension was the ever-increasing yield of mineral wealth. In itself this was encouraging, but many colonial interests seemed likely to suffer from the investment of much capital in unproductive mines, and from the withdrawal of labour of various kinds to the new pursuit.

The question of royalties on minerals was revived on the 5th of March by the publication in the Government *Gazette* of a minute from the Governor informing the public of the rules that had been established for the future disposal of the waste lands of the Crown in South Australia, by which it was intended to secure a royalty of one-fifteenth upon all minerals raised from lands alienated from the Crown. Major Robe stated that the correspondence handed to him by his predecessor showed that the mineral wealth of the colony had attracted the attention of capitalists in England to a considerable extent, and a company in London had proposed to the Secretary of State for the Colonies to treat with the Government for a monopoly of all mines in South Australia belonging to the Crown, upon the basis of a lease, with rights of mining upon payment of a seignorage or royalty upon the produce of those mines. Lord Stanley rejected this proposal, but the question of reservation of royalties with a view to the ulterior benefit of the colony was submitted for the consideration of her Majesty's Commissioners of Woods and Forests, and to the Colonial Land and Emigration Commissioners, as well as to one of the first geologists in

England, and subsequently to her Majesty's law advisers. No objection was raised by any of these to the proposed imposition, and as regarded the colonists themselves, Major Robe said in a minute to the home authorities :—

"I do not anticipate that there will be much difference of opinion amongst the colonists upon the question of the expediency of reserving a moderate royalty on metallic minerals when it is declared, under authority, that the proceeds thereof, after deducting the cost of collection, will be applied to the same purposes as the gross proceeds of the sale of the waste lands of the Crown under the Act 5 & 6 Vict. c. 36. Instead of large present receipts, founded, perhaps, on gambling speculation as to the chances or probabilities of future results (which receipts will cease as soon as all the mineral land has been selected), there will be provided in aid of a constant stream of emigration from the United Kingdom, a growing income proportioned to the advancing wealth of the colony. Such is the view taken by the Commissioners and by her Majesty's advisers, and in that view I entirely concur."

But the colonists did not, nor did they agree with the "few short rules based upon the principle of a royalty of one-fifteenth of the produce" which the Governor had drawn up.*

* The published regulations stipulated for a right of free access to all mines by duly appointed servants of the Crown; a right to select, for free occupancy, a portion of land not exceeding a quarter of an acre, near the mouth of any mine, for a residence or store "for the person or persons appointed to receive the Queen's dish or dues;" the right of commuting from time to time, for periods not exceeding twelve months, the Queen's fifteenth in kind for payments in money; the right of recovering such money by distress; the reference of all questions to the Governor in Executive Council, for decision; the sale of land, as heretofore, with the exception of the reservation stated; the reservation on lands open for selection without competition; the leasing of mineral lands for periods not exceeding twenty-one years, such leases to be subject to competition at public auction; the forfeiture of the leases for non-payment, underletting without license, etc.; the appropriation of the proceeds from sale or lease of lands and royalties; the fees payable for deeds, leases, and registration.

Nor did they agree with the law officers of the Crown, who gave it as their opinion that there was nothing incompatible with the provisions of the Act in the plan proposed. "The waste lands of the Crown," they said, "if alienated and conveyed, must be conveyed in the manner prescribed by the Act, but there is nothing in its provisions restrictive of the right which the Crown possesses to reserve to itself any portion of its property or interests, or which makes it compulsory to part with them."

The publication of the Governor's minute, together with the regulations for carrying it out and the opinion of the law officers of the Crown thereon, was the signal for a great demonstration against the measure. On a vacant acre at the corner of King William Street and North Terrace a platform, or hustings, was erected, which was crowded with members of Council, justices of the peace, and some of the most influential colonists, who, surrounded by a large and excited audience, characterized the action of the Government as "illegal, unjust, and impolitic, and, if persevered in, highly injurious to the best interests of the colony, as it would check the industry and exertions of the settlers, and discourage emigrants from Great Britain."

They argued that it was illegal, inasmuch as it set at naught the guarantees of the Act of Parliament, and unjust, as it was in direct contravention of the original tenure upon which the waste lands were alienated from the Crown and thereby gave to the colony one of its peculiar features.

One of the resolutions moved at the meeting by Mr. E. Stephens, J.P., and seconded by Mr. J. Baker, J.P., set forth that "the repeated attempts of the Colonial Office to set at naught in this colony the stipulations and solemn engagements guaranteed to the colonists by Acts of the Imperial Parliament are subversive of that confidence and respect which the settlers ever have entertained, and are desirous of continuing to entertain towards the parent State."

A short and typical specimen of South Australian

oratory in those early days may not be out of place here. In moving this resolution Mr. E. Stephens said—

"Her Majesty never had under that flag"—pointing to the royal ensign waving from the flagstaff at Government House—"a more devoted and loyal people than she has in South Australia. Under every infliction and every injury their loyalty has been unquestioned. But there were points at which they felt they could endure no longer, and no reckless and ruthless hand should destroy their rights or involve their privileges with impunity, and if such attempts were sanctioned by their rulers, nay, if they were not discountenanced by them, their loyalty and their devotedness were indeed endangered. It was true they had left the home of their fathers, but they were Britons still. They had left their native soil, but not for a foreign land; they had come hither to perpetuate her institutions, to introduce her laws, to share her privileges, to be governed by her wisdom, to link their destinies to hers; but they came also to enjoy her freedom. They came forth alone and unaided by the parent State to a land whose existence was almost unknown, to extend the boundaries of her empire, and by their energies, their industry, and their capital to add another flourishing province to her dominions. And did England out of her treasury assist them? Did she give to their departure pomp and circumstance? No. They crossed the wide waste of waters in humility, but with fixity of purpose, to make for themselves a home, and to found an empire in the wilderness. Not one shilling did England contribute. Nay, more, let it never be forgotten that before she suffered them to quit her shores she compelled them to leave behind twenty thousand pledges in the shape of so many pounds sterling, that they should be no burden to the parent State. These recent attempts by the Home Government to depart from the terms of the Act constituting the colony could be likened to so many nibbles at the seal of the bond entered into by the mother country and the colonists, and this royalty imposition was the last and most flagrant and most unjustifiable attempt to rob the colony of one of its guaranteed and peculiar features."

The ringing cheers that greeted this speech proved not only the spirit of sturdy independence in the colonists, but also the futility of sending as their Governor such a man as Major Robe. Petitions to both Houses of the Imperial Parliament were very numerously signed, and so this stage of the opposition closed.

The next step was taken in the Legislative Council on the 30th of September, when the New Waste Lands Bill was introduced by the advocate-general. The second reading was opposed by Mr. J. Morphett, who moved as an amendment that the Bill be read that day six months. This was seconded by Major O'Halloran, and supported by Messrs. Bagot and Davenport; but, upon a division, the amendment was lost, and the original motion carried.

Thereupon a scene ensued—one of the historic scenes of the colonial Legislature. Mr. J. Morphett rose from his seat, and, followed at once by Major O'Halloran and Messrs. Bagot and Davenport, left the council chamber, and by so doing left the august and astonished body without a quorum. The audience in the strangers' gallery shouted "Bravo!" while the Governor and his executive stood dumfounded. When silence was restored Major Robe declared the Council adjourned.

A week later the Council reassembled, and the Governor expressed in mild terms his disapproval of the unconstitutional mode of opposing the Government pursued by the non-official members; but the recalcitrant members justified their conduct, and retorted that it was the only course left open to them, as "his Excellency invariably neutralized the votes of independent members in every case when the votes were equal, and on every measure resisted by the non-officials."

On the motion for going into committee on the Bill, the recusant members proposed, seconded, and supported an amendment that it was inexpedient to do so until the fate of the measure proposed to be introduced into the English House of Commons became known. When the Council divided, the Governor again exercised his casting vote, and in announcing the result of the division said—

"Having vindicated the dignity of the Crown and asserted its right to insist on the presence of members, he had no hesitation in saying that he should, in deference to the strongly expressed opinion of all the non-official members, and in compliance with the earnest appeal of their senior (Major O'Halloran), authorize the withdrawal of the Bill."

Notwithstanding the unpopularity of the Governor, he took no steps whatever to mend his ways. On the contrary, he recklessly plunged into a fresh sea of controversy on a subject concerning which men are more tenacious of their opinions than on any other.

While the royalties question was still the topic of the day, the members and adherents of the Church of England called a public meeting to memorialize the Governor to make a grant in aid of religion from the public funds. Of course this stirred the Dissenters to action, and they attended the meeting in such force that when the first resolution was proposed by the Church party, affirming that such a grant was desirable, an amendment was moved by the Dissenters, and was carried by an overwhelming majority. The meeting being then in their hands, they passed resolutions condemning State aid to religion, and adopted a memorial to the Governor, urging him not to give effect to the views of the Church party. A deputation of leading men was appointed to present the memorial to the Governor, and in due course they waited upon him. The document having been read, they waited anxiously for his reply. It came in these terms: "I have no remarks to make, gentlemen;" and, bowing, he dismissed the deputation. Whether the discourtesy were intentional or not, it was, to say the least, irritating.

While feeling was still running high on this subject, and in the same session in which the royalties question had been so warmly discussed, Major Robe threw down the gauntlet for a pitched battle with the religious sects, by introducing the question of State aid to religion into the Council. He did so in these words: "The provisions heretofore made from the revenues of the province for purposes of religion and religious instruction are quite inadequate. Judging from returns lately laid before Parliament, it would appear that South Australia is one of the most backward of all the colonies of the British Empire in providing from its public resources for the means of worshipping that Being to whom we owe our existence and all the blessings we enjoy. This should not be; it is not in accordance with the spirit of the colonists themselves. Let it no longer be a reproach upon the Government and the legislative body of the province having control over the public finances. The members of the Church of England, forming more than half of the entire population, have lately received the benefit of two additional clergymen sent among them, but for these we are mainly indebted to the pious zeal of our friends in England. The due apportioning of Government aid among the different sects of professing Christians is a question of some difficulty, but it is not, I trust, unsurmountable."

In this speech Major Robe, more explicitly, perhaps, than in his other oracular utterances, showed his total incapacity to grasp an idea of the principles on which the colony was founded. A Tory of the Tories, relying on the vote of the officials in the Legislative Chamber and his own casting vote, and unduly prejudiced in favour of his own opinions, he had set his mind on carrying a measure which the most bigoted would have been ready to acknowledge was diametrically opposed to the ideas of the fathers and founders of the colony, to the Act of Parliament establishing it, and to the wishes of the large majority of the colonists.

The history of this principle of disassociation of Church and State is one of the most interesting in colonial annals. Let us now follow the present phase of it.

On the second day of the session Mr. J. Morphett, destined hereafter to take a high place in the councils of the province, presented a petition, couched almost in the identical words of the Governor, praying for Government aid to religion and education. It added that the petitioners could not close their minds to the fact that the voluntary principle had hitherto proved utterly inadequate to supply the needs of the colony, and that they considered the true interests of every Government were best consulted by promoting the moral and religious well-being of the community.

There were hundreds of men who, on the strength of the voluntary principle being the law of the land, had emigrated to South Australia, and this was the signal for them to be up and doing. They held a meeting at the "Company's" offices in North Terrace to discuss measures for the defence and maintenance of religious freedom, and set forth in an elaborate memorial a long array of all the stock arguments against the proposal of the Governor—arguments too well known to need specifying in detail—and concluded with the prayer "that every denomination should stand on its own basis, without State interference, favour, or support, and that no legislative enactment might be passed, or grant made, for support of religion in South Australia."

Despite motions in the Legislative Council by Mr. (afterwards Sir Samuel) Davenport and Captain Bagot, urging delay, and a petition from the advocates of voluntaryism, got up and signed in twenty-four hours by two hundred persons, including many ministers of religion, also urging delay, on the 16th of July Mr. J. Morphett moved in the Council "that his Excellency be requested to introduce with the estimates for the financial year 1847, a sum of money for religious and educational purposes, to be apportioned among the different denominations of Christians in the province in the rate of their numbers according to the late census returns, and to be applied by their respective bodies either in building places of public worship, the support of ministers of religion, the erection of school-houses, or the maintenance of schoolmasters or schoolmistresses; the sums, as apportioned, to be paid to, and appropriated by, a limited number of individuals in the nature of trustees to be nominated by the respective bodies; the trustees to furnish a report to his Excellency the Governor of the appropriation, accompanied by a proper statement of accounts to be laid before the Council."

The speciousness of this motion will be seen as we proceed. Amendments were moved against it, but were lost, and, the vote having been taken, the matter was allowed to rest for a time so far as the action of the Government was concerned.

Meanwhile, meetings were held, and the discussion of "political religion" became the order of the day. Deputations were sent to the Governor conveying memorials, the burden of which was in many cases that the vote of the Legislative Council in aid of religion without regard to its truth or error was a violation of the rights of conscience, by compelling individuals to contribute to the support of modes of worship or forms of doctrine which they believed to be unscriptural and erroneous; that it was a misappropriation of the public funds, a direct breach of the public pledges given at the foundation of the colony, and not justified by the then present circumstances of the province; and that it was, consequently, a measure inexpedient and unjust.

In the suddenness of its introduction, and the haste in which the vote had been passed, the advocates of voluntaryism had been taken at a disadvantage. True, there had been, during the administration of Captain Grey, a skirmish on the subject, but it was conceived that the ghost of a "State-aided Church" had been laid. Now it was determined that, whether on the present issue they lost or won, such steps should be taken that, when another opportunity arose, they would be in a position to fight the question to its bitter end. Accordingly, a society was formed, called "The South Australian League for the Maintenance of Religious

Freedom in the Province," its object being not only to oppose the present grant so far as it was still possible, but to adopt such measures as should prevent the perpetuity of any such action in the colony.

In a young colony, where the settlers are bent on making provision for their wives and families, and of seeing them in comfortable circumstances before the bread-winners shall be overtaken by illness or old age; where the restraints of the mother country are to a great extent thrown off, and every one feels himself to be his own master; when the old religious ties have to some degree been broken and the enthusiasm of Christian work has received a check by the breaking up of old associations, it is a good thing to see large bodies of men, at great self-sacrifice, take up with enthusiasm a question of this kind. If the moral history of South Australia were to be written this episode which we now chronicle would probably be represented as the sowing time of the great harvest of moral and spiritual good which was developed in later years.

One of the first steps undertaken by the League was to publish an address setting forth the position they proposed to occupy. "In all political matters we know that obedience is due to the Government. We may doubt the expediency or even the justice of their measures, but we are still bound to obey them, except in those rare cases which we may hope will never arise in this colony. But in religion we owe no obedience to the State. This is a matter beyond the control of Government and in which they cannot rightfully interfere. If the State should overstep its legislative boundaries in this matter, resistance is always the right, and may often be the duty, of every individual. It is a point upon which there can be no concession and no compromise, and at all times and under all circumstances we are bound to protest against, and, so far as may be done by lawful and peaceful means, to impede the execution of laws which violate these our highest and most essential rights. We are ready to 'render unto Cæsar the things that are Cæsar's,' but we render to God, and to God only, the things that are God's."

It was maintained, and maintained truly, that this principle was recognized in the Act of Parliament, and by the Commissioners originally appointed to carry it into execution; that in all printed statements this was set forth as an inducement to emigration, and that they were justified in requiring a fulfilment of the pledge which induced so many of them to emigrate.

The machinery of the League was soon in working order, information was disseminated, memorials to Queen and Parliament prepared, and it was soon apparent that the members were actuated by a purpose, and would shortly become the most able and active organization ever formed in the colony.

Meanwhile numerous petitions were presented in the Council Chamber for and against religious endowments, until, on the 19th of August, the question of a grant was formally introduced, when Mr. Morphett moved that the sum of £1110 10s. be placed upon the Supplementary Estimates for 1846, to be appropriated in accordance with the terms of his previous motion, with the addition that the trustees should be appointed in such manner as the Governor might by proclamation direct, subject to the proviso that such trustees should, on the 31st of March, 1847, make a report to the Governor, to be laid before the Legislative Council, of the manner in which the moneys had been applied.

An amendment was moved, but it was found that the mover and seconder were the only opponents to the grant.

It must be admitted that the sum was not a large one, although on a question of principle, of course, this was immaterial. The proportion for the Jews, who had petitioned to be included, was found to be £2 18s. per annum!

Less than a month later, the conduct of the Lieutenant-Governor and of the Legislative Council in voting this money in opposition to the declared sentiments of the great majority of the colonists was the subject of an appeal to her Majesty and to the Imperial Parliament for protection, the memorial to the Queen being signed by 2530 persons.

Eventually good came out of the apparent evil. The carrying of such a question in opposition to the wishes of the large majority raised at once the desire for a more popular system of representation, and zealous efforts were forthwith inaugurated to this end.

Before the year closed the Governor, who had been the cause of all the strife, had grown weary of his office, for which it must have been obvious to himself, as it was to everybody else, that he was unfit, and had appealed to the Home Government to relieve him of his responsibilities.

Notwithstanding the fact that the year 1846 was a year of controversy and political discontent, in other respects it was marked by progress and prosperity. On the 14th of January, 1846, the announcement was made of Captain Sturt's return from the interior, after an unsuccessful attempt to proceed beyond latitude 24° 30' and longitude 138° to the north-west and latitude 25° 45', longitude 139° 13' northwards. Both he and his party had suffered greatly from scurvy.

The arrival of the party at Adelaide was an event of deep interest, especially to those who had witnessed its outfit and start some eighteen months previously. The procession was as novel as it was interesting—the long beards of the brave fellows almost hid their faces, and, on account of the exposure to which they had been subjected, they appeared more like a race of beings from the regions into which they had penetrated than Europeans. The wheels of the drays were caulked and stopped up with whatever materials could be spared to fill up gaps and cracks to keep them together; the woodwork of the drays showed that every particle of oil and turpentine had been extracted by the heat of the sun. But the most singular object of attraction was the remainder of the flock of sheep following, from habit, the last of the drays, as quietly and regularly as a rear guard of infantry. As the expedition moved slowly up Rundle Street and King William Street, the spectacle appeared too impressive and suggestive to excite shouts or greetings, but many and hearty were the welcomes given when the party halted in Victoria Square.

In the early part of the year (1846) the Governor, accompanied by his private secretary and Mr. Burr, deputy surveyor-general, proceeded in the Government cutter, which on this occasion was commanded by Captain Lipson, R.N., harbour-master, for the purpose of examining the bays on the south-east coast of the colony, of which little was then known. The Governor reported favourably of Lacepede Bay and of Guichen Bay, at which a township had been laid out and was about to be offered for sale. During his six weeks' trip, in which he traversed about four hundred miles by land and as much by sea, he gained and imparted so much valuable scientific information, that towards the end of the year he was induced to take another trip, this time to Spencer's Gulf, to inspect the ports and inlets along the coast. On his return he officially reported the results of his visit, and in the course of his geological observations remarked that on the western side of the head of Spencer's Gulf the hills were of red sandstone, in strata nearly horizontal. "In other parts of the globe," he said, "coal is very frequently associated with this formation." At Lipson's Cove he observed that the rocks seen were gneiss and hornblende schist, nearly vertical and having a general course north and south. "This formation," he wrote, "is, in other countries, frequently rich in metallic ores." If Major Robe could only have made known how rich and extensive the mineral deposits on Yorke's Peninsula were, he would have made his name immortal. But the great discovery was not made until fifteen years later.

The only other attempt at exploration this year was undertaken in July by Mr. J. A. Horrocks, who, with a small party and a camel, set forth to explore the then unknown country north-west of the ranges of Mount Arden. Progress was reported from time to time, but in September came the sad tidings that by the accidental discharge of a gun Mr. Horrocks had been shot; mortification set in, and he died. The expedition, therefore, returned to Adelaide.

Wealth and prosperity, by the end of 1846, had now fairly taken the place of previous depression. Agricultural operations had been extensively increased, large land sales effected, vast mineral treasures developed, and trade and shipping considerably augmented. The result of this commercial revival was the recommencement of immigration.*

The new year (1847) opened auspiciously. Intelligence was received that Lord John Russell had succeeded Lord Stanley as Secretary of State for the Colonies, and that one of the first acts of the new Secretary had been to expunge the royalty clause from the imperial Waste Lands' Bill. In this direction, therefore, the horizon appeared clearer, but in another the clouds of religious dissensions were still gathering blackness.

In April the Governor submitted to the Legislative Council the reports of the trustees, showing how the grants in aid of religion and education had been distributed. A discussion ensued, in the course of which the Governor said he considered the plan adopted in New South Wales for the distribution of money in aid of religion and education was preferable to the one being carried out in South Australia, the principle of the former being to assist voluntary efforts in the proportion of half or equal the amount so raised; and a few days later he laid before the Council "A Bill to promote the Building of Churches and Places of Worship and to provide for the Maintenance of Ministers of Religion." It proposed that whenever a sum of not less than £150 had been raised by private contribution towards a church or chapel, a grant in aid should be allowed of any sum not exceeding the amount of the

* Four vessels arrived from England in one day, and 655 persons landed in one week.

private contribution, provided that no grant should exceed the sum of £300. As regarded ministers' stipends, when one hundred persons residing within a reasonable distance of a proposed place of worship subscribed to a declaration setting forth their desire to attend the same, the sum of £100 per annum would be granted towards the minister's stipend; when two hundred persons subscribed, the sum of £150 would be granted; and when five hundred subscribed, £200, which was to be the maximum rate in aid of stipends. Various other scales for a lesser number than one hundred subscribers were introduced into the Bill, together with elaborate clauses relating to the duties and obligations of trustees.

This Bill (which was designated by the *Observer* "a legislative curiosity") set the members of the League for the Maintenance of Religious Freedom to work in earnest, as it preserved all the objectionable features of the one it was intended to supersede and would infallibly perpetuate and augment the dissatisfaction, strife, and alienation caused by the former measure, more especially as this was framed on a model to suit the exigencies of a penal settlement.

On the second reading of the Bill the advocate-general undertook the defence of the measure, and a warm discussion followed. When the Council was in committee on the Bill many amusing views were propounded and some curious theological arguments adduced. Thus, one member (Mr. Hagen) was of opinion that the word "Christian" should precede "worship," and read "places of Christian worship." Major O'Halloran objected, on the ground that all those who contributed should benefit, whether Chinese, Hindoos, or New Zealanders, and by the proposed title the Jews would be excluded; to which the Governor replied, "He only understood the Council was legislating for the Christian religion—the Bill for the promotion of Mahommedanism was not yet before them!"

Meantime the League was busy in pulpit, press, and platform, all over the province, while Mr. George Fife

Angas, to whom the petition for aid in the mother country had been sent, was using every endeavour to bring the matter under the notice of members of Parliament and others in Great Britain interested in the question. But, notwithstanding all this, the Bill was read a third time and was carried.

During the session of the Council an elaborate financial statement was made, showing that the land sales had enabled the Governor to appropriate the sum of £160,000 to immigration purposes, and that arrangements had been made for the despatch from England of one vessel per month. A large sum was also available for public works and buildings. In the matter of education a Bill was introduced fixing the payment of teachers as follows:—Minimum rate for twenty scholars, £26, and maximum rate for fifty scholars and upwards, £50; for every advanced pupil, teachers should receive £1 per head additional. A Board of Education was constituted to carry out the provisions of the Bill.

On the 5th of October the Governor laid important despatches on the table from the Secretary of State, relative to (1) the Corporation of the city of Adelaide, advising the Council to bring in a Bill to establish it, if the colonists thought fit; (2) the threatened combination of the Land League, which Earl Grey regretted, as if the price of land were kept down by this means the flow of immigration would be checked; and (3) an acknowledgment of the petition to the Queen against State support to religion. It ran thus: "You will acquaint the petitioners that I have not been able to advise the Queen to assent to the request; on the contrary, it has been my duty humbly to submit to her Majesty my opinion that the course pursued by the local Legislature in applying some part of the local revenue towards the promotion of religion, knowledge, and education in the colony merits her Majesty's entire approbation, and it is not in any respect at variance with the terms of the Act of Parliament under which the colony was originally founded. The Queen has been graciously pleased to adopt and sanction that opinion."

A further despatch informed Major Robe that the Government had acceded to his request by removing him from the civil to the military service, and that Sir H. E. F. Young had been appointed as his successor in the government of the province. It soon transpired that Major Robe had been appointed to the rank of lieutenant-colonel in the army, and that his future work would be that of deputy quartermaster-general at Mauritius.

On the 5th of October the Council was adjourned *sine die,* but was called together again on the 9th of November to consider an important despatch on the subject of steam communication with the mother country, proposals for the conveyance of mails having been received by the Secretary of State from the Peninsular and Oriental Company and the Indian and Australian Company.

The estimated amount of postage charged upon letters and newspapers conveyed between the United Kingdom and the Australian colonies for the year ending October, 1847, was £14,799 14s. 4d. Preference was given to the Cape route as best for South Australia, and £3000 was agreed upon as the share of that colony towards the subsidy.

It was thought that this would be the last session in which Major Robe would take part, but unforeseen circumstances arose to delay his departure, and when, on the 2nd of June, 1848, the Legislative Council was opened, he was ready with the annual estimates—a duty that he had little anticipated would devolve upon him again. During that long interval there had been a comparative cessation from strife; no startling episodes had occurred, the stream of prosperity had been gliding along smoothly, and the foundation and development of new enterprises had not been neglected.*

Only one set of circumstances demands any detailed notice here, as it bears upon the "great controversy"

* See "Chronological Summary of Events" at end of work.

of that day and of a greater one looming in the distance.

In religious circles in the mother country there was a great revival of zeal on behalf of the missionary and colonial work of the Church, and the Baroness (then Miss) Burdett-Coutts had offered an endowment of £800 a year each for the foundation of four colonial dioceses, that of Adelaide being among the number. The preferment to the latter see fell to the Rev. Augustus Short, D.D., who, with the three other bishops, was consecrated in Westminster Abbey on the 29th of June, 1847, the occasion being one of unusual solemnity, the ceremony lasting over four hours. In December of that year Dr. Short arrived in Adelaide, and was formally inducted at Trinity Church, when her Majesty's letters patent were read, constituting South Australia a diocese, and "appointing Dr. Short to be the bishop thereof, under the style and title of Lord Bishop of Adelaide."

He arrived in critical times, while the Church and State storm was raging, and of course every step he took was watched with eager and jealous eyes. Before he had been long in Adelaide, the bishop, acting upon advice given to him before leaving England, and furnished with a formal land grant under the hand and seal of the Governor, proceeded to claim an acre of ground in Victoria Square as a site for a cathedral. But he had reckoned without his host. The local authorities declared that the document was *ultra vires*, and legal proceedings were commenced. For years the case dragged its weary length along, and it was not until 1855 that the Supreme Court decreed that Dr. Short could not enforce his claim, it being held that, though the Governor could grant waste lands, he could not interfere with the public reserves, of which Victoria Square was one.

On the 2nd of August, 1848, Colonel Robe took leave of the Legislative Council, and in concluding his speech said, "In relinquishing the duties which have devolved upon me under the appointment of her Majesty, I look to my Sovereign alone for any expression of approbation."

This was highly characteristic of the man. As an officer in the army he had learnt to obey orders to the letter, and expected prompt and submissive obedience from those over whom he was placed in authority. But he had found that the free subjects of a free colony would not submit to be treated as subalterns in the army, and, this being the case, he had wisely altered his manner and plans of procedure long before his removal from the colony. Although from his previous habits the position of Governor was not congenial, the knowledge and experience which length of residence gave him, both of the country and people, led him to become greatly attached to both, and his despatches for some time previous to his departure manifested the warm interest he took in the rise and progress of South Australia.

With all his official faults he was a man of stern inflexibility of character, and of a high sense of duty; a master in official routine, and a prince in hospitality.

Not a few, both in the colony and at home, would have liked to see Colonel Gawler restored to the post from which he had been so hastily and ungenerously recalled. Mr. G. Fife Angas was one of these, and in a letter to Earl Grey, under date 2nd of June, 1847, he says—

"If Major Robe is about to remove to the Mauritius, it would afford a gracious opportunity to restore Colonel Gawler to South Australia. His noble and distinguished conduct there, by which he laid the foundation of its future prosperity under the judicious government of Governor Grey, has not been well understood in this country, and thereby great injustice has been done to that upright and sensible officer. He would be sure to meet with a popular reception, the more so were he to be the bearer of a Constitution founded on simple, practical, and liberal principles. . . .

"The colonists justly complain," added Mr. Angas, "of the frequent change of their Governors as being very injurious. No sooner does one become acquainted with the localities and the people, and they with him, and a cordial feeling has sprung up on both sides, than he is removed—a system which, if pursued in principle by a great mercantile house in the management of its foreign establishments, would involve it in confusion and ruin."

The wish for Colonel Gawler to be reinstated was not gratified, but in the successor to Major Robe the colonists found an ideal Governor and a man after their own hearts.

CHAPTER IX.

ADMINISTRATION OF SIR HENRY EDWARD FOX YOUNG.

August, 1848—December, 1854.

Antecedents.—Suspension of Royalties on Minerals.—Irish Orphans. —A Policy of Progress.—Municipal Corporation for Adelaide.— A New Constitution.—Federation proposed and rejected.—The " Political Association."—Universal Suffrage and the Ballot.— A Lost Constitution.—Elections to New Legislative Council.— Statistics.—State Aid to Religion permanently abolished.— Education.—City and Port Railway Bill.—Pensions.—Californian Gold.—Anti-Transportation League.—The Victorian Gold-fields.—Exodus from South Australia.—State of Adelaide and Suburbs.—A Drain on the Banks.—Proposed Assay of Gold into Stamped Ingots.—The Bullion Act.—Government Assay Office opened.—Mr. Tolmer and the Overland Gold Escort.— Exciting Adventures.—Gold at Echunga.—Increased Cost of Living.—Navigation of the Murray.—Captain Cadell.—The Governor explores the Murray.—The " Murray Hundreds."— Dreams that never came true.—A Parliament for South Australia proposed.—Opinions on a Nominee Upper House.—A Civil List Bill.—Establishment of District Councils.—Roads and Railways.—Defence of the Colony.—Military Ardour.

THE emigrant ship *Forfarshire* arrived off the lightship on the 1st of August, 1848, with Sir Henry Edward Fox Young and Lady Young on board. Unfortunately, through inadvertence, no pilot was in readiness to board the ship, not a Government boat was at hand, nor a solitary head of any Government department present to receive the new Governor. On arriving at Government House there was, through another negligence, neither guard of honour to receive him, nor any members of the Executive to bid him welcome. It was a cold reception, but it was amply atoned for afterwards.

Sir Henry Edward Fox Young was the son of Colonel Sir Aretas William Young, and was born at Brabourne, near Ashford, Kent, on the 23rd of April, 1810, being named after his godfather, General Edward Henry Fox, brother of the Whig statesman, the celebrated rival of Pitt.

Sir Henry was educated at Dean's School, Bromley, Middlesex, and was intended for the Bar, but on quitting school he joined his father at Trinidad, and received an appointment in the colonial treasury in that island. This, rapidly followed by other colonial promotions, prevented him from being called to the Bar. At Demerara he served under Sir Benjamin D'Urban as aide-de-camp, and was then promoted to St. Lucia, where for a time he filled the several offices of secretary, treasurer, and puisne judge of the Supreme Court of Justice. He was then transferred back again to Demerara, and later on, was appointed Lieutenant-Governor of the eastern districts of the Cape of Good Hope, whither, a few weeks before, Sir Henry Pottinger had been despatched as Governor and High Commissioner for the settlement of Kaffraria. The Kaffir War was unexpectedly renewed a few weeks after his embarkation from England, and the Home Government, under the impression that a civil Lieutenant-Governor could not under these circumstances be required, removed Sir Henry Young to South Australia without waiting for the report of Sir Henry Pottinger from the seat of war, whose despatches endeavoured to frustrate any intention to remove Sir Henry Young, and recommended that, notwithstanding the breaking out of war, the services of the civil Lieutenant-Governor should be continued, as his services had been very valuable at Grahamstown during the brief period (some eight months) in which he had remained in that position.

A fortnight before leaving England, Sir Henry married

Augusta Sophia, daughter of Mr. Charles Marryat, and niece of Captain Marryat, R.N., the well-known novelist and author of the code of signals bearing his name.

The day after his arrival, Sir Henry Young was introduced to the members of Council, and received an address of welcome and congratulation from the colonists. In his reply he pointed out that the sphere of official government was wisely limited, and that the numerous methods of social advancement in all free countries should derive their origin, maintenance, and progress from the energies and resources of private individuals. In this connection he spoke of the importance of diffusing scientific information applicable to agriculture, wool-growing, and such-like industries, more particularly calling attention to the mining interests, which would be enhanced by the formation of self-supporting voluntary associations to receive, record, and arrange any accounts and specimens transmitted to them of mining operations, and thus preserve valuable facts that might otherwise be lost to practical science. It was evident from the first that "progress" was the key-note of his administration.

On the 9th of August the Legislative Council assembled to hear and act upon a despatch from Lord Grey, calling attention to the insufficient salary attached to the office of Governor, and "strongly recommending that an increase of £500 per annum should be made to the salary of the present Lieutenant-Governor, raising it to £2000 per annum." A Bill was brought in accordingly, which passed through its several stages on the 15th of August, and secured the much-needed addition.

The first public step of the new Governor was a bold and politic one. It was no less than a notification in the Government *Gazette* that, pending the further signification of her Majesty's pleasure, the imposition of royalties on mineral lands would be suspended, and not inserted in future land-grants. This gratifying information gave the most profound satisfaction, and Sir Henry was overwhelmed with the thanks of the colonists.

The formal authorization of the step by the Secretary

of State was not officially announced until July of the following year, and if, as is supposed, the relinquishment of the royalty dues was taken on the Governor's own initiative, it was a step almost unprecedented in its boldness.

One of the early questions demanding his attention was a proposal from the Colonial Land and Emigration Commissioners, approved by the Secretary of State, to receive "certain classes of orphans of both sexes in Ireland, between the ages of fourteen and eighteen." The Commissioners and Lord Grey considered that these orphans, at that time maintained in Irish workhouses, would keep up the supply of labour required in the colony. Little did the colonists imagine the extent to which the plan proposed would be carried out, nor were they desirous that any immigration of the kind should be confined to the Irish. But, as there were no valid objections to urge, they assented, and a committee was appointed for the protection and guardianship of the orphans. The committee included Dr. Short, Bishop of Adelaide, Dr. Murphy, Roman Catholic Bishop, and representatives of the Nonconformist bodies. It was unfortunate that at about this time there was a large addition to the population of the colony. In one week in December no fewer than 1131 persons arrived, about 600 of whom had paid their own passages, the remainder being Government emigrants. To assist newly arrived immigrants and others in obtaining employment, the Colonial Labour Office was opened early in the following year (1849), under the direction of a committee, and was supported in the first instance by subscriptions, as no fees were charged for arranging engagements. It was found a great accommodation to both employers and employed.

This rapid influx of immigrants was the beginning of what was to be hereafter a source of considerable trouble. Owing to the unsuitable class of persons sent out, it soon became necessary to find relief for the destitute poor, and a Board was appointed to take the matter up. The first shipload of Irish orphan girls arrived in June, 1849. They were kindly received and accommodated with lodgings in the Native School location on the North Park Lands, and were visited by a committee of ladies who advised them as to their future.

When, in November, 1848, the Governor opened the Legislative Council, hopes were entertained that he would have made some important revelation with regard to a new Constitution for the colony, but instead he stated it to be merely his intention to forward certain Bills left undisposed of by his predecessor, and to introduce a Bill for the guardianship and apprenticeship of orphan immigrants. But he made a statement in which he foreshadowed his whole policy :—

"It only remains for me, on the first occasion of transacting ordinary business with the Council," he said, "to give my sincere assurance that whether the lapse of time that may occur before representative institutions be conceded to South Australia be long or short, and my wish is that it may be but brief, I am cordially desirous, as far as my power extends, to join with this Council as now constituted only in such legislation as shall be in unison with the general opinion of the colonists"—a policy in direct opposition to that of his predecessor.

The real work of the Legislative Council under the new Governor did not commence until the 4th of July, 1849. In opening the Council the Governor read an elaborate minute of a very satisfactory character, in which he announced the payment to the emigration fund of £56,746 from the Crown reserved moiety of the land fund, thus extinguishing a long-standing technical claim.

The estimated expenditure for the following year (1850) was stated to be £108,555.

From the item of imports and exports it appeared that, for the first time since the foundation of the colony, the exports exceeded the imports, the latter being valued at £471,556, and the former at £485,951 (including sixteen thousand tons of ore).

In the early part of the previous year the citizens had petitioned for a resuscitation of the Corporation, and it was anticipated that this would be the main business of the session. In introducing it the Governor said, "The Bill to constitute a municipal Corporation for the city of Adelaide, and the Bill to provide a general board for the care and maintenance of the lines of roads, with local election boards for the management of the district or cross roads, are framed on so popular a basis as to be fit precursors of that more general system of representative government, the concession of which has been usually preceded by some experience of the working of civic, or parochial, or district municipalities."

Sir Henry Young, unlike his predecessor, knew exactly how to secure popularity. From the date of his first public utterances he laid it down as a matter of duty as well as of inclination to adhere to that line of policy which should frame all legislation in unison with the deliberate opinion of the majority of the colonists.

In concluding his speech on this occasion he reiterated that policy, and added, "Let us, then, whose mission it is, as a Legislature, to nurse this infant community in its advance towards the rank of a nation, so act for the permanent interests of present and future time, that our successors shall not be able to associate our proceedings with the origin of any short-sighted or illiberal measures. In this honourable and responsible aim it will be my pride cordially to afford you my best co-operation."

On the 24th of September the long-looked-for new Constitution, for the Australian colonies generally, arrived in the *Grecian*, and supplied plenty of work for the Legislature and the public.

The Bill first provided for the separation of the district of Port Phillip from the colony of New South Wales, and the boundary of the new colony of Victoria. The Legislative Councils to be established in each colony were next determined. These bodies were limited to twenty-four members, two-thirds of whom were to be elected, and the remaining third nominated. Power was then given to make laws, to raise taxes and appropriate public money, and to establish district councils after the formation of Legislative Councils. Further power was given to establish a General Assembly for the Australian colonies; and, lastly, with the assent of her Majesty in Council, to alter the constitution of the respective Legislative Councils, if necessary.

The most important features of this Bill were, of course, the grand federal idea set forth in the clauses for the establishment and guidance of the General Assembly, and the power to alter the constitution of the Legislative Councils. In regard to the latter the Bill provided that it should be lawful for the Governor and Legislative Council of each colony, after the establishment of the Legislative Council stipulated for by the Bill, to alter from time to time, by any Act or Acts, "the provisions or laws for the time being in force under this Act, or otherwise concerning the election of the elective members of such Legislative Councils respectively, the qualification of electors and elective members, and generally to vary in any manner not hereinbefore authorized the constitution of such Legislative Councils respectively, or to establish in the said colonies respectively, instead of the Legislative Councils, a Council and a House of Representatives or other separate legislative houses, to consist respectively of such members to be appointed or elected respectively by such persons and in such manner as by such Act or Acts shall be determined, and to vest in such Council and House of Representatives or other separate legislative houses the powers and functions of the Legislative Council for which the same may be substituted, provided always that every Bill which shall be passed by the Council in any of the said colonies, for any of such purposes, shall be reserved for the signification of her Majesty's pleasure thereon; and a copy of such Bill shall be laid before both Houses of Parliament for the space of thirty days at the least before her Majesty's pleasure thereon shall be signified."

We have given this prosy quotation in full, as it sets forth in exact terms the "case" on which, in the near future, ten thousand arguments were to be founded.

The clause providing for the establishment of the General Assembly set forth that it should be lawful for the Governor-General "to convene, at such time or times and at such place within any of the said colonies as such Governor-General shall from time to time think fit to appoint, a General Assembly for all the said colonies, to be called 'The General Assembly of Australia,' which said General Assembly shall consist of such Governor-General and a House of Delegates, and such House of Delegates shall consist of members to be elected by the respective Legislative Councils of the said colonies of New South Wales, Victoria, Van Diemen's Land, and South Australia in the proportion following; that is to say, two members from each of the said colonies for every 15,000 inhabitants thereof, the number of the inhabitants being calculated according to last authentic enumeration at the date of the election, and such members shall be elected and all laws to be made and enacted by such Assembly shall be made and enacted and the business of such Assembly shall be conducted in such manner and form, and subject to such rules and conditions, as her Majesty by Order in Council shall direct, provided always that the first convocation of such Assembly shall have received from the Legislative Councils established under the said firstly recited Act of the sixth year of her Majesty, or this Act, of two or more of the said colonies, addresses requesting such Governor-General to convene such Assembly."

Other powers and provisions followed, which it is not necessary to record here.

Long before the colonists were called upon to give expression to their opinions on this federal scheme, Mr. G. F. Angas, in a letter to Earl Grey, of which the following is an extract, had very fairly represented their views:—

"2, Jeffrey's Square, St. Mary Axe, 4th of July, 1849.

"Time does not press with the federal government question because the habits, disposition, social condition, and productions of each colony are so diverse, the distances so great, and the means of conveyance so few and inconvenient, while the aggregate population is so small, that for twenty years to come it will be quite impracticable to work out the scheme of a General Assembly. Until the three or four young colonies become more advanced in population, wealth, and social progress, and get experience in the working of their separate political institutions, it is not very improbable that the attempt to form a General Assembly would embroil the whole of them in discord and dissatisfaction with each other, and with the parent State. The four new colonies would be swamped by the two older penal ones, and, as public opinion at present exists, they could not agree upon the locality and measures required by a General Assembly."

The first to take action in the colony on the new Constitution was Mr. J. Morphett, who submitted to the Governor a series of resolutions which were published in the Government *Gazette*, as the Council was not then sitting. These resolutions affirmed that "it is essential to the welfare of this colony that the Imperial Parliament should, in framing a Constitution for South Australia, adopt the principle of municipal government, adhering, as far as the different ages of the two places would admit of it, to the form and system of the Government of Great Britain;" that is, a Governor and two chambers, one in the nature of an Upper Chamber with hereditary members nominated by her Majesty, and a Second Chamber to consist of members elected by the people.

These resolutions were added to and amended in a committee of the Legislative Council, and at the same time emphatic motions were passed against the proposed federal scheme, on the ground that it was inexpedient, inasmuch as there was a great dissimilarity in the pursuits and interests of the several provinces, that the overwhelming preponderance the larger provinces would have in the Assembly would be greatly injurious to the lesser, and that there was no point, so far as could be seen, upon which benefit would accrue to any of the provinces by the establishment of such an Assembly.

Out of doors the views of the colonists took this form. They were grateful to Earl Grey, Mr. Hawes, Lord John Russell, Mr. Labouchere, and the members of the House of Commons who had brought in the Bill, and so far as the concession of a representative government for South Australia was concerned they hailed it as a wise, liberal, and comprehensive measure. But they drew the line there, and protested vigorously against a General Assembly of the Australian colonies, or a federal union, as unconstitutional and endangering colonial independence, and maintained that, as they were prepared to bear the whole expenses of their civil government, they had a constitutional right to regulate, by means of their representatives in council, the mode of raising and appropriating the colonial revenue, free from all control of her Majesty's Treasury.

The discussions on the formation of a Constitution were varied by lengthy debates on roads and road-making, as a Road Bill passed through the Legislature at this time, and a Central Board was appointed for carrying it into effect. We shall not, however, concern ourselves with details of the ordinary course of legislation in this place, but proceed to tell the whole story of the new Constitution.

The rule of Sir Henry Young was an era of progression. Settlers were now more or less settled—prosperity had set in—and the colonists, losing sight of their own immediate and personal interests, were now directing their attention more than they had ever done before to the good of the colony as a whole, and to the duty of "making a nation." They could not have had a better leader than Sir Henry Young—a man of broad mind, liberal views, great intellectual capacity, and withal a thorough friend to free institutions.

The somewhat unpopular rule of his predecessor, Major Robe, had not been an unmitigated evil. It aroused in the colonists a determination to stand together and fight for their political rights, and it awakened, even in the most indifferent, a spirit of sturdy independence. The times were ripe for action, and with the Hour came the Man.

Ideas were developing apace. As the time drew near to elect representative members for the new Legistive Council, the advocates of popular, or democratic, principles strained every nerve to obtain as large an infusion as possible into the new body of the element they considered most essential to their own welfare. An "Elective Franchise Association" was formed, with this astounding platform—universal suffrage, vote by ballot, annual elections, no property qualification for representatives, and no nominee members! Later on in the year the "South Australian Political Association" was formed, and in a short time it had branches in various parts of the colony, its programme being mainly the advocacy of universal suffrage and the ballot. The formation of the association marked an epoch in the political history of the colony. From the first it excited a powerful influence, which increased as the years went on, and many elections in some of the most important constituencies were decided by its action, the conservative element being threatened, if not with extinction, at least with paralysis of its power.

The year 1851 opened with active preparations for popular representative government, and the *Ascendant*, the vessel that was to bring out the new Constitution, was awaited with feverish anxiety. A curious story attaches to this episode. In that same vessel Mr. George Fife Angas, one of the fathers and founders of the colony, and the originator of the South Australian Company, left England to take up his residence on his large estates in the Barossa District. It had been an ambition of his to be the personal bearer to the colony of the official copy of the New Constitution Act, and application was made to the Colonial Office to this end; but it was found to be contrary to precedent and red-tape triumphed, the important document being sent from the Colonial Office in charge of a clerk, who was instructed to take it on board the *Ascendant* and deliver it into the hands of the captain. But he had gone ashore, and as the ship was on the point of sailing, the clerk, either through negligence or from not understanding the importance of the papers with which he was entrusted, gave the package to a steward, who, being very busy, thrust it into the nearest place of safety. The ship sailed, and if the captain gave a thought to the matter at all, he merely supposed that there had been some delay or fresh arrangements had been made. On arrival in Adelaide, the proper authorities came on board to demand their Constitution and receive it with due honour, for advices from England had informed them that it would arrive in the *Ascendant*. The captain, of course, protested that he had seen nothing of it, and there was a great hue and cry for the lost Constitution, until one day shortly after, in turning out the captain's soiled linen for the laundress, it was found, to the great amusement of every one, at the bottom of the bag, where the steward had hurriedly placed it for security! *

The " Act for the Better Government of her Majesty's Australian Colonies" was received with elaborate explanatory despatches, followed, a short time afterwards, by an announcement of the appointment by her Majesty of Sir Charles Augustus Fitzroy, knight, to be Captain-General and Governor-in-Chief of South Australia, and of Sir Henry Young to be Lieutenant-Governor, a title he had held throughout, but which was now to be held upon a different tenure. It will be remembered that it was assumed by Major Robe for prudential reasons, namely, to prevent his predecessor, Captain Grey, from becoming liable for any of his dishonoured bills; now it was to be held in prospect of the federal scheme which had been pro-

* Quoted in " Life of George Fife Angas."

pounded. As, however, the Australian colonies were not ripe for this movement, no further steps were taken, and Sir Charles Fitzroy never attempted to exercise any control over his lieutenant or over the colony.

A *Gazette Extraordinary* was issued proclaiming the new Constitution, and immediately afterwards the first candidate for legislative honours (Mr. F. S. Dutton) entered the field, followed by several other leading and influential men. Meanwhile the Council was called together, and the "Bill to establish the Legislative Council of South Australia, and to provide for the Election of Members to serve in the same," was passed on the 21st of February. The new Legislative Council was to be composed of twenty-four members instead of eight as heretofore, of whom eight were to be nominated by the Crown, and sixteen members were to be elected by electoral bodies. And this, it was hinted, was by no means a final measure of reform.

In the course of his valedictory address to the old Council, the Governor said:—

"As there is no probability of this Council being again assembled, I cannot refrain from making one observation before we separate. Your successors, gentlemen, will have a field of universal extent and of universal responsibility, . . . yet the colonial annals cannot fail to record that the prosperity which, with the continuance of the Divine blessing, it may be the happy privilege of a new legislation to preserve, to develop, and to augment, took its rise and acquired a character of stability under the sway of the present Council. This is a distinction and a satisfaction of which you can never be deprived.

"It is permanently useful, too, as affording an incentive to your successors to take care that the public resources receive at their hands, not only no detriment, but universal productiveness."

Up to the time of the elections the Political Association, the Ballot Association, and the League for the Maintenance of Religious Freedom displayed great activity, holding meetings in various parts of the colony, with a view to secure representatives favourable to their claims. Without doubt, these societies exercised a considerable influence on the elections. A committee was formed, by whom the following questions were prepared and submitted to every candidate :—

1. "Are you in favour of, and would you vote for, the adoption of the ballot at elections?"

2. "Are you in favour of State grants for the support of religion, or would you strenuously oppose such a measure?"

3. "In the event of your being returned as our representative, how far would you extend the suffrage?"

4. "Would you use your utmost endeavours to obtain the constitution of an Assembly strictly representative, as opposed to nomination?"

5. "As to the duration of Legislative Councils, would you limit them to three years, or what are your views on this head?"

These questions were the means of eliciting considerable information from the candidates to whom they were addressed, placed the constituencies in a good position as to their men, and regulated mainly their course of action.

The League, in a large measure, acted independently, directing the full force of its energy to securing candidates pledged to oppose, tooth and nail, any State grant in aid of religion. Some recent events in Church circles had been favourable to the leaguers. While the lawsuit with regard to the site of the cathedral was still pending, popular feeling was further excited in consequence of the bishop having met the other colonial prelates and attached his signature to a minute affirming the doctrine of baptismal regeneration, which the Bishop of Melbourne had refused to sign. A great public demonstration by members of the Church of England followed, when the course pursued by Bishop Short was almost unanimously condemned in the strongest language. Before the storm had died away, the elections came on, and capital was made out of the conduct of the Bishop.

After innumerable meetings in nearly every part of the colony, the elections began on the 2nd of July, when the most profound interest in the proceedings was displayed, eager crowds thronging the gaily decorated polling booths, while more active partisans paraded the streets with banners, trumpets, and shawms.

To show how successful the League had been in these elections, it may be stated that, out of sixteen districts, only four candidates were returned favourable to Government support to religion.

The question next in importance was, of course, with regard to the Constitution to be framed by the new Council, or, at any rate, to be initiated by it.

When, on the 28th of August, the new Council * met in the new Court House in Victoria Square, an eager throng of spectators crowded the approaches, to witness

* The following were the first members elected for the new Council:—

East Adelaide	Mr. F. S. Dutton.
West Adelaide	Mr. A. L. Elder.
North Adelaide	Mr. J. B. Neales.
Yatala	Mr. R. D. Hanson.
East Torrens	Mr. G. M. Waterhouse.
West Torrens	Mr. C. S. Hare.
Port Adelaide	Captain Hall.
Mount Barker	Mr. J. Baker.
Hindmarsh	Mr. R. Davenport.
Noarlunga	Mr. W. Peacock.
Barossa	Mr. G. F. Angas.
Victoria	Captain John Hart.
Light	Captain C. H. Bagot.
Stanley and Gawler	Mr. Younghusband.
Kooringa	Mr. G. S. Kingston.
Flinders	Mr. J. Ellis.

The eight gentlemen nominated by the Governor to occupy seats in the new Legislative Council were:—

Mr. Charles Sturt	Colonial Secretary.
Mr. T. B. Finniss	Registrar-General.
Mr. R. D. Hanson	Advocate-General.
Mr. R. R. Torrens	Collector of Customs.

The non-official nominees were:—

Mr. John Morphett.   Mr. E. C. Gwynne.
Mr. J. Grainger.   Major Norman Campbell.

as much as possible of the inauguration of the new Legislature.

It was confessedly only an experiment, and the Imperial Government, in its wisdom, had placed in the hands of the members the power of introducing such modifications as might be necessary, although, as the Governor in his opening address observed, it was desirable that such a trial of the present Constitution should be given as would show that any modifications to be proposed hereafter should be to remedy " proved inconveniences and not merely theoretical requirements."

The Governor was able to report to the new Council that the general condition of the colony was in all respects satisfactory. The population was 63,700, exclusive of 3730 aborigines. The excess of immigration over emigration during the year was 6137. The imports were in value £887,423, or about £13 18s. per head; the exports, £571,348, or more than £8 19s. per head. There were 102 places of worship in the colony, and 115 schools; 174,000 acres of land were inclosed, and 15,000 square miles of Crown land occupied by squatters and depastured by sheep and cattle. The export of wool was 3,289,232 lbs., and the export of copper metal 44,594 cwt., and of copper ore 8784 tons. The sum of £140,000 was named in the estimates as the amount required for public works. Drafts of various laws were laid before the members, priority being given to the question of the continuance of aid from the public treasury to the erection of Christian churches and to the support of Christian ministers, the enactment for it having terminated on the previous 31st of March, after a three years' trial.

An Education Bill, as well as measures for giving enlarged powers to district boards, was also in the programme for the session, whose subsequent meetings, by the way, were held in the Council Chamber on North Terrace.

On the 29th of August the hour arrived for which the large majority of colonists had anxiously waited for more than three years—that is to say, ever since the date of the ill-judged action of Major Robe—when Mr. Gwynne rose to move the first reading of a Bill to continue "an Ordinance to promote the Building of Churches and Chapels for Christian Worship, and to provide for the Maintenance of Ministers of the Christian Religion." This was the signal for the great battle of the session to commence; but the opponents of the grant were determined to make the contest as brief and decisive as possible, and moved, as an amendment to its first reading, that "it be read that day six months."

This was carried by a majority of three, there being thirteen for the amendment and ten against it, the votes of all the members, with one exception, having been recorded on this important question. The arguments of the victorious party were briefly these:—

That all mankind have a natural and indefeasible right to worship Almighty God according to the dictates of their own consciences, and no man can, of right, be compelled to attend, erect, or support any place of worship, or to maintain any ministry against his consent; that no human authority can, in any case whatever, control or interfere with the rights of conscience; that no preference shall ever be given by law to any religious establishment or modes of worship; that no part of the revenue from the colony of South Australia, from whatever source it may arise, and that no part of the land and emigration funds, can be made applicable to the support of ministers or teachers of any religion or to the erection or repairing of any place of worship.

To supply the place of the Government stipends, it was necessary that some new machinery should be invented, and to this end the Bishop addressed a minute to the Church Society. In reply he received a report projecting and recommending a constitution for the Church, to consist of a diocesan assembly, composed partly of clergymen and partly of lay representatives chosen by the various Churches. This plan was adopted, but it was found almost as difficult to frame a constitution for the Church as the Legislature found it to be for the colony. When at length it *was* framed, the next aim of the Bishop was to obtain for it the force of law; but in this he signally failed, and the whole project fell through, notwithstanding the fact that a fresh newspaper, the *Adelaide Morning Chronicle*, was called into existence to advocate the claims of the friends of State aid to religion.

So decisive was the blow struck in that ever-to-be-remembered Council of 1851, that no attempt has again been made to introduce into the colonial Parliament the question of State aid to religion, and through the long years that have passed it has been found that the voluntary principle then adopted was best suited to the genius of the people. Amazing efforts were made by all denominations to supply the religious wants of their respective communities; the colony became remarkable for the number of its places of worship in proportion to the population; the Church of England, which, of all other Churches, deprecated the voluntary principle, found, on giving it a fair trial, that sufficient funds could be raised from private sources to build their churches and pay their ministers.

With the discontinuance of the Government grant in aid of religion came a measure for the promotion of education, providing for stipends to teachers, assistance in the erection of school-houses, and other regulations, the whole of which were to be under the control and management of a Board of Education.

One clause of the Bill provided that no minister of religion should be a member of this Board—a clause of which the Governor so highly disapproved that he sent a message to the Council urging that it should be rescinded. This interference the Council resented, and carried the Bill as previously passed by a majority of six.

Soon after this Education Bill was passed, the South Australian Preceptors' Association was formed, its object being to elevate the standard of education by the improvement of the educator, and to obtain a higher social grade for the teacher, so that the scholastic profession should have as recognized a position as the clerical, legal, and medical professions.

This first session of the Legislative Council under the new Constitution was perhaps the most important in the history of the colony, as it set at rest for ever the question of Church and State, and it inaugurated a system of public education which, with necessary modifications to suit the exigencies of the times, has continued almost to the present day. Among the less important items of the session were the City and Port Railway Bill, which was passed on the 25th of September; and the offering of a premium for any steamer or sailing vessel landing mails and passengers within sixty-seven days from Britain = £250 if landed at Nepean Bay, and £400 if landed at Port Adelaide; the total amount not to exceed £5000 in any one year.

An important discussion also took place on the question of annuities or pensions to Government officials. In consequence of Captain Sturt, the great explorer, who was also the colonial secretary, wishing to retire from public life, it was moved that a sum should be placed on the estimates as a suitable testimonial for the important services he had rendered by the discovery of the colony, and to provide for his comfortable retirement from public life.

Mr. G. F. Angas moved an amendment to the effect that a Bill be introduced "for the purpose of granting an annuity for life to the Hon. Captain Sturt, and that the proposed Bill have a clause inserted in it declaring that it is not to be considered as a precedent for retiring pensions to official persons in South Australia"—a system, said Mr. Angas, "servile in itself and calculated to induce improvidence." The amendment was carried by a majority of ten to six, and eventually the sum of £600 per annum was secured to the gallant captain—an act of liberality honourable to the colony, and bestowed upon one well worthy of such a token of regard.

While these things were going on in the Legislature there were matters out of doors which threatened mischief. The winter had been long and inclement; great distress existed among the working classes; the prices of provisions were unusually high, and few public works were in hand, the estimates having been long delayed. Moreover events were pending unprecedented in the world's history, and destined to affect the whole future of the Australian colonies.

In 1849 an emigration of the male adult population had been threatened, when the news arrived of gold being discovered in large quantities in California; but the first vessel laid on at Adelaide (the *Mazeppa*) only took about twenty passengers. The exodus was renewed in January, 1850, when two ships cleared out for California, followed by others in February and March, and conveying five hundred and seventy passengers in all. Happily these departures relieved the colony of many who could well be spared. From all the Australian colonies large numbers of doubtful characters were drained off to the Californian diggings, and this led the people of Van Diemen's Land to seize the opportunity and take steps to enlist the sympathies of the Australian colonies generally to save them from the further transportation of felons to their shores. An Anti-Transportation League was established in Tasmania, and South Australia, with New South Wales and Victoria, were invited to join and co-operate. The South Australians were quite ready and willing to do this, and at once sent some of their picked men to represent them in the League.

This League may be regarded as the first great federal action of the colonies named. One other colony, Western Australia, not only held aloof, but, while the four other colonies were striving to be relieved from the galling burden of convictism, she had servilely petitioned for the yoke, and the first shipload had been actually landed on her shores in answer to her prayers. In September, 1851, the delegates from the "Australian Conference for the Discontinuance of Transportation" arrived in Adelaide. A crowded meeting was held for their reception, and the colonists pledged themselves not to employ any persons thenceforth who might arrive in the province under sentence of transportation for crime committed in Europe; to prevent by all lawful means the establishment of English prisons or penal settlements; not only to refuse assent to any projects to facilitate the administration of such penal settlements, but to seek the repeal of all regulations and establishments for the purpose; and, finally, to support by countenance, advice, and money, all who might suffer in the promotion of this cause.

The feeling had become strong and fairly general that the total cessation of transportation to the colonies was essential to their honour, happiness, and prosperity, and that to secure this desideratum it was necessary that the Australian colonies should join in one great confederation to obtain deliverance from this curse of civilization, and, as we shall see, it was not long before this great end was practically obtained. Of course, having taken this important step, South Australia could not with any show of consistency continue to transport its own felons to Van Diemen's Land, and a measure was therefore adopted for the employment of convicts within the province, who should henceforth be sentenced to hard labour instead of "transportation beyond the seas." This led to the establishment of a stockade at Cox's Creek, and, subsequently, of the Labour Prison at the Dry Creek.

While these matters were going on, while excitement was running high on the questions brought forward in the new Legislative Council, already chronicled in this chapter, news reached the colony of the increasing richness of the gold discoveries in New South Wales, and of the still greater yield of the more recently found gold-fields in Victoria. At once there was a stampede of such working men in South Australia as could raise sufficient money for their passage and outfit, and they left for Victoria, at first by fifties, then by hundreds, and at last by thousands.

Soon after the exodus commenced, Mr. J. M. Solomon advocated following the example of Victoria and offering a reward for the discovery of a workable and paying gold-field in South Australia, and £300 was guaranteed by private subscription; while the Legislative Council not only determined to permit licences to be issued for the search for gold on unsold waste lands, and also to appropriate a sum of money for a geological survey of the colony, but offered £1000 for the discovery of a gold-field in the colony, the produce of which in two months should amount to £10,000. To this there was a poor response—a bird in the hand, like the Victoria fields, was considered to be better than half a dozen in the bush—and the exodus continued. "It is perhaps no exaggeration to say," said the report of the Chamber of Commerce for 1851, "that at least 15,000 to 20,000 individuals left South Australia during the prevalence of the gold mania," and this included the greater part of the most useful labourers, involving a cessation of almost all industrial production.

On the 27th of November a notice appeared in the *Adelaide Times*, stating that after the next issue it would be published weekly instead of daily, "in consequence of the falling off of business and the departures for the diggings." One by one the other papers were stopped, until the *Register, Observer, Times,* and *Morning Chronicle* were left the sole representatives of the press.

In 1852 came a crisis in the history of the colony. An abundant harvest had been gathered in with some difficulty, owing to the scarcity of labour; and hundreds of gold-diggers had returned with their rich gains and findings. But, with a surfeit of wealth, it could not be put into circulation. The banks had been drained of coin by the numbers who had left the colony, and with the absorption of a medium of circulation there came a stagnation of trade, and with it the discharge of nearly all those employed who had not voluntarily left their occupations and pursuits to proceed to the diggings. It thus happened that there was not in many instances sufficient business to occupy the time of even the former employer of labour, and one after another shops were closed, business suspended, and they too followed in the general wake and went to the gold-fields. Shepherds left their flocks in the sheep-yards; stockmen deserted the cattle-stations; farm labourers abandoned their teams and ploughs; dairy cows were left to run untended in the bush, and servants of all classes left their employers. The hands employed at the Burra-Burra mines were reduced from 1042 to 366, and subsequently to 100 Pumping engines were stopped, and dry levels only worked.

Rapidly and extraordinarily the contagion spread. In one week in January, 1852, no fewer than thirteen Government officers, and again in one week in February seventeen others, sent in their resignations. So many persons were leaving the colony in debt that a Bill was hastily passed to obtain summary payment of small debts, but it was rendered almost nugatory by the discharge of officers from the local court.

A great part of the police force resigned, and those who were left were in a state of disorganization, so that grave fears were entertained that in distant and unprotected stations the natives would commit depredations and otherwise become troublesome. For the city no fears were felt, as the thieves and bad characters generally had made their way to the diggings, a more lucrative field for their operations.

But for the intervention of the Chamber of Commerce, many of the letter-carriers would have been dismissed, at a time, too, when the business of the post-office was largely increased by the number of letters passing between the absentees and their families. Several of the minor departments were left without any clerical assistance whatever. The Labour Office was removed to the Port, as if ready to take its departure with those for whose use it was established. The relieving officer and health officer were discharged. The Destitute Board, finding that the asylum was likely to be filled to overflowing with deserted wives and families, advertised that such as were left behind by men who had proceeded to the diggings would not be supported. The city surveyor, the inspector of weights and measures, and many others were under notice that their services would probably soon be dispensed with.

The city and suburbs presented a most desolate and forsaken appearance. Some fifty or sixty shops were closed in Hindley Street and Rundle Street alone.* Many private houses were deserted in consequence of the occupants having left the colony, or, in a great number of cases, because they had joined some other family, left without its male members, for company and protection. Sixty women and several families were thrown upon the asylum despite the notice of the Destitute Board. The Port was left with only one water-carrier, and Thebarton with only one man!

The great difficulty, putting all others in the shade, was, however, the want of cash. It was calculated that "each man must have taken with him on an average ten pounds in specie, to pay his travelling expenses and provide the necessaries of life until his labour at the diggings should be productive. This amounted to a drain of gold sovereigns from the bank vaults. Every bank-note in the possession of the intending emigrant would be converted into coin, as the only circulating medium on which he could rely over the border. Taking the lowest estimate of fifteen thousand emigrants, this would imply a drain on the banks of £150,000. Such a drain as this involved the necessity on the part of the banks of restricting their note circulation, and of diminishing their discounts of commercial bills, which had the effect of paralyzing trade, and left the already glutted markets without purchasers for their commodities." †

Several plans were proposed, such as allowing the banks an extended circulation; the issue of Government

---

* On one of these deserted houses the following facetious notice was posted up for the information of the tax-gatherer: "Mr. Collector, gone to the diggings, hope to pay you when I return."

† Finniss's "Constitutional History of South Australia," p. 71.

notes having twelve months' currency; the transmission of gold to England for conversion into sovereigns, and the assay of gold in the colony.

The Governor was memorialized to establish the latter, but he declined to do so, and urged a forbearance of creditors to debtors as the best remedy for the evil. The managers of the South Australian Company adopted the plan of taking wheat for rent, and some few tradesmen took gold-dust for goods, although, if this system of barter had become universal, the ruin of the colony, at least for a time, would have been inevitable. As it was, large numbers were continuing to leave the colony, who would have remained if there had been trade and employment in proportion to the gold lying useless.

It cannot be denied that the attractions of the gold-fields were very great, the news from Forest Creek being to the effect that five Adelaide men had procured no less than 250 lbs. weight of gold, which, at 60s. per ounce (the price then given in Adelaide), was worth about £9000. On receipt of this news thirteen out of the twenty-two vessels in harbour were laid on for Melbourne.

A letter from a well-known colonist,* written about this time, gives a graphic picture of the state of affairs :—

"February 25th, 1852.

"What changes have taken place in this colony since Christmas! The discovery of gold has turned our little world upside down; thousands have left the settlement for the diggings. . . . In Adelaide windows are bricked up, and outside is written, 'Gone to the diggings.' Vessels are crowded with passengers to Melbourne, and the road to the Port is like a fair—ministers, shopkeepers, policemen, masons, carpenters, clerks, councillors, labourers, farmers, doctors, lawyers, boys, and even some women, have gone either by sea or land to

* Mrs. Evans, of Evandale, daughter of Mr. George Fife Argas.

try their fortunes at the diggings. . . . Somewhere about £16,000 worth of gold has in less than two weeks found its way here. Many have done uncommonly well, earning £200 perhaps, or more, in a week, while some have not earned enough to pay for their food. . . . It is quite ludicrous to see how these labourers spend their gold. One man bought six silk dresses and six bonnets for his 'missus.'"

Early in the year (1852) one or two far-seeing men, foremost among whom was Mr. George Tinline, manager of the Bank of South Australia, became convinced that the assay of gold into stamped ingots of a fixed value was the only immediate and effectual way out of the financial difficulty. Again the Governor was memorialized by the Chamber of Commerce, and also by the merchants and traders of Port Adelaide, on the subject.

Long, elaborate and ingenious replies were returned, arguing the position but declining to entertain the proposition. The following, read in the light of subsequent events, is an extremely interesting specimen. The Governor directed the colonial secretary to—"Acknowledge the receipt of the memorial urging the local Government to receive, assay, and coin, that is, stamp gold, as a measure calculated to relieve the depression of the mercantile and trading community. Say that the depression under which the colony is labouring is not owing to an insufficient circulating medium, or to a want of banking accommodation. Remotely the depression is owing to credit having been obtained far beyond the value of the article on which that credit was given. More immediately the depression is owing to a great diminution or total cessation of the demand for property or merchandise of any kind resulting from the migration of the population to the gold diggings. Assaying and stamping gold would put the metal in a convenient and desirable shape for the merchants to purchase, and the banks to advance upon, but it would not relieve the commercial pressure. The discoverer of gold is no more entitled to claim a mint, or an assay office to give a circulating fixed value to his gold, than the wool-producer can demand a manufactory for his raw produce. To give a fixed and circulating value to gold-dust would make money more plentiful, but investments of money would not be made here in the absence of population, or during a drain of it from the colony. The gold-dust to which additional value is proposed to be given by affixing to it the character of a circulating medium, would circulate back again for re-investment in gold-dust, to be again raised in value by the assay office in Adelaide, during the short period in which, under these circumstances, an assay office in the adjacent colonies should be non-existent. Whilst this additional value was received by gold-dust, and the trade in it consequently increased, all other kinds of property would still remain unattractive as investments; for, in the absence of population, or during the drain of it from the colony, other investments would yield no current income or profit. In short, if even sovereigns, instead of gold-dust, were extracted from the bowels of the earth of the adjacent colonies, these coins would not be invested in South Australia, because they could be more profitably invested where the capital would be more productive than it is at present in this colony, owing to the drain of the population and the consequent stagnation of all industrial pursuits. Capital would follow labour. Under present circumstances, gold brought here is brought by mistake, and must inevitably go back again. The amount of the currency is fixed or regulated, not by legislative enactments, but by the natural law or course of business. In a colony in which trade is conducted upon an extensive system of credit, every temporary diminution of capital or wealth has the effect of lessening or annihilating the demand for, and the consequent value of property, and must be inevitably followed by a proportionate extent of temporary loss. The banks have it not in their power to deal with anything more than the temporarily diminished capital of the community. No support which they can attempt to afford to the trade in gold will prevent individual members of the community from participating in the loss which the colony at large has suffered by the migration of the population and the temporary stagnation of trade."

Excellent as, in many respects, the arguments of the Governor were, he was wise enough to know that the opinions of men better versed than himself in practical business might be more valuable than his own, and he never at any time put himself in direct antagonism to such opinions. Immediately on receipt of the communication we have quoted above, the Chamber of Commerce again urged the absolute importance of immediate steps being taken to meet the crisis which threatened the doom of the colony. The arguments used were so conclusive, the scheme for carrying out the proposal so well digested, that a special session of the Legislative Council was summoned to meet at an early date, "in order to the enactment of such a measure as may be best calculated to meet the present emergency."

On the 28th of January the Council met to discuss a Bill to enable the banks, temporarily, in addition to the notes issued by them and then in circulation within the province, to issue notes in exchange for, or to the amount of, any gold bullion purchased or acquired by the banks, at a fixed rate; to enable persons to demand from the banks notes in exchange for bullion at a fixed value; and to make the notes of the banks a legal tender, except at the banks, so long as the notes were paid on demand in specie or in bullion. The Bill further provided for the establishment of an assay office, in order, on payment of the cost of assay, to facilitate to the banks and other buyers and sellers of bullion, the ascertaining of the weight and fineness of bullion sent them for assay, and to constitute such assayed gold, when stamped, a legal tender.

It was remarkable that the Governor, who had shown so much shrewdness and capacity on almost every other matter brought before him for the good of the colony, was still opposed to this somewhat daring scheme, and in his address to the Council he stated :—

"The banking, commercial, trading, and other moneyed classes of the community, and also my official advisers in Council, concur in the utility of the specific measure now introduced. Whilst my unaltered views, as already published in replies to the memorials that have been presented to me, do not coincide with the common expectations that legislation can be made, or will prove, a means of speedy and general relief to the existing depression, my judgment is nevertheless entirely satisfied that the present measure is alike safe and innocuous, and confers on the colonists of South Australia only an approximation to the advantages, as regards the possession of bullion, which holders of that commodity would obtain on application at the British Mint."

After the address the Council at once proceeded to the sole and important business of the special session, and the Bullion Bill was read a first, second, and third time, passed, and assented to, on the same day!

Of course in assenting to this Bill the Governor took upon himself an enormous responsibility, and ran the chance of an immediate recall, but he was not the first Governor who had exercised discretionary power at a critical time, and, as we shall see, his action met with the warm approval of the Home Government.

"The responsibility assumed by Sir Henry Young, in assenting to the Act," says Mr. Anthony Forster,* "was far greater than that assumed by Colonel Gawler in drawing upon the Lords of the Treasury, for it subverted the currency laws of the Empire, and was clearly repugnant to Imperial statutes. To make it obligatory upon the subjects of her Majesty to accept, as money, gold which did not bear the Imperial effigy; and, worse still, to oblige them to receive, as equal in value to the Queen's sterling sovereigns, the promissory notes of any or of all the banks of the colony, was such an

* "South Australia: its Progress and Prosperity." London: 1866.

interference with the circulating medium as had seldom before been attempted."

The Government Assay Office was opened on the 10th of February, and Mr. B. H. Babbage (son of Mr. Babbage, the celebrated inventor of the calculating machine), and Dr. Davy were appointed Government assayer and assistant assayer respectively. Success set in at once. On the first day of opening the office, gold to the value of upwards of £10,000 was deposited by twenty-nine persons, and day after day it continued to pour in to an extent beyond the most sanguine expectations, so that premises had to be enlarged almost at once, and the staff increased.

No doubt the inducements held out to depositors of gold-dust were great, the value given to the ingots and proportionately to crude gold being far in excess of the ruling price in Melbourne, where, at the time of passing the Bullion Act, it was from 58s. to 60s. per ounce, whereas the standard value of assayed gold fixed by the Act in South Australia was 72s. This price, of course, became the great attraction to owners and traders to bring their gold-dust or nuggets to South Australia, while the high price there fixed—in comparison with the Melbourne quotations—still left a sufficient margin of profit to make the traffic in gold a profitable trade. Almost everybody dabbled in it, and a walk through the streets of Adelaide left the impression that the city was transformed into El Dorado, shop windows being placarded all along the line of streets, "Gold bought," "Cash for gold," "Advances on gold," "Highest price given for gold," and so forth.

Shortly after the passing of the Bullion Act and the opening of the Assay Office, large quantities of gold began to arrive by vessels from Melbourne, one bringing £11,000 worth, and another £25,000 worth. These importations were not so much the property of the South Australian diggers as they were profitable purchases on the part of merchants and traders. A plan was, however, soon devised to reach these diggers direct by means of an overland escort, and with praiseworthy promptitude the plan was put into execution, Mr. Tolmer, commissioner of police, being entrusted with the important undertaking. As this route was being largely used by parties going to the diggings —the journey with bullock drays sometimes occupying from six weeks to two months—and as small farmers found it more profitable to sell their wheat ground into flour at £40 per ton on the diggings rather than at £12 10s. in Adelaide, the road was put into order. During the month of February no less than 1234 passengers, 1266 horses and bullocks, and 164 vehicles of all descriptions had crossed the Murray by the Wellington Ferry. The arrival of the first overland gold escort, a spring-cart drawn by four horses and laden with over a quarter of a ton of gold, was witnessed by multitudes of excited people. To be exact, the first escort brought gold valued at £18,456 9s., which had been sent by three hundred diggers. Mr. Tolmer, who was some time afterwards made the recipient of a handsome testimonial for his public services, reported having accomplished the distance (338 miles) between Adelaide and Mount Alexander in eight days. Arrangements were made for the escort to run monthly so long as it continued to be of benefit to the South Australian diggers, and a Commissioner was appointed to receive and take charge of deposits of gold and direct postal communication on the gold-fields.

The second overland gold escort arrived at Adelaide on the 4th of May, with 1620 lbs. weight of gold, valued at £70,000, sent by 851 diggers, together with 1350 letters, and was welcomed by some thousands of people, who proceeded to the eastern part of the city to get the first glimpse of the cavalcade, which was greeted with thundering cheers and the strains of music.*

Many stories of extraordinary adventure have been

		Valued at		
* Third arrival, May 5th, with 28,206¼ ozs....		£100,131	0	0
Fourth arrival, August 10th, with gold	...	85,200	0	0
Fifth arrival, September 16th „	...	189,884	4	0
Sixth arrival, October 9th „	...	199,170	2	3
Seventh arrival, November 20th „	...	154,758	6	0

told of the times of which we now write, but few are more interesting than those in connection with the overland gold escort. One incident, as a specimen of many, may be recorded here. During a season of pitiless rain Mr. Tolmer made his arrangements to leave the gold-fields with 28,000 ounces of the precious metal, consigned to 1021 families. Through storm and tempest, and under the eyes of a notorious gang who endeavoured to steal his horses and thus cripple his means to resist an attack, he reached Forest Creek. Then, when he was about to make his homeward start, in crossing an alluvial flat the horses plunged a good deal on account of the soft nature of the ground; but when the heavily laden cart came quickly down the hill and reached the level ground, down it went into a perfect bog. The wheels cut into the soil and sank until they could go no deeper, the flat bottom of the cart resting on the surface, and the horses plunging the while, but unable to move their load. Many men had prophesied that the escort would never reach Adelaide, and Mr. Tolmer was greeted with loud laughter from some of the spectators and entreaties from others not to proceed, while those who had bet champagne that he would not accomplish his journey suggested that he should pay for the champagne before he started. But the ex-commissioner of police was a man of resource, and how he dealt with the difficulty may best be told in his own words:—

"I took no heed of their sarcasm," he says, "but coolly, as if on parade, gave the order 'Halt front! Dress! Prepare to dismount! Dismount!' I then dismounted myself, unlocked the two strong boxes fixed by bolts to the bottom of the cart in which the gold was packed, quickly seized No. 1 bag, which I quietly placed across my saddle, and then gave the word 'Left files, take your bags!' In a moment, like as many ants, each trooper secured his own particular bag, threw it across his saddle, and then stood to his horse. Then followed the right files, who did the same, and, lastly, the men who had the charge of led horses got their bags and secured them on their respective packs. The whole proceeding did not occupy ten minutes. Having remounted the men I again gave the order 'Files right! March!'

"As we moved on, Rowe gave the horses a touch of the whip which made them bound forward, causing the lightened vehicle to spring up like a Jack-in-the-box, and then quickly continue its way. I then doffed my cap, saying, 'Good-bye, gentlemen. I'll come back and drink your champagne, be assured!' Whereupon they cheered lustily. Some of them then mounted their horses and accompanied us as far as the Lodden, where we parted. . . .

"After crossing the river, which was much swollen, the water reaching above the saddle-flaps, I selected a spot and encamped for the night in some thickly timbered country. It rained incessantly all night, and while the storm howled through the forest, it threatened to occasion serious impediments to our progress. Early next morning we made a start, and on the road met some teamsters who assured me that the Deep Creek, near Mr. Bucknall's, was fordable, and that they had crossed with their drays that morning. On arriving at the creek, however, I found it greatly swollen, and to satisfy myself of its practicability I went across in the first instance and then returned, and quickly gave directions to the men to take possession of their respective bags; then, taking the lead across the ford, I gave strict orders to each trooper to follow closely my own horse, whilst Rowe was to remain on the bank with the cart. During the time occupied in the removal of each bag of gold from the cart, and making them securely fast on the led horses, the water rose rapidly, nevertheless a safe crossing was effected. The bags, of course, got thoroughly soaked in the crossing, as we were up to our waists in water, and had it not been for the dead weight each horse carried, the whole cavalcade would have been swept away by the torrent. As the last led horse reached the bank, I called out to the driver, Rowe, not to lose a moment, but to drive the cart (in which six bags of gold remained, also the mail, provisions, etc.) and quickly cross the ford; which he attempted to do, but the animal in the shafts was unable to arrest the impetus of the vehicle, which rushed down the declivity and became fixed in a flooded hollow at the bottom. Rowe then endeavoured to urge the horses on, but the two leaders plunged into deeper water, and were there held by the traces, whilst the force of the current bore the shaft horse down and prevented him from rising. Seeing this mischance, I threw aside my cloak and sword, and dashing into the water, swam my horse across to the drowning animal, laid hold of the reins, and assisted it to regain its footing and reach a less dangerous part of the creek. Rowe was afraid to venture further in the attempt to get it across the creek, and urged fairly enough that, as he could not swim, the task was too great. Mr. Bucknall, jun., who was amongst the persons attracted to the spot, volunteered to take Rowe's place, which offer I gratefully accepted; and, having removed the bags of gold by dropping them into the water, and saved the mail, I mounted one of the leading horses and headed him to the ford. The water had, however, still risen while the cart was being unloaded, and it was necessary to swim the horses over. In attempting to do so I had a very narrow escape of being drowned, for when the current was strongest the horse on which I was mounted lost its equipoise, turned over, and plunged out into the turbid torrent, that had now formed itself into a river of considerable magnitude. I had very great difficulty in extricating myself from the dangerous position I was placed in by this untoward event; and, to add to my embarrassment, the top of one of my large riding-boots was turned down by the action of the water, and my spurs became entangled in the straps. My presence of mind did not, however, forsake me at this juncture, and, having freed my limbs by adjusting my dress I struck out and was about to make for the bank, when I perceived the current was carrying the horses and cart down the course of the stream. Although greatly exhausted, I made another effort, and succeeded in laying hold of the reins to turn the horses towards a landing-place, and cut the traces of the two leaders, which, upon being freed, were swept down the stream and managed to scramble ashore on the opposite bank. The cart, in which were the provisions of the party, and other matters, and the shaft horse were then carried away and lost. There were from thirty to forty persons witnessing these exhausting efforts, and, with the exception of Mr. Bucknall, no one volunteered to assist me. One man indeed, acting under a generous impulse, threw off his coat, but the bystanders dissuaded him from 'risking his life to save a horse.'

"After recovering myself somewhat by sitting on the bank and resting my back against a gum tree, I set about to recover the six bags of gold, which were then in a deep part of the creek and about six or eight yards from the bank, which I succeeded in doing by diving, each time seizing a bag, with which I reached the bank by taking a few long strides. The next momentous task, attended with difficulty and risk of life, was swimming my horse backwards and forwards across the swollen torrent with the gold, which I likewise successfully accomplished; but on returning again for the fourteenth time, bringing over the mail, on account of the exhausted condition of both the horse and myself, we were swiftly carried down the stream, and, had it not been for Mr. Bucknall and one or two others, we must have been drowned; for, about a quarter of a mile below the ford, there was a rickety wooden bridge, submerged at both ends, with a space of about six inches between the under part of the arch and level of the water, against which the horse and myself were jammed. One moment longer, without the help before mentioned, we must both have been forced under the bridge by the strength of the current, and of course lost our lives.

"The horse which performed this almost incredible feat was a splendid animal, very powerful, and stood about sixteen hands high; as a fencer there was not his equal in the colony."

Referring to this incident a few years later in a petition to the House of Assembly, Mr. Tolmer gave a summary of the events, thus: "Your petitioner suggested and brought into active operation the gold escort, and was for several months engaged in travelling therewith, on one occasion swimming his horse nineteen times across the overflowed Deep Creek in Victoria, recovering nine bags, containing £30,000 worth of gold, which were in imminent danger of being swept away by the torrent, in consequence of one of the horses harnessed to the cart containing the gold being drowned and the cart itself lost; for which last-mentioned services the Legislature addressed his Excellency Sir H. E. F. Young, then Governor of this province, requesting him to award your petitioner as a gratuity £100; which gratuity your petitioner unfortunately never received, inasmuch as his Excellency did not accede to the prayer of the said address." *

The Bullion Act not only saved the mercantile community from impending ruin, and the colony from general disaster, but it secured the speedy return of the colonists who had left at a time when the absence of such an inducement might have led to their permanent removal. As early as the month of March, unsuccessful gold-diggers returned in hundreds, and the vacant offices in the various departments of the public service began to be filled up. In the months of April and May the arrivals exceeded the departures, and in June eleven vessels arrived in Adelaide, bringing 687 passengers from Victoria.

As the season drew near for ploughing and sowing many of the successful as well as the unsuccessful diggers returned to put in their crops, and things in

* There appears to be some discrepancy here, but we quote verbatim from "Reminiscences of an Adventurous and Chequered Career," by Alexander Tolmer, vol. ii. p. 245.

general began to assume their ordinary aspect, with the addition of an abundance of wealth, and of a far more than ordinary amount of business. The first to benefit extensively by the reaction were the drapers and clothiers. The wives of fortunate diggers seemed determined to welcome their husbands in a way commensurate with their suddenly acquired wealth, and many ludicrous instances of absurd and unbecoming extravagance in dress occurred.

When the land sales were resumed a large number wisely invested their savings in land and house property. A great impetus was also given to the wheat and flour trade, large quantities of which were exported every week to Melbourne, and in consequence the price went up in Adelaide from £12 per ton to £37, while other provisions rose proportionately as the rate of wages increased.

Owing to the increased cost of living, which for some time past had exceeded on the average one hundred and fifty per cent. on the cost of corresponding items when official salaries were fixed, an increase of salary to all Government officers claimed the attention of the Legislature in 1853, persons in the public service being the only class either deriving no advantage, or suffering loss from circumstances which had been so favourable to the condition of the large majority of the colonists. Moreover, official duties had become permanently more extended and more onerous by reason of the enlarged political and social station to which the colony had attained.

In August (1852) the dwellers in South Australia were again thrown into a state of great excitement by the reported discovery of a gold-field of their own at Echunga, about eighteen to twenty miles from Adelaide. A commissioner was appointed, Government officials and mounted police were despatched to the scene of action, huts were erected, the *Register* and *Observer* sent special reporters, all requisite machinery was soon in working order, and in a few weeks a thousand licences were issued. It was thought that a second Ballarat or

Mount Alexander had been discovered, but soon the excitement quieted down, and though many continued at the diggings, earning a fair, and in some instances a very good, rate of wages, the existing state of things in the colony was not seriously disarranged, although the state of the labour market was such that many public works sanctioned by the Legislature could not be commenced.

When the Council met again in September (1852) the Governor announced the extinction of the bond debt of £85,800, which had been hanging as a millstone round the neck of the Exchequer Department, and referring to the operation of the Bullion Act, he said—

"This Act, by which the requisite increase of the currency of the bank-notes was regulated on a basis of present convertibility into assayed and stamped bullion, and of eventual convertibility, at no distant date, into coin of the realm, has, up to the present time, in its practical results, almost compensated for the absence of a Mint, has surpassed the expectations of the most sanguine, and has completely vindicated the prudence and sagacity of the Legislature of South Australia."

The Bullion Act was assented to by the Queen, and her Majesty's Government communicated to the Lieutenant-Governor "their disposition not to interfere with the discretion of the local authorities, who have exercised so much ability in their mode of dealing with this subject."

Early in 1853 a handsome testimonial was presented to Mr. G. Tinline, manager of the South Australian Banking Company, for the important part he had taken in furthering the objects of the Bullion Act.

It should be mentioned that no sooner had the mass of diggers returned to resume their various avocations, and had gathered in the harvest of 1852-53, than another exodus was threatened by reports of extensive and astounding gold discoveries in Victoria. The nuggets found were said to weigh respectively 76 lbs., 85 lbs., 120 lbs., and 134 lbs. Hundreds sped away at once, but the more sober-minded were deterred by the fact that very few out of the many thousands at the diggings were successful.

The overland escort continued to run throughout the year (1853), but was discontinued in December, the gold diggings having spread over a much larger extent of country, rendering it more difficult to collect the gold, and in consequence greatly increasing the cost of the escort. Arrangements were then made with the Victoria Government for the transmission of gold by the vessels running between Adelaide and Melbourne; but, gold having risen considerably in value in Victoria, there was not the same inducement to send it to Adelaide.

Great service was rendered to the colony throughout the whole period of the gold rush by the *Register* and *Observer* newspapers. When the North Eastern mails were stopped, this establishment undertook the transmission of a weekly mail to Houghton, Gumeracha, Chain of Ponds, and other places. A "Diggers' Edition" of the *Observer* was also regularly forwarded to the gold-fields, by which communication was kept up between the South Australian diggers and their friends at home, numbers of personal messages being sent through its columns, and, having a special correspondent at the diggings, authentic information was conveyed from time to time of the success or otherwise of the South Australian diggers.

Another important series of events, with which the name of Sir Henry Young will always be intimately associated, was in connection with the navigation and opening up of the river Murray.

In 1849 a committee was appointed to inquire into the practicability and cost of establishing places of shipment at the heads of St. Vincent's and Spencer's Gulf, and at the Onkaparinga, and of opening up a communication from the river Murray to Encounter Bay, to report on the capabilities of these localities and of their requirements to make them available as shipping places for colonial traffic.

Also (it was an age of progress, and it was carrying out the ideas propounded in the first speech of the Governor), they were to report on the shoals, reefs, sunken rocks, soundings, extent of anchorage, winds and range of exposure, height of waves, currents, and all kindred matters touching the safety of shipping.

In opening the session of 1850, on the 23rd of May, the Governor called attention to the difficulty of a direct communication from the sea mouth of the river Murray —a difficulty which had hitherto baffled and disappointed the hopes and enterprise of the friends of South Australia, both European and colonial, and still remained insuperable. But, aided by the good services of Captain Lipson, R.N., and Mr. Richard T. Hill, C.E., he was satisfied that the long-coveted desideratum was practicable by the construction of a railway entirely over Crown lands, along the sea-board of Encounter Bay, connecting the Murray at Goolwa with Port Elliot. He argued that if his project were carried out it would not only immediately and directly benefit the province, but eventually would be of great value to the whole of Australia. There was not a ready response to this scheme, an undertaking nearer home—that is to say, the City and Port Railway—being considered of more importance. Nevertheless the larger scheme was destined to be the first to be carried on and completed.

On the 6th of June, 1850, Captain Bagot moved that a sum of £4000 should be placed upon the estimates of 1851 for the purpose of granting a bonus of £2000 each for the first and second iron steamers of not less than forty horse-power, and not exceeding in draught two feet of water when loaded, that should successfully navigate the waters of the river Murray from the Goolwa to, at least, the junction of the Darling. In August the bonus of £4000 was duly advertised.

On the 10th of September Sir Henry and Lady Young, accompanied by Mr. (afterwards Sir Arthur) Freeling and Mrs. Freeling, Mr. and Mrs. Torrens, and Mr. W. S. M. Hutton, started from Adelaide for the purpose of proceeding some distance up the Murray, to ascertain from personal observation, by taking soundings in various parts, the practicability of navigating the river. The gentlemen proceeded on horseback, and the ladies were conveyed in a carriage to the Rufus, two whale-boats having been sent up from Wellington for the use of the party. They started on the 25th from the Rufus, and reached the Darling on the 29th, thus satisfying themselves that, so far, the river could be successfully navigated. On the return trip they proceeded by water to the Goolwa, with two other boats in company. In crossing Lake Alexandrina they experienced a little rough weather. On arrival at Port Elliot the *Yatala* was in waiting to convey the party to Port Adelaide, where they arrived after an absence of about two months.

Soon after this, a marvellous exploit was performed by Captain Francis Cadell, who had arrived in Australia a few years before, and was as enthusiastic about the navigation of the Murray as Sir Henry Young was himself. Leaving Melbourne with a canvas boat carried on the back of a pack-horse, he arrived at length at Swan Hill Station on the Upper Murray, launched his frail craft, and, with four diggers he had chanced to meet, descended the stream to Lake Victoria, a distance of thirteen hundred miles. On his arrival in Adelaide, he announced the important result of his observations, namely, that the river could be safely navigated by steamers of shallow draught. The matter was taken up with great enthusiasm: the Murray Steam Navigation Company was formed, principally through the efforts of Captain Cadell and Mr. William Younghusband, for some time Chief Secretary of the colony; and a steamer, the *Lady Augusta*, so named after the wife of the Governor, was soon placed by the company upon the river.

On the first voyage (in 1853) she was commanded by Captain Cadell, who was accompanied by Sir Henry and Lady Young, a special party of ladies and gentlemen, and two representatives of the press. At Swan

Hill, thirteen hundred miles from the sea, the Governor addressed a despatch to the Duke of Newcastle, Secretary of State for the Colonies, acquainting him with the success of steam navigation on the Murray. The following is an extract from the despatch:—

"I have the honour and gratification of acquainting your Grace that the project of the steam navigation of the river Murray, the promotion of which has never ceased to engage my attention since my arrival in South Australia, has thus far been prosecuted with perfect success. The distance from the river Murray terminus near the sea at the Goolwa, in South Australia, to as far up as this place, is now ascertained to be an easily navigable course of thirteen hundred miles. The wool, with which this vessel is now about to be laden, is only the commencement of a large future carrying trade, beneficial to the greater part of the extensive continent of Australia. Under these circumstances I beg leave to make known to your Grace the conclusions at which I have arrived after personal observation in regard to the further measures it would be politic to adopt in order to promote the colonization of the vast basin of the Murray. . . . As respects measures actually progressing towards completion, I have briefly to state that the connection of the river Murray terminus, styled the Goolwa (a designation applied to it by the aborigines at Encounter Bay) with the sea at Port Elliot will immediately be effected by an animal-power iron tramway of only seven miles in length. The tramway connects the river at the Goolwa with Port Elliot, and is laid on jetties at both places. At Port Elliot there are means of supplying fresh water to the shipping, and the anchorage is furnished with moorings for large ships. These improvements will have cost the Government £23,000, in addition to £6500, which will probably become payable from the same source, as premiums for the introduction of river steamers. . . ."

After describing the extensive tracts of land on the banks of the river, the Governor continued:—

"Considering, therefore, the importance of facilitating the location on its banks of persons whose industrial pursuits would be promoted in connection with the carrying trade of wool, and the return supplies to the stockowners; considering, too, most especially, the probability that large numbers of British emigrants, whether intending in future to settle in Victoria, New South Wales, or South Australia, are likely to be attracted to the vast basin of the Murray when its navigability by steamers shall become known, and it is found to be a most convenient route to the gold-fields— I have come to the determination at once to submit to my Executive Council, on my return to Adelaide, the expediency of proclaiming the lands on both banks of the river within the bounds of South Australia to the extent of two miles, to be the 'Hundreds of the Murray in South Australia.' Surveys of villages will be made in select spots, as traffic and population require, and roads leading to and from the river will be reserved for public use and as a means of access to the back lands, whilst the alluvial flats, subject, at present, to periodical inundation, may, by embankment, be rendered perfectly available. . . ."

The return journey was successfully accomplished, and the arrival of the explorers in Adelaide was the occasion of great popular festivities. The promised Government bonus was presented to Captain Cadell; the Legislature directed a gold medal to be struck to commemorate the event; several other steamers were soon placed upon the river, not only by the Murray River Navigation Company, but also by enterprising colonists; popular opinion, at one time dead against the expenditure of so much money on the scheme, turned in its favour, and the Legislature which had stoutly opposed it, gave a grand banquet in the Council Chamber to celebrate "the unparalleled triumph."

However much the community generally approved, the squatters, who wished to remain the sole and undisturbed occupiers of the vast tracts of pastoral country adjacent to the Murray river, were by no means pleased. The Murray Hundreds, when declared, became for years a subject for the discussion and animadversion of those who considered that their rights and territory had been unnecessarily invaded and encroached upon, by reserving the whole of the water frontages for hundreds of miles on both side of the river, while the back country was destitute of water.

No one rejoiced more sincerely in the successful opening up of the Murray than Sir Henry Young. It had been his pet scheme from the commencement of his administration. He foresaw the development of a great water-way for the commerce of the adjoining colonies; he foresaw the valley of the Murray teeming with a wealthy industrial population; he prophesied that Port Elliot would soon be "the New Orleans of the Australian Mississippi."

It is painful to record that the dreams of the Governor never came true, and the sequel to the story we have briefly told here is a melancholy and disappointing one. Port Elliot was an utter failure, owing to its insecurity and want of accommodation. Over £20,000, in addition to the initial cost, was "thrown into the sea," in a vain attempt to construct a breakwater and so improve the port, which resulted in its silting up, and at length it was abandoned. An enormous sum was also spent upon Port Victor, seven miles away, which then became the port of the Murray. Almost every one who speculated in the Murray trade came to grief, some to utter ruin, and amongst them the gallant Captain Cadell; the Murray Steam Navigation Company was dissolved, and the whole scheme was threatened with total collapse. In process of time, however, as we shall see later on in this history, the Murray river trade got into other hands and met with varying success, but the sanguine hopes of Sir Henry Young have never yet been fully realized.

One subject on which there was considerable discussion in 1852, and great diversity of opinion, was the abolition of grand juries. Under the rule of Sir George Grey the first attempt was made to abolish them.

It was then enacted in the colony "that in order to dispense with the attendance of the grand jury, and otherwise to expedite the business of sessions of the peace, all criminal proceedings before any such court of general sessions shall be by information in the name of her Majesty's Advocate-General." The ordinance was disallowed by Lord Stanley, "but the local authorities," says Mr. Rusden in his "History of Australia," "persevered. In 1843 they pushed aside, without abolishing, grand juries by an Ordinance . . . which ordered that 'no person should be put upon trial . . . unless the bill shall first have been presented to a grand jury on the prosecution of her Majesty's Attorney or Advocate-General and shall have been returned by them a true bill, reserving always, nevertheless, to her Majesty's Attorney or Advocate-General the right of filing informations *ex officio*, and to the Supreme Court the right of permitting informations to be filed.' This Ordinance was allowed; and, the path being smoothed, the work of repudiating a great social duty was consummated in 1852 by another (when Sir Henry F. Young was Governor and Mr. R. D. Hanson the principal law officer), which declared that 'from and after the passing of this Act no person shall be summoned or liable to serve on any grand jury,' repealed the section of the Ordinance of 1843 above cited, and made presentment 'in the name and by the authority of' a prosecuting officer sufficient when the lives of her Majesty's subjects were imperilled. The motive of departmental convenience was thus allowed to prevail, although some colonists were of opinion that the grand jury system had worked well."

In 1853 there were matters pending in the Legislative Council which were to influence the whole of the future of the colony, and to impress the name of the Governor indelibly upon its annals.

As the time drew near for the sitting of the Legislative Council, every man in the colony was more or less on his mettle. The great question of a new Constitution, which it was hoped would secure responsible government and free political institutions from that time forth and for evermore, was to be discussed, and meetings were held in various parts of the colony to have a " first say " in moulding opinion.

When the Legislative Council met on the 21st of July, despatches were read intimating the royal pleasure, upon certain conditions, to grant to the Legislature of the province the complete control of its internal affairs and the entire management and revenue of the Waste Lands of the Crown.

Two Bills were therefore introduced, one for constituting a Parliament consisting of a Legislative Council and Assembly, and the other for granting a Civil List to her Majesty.

" In framing the Bill for constituting a Parliament," said the Governor in his opening address to the Council, " a principal object has been to continue the advantages of a popular Government with those which result from the existence of an independent body, identified with the permanent interests of the colony, and forming a security against hasty or partial legislation. With this view, the number of members of the House of Assembly is proposed to be increased, the elective franchise to be extended, the duration of the Assembly to be reduced from five to three years, and a more simple and, it is believed, efficacious plan of registration has been devised. It has been provided that the Assembly thus constituted shall have the same control over the revenue and expenditure which is possessed by the Commons House of Parliament in England, while the Legislative Council will consist of persons summoned by the Crown, who will hold their seats for life, and thus be independent both of the Government and of the people. Her Majesty's Government, after full consideration, has deemed it most accordant with the principles of the British constitution that the selection of members for the Upper Chamber should be vested in the Crown. Experience has shown that, where the principle of responsible government exists, no permanent opposition can be maintained against the deliberate and repeated will of the community as expressed through their representatives; and if these reasonable expectations should be disappointed, a power is reserved to the united Legislature of introducing such further amendments in the Constitution as may suffice to bring it into harmony with the circumstances and wants of the colony."

The idea of a nominee Upper House was distasteful to the majority of the colonists, and the newspapers had but recently informed them how it had been ridiculed in the British Parliament. In a debate upon the Australian Colonies Bill, the Duke of Newcastle had said:—

"The theory of a nominee Upper House arose from the old notion of Imperial government, and from an idea that it was necessary to bind the colonies and the mother country together by some means other than those of mutual interest; that while it may be desirable to give the colonists a representative body to attend to their interests, they must at the same time appoint a nominated body to attend to the interests of the mother country. Now, it appeared to him that in following this old-fashioned notion, the Government were in this instance and in others, since their accession to power, pursuing the shadow instead of the substance of a conservative principle."

He continued: "Let them in any way provide for the superior influence of the members of an elective Upper Chamber; let them insist upon a higher qualification, either of elected or electors; let them give them a longer tenure of their seats, or make the areas of representation more extensive; but let them not engraft upon this measure of freedom and contentment to the colony a scheme which must end in disappointment and be the cause of future quarrel."

Earl Grey, in alluding to the want of analogy between a nominee Upper Chamber and the House of Lords, remarked "on the perfect absurdity of talking of a nominee Legislative Council as an imitation of that House. It had not," he said, "the most distant or faint resemblance to the House of Lords, which was an institution altogether peculiar to this country, and which Parliament could no more create than they could create a full-grown oak. It had grown up as part of our institutions from the earliest times, and was like no other body in any country in the world, and no imitation of which had ever been in the slightest degree successful."

Not only was the idea of a nominee Upper House distasteful to the outside public in the colony, but it was also to the elective members of the Legislature, who, at a meeting held to discuss the situation, agreed to oppose it. The next important step was taken by Mr. J. H. Fisher, who moved for a call of the House on the second reading of the Bill. Before the second reading came on, Mr. Dutton brought forward the following motion :—
" That in the proposed Bill for constituting a Parliament for South Australia, this Council is of opinion that the Upper House should be elective."

The debate on this motion lasted for three days, and on a division was lost by a majority of eight, in consequence of several members, who admitted the principle, having entered into a compromise with the Government to the effect that " a nominated Upper Chamber should be accepted by the House, on condition that the Constitution should be amended after a period of nine years, should such be deemed expedient by two-thirds of the members of the Lower House, and whose wishes to that effect should be expressed in two consecutive sessions, with a dissolution of the Assembly between."

The second and third readings of the Bill were carried, each by a majority of five. During the progress of the Bill through its different stages, the House divided no fewer than eleven times.

Considerable discussion also attended the passing of the Civil List Bill, which went through the ordeal of a select committee. The sums suggested by it, however, were not adopted, much larger amounts being substituted by the Council.

The debate on the Parliament Bill of 1853 was,

perhaps, the very best in the history of the South Australian Legislature. Every man was in earnest, and seemed imbued with the idea that in the part he was taking he was assisting to make the whole future of the colony. Many of the speeches might rank among the finest specimens of oratory of the English-speaking peoples. Although, as we shall see later on, their Bill was defeated, not receiving the royal assent, the victory was morally complete. Its provisions laid down the principles, and created and shaped the public opinion which in three years' time was to carry everything before it with overwhelming force ; and to the Legislative Council of 1853 every colonist in South Australia, now and for all time, owes a debt of deep gratitude, as they were undoubtedly the fathers and founders of the most free political institutions compatible with the sovereignty of the mother country.

Another important event that marked the successful administration of Sir Henry Young was the establishment of District Councils. In every new colony the question of roads and road-making is a burning one, and dwellers in old-established cities can form no conception of the wild enthusiasm, the fiery oratory, the impassioned earnestness displayed over a discussion on road-making. It had been a leading topic for many years in South Australia, during which time the central Government had undertaken the formation and repair of the main lines of road out of the land revenue. But as the country became opened up in all directions, it was found that the expense of making and maintaining roads in the various districts could not be borne from the same fund. On the 25th of November, 1852, therefore, "An Act to appoint District Councils, and to define the power thereof," passed the Legislative Council, and gave to the various districts power to tax themselves for the making and management of their own particular roads, bridges, and public buildings ; to grant timber, publicans', depasturing, and slaughtering licences, to establish pounds for the impounding of stray cattle, and so forth. Long before

Adelaide had a Corporation, municipal arrangements and a measure of local self-government were extended to the country districts.

"District Councils," says Mr. Finniss, "as they are established in this colony, are but incipient stages of a more perfect organization, which time and enlarged population will produce. They certainly, by their adoption, relieved the central Government of much odium, responsibility, and administrative work. It would have been impossible to manage the expenditure required under the head of roads, streets, and bridges, to which the Crown moiety, as it was called, of the land sales fund was applicable, without local advice and assistance, so as to avoid the reality, or at least the imputation, of favouritism and corruption. Local taxation, which was included in the powers given to the local bodies, and was eventually to supply the place of the subsidies from the general revenues, could not have been resorted to without the intervention of local elective bodies and absolute local self-control. It would have been invidious, if not absolutely unconstitutional, to have taxed a particular district for the erection of a bridge, or any other requisite public buildings, whereas there could be no objection to leave it in the power of a properly constituted district authority to tax themselves for such purpose where the benefit would be chiefly local."

Closely allied to the question of roads is that of railways, and to Sir Henry Young has been given the complimentary title of "Father of the Railway System of South Australia." So early as February, 1850, a measure was proposed by him, and carried through the Legislative Council, entitled, "An Ordinance for making a Railway from the City to the Port of Adelaide, with Branches to the North Arm;" and, a month later, a private ordinance guaranteed to the Adelaide City and Port Railway Company certain divisible profits in the concern. But the times were not ripe for the scheme to be floated, and there was much squabbling among wharf proprietors and others with local interests to protect, so that neither of these ordinances was put into operation. In the enlarged and partly elective Legislative Council of 1851, a fresh scheme was submitted and carried, namely, "An Act to authorize the Appointment of Undertakers for the Construction of the City and Port Railway," and from time to time funds were voted and placed in the hands of the executive body appointed under this Act.

On the 16th of December, 1854, almost the last act of the Governor before leaving the colony was to give his assent to a Bill authorizing the formation of the Adelaide and Gawler Town Railway, and to provide for raising the money required for that purpose.

Although, while Sir Henry Young was in the colony, there was not a mile of railroad opened to the public, the great battle of Locomotive v. Tramway was fought out by him; the sum of £400,000 was authorized under his administration for railway purposes, together with a further sum of £100,000 for deepening and improving the harbour, and so increasing the prospects of prosperity for the Port Railway. These sums initiated the national debt of South Australia.

The question of the defence of South Australia had happily not been necessary to discuss until the year 1854, when the startling news reached the colony that England, in alliance with France, had declared war against Russia. Hitherto no sense of danger had been felt; the sergeant's guard of Royal Marines (the bodyguard of Captain Hindmarsh, the first Governor) had given place to small detachments of troops—generally a couple of companies under one field officer—furnished by the regiments stationed in the older colonies. Spasmodic efforts were made, in the time of Governor Gawler and subsequently, to establish a volunteer force, but without much effect, and in the year 1846 there was supposed to be in existence "the Royal South Australian Militia Force." But this, according to a facetious member of the Legislative Council, "consisted of officers only and no troops." It was added that the standing army of South Australia had been for some years a standing joke, and that on one occasion, when the force was called out for exercise, the drill-sergeant, with great dignity and authority, gave the word of command to the three privates who occupied the field, " to form a square ! "

But in 1854, when the population of the colony had risen to nearly 100,000, and when the peace of Europe had been suddenly and rudely disturbed, it was considered time to take some serious action in case of surprise by an enemy's privateer or man-of-war. Accordingly, a Board was appointed to inquire into and report upon the measures of defence requisite for the public safety in case of—nobody knew exactly what. Of course the committee recommended as much protection as would have been practicable if Russia had declared war against South Australia, but out of it came some tangible results. An armed body of volunteers was enrolled; £15,000 was voted for defensive preparations; a Militia Bill was passed; excitement ran as high as fever heat, and the Colonial Secretary (Mr. B. T. Finniss), who was appointed " lieutenant-colonel of the staff and inspecting field officer," was able to report thus :—

"Leading colonists joined the military movement; men who afterwards became members of Parliament and of Ministries, men of substance, proprietors of the principal trading establishments in the city, served as privates in the first muster of a South Australian armed force, and of their zeal, enthusiasm, and martial ardour there could be no doubt in the minds of those who witnessed the first passage of arms and who saw the suburban companies cheerfully submitting to the rule of drill-masters."

Happily, in this first passage of arms, the (sham) enemy was only butchered to make a South Australian holiday; the Militia Act remained in abeyance; the volunteers, with their good old Brown Besses, had some fine exercise, and were paid for each day's attendance; and the seventeen thousand odd pounds spent was a good investment, inasmuch as it was the means of giving peace of mind to every timid colonist. Eventually, as we shall see in the course of this history, an efficient military establishment was formed, but not until many years had elapsed.

On the 20th of December, 1854, the successful administration of Sir Henry Young came to an end, and he left the colony on that day to assume the Government of Tasmania, bearing with him the gratitude and the good wishes of the whole population of South Australia.

Pending the arrival of the new Governor, Mr. Boyle Travers Finniss, one of the earliest settlers, who came to the colony with the surveying party in the *Cygnet*, was appointed acting Governor. He had from the first held many important offices, and commanded the respect of all parties in the colony. There were no events of any importance to mark the term of his office, but the quiet, business-like, and unostentatious manner in which he conducted the routine of public affairs won for him universal approval.

CHAPTER X.

ADMINISTRATION OF SIR RICHARD GRAVES MACDONNELL.

JUNE, 1855—MARCH, 1862.

Antecedents of Sir R. G. MacDonnell.—Unemployed Irish Female Immigrants.—An Amusing Incident.—The Parliament Bill.—Election Riots.—Opening of the New Legislative Council.—Depression in Trade.—Retrenchment and the Civil Service.—A Mania for Select Committees.—Adelaide Waterworks and Drainage.—New Constitution Act.—Ballot and Universal Suffrage.—The First South Australian Parliament.—A Noble Record.—Questions of Privilege.—Originating Money Bills.—Frequent Changes in Ministry.—Torrens' Real Property Act.—Mr. Justice Boothby.—Australian Federation.—Poll Tax on Chinese.—Colony attains its Majority.—Assessment on Stock.—Free Immigration.—The Political Association.—The Destitute Asylum.—Labour Tests.—The Working Men's Association.—Defences of the Colony.—Wreck of the *Admella*.—A Terrible Week.—Political Parties.—Ministerial Programmes.—Archdeacon Hale and the Aborigines.—Poonindie.—Mr. G. F. Angas and Missions to Natives.—The Great Murray Railway Scheme.—Explorations.—Sir R. G. MacDonnell on the Murray.—Mr. B. H. Babbage.—A Fearful Death.—Mr. Stephen Hack.—Major Warburton.—John McDouall Stuart—Journeys to the Interior.—Mining Discoveries.—Yorke's Peninsula.—Wallaroo and Moonta.—A Mining Mania.—South Australian Wines.—A Review of Six Years.

AFTER a stormy and perilous voyage of unusual length, the steamship *Burra-Burra*, with Sir Richard and Lady MacDonnell on board, arrived at Port Adelaide on the 7th of June, 1855.

Next morning the vessels in the harbour and the

public buildings on shore displayed their bunting, and, under a salute of seventeen guns, the new Governor landed and was driven, with Lady MacDonnell, in a carriage and four to Adelaide, amid the enthusiastic cheers of some thousands of the populace who lined the streets.

Sir Richard Graves MacDonnell, a son of the Rev. Dr. MacDonnell, Provost of Trinity College, Dublin, was born in 1815, entered Trinity College in 1830, took his degree of M.A. in 1839, and Doctor of Laws by special honorary degree in 1844. He was called to the English Bar in 1841, but two years later he accepted the office, then created, of Chief Justice of the British possessions at the Gambia, where he performed useful work in consolidating the laws of that colony, and also found time to make extensive and adventurous travels into the interior of Africa. Afterwards he twice visited North America, when he travelled over Canada and a great portion of the United States. He returned to England in 1847, and tendered the resignation of his office with a view to settling down at the English Bar. But Earl Grey having offered him the governorship of the Gambia Settlements, he returned there, and ably filled the difficult office for three years. When visiting one of the native kings he fell into an ambush treacherously laid for him, and was within an ace of being assassinated. Such an outrage on the representative of England could not be allowed to go unpunished, and four hundred men under Major Hill, including Sir Richard, acting as captain of a volunteer company, marched into the country of the enemy, and inflicted summary chastisement. Several explorations by the Governor into the interior of the country resulted in extending the limits of British commerce. In 1852 he was gazetted to the Government of St. Lucia in the West Indies, and afterwards to St. Vincent. He was knighted by the Queen in February, 1855, and soon afterwards—the appointment of the Hon. Mr. Lawley to the Government of South Australia having been cancelled—Sir Richard set sail from England to succeed Sir Henry Young in the Governorship of that province.

One of the first subjects to engage the attention of the new Governor was the large number of unemployed Irish female immigrants in the colony. Some hundreds were in the depôts, and it was not known how many more were on their way out. By this large, and in some respects unsuitable supply, the Emigration Commissioners posed as benefactors to the colonists, but the boon threatened to become a bane of no small magnitude. This kind of labour was only suitable for the country, and even there it was a drug in the market. But circulars were sent to the stipendiary and resident magistrates and chairmen of district councils with a view of ascertaining how many immigrants would be likely to meet with engagements in each district, and the result was more successful than had been anticipated—until an unlooked-for contingency arose. Many of these Irishwomen preferred a town life to a country life, and returned to the Adelaide depôt on the slightest pretext, or without any pretext at all.

Many schemes were proposed to meet the difficulty; among them one by Mr. E. Stephens, who suggested that respectable settlers should be found to employ them in any fair and suitable work for six months, the employer to provide them with board and lodging, and five shillings per week to be paid from the colonial treasury. But this suggestion was not carried out.

A remedy for excessive immigration was most urgently needed. During the first eight months of the year (1855), 2800 adult single females were landed at Adelaide, of whom 2047 were Irish, or nearly treble the total number of English and Scotch females. It was feared that the seeds of permanent pauperism were being sown. Despite every effort made by the Government and by the magistrates and district councils throughout the colony to obtain employment for them, there were, on the day the Legislative Council met, 800 Irish female immigrants lodged and rationed, either in the rural depôts or in town, as against only 27 English and 18 Scotch. At other times there had been as many as 1100.

Additional accommodation had to be provided, and the expense of this, with maintenance, reached nearly £25,000 in one year, "an amount," said the Governor, "which I propose to charge against the immigration moiety of the land fund, on the ground that all expenses and rations of an immigrant from the time he leaves England, till his absorption in the general population, are as justly chargeable against this fund as the cost of his rations on board the vessel which conveys him to these shores." Special representations were made to the Home Government, urging the necessity of a total discontinuance, for a considerable time, of Irish female immigration.

There was no ill feeling on the question of nationality, although it was determined in some quarters not to give any encouragement to immigrants from Ireland, which was not equally extended to natives of England, Wales, and Scotland. There was ample room for all who could work as agricultural labourers, miners, mechanics, or in any kind of industry, and it was a simple matter of fact that, although 9111 immigrants were landed in the first three quarters of the year, scarcely any of them remained unemployed except the women from Ireland.

It was some years before the matter was settled. The Colonial Commissioners in England paid very little regard in those days to remonstrances from the colony, and as the land fund had been prolific, the Commissioners continued to pour thousands of Irish immigrants into the colony. A select committee, appointed to report on excessive female immigration, stated that the total excess of females over males in 1853 was 679; in 1854, 1604; in 1855, 2829. Of the adult single females who arrived in 1855, 851 were English, 217 were Scotch, and 2981 were Irish!

It was a curious fact that at this time, although there were many hundreds of women out of employment, the greatest difficulty was experienced in obtaining a really good domestic servant.

Eventually a check was put upon the undue supply of Irish female labour, and an agent, with a salary of £500 a year, was appointed by the colonial Legislature to assist the Commissioners in the selection of suitable emigrants.

An amusing incident in connection with this subject was narrated by Sir Richard MacDonnell some years later in a speech delivered by him at the Royal Colonial Institute. Referring to the fact that in one year the Emigration Commissioners in England sent out 12,000 emigrants, he said " his hearers might fancy how much the difficulty of the position was augmented when he told them that of the above number no fewer than 4004 were able-bodied, single ladies. He questioned whether any other man than he ever had previously such a number of single women thrust upon him. He confessed that he had never been so embarrassed. He did what he could for them; built them barracks, offered to pay their fare, and all expenses to any employers willing to take them off his hands, for he was sorry to have to add that they were occasionally very unruly. Now, as women in a state of rebellion are not so easily dealt with as men, he might mention that by a happy thought they were on one occasion reduced to obedience by the cooling effects of water from a fire engine." *

One of the greatest series of events under the important administration of Sir Richard MacDonnell was in connection with the framing and passing the Parliament Bill. On the 11th of August, 1855, a *Gazette Extraordinary* was issued containing a despatch from Lord John Russell with reference to the South Australian Parliament Bill, from which it appeared that Sir Henry Young and his advisers had misconceived the intentions of her Majesty's Government in granting certain enlarged powers to the local

* "Proceedings of the Royal Colonial Institute," 1875-76, vol. xii. p. 203.

Legislature. The Bill, therefore, was not taken as an expression of the wishes of the majority, and as it was supposed that the colonists, if allowed the opportunity of arriving at a free and independent decision as to what they considered the best form of constitution for the colony, would reconsider and amend the Bill, it was recommended that such opportunity should be given by the dissolution of the elective portion of the then existing Council.

Four days later the dissolution of the Legislative Council was announced. "The incubus of nomineeism," said the *Register*, "had pressed heavily on the natural energies of the people's representatives, and the elaborate and positive misinterpretation of Imperial despatches on the part of the Executive had proved a fatal snare to an inexperienced Assembly."

The first Representative Council was no more, and the people were now called upon to reconstitute the Legislature under different auspices and for greater purposes than before. The future welfare of the colony depended upon their action. They were not called upon to make an ordinary law, but to elect men to make a Constitution which should more or less determine the nature of all laws to be subsequently enacted.

"We are laying the foundations," continued the *Register*, "of a new political and social state. We are deciding whether public opinion shall be taken as the source of legislative authority, or whether the people are yet to be held in the leading-strings of Imperial domination."

The Government put forth an elaborate outline of a Constitution Bill for the consideration of the next Legislative Council, but the proposed measure was not received with any degree of approval, and it was evident that it was the result of hasty or ill-advised consideration. Sir Richard did not press his measure, and expressed the hope that when the new Council met they would hit upon the form of Constitution best suited to the country.

The writs for the election of members for the new Council were issued on the 17th of August, and from that time forth meetings were held in all parts of the colony to hear the opinions of the candidates for legislative honours.

Excitement culminated on the 20th and 21st of September, the days fixed for the election in most of the districts, and, as if to demonstrate the need for the ballot, scenes were enacted at some of the polling booths, such as few would desire to see repeated. West Adelaide took the lead in this unenviable particular. When from the balcony of the Exchange Hotel it was announced that Mr. Forster was at the head of the poll, the partisans of Mr. Fisher rushed to the balcony, with a yell, pulled down the flags and tore them to shreds, and then descended and charged the crowd. Police on foot failing to scatter the rioters, " mounted troopers, led by the commissioner of police, galloped with drawn swords into the thickest of the fight, and the admirable and determined movements of this body had a very salutary effect upon the infuriated partisans, several of whom were captured" (*vide* local paper).

On the 1st of November the opening of the new Legislative Council took place, on which occasion the new Council Chamber, handsome and well furnished, was occupied for the first time for the transaction of the business of the country.

In his introductory speech, the Governor alluded to the gratifying acknowledgment by her Majesty's Government of the rapid growth of the colony, as shown by its recent separation from the control of the New South Wales Government, and modestly mentioned the fact that the Governor of South Australia was no longer merely Lieutenant-Governor, but held the commission of " Captain-General and Governor-in-Chief of South Australia," formerly held by the Governor-General at Sydney.

It still remained the special privilege, however, of the Governor-General to originate measures applicable to the whole of the Australian colonies—all measures, in short, requiring as it were federal action for the promotion of great objects common to all the Australian colonies.

When the all-absorbing question of a new Constitution came before the Legislature, the Governor, notwithstanding the rebuff he had received in the rejection of his first proposals, informed the Council that he still retained the preference he had avowed for a single Chamber only during the youthful stage of the colony's progress, although aware that the proposition would not meet with many supporters. But whatever inconvenience might arise from a double Chamber, he felt it was better and wiser to adopt those inconveniences, if supported by public opinion and sympathy, than to strive for the most ideal form of government in opposition to the feelings of the community—sentiments which even Lord Chesterfield would have been justified in setting before his son.

The Governor then gave the full outlines of the new Constitution Bill, but it soon became evident that the Council was not very favourable to the proposed Government measure. To avoid the rejection of it altogether, the Government suggested a compromise, namely, that if its second reading were carried, the Council would not be pledged to any of its clauses, and with this understanding the Council agreed to go into committee on the measure.

The Bill, as altered and amended in committee, provided for two Chambers, both elective—one of eighteen members, to be elected by the whole colony as one constituency; the other of thirty-six members, to be chosen by a certain number of districts equally arranged, and divided on the basis of population. In the Legislative Council, or Upper House, six members were to retire every four years, and for the House of Assembly the elections were to be triennial. The qualification of voters for the former was to be a freehold of £50 clear value, a leasehold of £10 per annum with three years to run, a right of purchase, or a tenancy of the value of £25. For the latter a manhood suffrage, with six months' registration, was all that was required. All voting to be by ballot. Responsible government was to be secured by requiring ministers to be elected by the constituencies, and when elected only to sit and vote in their own Chamber. All money Bills to originate in the House of Assembly. All official appointments and dismissals to be in the power of the ministry, and no Governor's warrant for the payment of money to be valid unless countersigned by the Chief Secretary.

As regarded the civil list, it was provided that instead of a bonus for the risk of loss of office by non-election, a moderate annual allowance was to be made to the Colonial Secretary, Treasurer, Advocate-General, and Commissioner of Crown Lands in the event of actual loss of office.

After passing through a severe ordeal, the third reading of the Constitution Bill in its altered and amended form took place on the 2nd of January, 1856, and the Bill was passed.

The year 1855 had been characterized by great depression in trade, consequent mainly upon the dry seasons that prevailed during the year and the one preceding it, causing a very deficient harvest; this reacted on all branches of industry, and gave a decided check to the rapid progress the colony had been making for two or three years previously. With the quantity of grain and flour exported, and the shortness of the supply, fears were entertained whether a sufficient stock had been kept in the colony to last till the harvest; fears that happily proved groundless.

The impetus given to trade by the large quantities of gold sent and brought from Victoria in 1852-53 had raised the price of almost everything. Land had reached a fictitious value both in town and country; wages had increased to such an extent as to render it impossible to employ labour except for indispensable and very remunerative undertakings; and, as provisions were still high in price, there was a strong disinclination to lower the rates in the labour market notwithstanding the excessive supply.

During this and several subsequent years, all classes of the community were slow to believe that, as the extraordinary influx of gold had ceased, prices must approximate to something near their normal rates before the colony could again be in a stable, healthy, and really prosperous condition. The suddenness of wealth had induced habits of extravagance which were not so easy to break off as to contract, and the absolute necessity for retrenchment in affairs public and private produced a general feeling of dissatisfaction.

After passing the Constitution Bill, the Council might very gracefully have retired upon its honours; but there were still certain pressing interests of the colony to be protected, and, with a view to retrenchment, the next business of the Council was to institute a searching examination into the public departments and accounts. The public service had to a certain extent become disarranged from the same causes which had produced so great an effect on the community at large—the influx of capital from the gold-fields. An Estimate Committee was appointed on the previous 13th of November (1855), and during its sittings five several reports were laid before the House, all of which were adopted or received by the Council. The committee sat seventy-five days, examined forty-nine officials and other witnesses, and elicited answers to 6193 questions.

The investigations of the committee * excited almost as much interest as the discussion of the Constitution. Every department was overhauled; every item of expenditure was checked; and the estimates for the year were reduced to the tune of some £40,000. Of course, retrenchment began in the Civil Service, as it always does everywhere; and a manly protest by the Governor, transmitted in a memorandum to the Legislative Council, will be read with interest by every Civil

* The committee (appointed by ballot) was made up as follows :—Mr. B. T. Finniss, Colonial Secretary, Messrs. Baker, Dutton, Forster, Kingston, Reynolds, and Younghusband.

Servant, in both hemispheres, who may chance to see it :—

"The tone in which the Government service has been alluded to more than once by the committee ; the ever-recurring attempt to drive as hard a bargain as possible with a body of gentlemen willing to toil hard for the sake of the country—but not to be thanklessly driven as well as underpaid—the extreme economy enforced in extensive departments, such as public works and the police, in which another but most important class of the community is largely interested—all these and other concurring circumstances are fast producing results which, ere long, there may be time to deplore, but not to remedy. There is a feeling gradually springing up that the service, which had been a badge of honour, is being changed into a badge of humiliation, and in these colonies freemen, whether their station be humble or exalted, will not brook to be looked down on by any man or body of men whatever. Fairer fields for enterprise and better rewards for industry and character are even now being sought out by numbers who had chosen this colony as their home, and had made her service their ambition."

The action of the Governor in sending this memorandum—which took up several other points—was severely censured, and a vote was moved and seconded declaring it to be "an irregular and improper interference in the constitutional action of the House and its committees." The wording of the resolution was, however, supposed to be toned down by an amendment "that the Governor's memorandum contains matter which is offensive to this House, and that the good understanding between the Government and the Legislature is not calculated to be maintained by transmitting such documents to this Council." Happily, the Governor was not puffed into space by this "counterblast," and the incident is amusing mainly as showing the political amenities of that day.

Apart from this little misunderstanding, it was well known and generally acknowledged that the main object of the inquiry was to secure the greatest economy of the public money with a due regard to the maintenance of the public departments in an efficient and adequate manner, and with the least interruption of public works and matters connected with the general progress of the colony. The Government bore testimony to the value of the labours of the committee by largely adopting their suggestions.

The committee was greatly indebted to the efficient services of the very able Auditor-General, Captain W. L. O'Halloran, who aided them in many important particulars, and was mainly instrumental, in fact, in making their inquiries possible.

About this time there was a mania for select committees; in addition to the one we have referred to, others were appointed during the session on the following subjects:—The colonial agency; the excessive female immigration; the distillation laws; the treatment of lunatics; the discipline and management of the police force; and the proposed proclamation of the Sydney coinage as a legal tender in South Australia.

One other measure claiming a notice on account of its magnitude and importance was the Adelaide Waterworks and Drainage Act, by which the Colonial Treasurer was empowered to borrow £280,000 on the credit of the general revenue, to bear six per cent. interest, with four per cent. added as a redemption fund.* The Bill was passed at the close of the session, and it is somewhat remarkable that, considering the sum proposed to be borrowed, and the heavy taxes to which the citizens would be subject, very little notice was taken of the matter by the public until it was too late. It is not impossible that, as the proposal had been so long pending, and the citizens had seen so many unsuccessful attempts to bring it to an issue, they took it for granted the Bill would not be passed.

But the citizens were gainers in the end. The water supply had always been sadly deficient in quantity

* It was required also to set apart £28,000 annually to pay interest and amount of redeemable bonds.

and inferior in quality, and they had ever before their eyes the fear of epidemics and the risk of desolating fires.

The session, opened on the 1st of November, 1855, was prorogued on the 4th of June, 1856, and, notwithstanding two or three adjournments, was the longest held in the colony up to that time. No less than fifty Bills were introduced, of which thirty-five passed. In his closing address the Governor said, "The session about to close will long be remembered as that in which the principles were established and the broad foundations laid of the Constitution under which South Australia will, I trust, long continue to extend that prosperity which, under Divine Providence, has hitherto blessed the energy and honourable industry of her children. I confidently expect that the extended political power entrusted to the people of this country, and the universal suffrage conceded by the new Constitution, will prove, in reality, a safe and conservative measure; and, whilst conferring the utmost possible powers of self-government, will render stronger and more enduring than ever the cherished ties of affection and loyalty which link this province to the throne of our respected and beloved Sovereign. I have therefore felt much pleasure in recommending that the New Constitution Bill should receive the royal assent; and in the event of any of its clauses appearing to exceed the powers of this Legislature, that an imperial Act should be passed, ratifying the measure as far as might be judged expedient, in preference to returning the Bill for further amendment."

On the 24th of October, 1856, the Governor received important despatches from England, together with the new Constitution unaltered, which had been assented to by her Majesty at a Cabinet council held in Buckingham Palace on the 24th of June, 1856. It was entitled " An Act to establish a Constitution for South Australia, and to grant a Civil List to her Majesty." On the very same day that the despatches were received in the colony, the Governor proclaimed the new Constitution and the appointment of the new Ministry.* Contemporaneous with the proclamation in the colony of the New Constitution Act, the new Waste Lands Act was to have the force of law, transferring to the colonial Legislature the absolute control of the land fund. By this Act the Crown vested in the colonial Legislature the whole of the unsold and unappropriated territory of the colony, and the power also to use the funds arising from the disposal of the said lands in any way that might seem most advisable or desirable.

The old Council assembled on the 11th of November, and the session was brought to a close on the 11th of December, having only held seventeen sittings. It was the last session of the partly elective and partly nominee Legislature, but the Council was not dissolved till the issue of the writs for the election of the new Parliament. During the short time that the representatives of the people had been entrusted with the partial control of the affairs of the colony, they had worked with so much zeal and ability as to entitle them to a foremost position in the forthcoming elections. The members of the Executive had won golden opinions

---

* The new Ministry was composed as follows:—

Chief Secretary	The Hon. B. T. Finniss.
Attorney-General	„ R. D. Hanson.
Treasurer	„ R. R. Torrens.
Commissioner of Public Works	„ A. H. Freeling.
„ „ Crown Lands and Immigration	C. Bonney, Esq.

The civil list provided for the following salaries:—

Governor	£4000
First Judge	1500
Second Judge	1300
Attorney-General	1000
Crown Solicitor and Public Prosecutor	600
Chief Secretary	1300
Under-Secretary	600
Treasurer	900
Auditor-General	700
Commissioner of Lands and Immigration	800
„ „ Public Works	800

These salaries, of course, present a striking contrast to those fixed in the year 1836.

from the working classes, by securing the partial discontinuance of immigration.

Notwithstanding that so much of the time and thought of people and rulers had been taken up in discussing the new Constitution, the year was not barren in results for the general good in other spheres of action. The harvest had been abundant, and a proportionate exportation of wheat and flour had yielded liberal returns. The value of wheat and flour exported amounted to the enormous sum of £528,320 13s. 4d. Great progress, too, had been made in public works; the Adelaide City and Port Railway had been opened to the public, and the Gawler line as far as to Salisbury; while "railway extension" was one of the main topics of discussion. One of the finest bridges in the colony, to connect North and South Adelaide, had been constructed at a cost, including its approaches, of about £20,000. Commissioners for carrying out the great waterworks scheme had been appointed and operations had commenced. The lighthouse on Troubridge Shoal had exhibited its warning light for the first time, and the necessary sums had been voted for similar beacons on Cape Borda and Cape Northumberland. The number of immigrants was small in comparison with the previous year, and, owing to the severe censures passed on the Land and Emigration Commissioners in England, they were of a much better class.

The year 1857 commenced with extensive preparations for the election of members for the first Parliament of South Australia. Meetings of candidates were held in all parts of the country up to the time of the issue of writs for the several divisions and districts, after which time, as prescribed by the Act, no further addresses were permitted. This "gagging" clause was roundly condemned—more especially by candidates who were late in the field—as an infraction of liberty of speech, the right of free-born Englishmen.

Not a few, to whom the words "ballot" and "universal suffrage" suggested ideas of democracy, republicanism, and anarchy, thought that the knell of the colony's ruin had been sounded. As the time for the elections drew near it was found that to fill the fifty-four seats in the two Houses, namely, eighteen to the Legislative Council and thirty-six in the House of Assembly, there were twenty-seven candidates for the former and sixty-two for the latter, making a total of eighty-nine. On the day of nomination the discovery was made that nine candidates were unopposed.

The 9th of March was the day fixed for the elections, and it was announced that it would be a public holiday. Those who had witnessed the quiet and orderly manner in which the several candidates were nominated had no doubt come to the conclusion that what many considered the glory of an election had departed. There had been no banners and ribbons, no music and orations, no shouting and fighting. The returning-officer had simply opened and read the letters proposing and seconding the various candidates, and this, with three cheers for the Queen, concluded the proceedings.

The Electoral Act provided for the conduct of the elections in a similar quiet and orderly manner. There were to be no hustings, and the booths or polling-places were to be a specified distance from a public-house. No wonder, therefore, that on the day of election people were seen quietly resorting to the polling-places as if they were going to exercise a national right and perform an important duty. This done, there was no inducement to linger at the spot, as it was provided that there would be no declaration of the state of the poll until the final stage was reached. It was a striking contrast to the scenes enacted at the last elections, and all sober-minded people congratulated themselves upon the reform.*

---

* The result of the elections for the first South Australian Parliament was as follows :—

For the Legislative Council.

G. F. Angas, H. Ayers, C. H. Bagot, T. Baker, S. Davenport, Dr. C. Davies, Dr. C. G. Everard, J. H. Fisher, A. Forster, A. H. Freeling, E. C. Gwynne, G. Hall, Major T. S. O'Halloran, J. Mor-

For the election the colony had been divided into "districts" and "divisions," the former electing members for the House of Assembly, the latter for the Legislative Council. The members for the latter House were to represent the whole colony, hence the dividing of it for the purpose of facilitating the elections. The members of the House of Assembly were to represent the districts which elected them, and the number of representatives for each district was regulated, as far as practicable, on a population basis.

By direction of her Majesty the members of the Legislative Council and the Speaker of the House of Assembly were to have the title of "Honourable" conferred upon them, and were officially to be addressed as such while occupying seats in the said Council, and the Speaker while holding office in such capacity. The members of the Executive Council (or of the Ministry) were also to enjoy a similar privilege or honour.

On the 22nd of April the new Parliament met, about a thousand persons assembling on North Terrace to witness and cheer the arrival of the members and the Governor.

phett, A. Scott, W. Scott, E. Stirling, and W. Younghusband, = eighteen.

For the House of Assembly.

City of Adelaide: R. R. Torrens, R. D. Hanson, F. S. Dutton, B. T. Finniss, J. B. Neales, W. H. Burford.
Port Adelaide: J. Hart, J. B. Hughes.
West Torrens: L. Scammell, J. W. Cole.
Yatala: J. Harvey, C. S. Hare.
Gumeracha: A. Blyth, A. Hay.
East Torrens: G. M. Waterhouse, C. Bonney.
The Sturt: T. Reynolds, J. Hallett.
Noarlunga: T. Young, H. Mildred.
Mount Barker: F. E. H. W. Krichauff, J. Dunn.
Onkaparinga: W. Milne, W. B. Dawes.
Encounter Bay: B. H. Babbage, A. F. Lindsay.
Barossa: W. Duffield, H. Dean.
The Murray: D. Wark.
Light: J. T. Bagot, C. Smedley.
Victoria: R. R. Leake.
Burra and Clare: G. S. Kingston, M. Marks, E. J. Peake.
Flinders: M. MacDermott.

There is something really amusing, but at the same time very splendid, in this inauguration of a Parliament for South Australia. Let the reader try and realize it. The whole population of the colony was estimated at 109,000; that is to say, fewer by some hundreds than are to be found to-day in such towns in England as Brighton, Bolton, Portsmouth, Leicester, or Cardiff, and considerably less than half the population of Bristol, Nottingham, or Bradford. The territory of the colony, on the other hand, was nearly three times as large as that of the whole of Great Britain; that is to say, it comprehended an area of 300,000 square miles, or 192 millions of acres. Only twenty years before, the land was practically uninhabited, with here and there a wattle-and-dab hut, or a canvas tent; population, and a certain amount of wealth, had poured in from all quarters, but ruinous reverses had been experienced. Out of these the people had struggled, holding on with tenacity to each success until it had been made more successful; throwing off one by one the leading-strings of paternal government until they attained political manhood.

To this handful of people, sixteen thousand miles, by sailing ship, away from England, composed of men, not as a rule those who had made their mark in the old country, or who were acquainted by practical experience with the usages of the Imperial Parliament, but simply a body of sturdy, loyal, and enterprising Englishmen seeking in one of the rising commonwealths of Greater Britain to perpetuate the institutions of their native land—to them was committed a system of responsible government involving the principles of universal suffrage, vote by ballot, equal electoral districts, and triennial Parliaments, together with the absolute control of revenues hitherto under the Crown, namely, the proceeds of the sale and lease of the waste lands within the province, and the unfettered management of the public purse, whether in taxation or expenditure. It is equally a wonder that the Imperial Government should have had sufficient confidence in the ability, loyalty, and discretion of the South Australians to entrust them with such a responsibility, as that men should have been found prepared and eager to accept it. "It must be confessed," said the London *Times* in a somewhat sarcastic article, "that it is rather an odd position for a new community of rising tradesmen, farmers, cattle-breeders, builders, mechanics, with a sprinkling of doctors and attorneys, to find that it is suddenly called upon to find Prime Ministers, Cabinets, a Ministerial side, an Opposition side, and all the apparatus of a Parliamentary Government—to awake one fine morning and discover that this is no longer a colony, but a nation, saddled with all the rules and traditions of the political life of the mother country."

Saddled with cumbersome and costly Government machinery the colony certainly was, and, in addition, it was subject to abuses to a great extent irremediable. For example, the power of governing was placed, by universal suffrage, in the hands of those who not only possessed the smallest stake in the colony, but were the least intelligent. It is amusing to remember that while the Constitution Act was under consideration, an endeavour was being made to establish an educational test, at least to the extent of reading and writing, as some guarantee of fitness for the exercise of the franchise; but even this was overruled by the democratic element in the Council as constituted at that time.

Nevertheless, with all the drawbacks, inevitable in the circumstances, the colonists hailed responsible government with enthusiasm, and after it had been tested by experience, they would not for any consideration have returned to the old state of affairs.

There was much work to be done on that auspicious day when the first South Australian Parliament met—the reading of the proclamation for assembling the Parliament, and of the commission for taking the usual oaths; the election of President for the Legislative Council (the Hon. J. H. Fisher), and of Speaker for the House of Assembly (Mr. G. S. Kingston), and to arrange the order, by lot, in which one-third of the Council should retire every four years. Then came the opening address, dealing first with the financial state of the province and then with the measures which would claim the attention of Parliament, including a Bill with regard to waste lands, an Education Bill (leaving untouched, however, the principle of the existing law), and other Bills relating to public works.

It was not to be expected that all the new machinery, now put into motion for the first time, would work well and smoothly at the start off, and it was not long before there was a decided "hitch." The first important disarrangement threatened to produce a deadlock. The occasion which brought the two Houses into collision was an amendment by the "Council" of a Bill passed by the "Assembly." The alteration made affected the principle of the Bill, and went so far as to strike out a clause providing for the repeal of the dues upon shipping. This was considered by the Assembly to be a breach of its privileges, and they passed a resolution calling upon the Council "to reconsider the Bill, inasmuch as it is a breach of privilege for the Legislative Council to modify any money Bill passed by this House."

This resolution was met by another in the Council, that "the policy pursued by the Ministry in attempting to legislate by resolution only in one branch of the Legislature is detrimental to the interests of the colony, subversive of the Constitution, and calculated to bring about a collision between the two Houses of Parliament." This resolution was, however, withdrawn, and the alternative course was—a battle on the question of privilege or a peace conference. The former course was chosen, and, after an adjournment for the preparation of the estimates, the matter came on for debate.

It would not interest the general public to follow the long and wearisome discussions that ensued; suffice it to say that for a considerable time public business was delayed; a long-winded opinion of the President, who was learned in the law, was obtained; much good temper, time, and eloquence were wasted on both sides, and in the end only a feeble compromise was effected. Still there were some points of interest in the great "Privilege Question," as it was called, that are worth recording. When it was found that there would be a deadlock unless some way of escape could be devised, a conference was agreed upon, and committees were appointed by both Houses to draw up "reasons" for the position taken up on either side. Those of the Legislative Council were to the effect that there was no analogy between the Imperial Parliament and the Parliament of South Australia, inasmuch as the British Upper House was hereditary and that of the province was elective, and as such was as much a guardian of the public purse as the Assembly, and further, that, with the exception of "originating" money Bills, the powers of the two colonial Chambers were equal. It was contended that the word "originate" should be taken in its sense, and applied only to the introduction of any money Bill. The Assembly, on the other hand, stood up for the analogy between the powers possessed by the British House of Commons and the colonial House of Assembly, and that, notwithstanding the fact that the term "originate" had not been defined by either legislative or judicial interpretation, both Houses must be influenced by reasons drawn from analogy as to the practice and privilege of the Imperial Parliament, and that, of course, reason and practice were conclusive in favour of the view of its privileges taken by the House of Assembly. That House further contended that as the right of the House of Commons to originate money Bills was claimed by that House, and had always been allowed by the Crown and the Lords as a common-law right, the claim of the House of Commons of excluding the House of Lords from modifying or altering such money Bills was a Parliamentary privilege inherent in, and flowing from, that right; therefore, as the Constitution Act vested in the House of Assembly the exclusive right of originating money Bills, the right to exclude the Legislative Council from modifying or altering such Bills was by direct and necessary implication also conferred.

Such being the attitude of both parties, public business was at a standstill until the feeble compromise aforesaid was effected. Briefly, it was as follows:—That while the Assembly should originate all money Bills, it should be competent for the Council to suggest alterations; but should those suggestions not be heeded, the Bills might be returned by the Assembly for reconsideration, and be either assented to or rejected by the Council. The Council still claimed its right to deal with the monetary affairs of the province, but would not enforce its right to deal with the ordinary details of the annual expenses of the Government.

These "concessions" were almost unanimously agreed to, and the crisis was averted for the time being.

Another important feature in this first session of Parliament was the frequent changes in the Ministry. The first, consisting principally of the Executive members of the former Legislature, held office until the 20th of August, having, after several defeats, tendered their resignations on the 10th of that month. The next was known as the Baker Ministry (Hon. John Baker, Chief Secretary), and held office from the 21st to the 27th, when, on a vote of want of confidence moved by Mr. Torrens, they resigned, and the Torrens Ministry came in and held office from the 1st to the 24th of September, when, Mr. Hanson having moved an adverse vote declaring a certain proclamation of the Governor to be "unwarranted and illegal," he was called upon to form the Hanson Ministry—and so on.

During this session Mr. (afterwards Sir) R. R. Torrens introduced his celebrated Bill for the transfer of real property, which has created more interest and brought about a greater reformation in the law of real estate than any measure ever enacted thereon either in England or in the colonies. No serious objections were raised against it at the time, and the Bill passed its third reading in the House of Assembly on the 15th of December with a majority of twelve, and in the

Legislative Council on the 26th of January, 1858, with a majority of five.

The design of Mr. Torrens was not only to dispense with transferring real estate in the first instance by deed, but also in every subsequent transaction where a deed would have been considered necessary.

"The first great principle of the Act," says Mr. Harcus, "is the transferring of real property by registration of title instead of by deeds; the second is absolute indefeasibility of title. The system is very simple and very inexpensive. The certificate of title is registered in the official registry at the Lands' Titles Office, the owner obtaining a duplicate certificate. All transactions affecting the land appear on the face of the certificate, so that at a glance it may be seen whether the property is encumbered or any charges are made upon it. If an owner wishes to mortgage his land, he takes his certificate to the office and has the transaction marked upon it. If he wants to sell, he passes over the certificate to the purchaser, and the transaction is registered. Any man of ordinary intelligence can do all that is necessary for himself, when once his property is brought under the Act." *

The cost was nominal. A percentage of one halfpenny in the penny was paid, when the land was for the first time brought under the law, to ensure the soundness of the transaction, and from this fund the State guaranteed to protect rightful proprietors when lands were brought by others under the Act. It was satisfactory to know that this provision was almost superfluous. When the accrued fund had reached £30,000, only £300 had been required to meet demands.

After accomplishing his arduous task, Mr. Torrens took a trip early in 1860 to the neighbouring colonies, where he met with a series of ovations, and was hailed as a general benefactor, each colony being anxious to put a similar law into operation. On his return he was appointed to the office of Registrar-General for

* "South Australia: its History and Resources," by W. Harcus.

the purpose of carrying out the measure. Various honours were heaped upon him, and he was subsequently knighted. It was not to be expected that Mr. Torrens would be able to carry everything before him in peace. In 1860 two cases of litigation arose relating to breaches of contract on the part of purchasers of land, and resulted in a keen contest between the legal profession and the friends of the Act. The decision of the judges was adverse to the Act, and it was determined to carry the case to the Court of Appeal, when Mr. Justice Boothby made the singular discovery that under the New Constitution Act no such tribunal existed!

It was while this case was under judicial consideration that fourteen members of the legal profession drew up a lengthy petition to the Duke of Newcastle, Secretary of State for the Colonies, praying that the Real Property Act might be referred to the law officers of the Crown for their opinion as to its legality and validity, before it received the assent of her Majesty.

Several colonial lawyers had, prior to this, addressed a letter to the Attorney-General, in which they expressed their opinion that the new Act was repugnant to the laws of England, and offered to draw up a fresh Bill. This offer was declined with thanks.

Then occurred a long series of public meetings and debates. The long-winded and utterly wearisome discussions would not interest anybody if they were reproduced, even in the briefest outline, here. Like most other reforms, this important and beneficent one had to encounter and overcome opposition from nearly all quarters—its advocates in their excess of zeal overstated its strength, while its opponents left nothing undone to find out its weak points. It was not in human nature that lawyers who had made small fortunes by their tedious " provided always " and " and whereas " could sit still and contemplate these time-honoured forms, which had been considered indispensable to a good title, being ruthlessly swept away; still less could they gaze upon vanishing six and eightpences and thirteen and fourpences with equanimity. What wonder, therefore, that they aroused themselves and fought to the death!

But the go-ahead South Australians were neither to be browbeaten nor hoodwinked. They saw that the old system of conveyancing (still adored in some old-fashioned countries—the mother country, to wit) was costly and cumbrous, and failed to give that security which is the only excuse for costliness, whereas the new system under the Real Property Act was simple, cheap, and secure. Moreover, it was specially adapted to meet the need of a colony where land was a common possession and a matter of daily bargain, instead of being the luxury of the few, and when once possessed was rarely parted with, except under circumstances of necessity.

Of course, there were imperfections in the system on its first introduction, but this is not so much a matter of wonder as that these imperfections were so few and were easily remediable, while its needs of amendment pale into insignificance beside the protracted legislation which has been found necessary in the mother country to bolster up the principles of the old system, to remove its anomalies, and to simplify its procedure.

From these discussions on the Real Property Act, there sprang up another—one of the most painful, and withal notable, in the annals of the colony. It may be well, perhaps, to tell the story in this place, although the case dragged its weary length along for years. The facts were briefly these :—

Mr. Justice Boothby having expressed his doubts as to the validity of certain Acts passed by the colonial Legislature, on the ground of their repugnance to the laws of England, rendered himself obnoxious to the Parliament, the press, and the public, and this was greatly increased when he went so far as to absolutely decide in the Supreme Court against the validity of the Real Property Act and other Acts which had not then received the royal assent. A motion for the appointment of a Select Committee "to examine into the recent decisions and conduct of His Honour, Mr. Justice Boothby, and to report thereon" was opposed by Mr. G. F. Angas on the ground that the whole matter turned upon hearsay and newspaper reports. But the motion was carried, and Mr. Angas was one of those chosen to act upon the committee.

Before this tribunal Mr. Boothby declined to appear; and this fact, perchance, added to the bitterness of the report of the Committee, a report from which Mr. Angas very strongly dissented, on the ground that the evidence adduced distinctly proved that the colonial judges had power to declare illegal and invalid Acts which had been passed by the Legislature of the colony, assented to by the Governor, and left to their operation by her Majesty, which was borne out by various decisions of the Courts of Law in other colonies and in England, and was consistent with the recognized and admitted principles of constitutional law. On this and on many other grounds, he stood out in defence of Mr. Justice Boothby, and a storm arose. So great was the outcry that meetings were held in various parts of the colony for the purpose of hearing the respective members give an account of the action each had taken in the matter.

By-and-by a petition was sent to the Queen, praying her to remove Mr. Justice Boothby from the bench, but it failed in its object; and instead of the judge being reprimanded, as some confidently anticipated, the colonial Legislature received a severe censure from the Home Government.

Not satisfied with this, a second address to the Crown was forwarded in 1866, to which the Secretary of State for the Colonies replied that the *ex parte* statements against the judge were insufficient grounds for his removal, and that unless the colony would agree to have the question argued before the Judicial Committee of the Privy Council, the local Government must deal with the case themselves.

This they resolved to do, and in June, 1867, a series

of charges were preferred against Mr. Boothby, who simply protested, but took no steps to defend himself.

The specific charges laid at his door were presented to Parliament in the following resolutions:—" (1) That he persistently refuses to administer laws duly enacted by the Parliament of South Australia. (2) That he declines to give effect to the Imperial statute known as the Validating Act. (3) That he is accustomed from the Bench to impugn the validity of the local Court of Appeals. (4) That he refuses to conform his judgment to the decision of the Supreme Court. (5) That he obstructs the course of justice by perversity and habitual disregard of judicial propriety. (6) That he has delivered judgments and *dicta* not in accordance with law."

The matter was ably and lengthily debated in the Legislative Council, but on the motion for the removal of Mr. Boothby, Mr. Angas seconded an amendment for inquiry and report by a Select Committee, which was lost. In his speech he pleaded for justice and impartiality, for calm and dispassionate inquiry, instead of "presenting to her Majesty's Privy Council mere declarations sought to be proved by newspaper reports, and even by the reports of the very men who made the allegations."

The Government carried their point, but it was afterwards generally admitted that it would have been better in every respect to have acted on the representations of Mr. Angas and the few others who held the same views.

The whole case was difficult and delicate throughout, and was dealt with in a manner which did not reflect great credit upon the chief actors in it, and brought upon them the severe censure of the Imperial Government.

The colonial Parliament took upon itself the grave responsibility of removing Mr. Boothby from office, and he at once declared his intention to appeal to the Judicial Committee of the Privy Council; but illness, brought on by ceaseless vexation and anxiety, supervened, and on the 21st of June, 1868, his death terminated the controversy.*

We must now go back to the year 1857, to the close of the first session of the first South Australian Parliament. It had been one of peculiar interest and importance, and had accomplished an amazing amount of work, notwithstanding its endless discussions. Twenty-seven select committees had been appointed, seven by the Legislative Council and twenty by the House of Assembly, while forty Bills had been introduced, twenty of which passed both Houses.

During the year the federal movement between the colonies occupied much attention out of doors and in Parliament. It appeared that the Australian Association in England had addressed her Majesty's Government on the subject, and a draft Bill had been prepared, providing for the federative union of the colonies, to embrace such objects as lighthouses along the coast, railways, navigation of inland rivers, a postal system, and other affairs in which the colonies were collectively interested. Select Committees inquired into the subject, and did not report dead against it; but the idea of federation was altogether unpalatable to the majority, and the matter was for the time being allowed to drop.

One step of a federal character was, however, taken by the Parliament this session in levying a tax upon the landing of Chinese in the colony—the Celestials having adopted the plan of disembarking by thousands in South Australia and walking overland to avoid the "head money" levied in Victoria on all such arrivals in that colony by seaboard. Some of these visitors proceeded up the Murray, but the large majority were landed at Rivoli Bay or Guichen Bay, where they obtained guides to conduct them to the Victoria gold diggings. The landing tax was considered by the majority as being mainly for the benefit of the sister colony, but it was denounced as illiberal, and was, after

* Quoted from the "Life of George Fife Angas," pp. 377-380.

a time, repealed. It served, however, to illustrate some of the difficulties that must attend federal action.

On the 28th of December, 1857, the colony attained its majority. In many respects it was the most eventful year of its history, and it is not a little remarkable that it should, while in its twenty-first year, have been entrusted with the entire management of its own affairs by the introduction of responsible government. There were other coincidences of the year. The first pile had been driven for the erection of a jetty at Glenelg, the first landing-place of the early settlers on the mainland; the first wire of the intercolonial telegraph for connecting South Australia with the neighbouring colonies had been fixed; the railway had been opened to Gawler, one of the largest country towns.

Notwithstanding all the drawbacks of infancy—and they had been many and severe—the colony stood in a strong, vigorous, and healthy position at the age of maturity (reckoning according to the years of manhood).

The population, in 1857, was estimated at 109,917; the land alienated from the Crown from the foundation of the colony was 1,557,740 acres, the purchase money amounting to £2,045,324 11s.; the quantity of land in cultivation was 235,965 acres; the number of horses, 26,220; of cattle, 310,400; of sheep and lambs, 2,075,805; the value of imports, £1,623,052; of exports, the produce of the country, and mainly cereals, minerals, and wool, £1,744,184; the number of flour mills was 70; of manufactories, 226; of post-offices, 110; of letters passed through the post-office, 934,550; of newspapers, 849,946; number of day schools, 167, with 7480 scholars; number of Sunday schools, 192, with 10,576 scholars; places of worship, 300, with accommodation for 50,000 persons; births, 5183; marriages, 1218; deaths, 1304.

The celebration of Foundation Day was to have been a brilliant affair, but a drenching rain marred the proceedings, which were to have included the affixing a plate with a suitable inscription on the old gum tree under whose branches the colony was proclaimed in 1836, the land on which it stood having been given to the Glenelg Corporation by the generous owner, Mr. J. Hector; but the ceremony was dispensed with at that time.

The second session of the first Parliament was somewhat barren in subjects of general interest. A Bill for levying an assessment on stock led to the appointment of a Select Committee, who recommended that the measure should be withdrawn; but, notwithstanding this, the debate on the second reading extended over seven days, and it finally passed both Houses without a division. It was estimated that the revenue raised from this source would amount to between £20,000 and £30,000 per annum; but it was found to be a difficult measure to carry into effect, and created a great deal of dissatisfaction on the part of the squatters. The annual value of the land held on lease at the time of passing the Bill was estimated at from £80,000 to £100,000. The distillation question, and taxation generally, were also referred to a Select Committee, who reported that, in their opinion, a system of collecting revenue by a duty upon imports possessed advantages over any system of direct taxation, and rendered any change inexpedient at that time. A total repeal of the distillation laws was recommended, and concurrently a reduction of the duty on imported spirits to four shillings per gallon, and further reductions annually, until a minimum duty of one shilling per gallon was reached. But no definite action was then taken.

During the year (1858) a cloud "no bigger than a man's hand" made its appearance, and before long spread far and wide. A movement was set on foot by the working classes to obtain, if possible, a total discontinuance of free immigration, on the ground that it was unnecessary while so many in the colony were out of employment. On the other hand, the view was taken that the prevailing rate of wages rendered the profitable use of capital impossible. Certainly a country possessing unlimited resources of various kinds, and growing food for a population considerably larger than it contained, ought not to have been in the position in which South Australia then was.

The matter claimed much of the attention of the third session of the first Parliament, which was opened in April (1859), much earlier than usual, consequent upon an alteration in the commencement of the financial year.*

In July a "Political Association" was formed, the approaching termination of the existing Parliament presenting a favourable opportunity to the working classes for ventilating their grievances generally, and for making arrangements for the return of members who would defend their rights and promote their interests. The "creed" of the Association was as follows:—

"(1) We believe the time has now arrived when immigration at the public expense should cease. (2) We believe that property should never be considered in comparison with manhood; that the happiness and well-being of the mass is paramount to the aggrandizement of the few. (3) We believe that all citizens should have equal political rights. (5) We believe that members of the Legislative Assembly should be paid. (5) We believe that all lands alienated from the Crown and unimproved should be taxed. (6) We believe in law reform. (7) We believe the press should be free and unshackled."

Men are said to be almost always better than their creeds, and the working men of South Australia, perhaps, did themselves an injustice in issuing this bald

* On the fourth day of the session a singular circumstance occurred in the House of Assembly, which nearly necessitated another formal reopening of Parliament. After the ordinary summons to the members, there was not a quorum in the House. The Speaker, without considering that the days of meeting had not been fixed, adjourned the House until one o'clock next day; but remembering that he had no power to do this, he recalled the departing members, and a few more dropping in who had either not heard or had disregarded the previous summons, a House was constituted.

programme. Their object was a political crusade against the wealthier classes. Times were bad, there was lack of employment, destitution had ensued; dissatisfaction had laid a firm hold on mechanics and artisans, and everything was ripe for the advent of the social demagogue who had a panacea for every evil.

Many meetings were held. The first resolution passed at the first meeting was in these simple and modest terms: "That his Excellency would be pleased to remove from his councils the present Ministry." Another, at a subsequent meeting, was to the effect, "The widespread destitution is attributable to absenteeism, and to the drainage of money from the colony for immigration;" while another characterized a vote of £2000 for the introduction of free immigration as "a policy wanting in humanity, insulting to the understanding of the meanest capacity, likely to compromise the present peace and order of the community, and opposed to the future prosperity of the colony."

Memorials to the Governor were drawn up, and deputations appointed to present them. Sir Richard MacDonnell was a practical man, and he dealt wisely and well with his democratic petitioners.

"In my opinion," he said to one deputation, "the want of the colony is the want most felt by all new countries worth inhabiting, namely, more people to inhabit it and cultivate the soil. The way to make the country wealthy is not necessarily by stopping the influx of people. I have never known immigration, well conducted, to interfere with legitimate wages; but, on the other hand, an influx of inhabitants, unattended with a corresponding influx of capital, is not, I admit, the way to promote the healthy and prosperous settlement of any country." Then, after urging them to use their political power wisely at the next general election, he met a complaint that had been made against the Government for not employing more labour in public works.

"If you will allow me to offer you advice," he said,

"it would be that you should avoid this growing tendency to look to Government, instead of to yourselves, and to cling to it in every reverse or difficulty, rather than to rely on your own willing hearts and strong arms. There is a fair field for the workman here, as compared with England; and if the disposition to which I have referred is persisted in, it will be a curse to the working man, and the most serious impediment to the prosperity of the colony. . . . The necessity for that self-reliance which can seek and make employment is all the more evident because, before long, we cannot calculate upon such large proceeds from the sale of Crown lands as we have hitherto enjoyed, and you must remember that it is from these sales that the principal amounts have been derived for public works. . . ."

As the rules of the Destitute Asylum did not admit of relief being granted to able-bodied individuals in good health, the Government established a labour test to meet the case of those who could not obtain work from any other source.* The rate fixed for taskwork was so arranged as to allow men to earn from three shillings to five shillings per day, and when they could not be employed in this way, four shillings per day was to be the rate of payment.

This was considered by the men as insufficient, and the inevitable memorial to the Governor, urging that six shillings should be the minimum price, was sent in.

Sir Richard, in reply, said he was grieved and disappointed to find so many workmen in the vicinity of town still looking to labour tests as a continuous means of obtaining a livelihood, instead of merely using them in the way intended, namely, as temporary makeshifts, whereby the industrious might gain time to look out for more permanent and congenial employment, plenty of which might be found, if diligently sought for. He justly considered that any man who could earn four shillings, and nevertheless remained idle because he

* The Government adopted a similar plan to that pursued by Governor Grey in 1841, except that the test rate of 1859 was more than double that of 1841.

could not earn six shillings, might be considered as squandering the money he refused to take, and disqualified himself from obtaining the highest wages accorded to others of his class.

It was these circumstances which led to the formation of the Working Men's Association, and subsequently the Political Association, with its branches in various parts of the colony—an association which exercised a powerful influence in the election of members for the ensuing Parliament by returning men who were pledged to represent their interest, and, in some cases, theirs only. From the results which followed it was clear that the other classes of the community had not realized the power which the ballot and universal suffrage had placed in the hands of working men.

The great depression in the labour market at this time could be mainly traced to two causes—one a deficiency in the wheat crop for four successive seasons, leading gradually to a crisis, and the other a partial recovery from the disarrangement caused by the exodus to the gold-fields, and the subsequent high rate of wages obtainable when the influx of gold into the colony took place, creating a fictitious, superficial, and temporary state of prosperity, leading in its turn to a large amount of improvidence, an erroneous view of the value of money, and other more serious evils.

Early in July, 1859, news reached the colony that Austria had declared war against Sardinia, and that active preparations were being made in England, in the event of other European powers being so involved as to necessitate Britain taking a part in the contest. In August came the intelligence that hostilities had commenced, that France had joined the Sardinians, and that some desperate battles had been fought and won by those united Powers. A proclamation by the Queen was forthwith issued by the Governor, declaring the neutrality of Britain and requiring the "strict observance of this attitude on the part of all the colonies and dependencies of the British Empire."

While South Australia was quite prepared to obey this order both in letter and in spirit, it was considered necessary to follow the example of the mother country in making preparation for any emergency. France was as much distrusted in Australia as in England, and the existence of a French naval station at New Caledonia, no great distance from the Australian coast, led the colonists to be on the alert. A Militia Bill and a Volunteer Force Bill were therefore passed through the Legislature, and the Government proceeded to enrol the militia, but it was understood that if two thousand volunteers offered their services the militia would not be called out except in case of absolute necessity.

Energetic steps were taken to enrol sufficient volunteers, and rifle corps were formed in most of the districts, the Government undertaking to provide rifles and ammunition on certain conditions, together with a small sum towards uniform. Major Nelson, of the 14th Regiment, the officer in command of the military, was appointed inspecting field officer. By December, sixteen companies were formed, upwards of six hundred volunteers enrolled, rifle butts had been erected on the South Park-lands, ball firing had been regularly practised, and two artillery companies had commenced target practice.

Meanwhile Australia had been constituted a separate naval station, independent of the East India and China station. Captain Long, of H.M.S. *Iris*, was appointed commodore of the second class; the *Iris*, *Elk*, *Niger*, *Cordelia*, and *Pelorus* forming the Australian squadron.

An event occurred in this year (1859) which will ever be remembered by South Australians as one of the saddest, most tragic, and most exciting in the annals of the colony.

In 1858 there arrived in the colony a splendid new steamship, the *Admella*, for the Adelaide and Melbourne trade, her name being a contraction and conjunction of the names of these two cities. On Monday, the 8th of August, 1859, a telegram was received in

Adelaide from Mount Gambier, announcing that the keeper of the lighthouse at Cape Northumberland had reported the total wreck of the *Admella* at some little distance from the cape, and the probable loss of nearly all on board. The news, it was stated, had been communicated by two of the crew of the ill-fated vessel, who had arrived at the lighthouse in an exhausted condition.

When this startling and melancholy intelligence was circulated there was distress and excitement in Adelaide such as had never been witnessed before. It was known that the *Admella* had left Port Adelaide on the 5th with between sixty and seventy passengers on board, most of whom had relations and friends in the city. The telegraph office was in consequence besieged, and intense excitement prevailed. Unfortunately, no precise information could be obtained, fragments of news only arrived at intervals, and the suspense was painful in the extreme.

Early on Tuesday morning telegrams were received stating that the steamer struck on a reef during foggy weather on Saturday and broke into four pieces, the boats had been washed adrift, and when the two men left, bodies were floating around them. Passengers had offered money, jewellery, everything they had, to be brought ashore, but the raft would only bear the two sailors; the second mate had tried to reach the shore, but was drowned in the attempt. Only the poop of the vessel was out of water, and the wreck was at least a mile from the beach and twenty-five from the lighthouse. A ray of hope came with the tale of sorrow. The two men who had reached the shore were so bewildered that no reliance was to be placed upon their report as to how many were alive on the wreck.

Meanwhile all that could be done in Adelaide, over two hundred and fifty miles away, was done. The *Corio* had been despatched from the Port to render assistance. Then came hours and days of intensely anxious suspense. Business generally was at a standstill; both Houses of the Legislature met and adjourned (two sons of the President of the Council had taken passage in the vessel, and their fate was unknown).

Thus Tuesday passed away. Wednesday brought tidings that those on the wreck had exchanged signals with those on shore, but neither boat nor steamer was in sight. By the aid of a telescope twenty persons were seen on the wreck, and a Mr. Rochfort was recognized as one of them. A lifeboat had been despatched, but she could not be got through the surf. Towards evening a steamer three miles off was seen approaching, but the sea was too rough for her to attempt a rescue. This was the last news received on the fifth day that the survivors had been on the wreck, and the third since the news reached Adelaide. Excitement was at white heat, and it is scarcely an exaggeration to say that half the citizens of Adelaide spent a sleepless night.

Early on Thursday morning the telegraph office was thronged by a pale and anxious crowd. The first telegram announced that the *Corio* was close by the wreck, that Rochfort, the captain, the first mate, Mr. Magarey, and a woman were recognized, but that the surf was too strong for any boat to live in it. Later in the day came other telegrams stating that the survivors were fewer, two having been seen to drop into the sea since daylight; that the *Ladybird*, despatched from Melbourne, and the *Ant* from Guichen Bay, were on the alert to render assistance; that the lifeboat of the *Corio* had been launched, but could not reach the wreck—it had got inside the reef and been thrown up on the beach, and the survivors witnessing the mishap had sent up a despairing shout, distinctly heard on shore, as if their last hope had gone. The wreck stood above high water as high as a man could reach, and, the hull having canted over to port, the survivors were sitting or lying on the starboard bulwark. A reward of £500, it was reported, had been offered by one gentleman to any person who would bring a single individual from the wreck alive. Such were some of the gloomy and disheartening tidings of the day.

Friday brought news of gallant but unsuccessful attempts by shore boats and the Portland lifeboat to reach the wreck, but the sea was running mountains high, and the brave men gave up their efforts in despair, not, however, until serious injury had been done to some of their number. As the telegrams brought information of their vigorous but unsuccessful attempts, it seemed to the anxious inquirers at Adelaide that all human help was in vain, and when some one proposed a special prayer-meeting, crowds left the telegraph office and proceeded to the Wesleyan chapel in Pirie Street.

On Saturday there was very little news; hope deferred had made the heart of the people sick, but they wandered about the streets, hardly losing sight of the telegraph office until evening, when the following telegram was posted up:—

"Glorious news! Twenty-two saved, including Rochfort, Hurtle Fisher, Captain McEwan, Andrew Fuller, and Thomas Davey. Other names not known. Nineteen gone on to Portland in the *Ladybird*. Three on shore. The nineteen were rescued by the lifeboat of the *Ladybird*, and the three by the Port lifeboat in charge of Germain. These taken off the wreck at eight o'clock this morning. Poor George Fisher drowned. Sufferers all much exhausted. . . ."

Further particulars came at intervals, and on Monday the first mate was sufficiently recovered to give full details, which were at once wired to Adelaide.

Thus ended a week of the most intense interest, anxiety, and suspense ever experienced in South Australia. By the calamity at least eighty lives were lost, under the most heart-rending circumstances. Large subscriptions were raised for the rescuers (over £3000), and also for those of the sufferers who needed help, and medals were awarded to those who had conspicuously distinguished themselves for bravery.

On the 1st of March, 1860, the first South Australian Parliament was dissolved by proclamation. When the writs for the new elections were issued, the Political Association set to work in right good earnest to secure the return of members who should make South Australia the paradise of working men.

The elections took place on the 13th of March, with the result that many important changes were made in the new Parliament, insomuch that the *Register* thus defined the position: "We cannot enter into any analysis of party gains and losses, for the very cogent reason that we have had no defined parties.* The old titles Whigs and Tories never had significance here, and even the terms Liberal and Conservative fail to convey any definite meaning. Here, we who wish to maintain the democratic institutions we have established are to all intents and purposes Conservatives, while the party whose political bias would in Britain be deemed Conservative are, in the very nature of things, Destructives here. The great majority of the people of South Australia are Democratic-Conservatives, and the minority consists of two factions having nothing in common but their opposition to the majority."

The second Parliament of South Australia assembled on the 27th of April, 1860.† The Governor stated,

---

* "Parties are divided upon particular subjects. There is a squatting party and an anti-squatting party; a Government House party, and a party opposed to Government House; a religious endowment party and a party unfavourable to religious endowments; but as to well-defined lines of political demarcation, you might as well look for ink-spots in the moon. This want of party organization has produced a chronic state of ministerial instability. In the nine years of responsible government in South Australia, there have been fifteen absolute changes of Ministry, besides several changes in individual offices. In order to save the country from the expense of frequent elections in the event of ministerial crises, and to facilitate a speedy readjustment of the Government machinery, it was provided that a member accepting a responsible office should not be required to go back to his constituents."—A. Forster, 1866.

† The days of meeting for the Council were three in each week, Tuesday, Wednesday, and Thursday; for the House of Assembly four, Tuesday, Wednesday, Thursday, and Friday; the time of meeting for the House of Assembly being half-past one.

among other things, that, the volunteer force being sufficiently strong, the militia would not be called out at present, although steps had been taken to have it in readiness. The number of destitute poor had diminished, and there were not at that time any able-bodied labourers dependent on the Government for employment.

Before the reply to the Governor's opening address had passed the House of Assembly, a serious change in the Ministry was announced, originated by the resignation of Mr. Finniss as Treasurer. Other changes followed. The Hanson Cabinet went out, and Mr. T. Reynolds took the reins.

As every young man has his escapades of one sort or another, and has to learn wisdom by experience, so it is with young Governments. South Australia was feeling its way, and it had a number of excellent men pressing to the front, anxious to do good in their time, and to leave their names inscribed on the scroll of fame. But no new man could then come to the front in political life unless he could introduce a bigger programme than his predecessor, and this is the one Mr. Reynolds set before the country :—

(1) Retrenchment, the principal part of the policy of the new Ministry;

(2) Repeal of the *ad valorem* duties;

(3) Abolition of harbour and light dues, and remodelling of pilot service;

(4) Amalgamation of Harbour Trust, Trinity Board, and Local Marine Board into one body, to be called the Marine Board;

(5) Establishment of circuit courts;

(6) Opening up of Northern Country for profitable occupation;

(7) Such alterations in the mode of disposing of the Crown lands as may be necessitated by the legislation of the neighbouring colonies;

(8) Placing the salaries of all members of boards on the estimates, so as to bring all official expenditure under the control of the Assembly;

(9) Reform of the Civil List for the purpose of retrenchment;

(10) Reform of the Constitution Act by substituting some lay officer in the Cabinet for the professional one of Attorney-General;

(11) Amendment of the Real Property Act in accordance with the views of the Registrar-General, Lands Titles Commissioners, and their solicitors;

And eight other items equally sweeping and radical.

With such a programme as this a long sitting of Parliament was inevitable. At all events, from the composition of the new House, the Ministry saw that the way was clear for many and great reforms, and the old party that had, comparatively, so long administered the affairs of the colony, knew by the result of the elections that the constituencies had determined to secure, if possible, some radical changes.

The Ministry was decidedly popular, and the two Houses worked together much more harmoniously than could have been expected. Moreover, the personal composition of the Parliament at the close of the session was precisely the same as at the commencement—a rare circumstance in those days. It indicated a fixity and settlement in the political condition of the province, and showed that the constituencies had not, after all, made an unwise selection of men to represent them.

In following the story of the settlers we have to some extent lost sight of the aborigines, and we must now go back in their history to the time when Archdeacon Hale conceived an idea which, more than any other previously advanced, seemed to meet the need of the natives. The great difficulty had always been to check their vagrant habits, and to overcome this evil the Archdeacon resolved to attempt the establishment of a native institution in some locality as far removed as possible from the centres of European population, and also at a distance from the usual haunts of the aborigines. By thus isolating the children of the natives and forming them into a little colony he concluded that a mutual attachment would grow up between the sexes, and in course of time, after acquiring a moderate amount of education, combined with a knowledge of husbandry and of some of the most useful trades, they would marry and continue to practise the civilized habits they had acquired.

In May, 1850, the plans of Archdeacon Hale were sufficiently matured to enable him to commence operations. The spot selected for his praiseworthy and self-denying experiment was Boston Island, about three and a half miles in length, of the average breadth of one and a half miles, and stretching along the eastern side of Boston Bay, thus partly forming the harbour of Port Lincoln, from which township it was about four miles distant.

The party at first consisted of eleven persons; eight natives (four of each sex), the Archdeacon, Mr. Minchin, and Mr. Rayner. The only accommodation they had was a tent for the females and another for the stores, and for the rest a breakwind of wattle branches and the canopy of heaven for a roof.

"Our object in choosing this locality," said the Archdeacon, "was principally seclusion, that we might be cut off from the society of blacks living in a wild state, and protected from the unwelcome intrusion of evil-minded persons amongst the whites. These advantages we set against the formidable disadvantage that no permanent fresh water had as yet been found upon the island."

After a fruitless search for water the island was abandoned, and Poonindie, on the mainland in Louth Bay, near the river Tod, was selected as the site for future operations. Here the Archdeacon and his party forthwith reared three substantial stone houses and nine log huts; a block of about three thousand acres of surveyed land was rented for the institution, and by purchasing the sheep depasturing on the surrounding runs the use of about twelve square miles was acquired as a run. In a few months the settlement was formed, many acres were cleared, fenced, and sown, and wells were dug. In all these operations the natives assisted, being paid at the rate of sixpence a day, which it is said they never squandered, but expended in clothes for themselves, or articles for their houses. In process of time the native school at North Terrace was discontinued, about fifty children being drafted from thence to Poonindie. There a capacious chapel and schoolroom were erected, and additional huts were reared for married couples, of whom there were as many as seven or eight.

The institution grew and flourished, and so long as the Archdeacon had the superintendence of it the expenses of management were kept under by the services rendered by the natives.

In 1856 the appointment of Archdeacon Hale to the bishopric of Perth necessitated his giving up the charge of the institute, and Dr. Octavius Hammond became his successor. When the Archdeacon resigned there were sixty individuals maintained and under instruction, but within the subsequent fifteen months no fewer than twenty were removed by death, and a period of depression and anxiety set in.

Meanwhile, in 1858, the "Aborigines' Friends Association" was formed, and the Hon. G. F. Angas was appointed its first president. The object of the association was "the moral, spiritual, and physical wellbeing of the natives of this province." Under the auspices of this association the Point MacLeay Institution for Natives was inaugurated, Mr. G. Taplin being the superintendent. For the first few years it was tolerably well supported by contributions from the Government towards food and clothing, and partly by private contributions. Then came a falling off, due in great measure to the sad fact, applying equally to the Poonindie Institute, that there was a great mortality amongst the native inmates, and the inference could not be overlooked that the confinement of the schools, and the comparatively close application of the mind to study, had a prejudicial effect upon the health of these children of the bush.

In 1860 a Select Committee of the Legislative Council was appointed, of which Mr. G. F. Angas was a member, " to inquire into the appropriation of the funds set aside from time to time for the use and benefit of the aborigines, and to suggest such measures as were likely to tend to the future and permanent benefit of the natives and the community at large"—a broad subject, but it was taken up heartily, especially by Mr. Angas, who had been among the first to care for these poor creatures.*

The recommendations of the committee were excellent, but, in view of the fact that every previous effort to permanently benefit the natives had ended more or less in failure, the prospect of these recommendations being carried out was more than doubtful. Even Mr. Angas, who from the first had been more hopeful than any one for the future of the natives, and had been probably the largest contributor to agencies working for their good, was forced to arrive at the following conclusions:—" The committee submit as their strong conviction that permanent benefit to any appreciable extent from attempts to Christianize the natives can only be expected by separation of children from their parents and from the evil influences of the tribe to which they belong. However harshly this recommendation may grate on the feelings of pseudo-philanthropists, it would in reality be a work of mercy to the rising generation of aborigines." The report concluded with the old sad story: "All the evidence goes to prove that they have lost much and gained little or nothing by their contact with Europeans, and hence it becomes a question how far it is in our power, or what is the best possible means of compensating

---

* It will be remembered that the first systematic attempt to instruct the natives was made by Messrs. C. G. Teichelmann and W. C. Schürmann, who were sent out from the Lutheran Missionary Society at Dresden, under the auspices and mainly at the expense of Mr. G. F. Angas.

them for the injuries they have sustained, or of mitigating the evils to which, so far as they are concerned, our forced occupation of their country has led."

Among the causes of their rapid decrease in number the following were specified :—(1) From infanticide to a limited extent. (2) From certain rites performed upon young men impairing their physical powers. (3) From the introduction among them by Europeans of more aggravated forms of disease than were known to exist prior to our occupation of the country. (4) From the introduction and use of intoxicating liquors, a habit which is prevalent to excess among the natives, who, despite existing laws to the contrary, are frequently aided by Europeans in obtaining supplies. (5) From the disproportion of the sexes.

Some idea of the ratio of decrease may be gained from the fact that within an area of 2800 miles, the population, which in 1841 numbered 650, was in 1856 only 180.

The first and only reliable census of the aboriginal population was taken in 1861, when it was found that there were 2375 males of all ages, and 2022 females, or a grand total of 4397.

For several years it was a custom to assemble the natives at Adelaide on the anniversary of the Queen's birthday, and give them a feast. It was inaugurated by Governor Gawler, who gave them the good old English fare of roast beef and plum pudding, and he was long remembered by the aborigines as "bery good Gubner," who gave them "plenty tuck out." Blankets were also given on these occasions to the aged and infirm. In the first year, 1841, only 283 persons assembled, but the numbers gradually increased, till in 1845 about nine hundred presented themselves. This was inconvenient, more especially as quarrelling and fighting generally ensued, and therefore the plan of distributing the Queen's bounty in the native settlements was adopted. But the numbers in attendance fell year by year, and in 1856 the custom was discontinued. Alas, and the pity of it! the day was fast approaching when there would be no aborigines left to assemble.

Although the natives of Australia were not comparable in intelligence to the Maoris of New Zealand, they were not the degraded set of human animals that some writers have described. They had in them the germs of better things, and in proportion as they were educated, the better qualities came into play. Among these was generosity and a keen sense of humour—phases of character not generally ascribed to them. An illustration of both these points may be given in an anecdote of the experience of the Rev. — Reid, a zealous clergyman, bent on Christianizing the natives on the Coorong, and who literally died in their service, as he was capsized in his two-masted open boat when on a mission to them, and was drowned. On one occasion he found some of these Coorong natives cooking mullet. As they were about to eat, Mr. Reid, wishing to improve the occasion, said, "Who gave you that fish?" "Me catch'm," was the answer. "No," said the pious minister, "God gave you that fish. God gives black fellow everything." The natives gave some quick, merry glances, and went on with their meal. Towards the end, as there was food in plenty and Mr. Reid was hungry, he said, "You give me some fish." At once the answer came, "What for me give you fish? You ask'm God; Him give you plenty." Whereupon there was a roar of laughter; but, nevertheless, two or three fish were at once thrust into the clergyman's hands.

During the administration of Sir Richard MacDonnell, many important explorations and discoveries were made and public works undertaken, which deserve more than a passing notice here. Let us glance at a few of these events in detail.

On closing the session of the Legislative Council in June, 1856, the Governor alluded to a project for connecting by rail the capital of the colony with the Murray—that great river which traverses with its navigable stream of two thousand miles the three extensive British colonies of New South Wales, Victoria, and South Australia, receiving tributaries which in their turn traverse many hundred miles of valuable country, and afford the cheapest and best of all carriage where obtainable in a new country—namely, internal water carriage.

In strong and vigorous language, the Governor briefly foreshadowed a scheme for carrying into effect his pet idea. But public opinion was not so strongly in favour of the great Murray Railway scheme as he was. The public did not relish the idea of the enormous debt it was proposed to incur, nor were they unanimous in considering the undertaking even desirable. By many the Goolwa and Port Elliot tramway connecting the Murray with the seaboard was considered amply sufficient for the purposes of traffic, while others recognized the importance of saving time and distance by direct railway communication between the upper waters of the river and the capital. The question was also one of rival northern and southern interests, as the railway in the north would, to some extent, affect the trade at the Goolwa end of the southern districts; and so, for a time, the matter was allowed to lapse. Meanwhile, about the middle of August, 1856, Sir Richard MacDonnell, accompanied by Lady MacDonnell, the Private Secretary, Surveyor-General, and Mr. Younghusband, started for a trip up the Murray. They proceeded to Moorundie, and there embarked in the steamer *Melbourne*, having the barge *Eureka* alongside with a cargo of 160 tons, intended principally for Albury. The *Melbourne* left Moorundie on the 25th of August, and on the 25th of September the party disembarked for the purpose of visiting Beechworth. Here, as at all other places visited, the Governor was kindly welcomed with every mark of respect. On the 30th they left Beechworth and returned to Goolwa by way of Albury, the distance between these two places being estimated at eighteen hundred miles. The party returned to Adelaide on the 23rd of October, after an absence of over two months. The trip was taken for the purpose of personally inspecting the capabilities of this great river for traffic and commerce; but, of course, it did not add much to the sum of geographical knowledge. It was, however, only one of many journeys taken by the Governor, who was so excellent a traveller as to entitle him to a place among the explorers of South Australia.

From 1857 onwards, a series of explorations was undertaken by the South Australian Government, and nearly all of them were in the direction where Eyre and Sturt had previously travelled. But what was then called Lake Torrens presented for a long time an impenetrable barrier to the exploration of the northern interior; nevertheless, as we shall see, each successive attempt helped to make the great discovery of Mr. J. M. Stuart possible.

In 1856 the Legislative Council voted the sum of £1000 to aid in a search for gold, and Mr. B. H. Babbage, Government geologist, who was entrusted with the command of the expedition, set forth northwards in September. He did not find gold, but not far from Eyre's Mount Hopeless he discovered an extensive creek, which he named MacDonnell, after the Governor, and a fresh-water lake, which he named Blanchewater, in honour of Lady MacDonnell. The country thus discovered was visited in 1857 by Mr. G. W. Goyder, Deputy Surveyor-General, who was sent out to establish a trigonometrical survey of the neighbourhood. Mr. Goyder reported the discovery of a magnificent and extensive fresh-water lake and a creek, to which he gave the name of Freeling. To follow up this discovery, Captain Freeling, the Surveyor-General, organized a party, and left Adelaide in July by steamer for Port Augusta, and reached the scene of Goyder's supposed discoveries. But, unfortunately, he was not able to confirm Mr. Goyder's report; on the contrary, he wrote as follows:—

"I much regret that what there is to relate is decidedly unfavourable to the extension of discoveries in the direction mentioned, and by the means proposed. The extensive bays described in Mr. Goyder's report, the bluff headlands, the several islands towards the north and south shores, the vegetation covering them, and their perpendicular cliffs have *all been the result of mirage*, and do not in point of fact exist as represented." One of Mr. Goyder's party, who accompanied Captain Freeling, stated that the water had receded half a mile since his former visit. The captain and some of the party waded into the mud for a considerable distance, and at the farthest point reached, he described the view as desolate in the extreme, the same shallow waters, low islands, and mud extending round three parts of the horizon. So ended a fruitless journey.

In 1856 Mr. B. H. Babbage made certain proposals to the Commissioner of Crown Lands with reference to the outfit of an expedition to explore Lake Torrens more thoroughly, and, after crossing it at a certain point, to proceed to the north-west as far as possible. The Government, with the sanction of Parliament, was entrusted with the necessary outfit; Mr. Babbage was appointed leader of the party, and Mr. Harris, of the Survey Office, second in command. In February, 1857, the expedition set forth, the route being through the districts occupied by the most distant sheep and cattle stations, from whence the movements of the explorers were reported—disadvantageously, for Mr. Babbage seemed loth to take a plunge into the wilderness, and the delay called forth such dissatisfaction from the people that it became the subject of inquiry in Parliament, and eventually of his recall, Major Warburton, Commissioner of Police, being appointed in his place. But the whole expedition did not result in any appreciable advantage to the colony, and ended in disappointment to all concerned, as well as with an expenditure of £5552.

One painful discovery made by Mr. Babbage was that of the dead body of a gallant explorer. Messrs. W. Coulthard, Brooks, and Scott had gone forth on an expedition in search of a good sheep country, and when north of

Port Augusta announced to some returning travellers their intention to push forward in the direction of the Pernatty Lagoon. They were warned of the extreme hazard of the undertaking, owing to the intense heat and lack of water, but, disregarding the caution, they went their way. When searching for water, Coulthard got separated from his companions and was lost in the bush. Every possible search was made by Messrs. Brooks and Scott, but without avail, and no one ever saw him again alive. But Mr. Babbage accidentally found his remains, and near to the body a shepherd's tin canteen, on which was scratched one of the saddest records ever penned. It was as follows:—

"I never reached water. I do not know how long it is since it is that I left Scott and Brooks, but I think it Monday, bleeding Pomp to leive on his blood. I took his black horse to look for water and the last thing I can rember is puling the saddle off him and letting him go   until now is not good   long it may be wether 2 or 3 days I do not know   I am not shure   My Tung is stiking to my mouth and I see what I have rote and know this is the last time I may have of expressing feeling   Blind (?) altho feeling exce   for want of water   My ey Dazels my tong burn   I can see no way God help——"

The earlier words were firmly and clearly marked, but towards the end they became almost illegible scratches, made, it is evident, when the poor fellow, blind and half mad, was in the agony of death. To add to the sadness of the story, it was found that within half a mile of the bush where Coulthard lay down to die, there was a waterhole with an abundant supply of water.

About this time (1857-8), a number of explorations were originated. Mr. Stephen Hack, accompanied by Mr. Harris of the Survey Department, tried to penetrate to the north-west, but was unable to pass the dense scrub. A private party, consisting of Messrs. D. Thomson, M. Campbell, and C. Swinden, started from the head of Spencer's Gulf for a trip northwards, and came upon the large lagoon called by the natives Pernatty, two remarkable hills (Bonney's Bluff and Bottle Hill), and a creek which they named the Elizabeth. They were only away for a few days, as they had not much provision with them; but their discoveries were important, although it afterwards transpired that some of the country had previously been examined.

Of the two expeditions under Major Warburton, the Commissioner of Police, the one in which he was sent to recall Mr. Babbage was most fruitful in results. On his return journey he conceived the idea of crossing the supposed bed of Lake Torrens, and reaching the settled districts by this entirely new route. The passage was a complete success, for instead of having to wade through water, or plunge through mud, as indicated in the maps then extant, the major found good dry land, and no obstacles other than those ordinarily met with in new and untrodden paths.

Later, Major Warburton and Mr. Samuel Davenport examined some of the country from Streaky Bay to Lake Gairdner, as well as the Gawler Range district, but no striking discoveries were made.

Two expeditions made by the Governor, Sir Richard MacDonnell, in the year 1859 deserve some notice here. Of the first he gave an account to the Hon. G. F. Angas, who was at that time on a visit to England, as follows:—

"Nepean Bay, Kangaroo Island, Feb. 17, 1859.

"I am just returned from a very rapid and successful exploring expedition up the Darling in Cadell's steamer, the *Albury*. I regard all these expeditions as an extension of this colony's commercial boundary, which, after all, is its real boundary for many important purposes. It will interest you to learn that I only left Adelaide on the 23rd ult. (January), and having embarked at Blanche Town on board of the *Albury* after a ride of seventy miles (via Angaston) from Gawler through a fierce hot wind, I reached the junction on the 26th and slept on Mount Murchison, 290 miles by land and 600 by water from the junction, on the 5th instant, whilst I now write to you from Kangaroo Island on the 17th, having between the 23rd ult. and this morning steamed on Australian rivers nearly 2400 miles, and ridden about 200.

"I have just been telling Sturt how smoothly I have been gliding through scenes of his hardships and disasters. We are certainly progressing, as you may judge when I tell you that an order dated from Sydney the 23rd of January to deliver four tons of goods at a station 400 miles up the Darling, was executed on the 3rd of February, only eleven days after the order was given at Sydney. . . ."

The Governor's second journey was made in October of the same year, for the purpose of seeing the discoveries of Sturt, Babbage, and Warburton in the north. The farthest point reached was a range of hills which he named the Denison Range in honour of the Governor-General. Sir Richard was absent for nearly three months, and during that time he rode on horseback 1800 miles, endured the hardships of heat and thirst common to explorers, and proved himself to be an excellent bushman.

But all the explorations of this period, valuable as they were, pale into insignificance beside those of John McDouall Stuart, South Australia's greatest explorer. His achievements have been so often and so fully told in detail, that it will not be necessary to give more than the barest outline here.

In April, 1859, Mr. Stuart, the draughtsman of Captain Sturt's expedition, went out northwards and travelled through the Pernatty country in search of pastoral runs for Messrs. Chambers and Finke. He was accompanied by Mr. Kekwick and one attendant, and was provided with nine horses. On the 17th of July Stuart returned to Adelaide, and reported that he had succeeded in reaching the then northern boundary of the colony in about latitude 26° south, and that the country traversed consisted mostly of immense plains interspersed with numerous hillocks, from the summit of which springs of water gushed out. Ranges, rivers, and creeks were also met with by this small and intrepid party; in short, a most fertile and interesting tract of country was reported to exist where it was previously supposed that only scrub, sand, and saline lakes were to be found. To complete the glowing picture it was rumoured that an auriferous country had also been discovered. This rumour was re-echoed some time afterwards by the Royal Geographical Society, to whom some particulars of the expedition, not known elsewhere, were communicated. So highly did the Society appreciate Stuart's labours that they awarded him a handsome gold watch.

When Stuart returned to Adelaide Parliament was in session, and in order to encourage him, or some other explorer, to cross the continent and reach the northern coast a sum of £2000 was voted as a reward for the accomplishment of this feat. Mr. A. Tolmer was the first competitor, but before he had got beyond the reach of the settled districts, owing to difficulties with the horses and dissensions among his men, he gave up the attempt.

Meanwhile, Stuart, with the assistance of Messrs. Chambers and Finke, quietly and unostentatiously made his arrangements for penetrating as far as possible into the northern interior. As he preferred travelling by land rather than sea, he applied for a vessel to be sent to the northern coast for the purpose of taking supplies, and of bringing him and his party back in the event of their reaching the other side of the continent. Very little was known of his movements except that he had started with a small expedition for the interior.

About this time, that is to say in August, 1860, the Victorian Government, stimulated by the action of South Australia, sent forth an expedition, with the same object in view, under the command of Robert O'Hara Burke, with whom was associated Mr. W. J. Wills and others.

On the 7th of October Mr. Stuart and his two companions returned to Adelaide. In consequence of scarcity of water, the hostility of natives, and the smallness and weakness of their party, the attempt to cross the continent had been unsuccessful. Nevertheless the results of the expedition were of exceptional interest. Its promoters, Messrs. Chambers and Finke, in placing Mr. Stuart's journal in the hands of the Government, stipulated that it should not be published for a certain period, so that the benefit of the discoveries made should be secured to Mr. Stuart, who was ready to continue his task when opportunity should offer. The publication was deferred until, in a further attempt to cross the continent, Mr. Stuart had arrived outwards as far as Chambers' Creek. No sooner was this valuable document issued than a special messenger was despatched by the Victorians to place Mr. Burke in possession of the information gained by Stuart in the interior, but scarcity of water prevented the messenger from accomplishing his task.

From Stuart's journal it appeared that he left Chambers' Creek on the 2nd of March, and on the 22nd of April reached the centre of the continent, where, on a high mound which he named Central Mount Stuart, he built a cairn of stones, and planted the British flag upon it. On the 26th of June, on reaching a large creek, the party were attacked by a number of powerful natives, and it was found necessary to beat a retreat as soon as possible. Some of his hairbreadth escapes, and the motives which induced him to abandon his cherished object, are given in a letter to Mr. Chambers, from which we quote:—

"After making the centre I was assailed by that dreadful disease, the scurvy, which completely prostrated me and rendered me quite helpless. Still I persevered, and endeavoured to reach the mouth of the Victoria river on a north-west course, but was obliged to relinquish the attempt three separate times through the want of water. . . .

"I was now forced to go back to the centre. Three miles to the north of the centre is a high hill, on which I planted the flag, and named it Central Mount Stuart. From this I could see ranges to the north-east, which gave me a better idea of the country for water, and I thought I might get an opening that would lead me to the north-west of Gum and Spinifex Plain. I therefore proceeded in that direction to latitude 19° 22′, longitude 134° 18.′ From this I again made another attempt to make the Victoria on a north-west course, but again I was obliged to retreat from the want of water. We were one hundred and eleven hours, without a drop of water under a burning hot sun and heavy sandy soil to travel on. After this journey I gave up all hope of making the Victoria, and tried for the Gulf of Carpentaria."

But in this attempt dangers, difficulties, and insuperable obstacles beset him at every turn, and finally there was a desperate encounter with the natives.

"I took into consideration," Stuart adds, "the position in which I was then placed—my horses tired and weary, three of them unable to be longer than one night without water; the men complaining six weeks before this of being so weak from want of sufficient food that they were unable to perform their duty—their movements were more those of men of a hundred years old than of young men of twenty-five—and myself being so unwell that I was unable to sit in the saddle the whole day without suffering the most excruciating pain; our provisions scarcely sufficient to carry us back, and now being in the midst of hostile natives who were wily, bold, and daring, so much so that I could see at once that my party would be unable to cope with them, although we gained the advantage at first. . . ."

These were among the amply sufficient reasons which induced Mr. J. M. Stuart to return, and it was fortunate he did so at once, for on his journey back he found many of the water-holes dry, which he calculated would have lasted much longer.

The furthest point reached on this journey was about the nineteenth degree of south latitude, or about 1300 miles from Adelaide in a straight line, and about 300 miles from the north-west coast of the Gulf of Carpentaria.

The fact of this extraordinary feat having been accomplished was doubted by many, and even denied by one writer in Victoria, but the publication of the letter, from which we have quoted above, silenced alike the doubters and deniers.

On the return of his party to Adelaide, a great demonstration was made in honour of the intrepid explorers, and the Government voted the sum of £2500 to fit out an expedition to enable Mr. Stuart to make another attempt to accomplish the feat of crossing the continent.

On the 2nd of November, 1860, Mr. Stuart left Adelaide to follow up his adventurous task. He was accompanied by Mr. Kekwick, as second in command, F. W. Thring, third officer, and a brave following, namely, E. E. Bayliffe, J. H. Ewart, B. Head, A. J. Lawrence, W. Masters, J. A. Thomas, D. Thompson, J. Wall, and J. Woodforde. On the 1st of January, 1861, they started from Chambers' Creek, and nothing more was heard of them until about the middle of September. Then came the startling report that the party had actually crossed the continent. But rumour lied, and from subsequent intelligence it was found that although they had reached the latitude of the head of the Gulf of Carpentaria, they had not succeeded in getting to the seacoast on the other side of the continent. After penetrating some considerable distance beyond the point previously reached, the first great difficulty arose from meeting with some large plains, which he named Sturt's Plains, after the great Australian explorer. Stuart concluded that these plains had been at one time the bed of a large fresh-water lake; they were covered with luxuriant grass, in many places above the horses' knees, but the ground was very rotten and difficult to travel over. The plains were skirted by an impenetrable scrub and dense forest, which completely arrested further progress, although gallant attempts were made in all directions. In the neighbourhood of the plains, however, a splendid sheet of water was found, 150 yards wide, nine miles long, and seventeen feet deep in the middle. This valuable discovery—named Newcastle Waters in honour of the Secretary of State—raised the hope that, after all, the progress of the party would be possible; but at the end of nine miles the deep water was succeeded by a chain of ponds, and beyond, scrub and forest even denser than those that had before driven them back. Again and again they tried to force their way, but it was hopeless, and on the 11th of June Stuart wrote as follows:—

"Tomkinson's Creek.

"Shoeing horses and repairing saddles and bags to carry our provisions back. We have now run out of everything for that purpose. We are all nearly naked; the scrub has been so severe on our clothes, one can hardly tell the original colour of a single garment—they are so patched; our boots are also gone. It is with great reluctance I am forced to return without a further trial. I should like to go back and try from Newcastle Waters, but my provisions will not allow me. I started with thirty weeks' supply, at seven pounds of flour per week, and have now been out twenty-six, and it will take me ten weeks before I can reach the first station. The men are also failing and showing the effects of short rations. I only wish I had sufficient to carry me on until the rain will fall in next March. I think I would be able to make both the Victoria and the Gulf. . . ."

Although considerable disappointment was felt and expressed by the colonists when it became known that Stuart had again failed to cross the continent, a warm reception was given to him and his brave companions, and even before the whole of the party arrived in Adelaide, steps were taken by the Government to once more send Stuart out with a party well equipped in every particular.

In all the explorations up to this time Sir Richard

MacDonnell had taken the most profound interest, and had given the most cordial assistance. It was a matter of the deepest regret to him, as it was to the colonists generally, that the term of his administration ceased before the party, reorganized and sent out in the beginning of December, 1861, returned crowned with victory. We shall defer the narration of Stuart's final exploration, therefore, until we come to the story of the administration of Sir Richard's successor.

Between 1859 and 1861 important mining discoveries were made, which had an altogether exceptional influence upon the material advancement of the province. As early as the year 1847 minerals were known to be in existence on Yorke's Peninsula, although no one was aware of their richness or extent, and it was not until 1861 that the two great mines in this locality, the Wallaroo and Moonta mines, attracted public attention. Singular to relate, both these mines, as in the case of the renowned Burra-Burra and others, were discovered by shepherds. It was in December, 1859, that a shepherd named James Boor, in the employment of Mr. (afterwards Sir) Walter Watson Hughes, picked up some specimens on the sheep run where he followed his flock, and these, upon analysis, proved to be rich in copper. In February, 1860, four Cornish miners appeared upon the scene, and the result of their labours led to a speedy increase of hands and the extensive application of machinery. Mineral leases of the land were immediately secured, a company was formed, and success set in. The richness of the Wallaroo Mine may be judged from the following figures: "The ore raised between March, 1860, and December, 1884, amounted to 428,333 tons gross weight, of a net value of £1,970,533, and represented a production of copper of 41,025 tons, of an estimated net value in the colony of £2,873,121. The mine gave employment, when in full work, to a very large staff, there being at one time as many as 1003 men and boys engaged in the workings." *

* "South Australia," by John Fairfax Conigrave.

Splendid as these results were, they were eclipsed by those of the Moonta Mine, discovered in May, 1861, by a shepherd named Ryan, also in the employment of Mr. W. W. Hughes. The claim of Ryan was disputed by Mr. E. R. Mitford, the editor of *Pasquin*, a clever satirical writer, who alleged that he had made the discovery as early as 1848, but had not taken any steps until public attention was turned to the Peninsula as a mining district. Mr. Mitford endeavoured to establish his claim, first through the Crown Lands Department, and next by petition to Parliament, where a Select Committee decided against him.

When the shepherd Ryan made the discovery of a valuable deposit of copper ore at no great distance from his hut, and, like the Wallaroo, only a few miles distant from the sea-coast, he was in a dilemma. The fact was Ryan was not a teetotaller, but, on the contrary, was rather given to too free indulgence in "the cup that cheers, but inebriates," and the friend to whom he first confided the news of his discovery was slow to believe him, as "lucky finds" had turned the heads of many much more sober men. It appears that there was some doubt in Ryan's mind whether he would secure the claim for himself and a partner, or allow his employer to become the fortunate holder. Whether the latter was his intention or not will probably never be known, but Mr. Hughes and his friends got scent of the matter, and lost no time in lodging a claim for five sections somewhere not very far from the locality indicated. Meanwhile Ryan took a trip to town and entered into an agreement with Mr. S. Mills to share with him the discovery, and Mr. Mills proceeded to the Land Office to lodge a claim. No sooner were the doors of the Land Office opened than the rival claimants entered, but the agents of Mr. Hughes being more expeditious in filling up the forms of application succeeded in first handing in their claim. To tell the whole story of the events that followed, and all the circumstances connected with the Tipara Mineral claims—as the Moonta sections were then generally designated—would fill a moderately sized volume. The whole matter was finally referred to a Select Committee of the House of Assembly, appointed in 1863, who asked and elicited answers to upwards of seven thousand questions. Their report decided adversely to Mr. Hughes's right to the property, and in favour of Mr. S. Mills, as the party authorized to lodge the claims by the legitimate discoverer, Ryan, and this decision of course invalidated the claims of Mr. Mitford also, so far as the committee was concerned.

But the report of the Select Committee was not adopted by the House, the Assembly considering that the case should be relegated to the limbo of the Law Courts. Mr. Hughes, however, secured thirty sections in the vicinity of the first discovery, and twelve of these were subsequently leased to the proprietary. The property was at first represented by forty shares, some of which were given away in a most liberal manner, and the whole were subsequently subdivided. The Moonta Mine soon proved to be more productive than the famous Wallaroo Mine. "From the opening of the Moonta Mine in 1861, to the 28th of February, 1885, the total quantity of ore raised amounted to 447,969 tons (gross weight) of twenty-one cwts., of a value in the colony of £4,468,124, representing a total production of refined copper of 85,104 tons, the value of which to the colony may be approximately stated at £5,879,226." *

In 1861, in consequence of further mineral discoveries on the Peninsula, some hundreds of claims for mineral leases were lodged at the Crown Lands Office. Mining became a mania; tradesmen and others left their ordinary occupations to pay a visit to the Peninsula, nearly all of whom found, or thought they had found, "good indications." If two or more hit upon a likely spot it became a race which should first reach the Land Office to lodge the claim.

Several other mining companies were formed, or "mining ventures" were entered into, while the mania

* "South Australia," by John Fairfax Conigrave.

lasted, the total capital of those who advertised amounting to about half a million sterling; but after the expenditure of much money in prospecting, sinking, and advertising, they were nearly all wound up, leaving the colonists in general, and the tradesmen in particular, poorer but wiser men. During the time that the excitement lasted it was believed that a larger sum was realized by the sale and transfer of shares than was payable in dividends by all the companies for a year to come. Those who had resided in the colony during the mining mania of 1845-46 well knew that, with the exception of the Burra-Burra Mine, the most profitable period in the history of all other mines had been while there was sufficient enthusiasm to raise the shares to a premium, and those "who knew a thing or two," as the vulgar say, managed to feather their own nests.

The large population attracted to the Peninsula by the prosperity of the great mines led the Government to lay out two townships, one at the shipping place, named Wallaroo, and one a few miles inland, named Kadina. So completely did the mineral discoveries change the face of the country that in three or four years the land, which had previously been a mere sheep run, possessed two flourishing towns with substantial buildings, and a large population.

One great drawback experienced in both townships, as well as at the mines, was the want of water, to supply which distillation was, in the first instance, resorted to, the salt and brackish water from the mines being used for this purpose. A high price had to be paid for this unpalatable liquid, and housekeepers and teetotallers had a poor time of it. All new buildings, therefore, had the roofs so constructed that they should store every drop of rain water that fell on them, and this was found to be a great improvement upon the distilled water.

About this period another very important branch of industry, destined in the near future to become a staple in the South Australian market, was coming into prominence. In a letter to Mr. G. F. Angas, written in 1860, Sir Richard MacDonnell said:—

"I have lately been going through the dozen duplicate samples of wine which you sent me from Tanunda, and at least eight of them are excellent. I have been quite surprised at their quality, but I have no doubt this country will be a good wine-producing country. People are setting to work energetically planting vines in all directions, and in four years I have no doubt we shall obtain a tolerable footing in the English market."

The Governor was not far out in his calculation, but it was not until 1871 that any trade of importance was done with England. Vines were sent out by the South Australian Company as early as 1835–36, but the first vineyard proper was planted by Mr. John Reynell, on his property at Reynella, about twelve miles from Adelaide, in 1840. In 1846 Mr. Patrick Auld commenced the celebrated "Auldana" vineyard. In 1863 the justly famous "Tintara" vineyard was planted by Dr. Kelly. It must be confessed that at first Australian wine was sorry stuff, but year by year planting went steadily on. It was found that soil and climate were suited to the production of every kind of wine, but more especially of generous wines of the claret and Burgundy type, while some, such as the "Highercombe," more resemble Chablis. We shall have more to say about the marvellous development of the wine trade of South Australia later on, but it may give an indication of its enormous growth to state here that in four months ended the 31st of May, 1890, one firm alone (Messrs. P. B. Burgoyne & Co.) imported into England 123,658 gallons! A year or two later than the date of Sir Richard MacDonnell's letter, from which we have quoted, Mr. Anthony Forster, an old and experienced colonist, wrote upon the wines and vine culture of South Australia as follows:—

"South Australia has made immense progress in the development of agricultural, pastoral, and mineral wealth. These are the three great staples of the country, to which wine may be added as a fourth. The production of the latter is increasing largely every year, and promises to become a considerable source of income to the horticulturist, as well as a protection to the community against the excessive use of more stimulating beverages. The wine produced is of a light but excellent description, well suited to the requirements of a warm climate, and free from the noxious adulterations so frequently discovered in imported wines."

When Parliament was called together on the 20th of April, 1861, the Governor announced, among other things, the receipt of a despatch from the Duke of Newcastle, stating that her Majesty would be advised to introduce a Bill into the Imperial Parliament to give her Majesty power to annex to South Australia the tract of land lying between the western boundary of South Australia and the eastern boundary of Western Australia, and also, at some future time, to extend the colony northward.

During the session the Immigration Question gave rise to a long and spirited debate, and resulted in the passing of resolutions in both Houses for the resumption of free immigration, leaving it to the Ministry to exercise a certain amount of discretion in the matter.

On the 3rd of December the protracted labours of the session were brought to an end, and as it was the last occasion on which the Governor expected to meet the Parliament of South Australia, he delivered an address of more than ordinary length.

In congratulating the members on the aspect of affairs in the colony, he said, "If there is less excitement than at some former periods there is more substantial prosperity and solid advancement. All classes of the labouring population find ready and remunerative employment, while, owing to the low prices of provisions and other necessaries of life, their material comforts are greater than they have been for many years. Fresh tracts of country are being continually occupied; new sources of mineral wealth are being opened up, and Divine Providence has again favoured us with abundant crops."

He congratulated them on the boon conferred by the Real Property Act, providing for increased facilities, cheapness, and simplicity in all dealings with land; on the volunteer movement and the additional security of the colony; and on general subjects connected with the administration.

In looking back on the past six years of the history of the colony—the period covered by his term of office—he said:—

"When I landed here in June, 1855, there was not a mile of railway opened in the colony; now there are fifty-seven miles in use, over which annually rolls a traffic of more than 150,000 tons and 320,000 passengers. Your coasts have been lit with three additional first-class lights, and three additional harbours have come into extensive use. Your population has grown from 86,000 to nearly 130,000, whilst the exports of colonial produce have risen from less than £691,000 in 1855 to £1,808,000 for the year ending the 30th of June last. When I landed there were scarcely sixty miles of made road in the colony, whereas now, independent of those in the city, there are over two hundred miles; and instead of 160,000 acres only in cultivation, there cannot be less now than 460,000—a number greater in proportion to the population than obtains in any other portion of her Majesty's dominions, or, indeed, in any other part of the world with which I am acquainted. It is, moreover, since 1855 that the first telegraph post was erected in this colony, and yet you already possess 600 miles of telegraph communication, and nearly 1000 miles of wire, together with twenty-six stations. It is also since 1855 that the explorations of Mr. Stuart and others have added so much to our geographical knowledge, filling up the large blank spaces which had so long defaced the map of South Australia, and usefully opening up the country to further settlement. Above all, it is since my arrival here that the great experiment has been tried of entrusting the general mass of the people, through their immediate representatives, with power to control completely the taxation and expenditure of the country and direct its general legislation."

On the day of prorogation valedictory addresses were presented from the members of both Houses to the retiring Governor, and expressions of regret on their part, no less than on his, were warmly exchanged.

On the evening of the 23rd of December, a large body of German colonists, having resolved to present a valedictory address to Sir Richard, formed a torchlight procession, and, preceded by a band of music, and accompanied by the members of the Liedertafel, proceeded to Government House. Some thousands assembled to witness the novel and effective demonstration. Two hundred and fifty torches were lighted, Bengal lights were burnt, and finally a bonfire was made of the torches. The address was signed by 1326 German colonists.

The name of Sir Richard MacDonnell will ever remain identified with the most interesting and most important period of South Australian history—the transition of the colony from a state of comparative dependence to the enjoyment of a Constitution which, while it imposed an enormous, weighty, and responsible trust, involving the almost absolute control of all local interests, at the same time gave an independence which should endure and carry its blessings with it, through all time.

So great a favourite was Sir Richard, and so essential to the welfare of the colony was his presence regarded that a memorial was drawn up, praying her Majesty to extend his term of service; but, as Sir Richard pointed out to the leaders of this movement, he could not forward a document of the kind in which he himself might be regarded as personally interested, and, moreover, at that time a despatch had been received from the Duke of Newcastle, stating that Sir Dominick Daly had been appointed his successor.

CHAPTER XI.

ADMINISTRATION OF SIR DOMINICK DALY.

MARCH, 1862—FEBRUARY, 1868.

Coming and Departing Guests.—An Irish Gentleman.—Warlike Times.—Volunteering.—Explorations.—McKinlay.—Burke and Wills.—Return of J. M. Stuart after crossing and recrossing the Continent.—A Great Ovation.—Geological Survey by Mr. Hargreaves.—" No Man's Land."—Ministerial Difficulties.—The English Mail Service.—An Intercolonial Conference.—" No Confidence " Motions.—Retirement of M.P.'s.—Red Rust in Wheat.—Party Spirit.—The Northern Territory.—A Terrible Responsibility.—Waste Lands in North Australia—A Survey Expedition.—Mr. B. T. Finniss Government Resident.—A Pioneer Expedition.—Misunderstandings.—Recall of Mr. Finniss.—Mr. G. W. Goyder sent out.—The Squatter Question.—Revaluations of Land.—Unprecedented Drought.—Loss of Stock.—Visit of H.R.H. the Duke of Edinburgh.—A Round of Gaieties.—Attempted Assassination of the Duke of Edinburgh at Sydney.—Death of Sir Dominick Daly.—Funeral.—Review of his Administration.

SIR DOMINICK DALY arrived at Port Adelaide early in the morning of March 4, 1862, so early, in fact, as to disarrange all preconcerted plans for his reception, and he and his family had to walk to the railway station. The ceremony of swearing-in took place at Government House the same day, when Sir Richard MacDonnell, "as a private individual," delivered a kindly and generous address of congratulation.

Later in the day the new Governor, accompanied by Sir Richard, reviewed the volunteer corps (numbering from six hundred to seven hundred) in the presence of some five or six thousand spectators. It was rather an anomalous demonstration, as it was originally designed in honour of Sir Richard, who had taken a lively interest in the volunteer movement during the whole period of his administration, and it now had to serve a double purpose—to "welcome the coming and speed the parting guest."

It must be admitted that the day of departure of a Governor who had made himself decidedly and deservedly popular was not the most appropriate day for the arrival and inauguration of his successor, but in the circumstances it could not be arranged otherwise.

Sir Dominick Daly's antecedents were good. In 1822, at the age of twenty-four, he left Ireland as private secretary to Sir Francis Burton, who in that year went out as Governor of Lower Canada. In 1827 Mr. Daly received the appointment of Provincial Secretary of Lower Canada, and upon the union of Upper and Lower Canada in 1840 he was promoted to the Secretaryship of the United Provinces, an office he held until 1848, during which period he became not only thoroughly acquainted with the routine work of colonial government, but also with the working out of responsible government.

Sir J. W. Kaye, the biographer of Lord Metcalfe, who was Governor of Lower Canada during a portion of this period, says of Mr. Daly:—

"He was an Irishman and a Roman Catholic, and although for the latter reason his sympathies were strongly with the French people, or had been so long as they were oppressed by the dominant race, his feelings, the growth of education and early association, were of a conservative and aristocratic cast. All Metcalfe's informants represented him to be a man of high honour and integrity, of polished manners and courteous address—a good specimen of an Irish gentleman. It was added that he was possessed of judgment and prudence, tact and discretion—in short, a man to be trusted."

During the four years he was in England he was entrusted with some important commissions by the Home Government, and in 1852 he was appointed to his first colonial Governorship, that of Tobago, one of the Windward Islands. In 1854 he was promoted to the Government of Prince Edward Island, and occupied that post for six years. In 1856 he was created a Knight Bachelor, and in 1859 returned to England, where he remained until he received the appointment of Governor of South Australia.

The time at which Sir Dominick assumed the office of Governor was one of some anxiety, reports having reached the colony that a war between England and the United States was not improbable in consequence of the seizure by a Federal war steamer of two passengers, Messrs. Slidell and Mason, Confederate commissioners to England and France, on board the English mail steamer *Trent* in the Bahama Channel. How an apology was demanded by the English Government, and how the United States Government surrendered the "rebels," thereby averting a war between the two countries, is matter of well-known history. The "great review," which signalized the advent of Sir Dominick Daly, occurring in such warlike times, was an appropriate demonstration. It so happened, too, that it was the closing term of the first really important volunteer movement in the colony—that is to say, it brought to an end the three years' service of the first enrolment of unpaid volunteers. Unfortunately, martial zeal was a difficult thing to sustain in the colony, and the unpaid volunteer system fell somewhat into disfavour, although in the following year a second enrolment was resorted to for a further period of three years. "In order to continue the renewal of the services of the trained volunteers they were offered, as an inducement to sign the new roll, the free gift of the rifles and accoutrements then in their keeping. But it was felt that the day was gone by when men would continue to attend drill without some compensation for loss of time, and this disinclination was shown in the gradual falling off in the numbers present on field-days." In 1866, therefore, an Act was passed—subsequently amended in many important details—which made the volunteer military force a paid body.

The association for rifle practice, originated and warmly supported by Sir Richard MacDonnell, continued to flourish, and developed into the "South Australian National Rifle Association," recognized by the Government and encouraged by a special Act of Parliament as an Auxiliary Volunteer Military Force.

The question of the defence of the colony was one that was continually cropping up, and in the days when the unpaid volunteer force was in full vigour many imaginary invasions took place, and on several occasions, in order to keep the force in a state of preparation, a prearranged signal would rouse the peaceful colonists from their slumbers to go forth in the dead of night to engage in sanguinary conflict with the supposed invaders.

Sometimes the volunteers rendered important service and gave to the colonists a sense of security they would not otherwise have had. For example: in consequence of the urgent necessity that existed for the presence of all the available troops stationed in the Australian colonies to assist in suppressing the war with the Maories in New Zealand, the detachment of the 40th Regiment located at Adelaide was allowed, in October, 1863, to leave the colony for the seat of war.

In April, 1865, a commission, appointed to inquire into the best means of protecting the coast in the event of invasion, gave in its report and recommended the procuring from England of ten or twelve guns of heavy calibre; the erection of batteries at such points of the coast as would most effectually protect the ports and townships within range of the enemy's guns from the sea; the purchase of a complete equipment for a full battery of rifled field artillery to be manned by a local force; the maintenance, under strict military discipline, of a paid force of seven hundred infantry and two hundred artillery; that encouragement should be given to the colonists to obtain a knowledge of the use of the rifle and of simple military movements with a view to their acting as volunteer auxiliaries to the paid body; and that a supply of the most approved rifles for at least two thousand men should be procured. Several of these recommendations were fully carried out.

The absorbing topic in the early days of Sir Dominick Daly's administration, and more or less throughout that whole period, was not "rude war's alarms," but the victories of peace, especially those gained by Australia's great explorers. Mr. J. M. Stuart had, as we have seen,* gone forth for the fifth time to attempt the gigantic feat of crossing the continent, and Messrs. Burke and Wills, under the auspices of the Victorian Government, had been sent out upon a similar errand. Unhappily the latter expedition, although successful in being the first to cross the continent, ended in a terrible tragedy.

Towards the end of 1862 there occurred some of the most exciting incidents in connection with South Australian exploration. In October information was received that Mr. McKinlay and his party, who had been despatched on an expedition with a view to render assistance, if not too late, to the Burke and Wills party from Victoria, and, if possible, to explore the neighbourhood of Lake Eyre, had returned by quite an unexpected route. It appeared that he proceeded direct to Cooper's Creek, where, from the accounts of the natives and the discovery of what was supposed to be the body of Gray, one of the missing explorers, he concluded that the whole of Burke's party had been murdered, and, accordingly, he sent messengers to Blanchewater with this painful intelligence. Before their return, however, he found memorials left by Mr. Howitt, who had been sent out by the Victorian Government, recording the terrible fate of Burke and Wills. When McKinlay's messengers returned, they brought fuller particulars of the tragedy, together with information that the Victorian Government intended

* See p. 345.

to despatch a party to convey the remains of the unfortunate explorers to Melbourne. In endeavouring to carry out his instructions to head Lake Eyre and return by the western shores of that lake, Mr. McKinlay was suddenly surrounded by a heavy flood, and was obliged, with his party, to remain for several days upon a sand-hill. It was with the greatest difficulty he made his escape, as the country was one vast sheet of water—that same country which had but a short time previously been a desert, dry, and without a sign of vegetation. The flood waters ran apparently into a basin so wide and deep that Mr. McKinlay was unable to pass by the head of the lake as instructed, and this led him so far towards the Gulf of Carpentaria, that he determined to push on there and obtain a supply of provisions from the Victorian steamer, sent to that gulf to assist any party successful in crossing the continent. He was disappointed in the expectation of obtaining supplies, and being short of the commonest necessaries, it was imperative that he should at once take the shortest route to settled districts. He accordingly made for Port Denison, where he obtained the needful supplies. Although he had departed from his instructions in making his bold dash to the northward, he had solved the great problem, and had succeeded in crossing over to the Gulf of Carpentaria almost in the footsteps of Burke and Wills.

A handsome public presentation was made to Mr. McKinlay, and the Legislature also voted the sum of £1000 as an acknowledgment of his valuable services.

But the idol of the people was, without doubt, John McDouall Stuart, whose return was awaited with almost feverish anxiety. In the mean time, however, and as if to bring home to them with renewed force the hazards and perils of interior exploration, they were to witness a scene which none who beheld should ever forget.

In December, 1862, the remains of the missing explorers, Messrs. Burke and Wills, were brought by Mr. Howitt and his party to Adelaide, from Cooper's

Creek, *en route* to Melbourne, from whence these gallant but unfortunate men had started with a view to cross the continent. The streets of Adelaide were lined by thousands of sympathetic spectators, who, with uncovered heads, surrounded by emblems of mourning, and amid the clangour of tolling bells, viewed the mournful procession as it passed on its way from the railway station to the barracks. Much respect was shown to Mr. Howitt, who, in addition to the objects of his special mission, had made important explorations affecting the interests of South Australia.

Only a few days after the remains of the daring but unsuccessful explorers, Burke and Wills, had left Adelaide by steamer for Melbourne, the gratifying intelligence was received from the far north that Mr. J. M. Stuart and his party had returned to the settled districts after successfully crossing and recrossing the continent. There was not a man in all South Australia whose heart did not swell with gratitude, pride, and satisfaction, on receiving this news, and every scrap of information was eagerly devoured. The party consisted of J. M. Stuart, W. Kekwick, F. W. Thring, W. P. Auld, S. King, J. Billiatt, J. F. New, H. Nash, J. McGorrerey, J. W. Waterhouse, amongst whom the Government grant of £3500 was divided.

It appeared that within three months after leaving Chambers' Creek, the party arrived at Newcastle Waters, from whence the work of fresh exploration really commenced. After several unsuccessful attempts to get beyond the dense forest and scrub already described, Stuart came upon a succession of ponds. Pushing forward past a permanent sheet of water, named the Daly Waters, in honour of the Governor, he entered upon a fine, well-watered country, and in about 150° of south latitude came upon the river Strangways, which, in a few days' travel, led to the river Roper. Mr. Stuart considered the country in the neighbourhood of the Roper the finest he had seen; the soil excellent, grass rich and abundant, the river banks richly lined with cabbage trees, cane, bamboo, and other shrubs. Passing to the northward, they followed down the river for some distance, and then made for the Adelaide river, which they reached on the 10th of July. Here, in the midst of lovely scenery and luxuriant vegetation, with birds of splendid plumage, and with abounding creeks and watercourses, they lingered for a few days, travelling gently down the river, and every step bringing them nearer to the sea-coast, a fact which Stuart kept from the knowledge of the rest of the party, in order to give them a joyous surprise. The story of the approach to the sea may best be told in Stuart's own words.

"At eight and a half miles came up to a broad valley of black alluvial soil, covered with long grass; from this I can hear the wash of the sea. On the other side of the valley, which is rather more than a quarter of a mile wide, is growing a line of thick heavy bushes, very dense, showing that to be the boundary of the beach. Crossed the valley and entered the scrub, which was a complete network of vines; stopped the horses to clear the way whilst I advanced a few yards on to the beach, and was delighted and gratified to behold the waters of the Indian Ocean in Van Diemen's Gulf, before the party with the horses knew anything of its proximity. Thring, who rode in advance of me, called out, 'The sea!' which so took them all by surprise that he had to repeat the call before they fully understood what was meant; hearing which, they gave three long and hearty cheers. The beach is covered with a soft blue mud; it being ebb tide I could see some distance; found it would be impossible for me to take the horses along it; I, therefore, kept them where I had halted them, and allowed half the party to come on to the beach and gratify themselves by a sight of the sea, while the other half waited to watch the horses until their return. I dipped my feet and washed my face and hands in the sea, as I promised the late Governor, Sir Richard MacDonnell, I would do if I reached it. . . . I returned to the valley, where I had my initials cut on a large tree (J. M. D. S.), as

I intended putting my flag up at the mouth of the Adelaide.

"Thus have I, through the instrumentality of Divine Providence, been led to accomplish the great object of the expedition, and take the whole party through as witnesses to the fact, and through one of the finest countries man would wish to pass—good to the coast, and with a stream of running water within half a mile of the sea. From Newcastle Waters to the sea-beach the main body of the horses have only been one night without water, and then got it within the next day. If this country is settled, it will be one of the finest colonies under the Crown, suitable for the growth of any and every thing. What a splendid country for producing cotton! Judging from the number of the pathways from the water to the beach, across the valley, the natives must be very numerous. We have not seen any, although we have passed many of their recent tracks and encampments. The cabbage and fan-palm trees have been very plentiful during to-day's journey down to this valley."

On the next day, Mr. Stuart having determined to recross the continent, he had an open space cleared, selected one of the tallest trees, stripped it of its lowest branches, and on its highest branch fixed the Union Jack with his name sewn in the centre, amid the cheers of the whole party. A paper, enclosed in an air-tight case, was buried one foot south of the tree, bearing this inscription:—

"SOUTH AUSTRALIAN GREAT NORTHERN EXPLORING EXPEDITION.

"The exploring party under the command of John McDouall Stuart arrived at this spot on the 25th day of July, 1862, having crossed the entire continent of Australia, from the Southern to the Indian Ocean, passing through the centre. They left the city of Adelaide on the 26th day of October, 1861, and the most northern station of the colony on the 21st of

January, 1862. To commemorate this happy event they have raised this flag bearing his name. All well. God save the Queen!"

The return journey was accomplished with difficulty: first, from the weak state of the horses; next, from the annoyances of natives, who set fire to the grass and otherwise hindered their progress; and, finally, from the severe sickness of Mr. Stuart. As the party neared the centre he was seized with a violent attack of illness, from which he did not expect to recover. He had been suffering from scurvy for some time previously, his eyesight nearly failed him, and at one time he almost lost the power of speech. It is sad to read an entry in his journal, under date of October 31, where, after "thanking Almighty God that, in His infinite goodness and mercy, He had so far prolonged his life," he adds—

"What a sad difference there is between what I am now, and what I was when the party left Adelaide! My right hand nearly useless to me by the accident from the horse; total blindness after sunset—although the moon shines bright to others, to me it is total darkness, and nearly blind during the day; my limbs so weak and painful that I am obliged to be carried about; my body reduced to that of a living skeleton, and my strength that of infantine weakness—a sad, sad wreck of former days."

It is difficult, nay impossible, to estimate the importance of Stuart's great enterprise, not only to the colonies of Australia, but to the world at large. It is equally impossible to find language that shall not appear exaggerated to characterize the heroism and indomitable pluck of this brave and noble man. It is true he was not the first to cross the continent, although he was the first to absolutely complete the route from the southern to the northern coast, for neither Burke nor McKinlay really saw the northern sea; but he was the first who laid down a line of route, describing every step of the way in chart and journal, by which any one might pass with comparative ease from Adelaide to Adam Bay. How his discoveries were utilized we shall tell elsewhere.

A great ovation awaited him on his return to Adelaide—fêtes and banquets were given in his honour; the Legislature awarded him the sum of £2000 and proportional gratuities to all the members of his party. The lease of a large area of land in the north was also granted to Mr. Stuart rent-free for several years, but his constitution was so shattered by the exposure to which he had been subjected in his various explorations that he did not live long to enjoy his hard-earned honours. In April, 1864, he proceeded to England in the hope that the voyage and residence in the mother-country might to some extent restore his health; but this was not to be, and he gradually sank till death put an end to his short, but useful, career.

Other explorations undertaken during the administration of Sir Dominick Daly were useful, but not of startling interest. With a view to ascertain whether a payable gold-field really existed in South Australia, which would not only give employment to many in the colony, but attract outsiders, the Government secured the services of Mr. Hargreaves, in 1863, for the purpose of making a geological survey of the settled districts. He started on the 31st of October, 1863, and returned to Adelaide on the 18th of June, 1864, having examined the country from Cape Jervis, sixty miles south of Adelaide, to a point 540 miles north of Adelaide. He reported that, although gold existed generally from Cape Jervis to Tanunda, and in paying quantities in the beds of the Torrens and the Onkaparinga, he did not consider the precious metal would be found anywhere in sufficiently large quantities to justify a "rush."

In September, 1864, Major Warburton started on an expedition to explore the country north and west of Mount Margaret, known as "No Man's Land;" but, after being absent about two months, he returned, finding it impracticable to proceed in the desired direction.

In June, 1866, he made another attempt to accomplish the same object, but was again compelled to abandon it, and returned to Adelaide, after an absence of twenty-one weeks.

During that year the Hon. Thomas Elder imported 121 camels from Kurrachee, which were landed at Port Augusta, and were found very useful to explorers in crossing the dry parts of the north country.

We do not propose to give in detail the history of legislation during the administration of Sir Dominick Daly. The constant crises, the ever-recurring resignations, the splits and compromises, which had, it may be, an absorbing interest in the passing hour, would be found of little interest now; nor do we propose to burden our pages with the names of the members of each successive Parliament, or even the titles of the multitudinous Bills they passed. We shall, however, glance at the general action of Parliament during the period under consideration, and then select for more detailed notice those measures which had a special and abiding influence on the colony.

The first meeting of Parliament under Sir Dominick Daly was held on the 25th of April, and the "vice-regal speech" was considered rather barren, so far as regarded the measures promised by Government. One of the first Acts of both branches of the Legislature was to send addresses of condolence to her Majesty on the irreparable loss she had sustained in the death of the Prince Consort.

In July the Ministry resigned on a question of "assimilation of tariffs," but, after explanations, the resignations were withdrawn.

In September the "Ministry, considering that they had not a sufficient majority to carry on the business of the country," again placed their resignations in the hands of the Governor, but an arrangement was made that the existing Ministry should continue in office until the prorogation on the 21st of October.

On that occasion Sir Dominick brought under the

notice of the House of Assembly the necessity that would soon arise for increasing the revenue of the colony, and expressed the hope that the approaching Conference at Melbourne would pave the way " for the introduction of a uniform tariff throughout the colonies, and for a mutual interchange, free of duty, of articles of colonial produce." Referring to the measure known as Sutherland's Act, his Excellency said it "recognized the sound principle, that increase of population is necessary alike to occupying fresh country and to imparting additional value thereto."

The Assessment of Stock Act, by freeing from the burden of assessment lands at present incapable of bearing this impost, would, he considered, do much to promote the occupation and settlement of that enormous territory made known by the researches and enterprise of Stuart, McKinlay, and other intrepid explorers, but which, owing to its distance from an available market, must otherwise have remained valueless.

For many years the English mail service had been a bone of contention in the Legislature, and at the same time an inestimable blessing to the editors of the local papers, inasmuch as the subject always made good "copy." The contention was that the geographical position of the colony was persistently ignored, and there was only one way of obtaining the mails without vexatious delay, namely, by sending a branch steamer for them to King George's Sound. In September, 1862, the Government accepted the tender of the Australian Steam Navigation Company for this service at £1300 per month, and for several years the anomaly lasted of the branch steamer arriving at Port Adelaide two or three days before the ocean steamer reached Melbourne, by which means the English news was telegraphed to the neighbouring colonies from Adelaide about the same time that the ocean steamer would be passing within two or three hundred miles of Investigator's Straits, on the way to Melbourne. By this absurd and unjust arrangement, South Australia was at the expense of a separate service, which supplied the earliest intelligence to those very colonies which placed obstacles in the way of obtaining the mails from the ocean steamers as they passed within a short distance of a South Australian port.

The first Parliamentary session under Sir Dominick Daly was not by any means a barren one; many useful Bills had been assented to, and one of the measures, that known as Sutherland's Act, deserves particular mention on account of its subsequent history. It provided that one-third of the proceeds arising from the sale of waste lands should be appropriated to immigration, another third to the construction of roads, bridges, and such-like work, and the remainder to public purposes, or, in other words, to secure the expenditure of moneys arising from the sale of waste lands for those purposes for which they were originally set apart. When the introduction of immigrants at the public expense had been discontinued, the one-third reserved for that purpose had been allowed to accumulate, and, after being used as a loan, had ultimately become absorbed in the general revenue.

During the session of 1862, therefore, the Legislature voted the sum of £25,000 for immigration, allowing time for Sutherland's Act to come into operation.

The first session of the third Parliament* under the Constitution Act of 1856 met for the despatch of business on the 27th of February, 1863, and adjourned on the 10th of March to the 9th of April, partly for the purpose of enabling the three delegates to the Intercolonial Conference to attend without putting the Legislature to inconvenience. The members selected to represent South Australia were the Hon. H. Ayers, the Hon. A. Blyth, and Mr. L. Glyde, M.P. The subjects to be discussed at the Conference were uniform tariffs, border customs duties, the postal question, coast lights, an Intercolonial Court of Appeal, and uniform weights and measures.

* At the general election which took place in November, 1862, about two-thirds of the members of the late Parliament were returned.

The Conference was duly held, and the report of proceedings was published in June. All the reforms contemplated in the programme were recommended, and many others in addition, such as the discontinuance of transportation to any portion of the Australian colonies, the encouragement of immigration, the improvement of navigable rivers, telegraphic communication with England, and various questions relating to law. But it is one thing to hold a conference, and quite another to carry out its recommendations. To wit, the new tariff agreed upon was introduced in the South Australian Parliament on the 1st of June, but was withdrawn on the 4th, because the New South Wales Government declined to co-operate!

The first session of the new Parliament was anything but peaceful. On the 30th of June the Ministry resigned and Mr. F. S. Dutton undertook the formation of a new Ministry, and succeeded; but when both Houses met on the 7th of July, the Ministry sustained a defeat in both Chambers, and on the following day sent in their resignations; whereupon Mr. J. T. Bagot was sent for to form a Government, but failing, the task was entrusted to Mr. R. I. Stow, who was also unsuccessful.

It is worthy of remark that, notwithstanding these failures, the extreme step of a dissolution was not so much as suggested. The Hon. H. Ayers came to the rescue and submitted a list of names which were approved and duly gazetted.

Soon after, difficulties arose on the question of borrowing money for public works, but they were tided over, and on the 12th of November Parliament was prorogued. Up to the very last hour, however, the Ministry was in jeopardy, a member being in the act of moving a vote of censure when the arrival of the Governor to prorogue the Parliament was announced.*

When the second session of the third Parliament was opened on the 27th of May, 1864, the Governor said,

---

* The Legislative Council had sat sixty-six days, and the House of Assembly 101 days.

" I believe I am warranted in saying that at no other period of the colony's history have we had greater evidence of substantial prosperity."

Many immigrants had recently arrived from Europe and had found immediate employment, and the demand for labour continuing undiminished, the Government anticipated a vote for immigration, and authorized the despatch of three vessels, to sail respectively in July, August, and September.

Active legislation soon commenced, but the session was marked by an irritating number of no-confidence motions, with their endless ministerial explanations and discussions, wasting an inordinate amount of time, and threatening serious consequences to the political welfare of the colony. And the curious part of it was that the extreme step of a dissolution was again not so much as suggested.

The outside public summed up the state of affairs in the form of a resolution carried with enthusiasm at a public demonstration: "That in the opinion of this meeting the scramble for office by members of the House of Assembly, regardless of public policy or political consistency, has delayed the business of the country, and is calculated to bring into contempt our present system of Government."

This had little or no effect. There were further skirmishes between the members of both Houses on the Squatting Question, and on the 29th of November such an attack was made on the Government that it was felt at length there was no other course left but to advise the Governor to dissolve the House, a course he consented to adopt and carry into effect so soon as the business then on hand was disposed of.

The first session of the fourth Parliament was opened on the 31st of March, 1865. The Hon. J. Morphett was elected President of the Council in place of Sir J. H. Fisher, who had retired after being connected with the Legislature for seventeen years. In the House of Assembly Mr. G. S. Kingston was elected as Speaker, Mr. G. C. Hawker, who had previously occupied that office, having retired for a time from parliamentary life.

Among the subjects touched upon in the Governor's opening speech was the Melbourne Conference, at which Victoria, South Australia, and Tasmania were represented for the purpose of taking joint action for the absolute termination of transportation to Western Australia, and his Excellency was happy to state that her Majesty's Government had been pleased to determine that such transportation should cease after a limited period.

Among the most useful measures of this session may be mentioned the Bill for providing for destitute persons in a more systematic manner than the one previously in operation, provision also being made for orphans and children of destitute persons. The erection of a commodious building, known as the Orphanage, at Magill, was one of the results of this Bill.

A marriage Bill introduced by the Ministry for placing all ministers of religion on an equality as regarded the celebration of Holy Matrimony was rejected, not so much on account of the principle involved, as on certain defects in its construction. A meeting of "friends of religious equality" was held in Chalmers', Church, North Terrace, when a committee was appointed to prepare a suitable Bill. This Bill was passed in the ensuing session, notwithstanding the strong condemnation of it by Roman Catholics in and out of Parliament.

In 1866 the ordinary routine of Parliamentary business was broken for a while in order to pay a tribute of respect to some of its leading members who were retiring from public life. These were Mr. J. M. Solomon, Mr. S. Davenport, Mr. C. Bonney, and Mr. G. F. Angas.

Special reference was made in the House to the loss the colony would sustain by these retirements, and men of all shades of opinion in politics expressed their regret. Notably was this the case in regard to Mr. G. F. Angas.

Mr. Baker, one of the most influential members, said, "In consequence of his early connection with the colony, his position in society, his experience, his knowledge of mercantile affairs, and everything connected with colonization, Mr. Angas was eminently entitled to their gratitude." Men who differed from Mr. Angas on many points joined in expressing the opinion that no other man had done so much to advance the interests of the colony.

Said Captain C. H. Bagot, an old antagonist, "I always regarded him as a deep-thinking, clever man, who never hesitated to declare what he thought was the right view, and was never overawed by popular clamour. This no doubt brought a good deal of obloquy upon him, but his conduct was always upright and consistent, and it was a matter of great regret that they had lost his services."

The verdict of the press coincided with that of the Parliament. "Although Mr. Angas," said the leading journal of the colony, "was not what is known as a popular politician, he nevertheless won general esteem by the independence, integrity, and painstaking industry with which his duties as a member were discharged."

Many years later, one who knew him well[*] added this testimony: "I may truly say that no member of the Legislative Council felt greater interest in its proceedings, nor evinced more ardour in his desire to lay broad and sound the laws for effecting the healthy development of the colony and the common prosperity of all classes of its people, than he did. In his statesmanlike view, the prosperity of each individual, and of each industrial class, was the most logical aim and the surest path to the attainment of the greatest good of all. To a heart full of sympathy with the best interests of the colony, he further elevated the character of a legislator by his long and extensive business experience, his high moral tone, and the consequent wisdom and prudence of his counsels. It is, however, as being

---

[*] Sir Samuel Davenport, K.C.M.G.

specially prominent amongst the Fathers and Founders of the colony that his name will lastingly claim the grateful recognition of all who have, or may, benefit by being colonists."

The fourth session of the fourth Parliament was opened on the 5th of July, 1867. For once the address in reply to the Governor's speech was passed in both Houses without a division, and the business was proceeded with in a way which must have greatly gratified the occupants of the Treasury Bench.

In the summer of this year the red rust in wheat was a source of much anxiety and loss to the farmers of the colony. It formed the subject of a debate in the House of Assembly on a motion to the effect that, as there was reason to fear that the occupiers of large areas of land would be unable to cultivate their land next season, the Government should obtain all possible information, and take all proper steps to avert so great a calamity. A select committee was therefore appointed to inquire into the matter and report.

The session was brought to a close on the 19th of December, 1867. During its continuance much less party spirit had been shown than heretofore, and for a time office-seeking seemed to have dropped out of fashion. The consequence was that there was more useful legislation, and a much larger number of Bills passed than in many previous sessions, while the astounding fact is worthy of special record, that not a single ministerial crisis occurred during the whole period.

It may not unnaturally be supposed by some readers that, in so small a community as Adelaide, the strong words and heated discussions in Parliament, the constant throwing over of leaders, the personal attacks on one another, the rivalry and defiance—all fostered and fanned into flame by the newspaper press—would give rise to much social unpleasantness, and tend to destroy personal friendship and good fellowship. As a matter of fact it did nothing of the kind. Let an old colonist, and an exceptionally well-informed man, tell the reason why. "The bitter rancour of political life, which is seen in some countries," says Mr. William Harcus,* " is comparatively unknown in South Australia. It is not that our public men do not feel strongly on political questions, but we are so closely mixed up in social and business life that we cannot afford to allow political asperities to pass beyond the region of politics. I have often seen two or more gladiators denouncing each other in the House in the strongest language allowed by rules of Parliamentary debates meet immediately after in the refreshment-room, when one would smilingly say to the other, 'Have a drink?' and the men who a few minutes ago were figuratively flying at each other's throats are hobnobbing like old friends, as they probably are. This is one of the pleasantest and most creditable features in a political life."

Having briefly glanced at the general routine of Parliament during the administration of Sir Dominick Daly, we must now turn to some of the burning questions which in that same period were engaging the attention, not only of the Legislature, but of every person interested in the welfare of the colony. The first in importance was the question of what was to be done with the newly discovered Northern Territory. And it is probable that, up to that date, such a gigantic question was never before in the world's history discussed and decided by a mere handful of men. Let the reader try, in the first place, to grasp the idea of what that Northern Territory, or Alexandra Land, was. To a great extent it was an unexplored country, save for the tracks made by the gallant explorers who had crossed the continent, and who had necessarily seen but a limited area. It consisted of 231,620 square miles of territory, or 35,116,800 acres, bounded on the north by the Arafura Sea, on the south by the 26th parallel of south latitude, on the east by the 138th meridian of east longitude, and on the west by the 129th meridian of east longitude.

Now, as South Australia had been the means of

* " South Australia; its History, Resources, and Productions."

discovering a practicable route across the continent, certain of the colonists thought they had a claim to at least a portion of the newly acquired territory, while others were of opinion that the whole should be handed over. And those others, as we shall see, carried the day. Originally the colony contained 300,000 square miles; then in 1861 "No Man's Land," a strip of land lying between its western boundary and the eastern boundary of Western Australia, containing 80,070 acres, was added to it, and finally the whole of the Northern Territory, thus bringing up the area to 903,690 square miles, or 78,361,600 acres, and making it by far the largest of the Australian colonies, with the exception of Western Australia.

When it is borne in mind that the population at this time was only about 165,000 souls, that the colony had only been in existence thirty years, that the art of government was only in its rudimentary stage so far as the colonial legislators were concerned, it must at least be conceded that the advocates of this enormous increase of territory were a bold and daring set of men. Let us now proceed to " set in order " their action in the matter.*

When Sir Richard MacDonnell was Governor, he took an enthusiastic interest in exploration, and more particularly in the adventurous attempts of Mr. J. M. Stuart to cross the continent. After Stuart's first exploration, Sir Richard, feeling confident that the goal would soon be successfully attained, wrote to the Duke of Newcastle, and suggested to the Home Government that it would be only an act of justice to the colony to extend its territory to those outlets on the northern coast which Mr. Stuart had shown would soon be connected by an overland route with South Australia. The Duke's reply to this was, that as the overland route had not really been opened, it was altogether premature to think of attaching the northern country to South Australia; besides which, it was certain that, at no

* For part of our information we are indebted to some admirable articles published in the *Register*.

distant date, independent settlements, which could not be governed from a distance, would have to be established on the northern coast. With this answer the subject was allowed to rest for a while.

The further explorations of Stuart, as well as those of Burke and Wills, McKinlay, and Landsborough having put the question of an overland route beyond doubt, Sir Charles Nicholson, who had been the first President of the Legislative Council in Queensland and was at the time Chairman of the Colonial Land and Emigration Commission, and who was in England when the result of the exploration became known, urged the Duke of Newcastle to lose no time in making provision for the Government of North Australia. He pointed out that the footsteps of the explorers would soon be followed by the squatters who occupied land on the outskirts of Queensland, and that unless the control of the new country were placed in the hands of some authority, lawlessness and disorder would prevail throughout the beautiful region which the labours of Stuart and others had made accessible. "Within a very few months," wrote Sir Charles Nicholson to the Duke, "the desire of occupying new country will tempt many persons, with their servants and flocks and herds, to locate themselves in this new district. The probability also is that many individuals who may have made themselves obnoxious to the laws, will, for the purpose of escaping the pursuit of justice, betake themselves in the same direction."

These and other considerations, such as the necessity of securing the rents of the lands occupied, and the desirability of encouraging settlement in so valuable a country, led Sir Charles Nicholson to recommend either that a new colony should be established, or that the whole of the North and North-west Territory should be placed under the guardianship—not of South Australia, by whose energy the country had been explored—but of Queensland!

Strange to say, the Home Government thought well of the latter suggestion, and after referring the matter to the Emigration Commissioners, at once offered the control of the country to Queensland. This was, naturally, more than the South Australians could stand, and the Government drew up a series of resolutions in Executive Council, and these were transmitted by Sir Dominick Daly to the Duke of Newcastle in December, 1862, with the result that in September, 1863, the Governor received a despatch from the Duke of Newcastle, placing that portion of the Northern Territory bounded by the 129th and 138th meridians of east longitude, and beyond the 26th parallel of south latitude to the Arafura Sea, under the charge of South Australia, with power "to revoke, alter, or amend the letters patent annexing the said territory."

While this concession was the occasion of loud congratulation among the majority, there were not a few far-seeing men, amongst whom was Mr. George Fife Angas, who strongly condemned any attempt to colonize the Northern Territory, predicting losses and failures as almost inevitable consequences on account of the inadequate means at its disposal for an undertaking of such vast magnitude. But their counsels did not prevail.

On the 1st of October the Treasurer introduced a Bill to provide for the disposal of land in North Australia, which was read a first time in the House of Assembly. It provided that 500,000 acres of country land might be sold in two several quantities of 250,000 acres each, the first lot at seven and sixpence per acre, and the second at twelve shillings per acre, and 1562 town allotments of half an acre each—one-half of the said lots to be open for sale and purchase in London, and one-half in the colony. The country sections were to consist of 160 acres, with which were to be offered a town allotment of half an acre. Provision was made in the Bill for the appointment of a Government Resident, and all other necessary officers for securing the order and good government of the Territory. The Treasurer, in introducing the Bill, stated that "the accounts relating to the new country were to be kept distinct from the accounts proper to South Australia. The object was to guard this colony from loss, and to settle the new country at as little expense as possible. The only advantage (he added) to be derived by South Australia was a market for its produce."

The regulations subsequently introduced in connection with the Bill reduced the original quantity to be offered in the first instance to two lots of 125,000 acres each, and holders of Parliamentary land orders were to be allowed to exercise their choice "at any time within five years from the date of the preliminary land order."

During the passage of the Bill through its various stages Mr. G. F. Angas renewed his protests from time to time, urging that it was an unwise thing for the colony, already possessing more than ample territory and with a limited population, to saddle itself with the responsibility of such an enormous appanage. He maintained that it was far beyond the capability of the colony at that time to manage successfully, and pointed out that settling the question of the land without making provision for the introduction of labour would not lead to the settlement of the country. He submitted an alternative scheme to the effect that, instead of planting a colony there, large inducements should be offered to squatters to take up the land, and that a Company—somewhat similar to the South Australian Company—should be formed and encouraged to attempt the growth of purely tropical products. Had his advice been taken the colony would have been saved enormous expenditure and annoyance. Many who wrote and spoke disparagingly of his views at the time afterwards acknowledged that they greatly erred in disregarding his wisdom and foresight.

On the 1st of March, 1864, offices were opened simultaneously in London and Adelaide for the sale of land in the Northern Territory, and on the 29th of that month the office at Adelaide was closed with the following result:—455 applicants for 118,880 acres of country land, and 743 town allotments of half an acre each, making a total of 119,251½ acres, the purchase money for which was £44,719 6s. 3d. The sales in London were materially assisted by the North Australian Company, which was formed for the purchase of land in the new territory, and applied for 25,000 acres.

The proceeds of these land sales were to be devoted in the first instance to the cost of surveying and settling the country, and, as there were no other funds available, of course the land sales took place before the surveys had commenced. The English buyers, therefore, speculated in faith; the choice of position was to be settled by lot, and the only guarantee they had was the pledge of the Government that within five years the land should be surveyed and ready for selection.

The sale of the land was immediately followed up by the South Australian Government with the outfit of an expedition to survey the quantity of land required, and to establish order in the newly acquired settlement. The command of the expedition was entrusted to Lieutenant-Colonel B. T. Finniss, who received the appointment of Government Resident. The choice was considered an excellent one. Mr. Finniss was an old and highly respected colonist, who had held the office of Treasurer of the colony, and, when Sir Henry Young left Adelaide, was acting Governor pending the arrival of Sir Richard MacDonnell. He was one of the fathers of the volunteer movement, and had a thoroughly practical knowledge of surveying. It seemed that he was *the* man to fulfil every requirement, and when a banquet was given before the expedition started, everybody seemed pleased with everything and with one another, and the future was seen as in a golden glory.

On the 29th of April the good ship *Henry Ellis*, well equipped in every respect, and amply supplied with stores, instruments, and weapons, set sail from Port Adelaide, having on board as officers of the expedition Mr. B. T. Finniss, Government Resident; J. F. Manton, engineer and surveyor; F. E. Goldsmith, surveyor and protector of aborigines; Ebenezer Ward, clerk in charge and accountant; Stephen King, storekeeper; John Davis, assistant storekeeper and postmaster; W. Pearson, J. Wadham, and A. R. Hamilton, surveyors; R. Watson and J. W. O. Bennett, draughtsmen, together with a strong party of labourers and seamen—forty-two persons in all, bound for Adam Bay, where it was thought a suitable site might be found for the first town, although absolute discretion was left to the Resident in this respect.

In May the Government schooner *Yatala* was despatched with a view to rendering any necessary assistance in navigating rivers, etc.

Unhappily, grievous dissensions arose among the party on board the *Henry Ellis*, which increased immediately after they landed in Adam Bay, and grew to a head when Mr. Finniss, against the strong protests and remonstrances of his officers, and the representations of the land purchasers, selected Escape Cliffs—one of the most inaccessible and improbable places imaginable—as the site of the first town.

In October intelligence reached Adelaide that misunderstandings of a most serious nature had arisen between the Government Resident and his subordinates, and that a collision had taken place between the Europeans and the natives, to whom summary and indiscriminate punishment had been administered. The position was a difficult one, and it cast a gloom over the prospects of the promoters of the annexation scheme. Nevertheless, a steamer, the *South Australian*, was despatched at once, with forty passengers to be employed in the Government service in place of any who might be desirous of returning. This steamer returned to Adelaide on the 1st of January, 1865, and in consequence of the information brought by her as to the site selected for the capital a meeting of land-order holders was held, who memorialized the Government not to determine on the site of a capital till the whole country had been examined. This request was acceded to as far as circumstances would permit, but to make a concession of this kind necessarily involved a tantalizing delay in the survey of the land.

In July, 1865, news reached Adelaide of the total disorganization of the survey party under Mr. Finniss. Some of the settlers had purchased a small boat, the *Forlorn Hope*, and, sailing by way of Champion Bay, reached Adelaide in safety, and laid a statement of the condition of affairs before the Government. Great indignation was expressed in all quarters, and Mr. Finniss was called upon for full and immediate explanation. All this was discouraging to those who had invested capital, and was embarrassing to the Government. But to meet any emergency that might arise, as well as to supply a pressing demand for stores and fresh provisions, the Government chartered the barque *Ellen Lewis*, which sailed for Adam Bay on the 25th of September, taking with her Messrs. McKinlay and John Davis, Dr. Milner, and ten other passengers, with stores, sheep, and horses.

The explanations of Mr. Finniss were eminently unsatisfactory, and he was recalled, Mr. Manton, the engineer and surveyor, being left in command.

The *Ellen Lewis* returned from the Territory on the 13th of February, 1866, with Mr. Finniss and a number of passengers on board. A Court of Inquiry was appointed by the Government to investigate the causes of the disagreements in the new settlement. The extent of the disruption that had taken place became painfully apparent by the number of charges and counter-charges that were brought under the notice of the Court. It was an aggravated repetition of the story of Captain Hindmarsh and the early settlers, and with such a warning within the memory of some who constituted the pioneer party to Adam Bay, it was somewhat surprising that they should have drifted into their present state of hopeless disorganization.

While the Court was sitting the *Ellen Lewis* returned to the Northern Territory with eleven passengers and a good cargo of live stock. On the 16th of May, 1866, a Special Commission of Inquiry gave in their report condemning Mr. Finniss' administration of affairs at Escape Cliffs, whereby the members of the expedition had been obstructed in the execution of their duties; condemning the selection of Escape Cliffs as the site of the first town; condemning him for lack of care in protecting the stores, and lack of skill in dealing with his men, and also in dealing with the natives with whom the party had come into collision. On the other hand, it was stated by the Commissioners that several of the persons comprising the expedition were totally unsuitable for the work entrusted to them. The inquiry was one of peculiar difficulty, owing to the extremely acrimonious feeling on both sides, and especially the strong personal animosity shown towards Mr. Finniss. The report of the Commissioners was accepted by the Government, and Mr. Finniss, although considering himself hardly dealt with, was removed from his position, or, as it appeared, resigned the office of Government Resident, on the 25th of May.

Meanwhile, Mr. Manton was left in charge, and the reports that came from time to time were unfavourable to his administration.

In September, 1866, Mr. McKinlay returned from an unsuccessful attempt to explore the country to the east of Adam Bay, and delay, vexation, and disappointment became the order of the day. Parliament and the Executive had no easy time of it, and after much deliberation it was decided to advertise for tenders for the survey of 300,000 acres of land.

On the 10th of December eleven tenders were sent in, and were handed to Mr. G. W. Goyder, Surveyor-General, to report upon. Only two were capable of serious consideration.

As a preliminary step, before any tender could be accepted, Mr. Goyder recommended that a competent officer should be sent at once to the Northern Territory, and should be instructed to visit the lands in the vicinity of the Victoria, and afterwards land at Anson Bay and the north coast of Port Darwin and Escape Cliffs, and, after deciding upon a site for the capital, to return and call for tenders, stating the actual nature of the country and the material required to facilitate the carrying out of the contract. Captain Cadell's services were secured for this purpose, and with a small party he set sail on the 26th of February, 1867.

After an absence of fifty weeks he returned and reported upon the advantages and disadvantages of the places visited. Instead of accepting any of the tenders, the Government decided to send Mr. Goyder as head of a new survey party (Mr. Manton and several of the original survey party sent out in 1864 having returned to Adelaide), and on the 27th of December, 1868, he sailed in the *Moonta* for Port Darwin, that place being considered the most suitable for the capital.

The tenders sent in had varied from £21,000 to £100,000, or from one shilling per acre to four shillings and ninepence halfpenny. Mr. Goyder's estimate for the work was £25,000, exclusive of cost of transit and of small vessels for river and mail services, but including salary and provisions to officers and men to and from the Northern Territory. This amount was also exclusive of a bonus of £3000 to Mr. Goyder, but included a bonus *pro rata* to the officers and men of the expedition.

While these arrangements were being made by the Colonial Government, the North Australian Land Company in England and several of the land-order holders were demanding a return of their purchase money, with interest, which tended still further to embarrass the Executive, and the impression was being extensively forced on the minds of many that the vast territory, asked for as a boon, might prove a bane to the colony.

How Mr. Goyder performed his mission, and how order was evolved out of chaos in the "white elephant" Territory, will be told in a future chapter.

Throughout the administration of Sir Dominick Daly, the "Squatter Question" was a subject of debate both in and out of Parliament, and not only during that period, but more or less throughout the whole history of the colony. The term "squatter," according to Mr. J. Henniker Heaton,* was first applied to persons in the territory of New South Wales, who, about the year 1835, without reasonable means of obtaining an honest livelihood, had formed stations in the interior, and then carried on predatory warfare against the flocks and herds in the vicinity. The term "squatter" is now used to describe one of the most useful and important classes of the community, principally the large pastoral tenants who rent the land from the Crown for grazing purposes. This signification was first applied in the year 1842, and has held its own ever since.

In the early days of the colony brave and adventurous men with a little capital went off into outlying districts with their sheep and a few shepherds, a certain amount of food, and the wherewithal of procuring more, and, building their rude huts, settled down to pastoral pursuits. In course of time the dangers which beset them in the earlier days from the attacks of natives were minimized, and as success attended the labours of the squatters, their general condition improved. But the tenure of the land they occupied was always more or less precarious, the condition upon which pastoral leases were held being that in the event of the land being required for agricultural purposes, the squatter must relinquish his "run" on receiving six months' notice, but would be compensated for the substantial improvements he had made.

Many of the squatters in a comparatively short time amassed large fortunes, while others were much better off financially than the dwellers in towns, and the consequence was that many considered it to be a mistake to lease land to them on the low terms that at one time prevailed. Mr. G. W. Goyder, the Surveyor-General, was therefore entrusted with the difficult task of fixing a new valuation on the renewal of the leases.

His valuations were so high that the squatters were

* "Australian Dictionary of Dates," by J. H. Heaton. London, 1879.

at first dumbfounded, but soon after raised such an outcry as to challenge public opinion on the whole question. There arose "squatter parties" and "anti-squatter parties" in Parliament. On one side the squatters were represented as having all the sweets of colonial life; on the other as poor, oppressed, and struggling men, to whom every consideration should be shown.

Strange to say, the re-valuations had scarcely been made, than there set in a period of almost unprecedented drought, and it continued for two years in succession. The grievances of the squatters then engaged the careful attention of the Legislature, and a Commission was appointed to inquire into the whole matter. As the position of those in the north was considerably aggravated by this calamitous drought, it was considered by many that they had a reasonable claim upon the sympathy and forbearance of the Government; but in consequence of the popular clamour raised against them as a class, it was not easy to obtain any concession for them from those who regarded themselves as representatives of "the people."

The facts elicited by the Commissioners were certainly calculated to turn the tide of popular prejudice which had set in against the squatters. But such was not the case. A wide-spread opinion prevailed that the "people's grass" had been leased to the squatters at too low a price, and that they were thereby enabled, in good seasons, to become wealthy in a short time. The squatters, on the other hand, contended that, as their leases could not possibly give them a guarantee against drought, it was unjust that they should pay for feed for their flocks and herds on land which did not yield such pasture.

The report of the Commission, under the head "Loss of stock through drought," was startling:— "235,152 sheep have perished out of 827,706 since the 30th of September, 1864, to the same date 1865, and 28,850 head of horned cattle out of 53,355. The horse stock has also suffered severely, 903 out of 2145 being reported lost. These losses do not include last year's increase of lambs and calves, for, with some trifling exceptions, not worthy of notice, all have perished."

Some of the most severe cases of loss were thus enumerated:—" Out of a herd of cattle of 8000 head two years ago, and which, according to the ordinary rate of increase, should now number 12,000, only 1600 remain; of 7000 sheep belonging to the same proprietor, only 800 have been brought away, and of 550 horses 520 have died. Another proprietor reports the loss of 1500 cattle out of 3000, and he has deserted the station, it being impossible to get supplies. Unless heavy rains fall before Christmas, the whole of the herd must die, it being utterly impossible to muster them, and even could that be done, they would not be able to travel away. Several others have lost three-fourths, and many half, of their entire stock. These losses have not arisen so much from want of water as from scarcity of food and length of drought, as in many cases the supply of water exceeds the feeding capabilities of the run."

In a return made by Mr. Goyder to the House of Assembly, towards the end of December, it was shown that the estimated loss to the revenue by making reasonable concessions to those lessees of the Crown who had suffered by the drought would be about £40,000.

Eventually a scheme was hit upon, and in closing the session of Parliament on the 16th of March, 1866, the Governor alluded to it in these terms: "It is with great satisfaction that I have assented in her Majesty's name to an Act for extending the term of occupation to the pastoral lessees of the Crown, believing that, while conferring a great boon on those who elect to take advantage of the measure, it will not be detrimental to the general interest of the community; and the subsequent Act, which allows the lessees the alternative choice of a remission of rent in some proportion to the loss of pasturage, is a wise concession, which the unparalleled state of the country demanded."

Thus, under very difficult circumstances, the matter was brought to a satisfactory result.

Public feeling with regard to the squatters was considerably changed in 1867, the drought having continued for an unexampled period. A series of resolutions were introduced by the Commissioner of Crown Lands and Immigration for affording relief by allowing them to surrender the leases they held, in exchange for others to be granted on more liberal terms, and a Bill to give effect to this was passed with very little opposition. Although the times were then so hard to the squatters, and many of them were unable to tide over their difficulties, some did not suffer in the end, and they continued in the future, as they had been in the past, among the most prosperous of the colonists.

The imminent wreckage of a Ministry in a peculiar form during the rule of Governor Daly deserves a passing notice, as it is among the historic incidents of the colony's history. On the 13th of April, 1865, Sir Dominick Daly, Sir Henry Ayers, Chief Secretary, several other Ministers, and a distinguished number of visitors, among whom was Lady Charlotte Bacon (the Ianthe of Byron), were being conveyed on the City and Port Railway—the Government speculation, which had cost over £250,000—by express train from Adelaide on a visit to H.M.'s sloop *Falcon*. Mr. Charles Simeon Hare, manager of railways, was in charge of the train, and he gave instructions to the engine-driver to put on "all speed." The result was a lurch, a crash, and two of the carriages were overturned and flung off the line. Happily the chain connecting the engine with the train broke on the instant, and the passengers escaped uninjured. A Commission of Inquiry sat for seven days, and the blame having been fixed on Mr. Hare, he was removed from office with compensation. It is reported that in after years he was wont to make merry in a subdued fashion on his exploit, and to say that, "though he never held office in a Ministry, he upset a Ministry and a Governor on top of it!"

The most memorable event of a general character

which marked the administration of Sir Dominick Daly was the visit of his Royal Highness the Duke of Edinburgh in the steam frigate *Galatea*. The intimation that Port Adelaide would be the first port in Australia that the Prince would visit was received with enthusiasm, and the loyal colonists took steps to give him as brilliant a reception as possible.

Towards the end of October (1867), when the arrival of the Prince was hourly expected, beachrangers were watching day and night on shore, and others in the Gulf, while the Adelaideans kept their eyes on the signal-staffs by day, and watched for the booming of cannon or the blazing of bonfires on Mount Lofty by night. But, in spite of all this vigilance, the *Galatea* steamed quietly up the gulf during the night of the 29th of October, and came to anchor in Holdfast Bay without any pilot, and without any visit from those who were on the look-out to intercept her.

Early next morning the telegraph flashed the news to the country districts, and all Adelaide and the suburbs were astir. When the public reception took place on the 31st, it was calculated that about 35,000 persons were present at different points, to witness or take part in the procession.

Never had Adelaide seen so great a show. Magnificent triumphal arches, miles of bunting, forests of evergreens, acres of red and gold cloth; merry peals ringing from the bells of the Albert Tower; the booming of cannon; the tramp of volunteers, joined by the members of friendly societies, the corporations of Adelaide and other municipalities, and the German Club; the clangour of bands of music, the thrilling voices of 4000 children singing the National Anthem; but, more impressive than all, the ringing cheers and the waving of handkerchiefs, as the first member of the Royal House of England passed along on Australian soil. At night there was a general illumination—a display of electric and magnesium lights and fireworks. Next day the Prince held a levée at Government House and laid the foundation stone of the Victoria

Tower of the new post-office, the day's proceedings terminating with a torchlight procession of 500 Germans. Great pains had been taken "to render this demonstration in every respect national; to include in it every German institution in the colony; to have every German township represented; and to get everything done exactly as in the Fatherland." This included transparent lanterns, the singing of the Liedertafel, and so on, and the whole thing was well done, and appeared to afford the Prince infinite pleasure.

On the 2nd there was a review of the volunteers and military on the North Park-Lands, and a presentation of colours to the Prince Alfred Rifle Volunteers by his Royal Highness. In the afternoon the Adelaide Amateur Athletic Club gave an excellent display of sports, and in the evening there was an amateur performance at the theatre by the officers of the 50th Regiment. Sunday, the 3rd, was spent by his Royal Highness on board the *Galatea*, and Monday was an "open day" so far as public celebrations were concerned, but steamers were running from the port to the royal frigate, and took from 2000 to 3000 visitors to see the *Galatea*.

On the 5th the Royal Duke laid the foundation stone of the Prince Alfred (Wesleyan) College, and in the evening there was a subscription ball in the Town Hall, at which nearly a thousand people were present. On the following day Gawler and Kapunda were visited, and in the evening there was a grand display of fireworks on Montefiore Hill, near Adelaide.

From the 7th to the 9th, the Agricultural and Horticultural Society held a special exhibition of colonial products and manufactures, and henceforth the society adopted the prefix of "Royal" to its title. Over 16,000 persons visited the exhibition.

On the 9th, it being the anniversary of the birthday of the Prince of Wales, a civic banquet was given in the Town Hall, at which 500 persons were present, and on the 11th the Duke and his suite left Adelaide for Lakes Alexandrina and Albert for sport, and returned on the 16th. Four days later, the Prince left Government House for the Port, accompanied by the Governor, of whose kindness and hospitality the Prince and his party spoke in the highest terms, and on the 21st the *Galatea* steamed down the gulf on her way to Melbourne, leaving the colonists to the reflection that though the visit of her royal captain had cost the colony between £20,000 and £30,000 such visits were likely to be of rare occurrence, and the loyal feelings they called into existence and fostered were certainly worth a few thousands, to say nothing of the sights and scenes they had witnessed and enjoyed during the gay holiday time.*

On the 12th of March, 1868, intelligence reached Adelaide of the dastardly attempt of one O'Farrell to assassinate the Duke of Edinburgh, while attending a picnic near Sydney. The news created a most painful sensation; prayers for his recovery were offered up at all the churches, indignation meetings were held, and an address to the Queen was drawn up and bore 63,689 signatures.

The telegrams announcing the Prince's progress towards recovery were awaited with anxiety, and the 3rd of May, good tidings having been received, was set apart as a day of General Thanksgiving for the preservation from assassination and for the restoration to health of the Prince.

The subsequent news of the execution of O'Farrell brought the tragic incident to a close, and by allowing the law to take its course, Australians generally felt they had done all that was in their power to do, to wash their hands of the foul deed for which they were in no way responsible.

Throughout the whole period of the preparations and the visit of the Duke of Edinburgh, Sir Dominick Daly took an active part, and although it was patent to every one that he was not in good health, he did not in any way relax his labours. On the 19th of December he

---

* Those who are curious in such matters will find elaborate details of each day's engagements in " The Cruise of H.M.S. *Galatea*," by the Rev. John Milner and O. W. Brierly. London: 1869.

brought a long and arduous session of Parliament to a close by the delivery of a brief speech, in which he reminded the members that the session then closing would probably terminate the existing Parliament, and that they would shortly be called upon to appear before their constituents. He congratulated them upon the Royal visit, and on the loyalty of the colonists; thanked the Parliament for the liberal means placed at his disposal for the reception and entertainment of His Royal Highness, and then touched in general and pleasing terms on the measures that had been passed during the session favourable to the pastoral, mining, and agricultural interests.

On the 19th of February, 1868, exactly two months after bringing the session to a close, the tolling of the large muffled bell in the Albert Tower and the half-mast-high flag at the entrance to the Government Domain told the sad tale that the Governor's earthly career was ended.

For some time previously he had been in a bad state of health; his lack of colour and of physical vigour had been noticed by every one, and medical men were prepared to hear that anæmia was the cause of death.

The end was sudden, and he died literally in harness; not only had arrangements been made a day or two before to hold a meeting of the Executive Council within an hour or two of the time that he breathed his last, but he was engaged in public business immediately before the final seizure.

The funeral took place on the 22nd of February, and, like the day when Sir Dominick arrived in the colony, the heat was almost unbearable. Nevertheless, some 14,000 to 15,000 persons lined the route to the cemetery, and, as all that was mortal of the late Governor was borne along on a gun-carriage and surrounded by military pomp, there was overwhelming evidence that his loss was deeply mourned.

An admirable review of Sir Dominick Daly's administration was given in the *Register*, and it expressed exactly the estimation in which he was held by the colonists from first to last. "Among the finest traits of an admirable character should be placed the tact and prudence whereby he averted the threatened calamity of religious discord. Among the grounds of our regret for his untimely loss it should not be forgotten what he suffered in the early part of his career on this point. His personal amiability and political impartiality soon lived it down, but while it existed it must have been a painful obstacle to the usefulness he had so sincerely at heart. No other person ever took office under such a serious disadvantage. None gained so steadily in public favour when he came to be known as he really was. There has been no other of whose career it could so truly be said that he left none but friends behind him. . . . Six years ago he came to us a stranger, and we received him, not without prejudices and misgivings. To-day we can all of us say in our hearts that we wish he had been spared many years longer to rule us. In his quiet, modest fashion, he had lived through much, learned much, and done a great deal more than the world gave him credit for. His career was singularly free from tinsel and dramatic effect, but all who study his biography will find in it the genuine characteristics of human worth. Remembering, as we ought, the peculiar difficulties of his position, we cannot be too grateful for the peace and prosperity which have attended his rule."

END OF VOL. I.

www.ingramcontent.com/pod-product-compliance
Lightning Source LLC
Chambersburg PA
CBHW051246300426
44114CB00011B/914